'This insightful and creative work provides a vivid example of why it is so important that we consider resilience. With great sensitivity to the voices of victims/survivors of conflict-related sexual violence, Clark helps us to understand what resilience theory can offer when unravelling the deep complexity of human experiences.'

Michael Ungar, Professor of Social Work,
Dalhousie University, Canada

'If "resilience" has become a buzzword, people often fail to define the term. In this book, Janine Natalya Clark not only deeply conceptualizes resilience, but offers a novel way of approaching it in terms of social ecology. By doing so, Clark makes an important contribution to transitional justice and many other fields concerned with resilience.'

Alex Hinton, Distinguished Professor of Anthropology,
Rutgers University, USA

'This ground-breaking book directs scholarly, policy and practitioner attention to people's capacity for resilience to conflict-related sexual violence. Using a novel social-ecological, comparative approach, Clark builds on the powerful stories of victims-/survivors in Bosnia-Herzegovina, Colombia and Uganda to show that interpersonal and ecological "connectivities" matter for resilience and transitional justice.'

Linda Theron, Full Professor of Educational Psychology,
University of Pretoria, South Africa

Resilience, Conflict-Related Sexual Violence and Transitional Justice

This interdisciplinary book constitutes the first major and comparative study of resilience focused on victims-/survivors of conflict-related sexual violence (CRSV). Locating resilience in the relationships and interactions between individuals and their social ecologies (including family, community, non-governmental organisations and the natural environment), the book develops its own conceptual framework based on the idea of connectivity. It applies the framework to its analysis of rich empirical data from Bosnia-Herzegovina, Colombia and Uganda, and it tells a set of stories about resilience through the contextual, dynamic and storied connectivities between individuals and their social ecologies. Ultimately, it utilises the three elements of the framework – namely, broken and ruptured connectivities, supportive and sustaining connectivities and new connectivities – to argue the case for developing the field of transitional justice in new social-ecological directions, and to explore what this might conceptually and practically entail.

The book will particularly appeal to anyone with an interest in, or curiosity about, resilience, and to scholars, researchers and policymakers working on CRSV and/or transitional justice. The fact that resilience has received surprisingly little attention within existing literature on either CRSV or transitional justice accentuates the significance of this research and the originality of its conceptual and empirical contributions.

Janine Natalya Clark is Professor of Gender, Transitional Justice and International Criminal Law at Birmingham Law School, University of Birmingham, UK.

Resilience, Conflict-Related Sexual Violence and Transitional Justice

A Social-Ecological Framing

Janine Natalya Clark

First published 2023
by Routledge
4 Park Square, Milton Park, Abingdon, Oxon OX14 4RN

and by Routledge
605 Third Avenue, New York, NY 10158

a GlassHouse Book

Routledge is an imprint of the Taylor & Francis Group, an informa business

© 2023 Janine Natalya Clark

The right of Janine Natalya Clark to be identified as author of this work has been asserted in accordance with sections 77 and 78 of the Copyright, Designs and Patents Act 1988.

The Open Access version of this book, available at www.taylorfrancis.com, has been made available under a Creative Commons Attribution-Non Commercial-No Derivatives 4.0 license.

Trademark notice: Product or corporate names may be trademarks or registered trademarks, and are used only for identification and explanation without intent to infringe.

British Library Cataloguing-in-Publication Data
A catalogue record for this book is available from the British Library

ISBN: 978-1-032-34725-7 (hbk)
ISBN: 978-1-032-34727-1 (pbk)
ISBN: 978-1-003-32353-2 (ebk)

DOI: 10.4324/9781003323532

Typeset in Bembo
by Apex CoVantage, LLC

In loving memory of Doreen May Clark

Contents

Acknowledgements	xi
List of Abbreviations	xiv
List of Figures	xvi
List of Tables	xvii
Note on Diacritics	xviii

	Introduction: Resilience, Conflict-Related Sexual Violence and Transitional Justice	1
1	Thinking About Resilience as a Social-Ecological Concept	21
2	Analysing Resilience Through Connectivity	46
3	Research Design, Methodology and Ethics	69
4	The Conflicts and Use of Sexual Violence in Bosnia-Herzegovina, Colombia and Uganda	98
5	Connectivity Stories of Resilience in Bosnia-Herzegovina	134
6	Connectivity Stories of Resilience in Colombia	169
7	Connectivity Stories of Resilience in Uganda	204
8	Resilience and Why Social Ecologies Matter for Transitional Justice	239
	Conclusion: Final Reflections and Connecting the Threads	273

Contents

Appendix 1 The Interview Guide	292
Appendix 2 Rape Cases in Bosnia-Herzegovina	295
Index	299

Acknowledgements

In 2017, I commenced a five-year research project, funded by a European Research Council Consolidator Grant (grant number 724518). This book constitutes the principal output. I would like to begin by sincerely thanking the European Research Council for giving me such a wonderful opportunity and for believing in the project. There have been many challenges along the way, but it has been a huge privilege to spend several years doing this research.

It was also an immense privilege to meet and speak to some of the women and men who participated in this study. In total, more than 400 victims-/ survivors of conflict-related sexual violence in Bosnia-Herzegovina (BiH), Colombia and Uganda shared parts of their stories and experiences, and this research would not have been possible without them. *Hvala puno. Muchas gracias. Apwoyo matek.*

Two postdoctoral researchers were employed on the project from the start. Thank you to Dr Yoana Fernanda Nieto Valdivieso and Dr Eunice Otuko Apio for their work on the project and in particular their fieldwork in Colombia and Uganda respectively. They also each read two of the draft chapters of this book and gave comments.

Several in-country organisations were involved in the research and played a fundamental role in supporting the fieldwork. In BiH, I wish to thank *Snaga Žene*, its director Dr Branka Antić-Štauber and in particular the psychologists Emina Altumbabić and Sabina Duman, as well as Sanela Zahirović. I am also grateful to Zlatica Gruhonjić, Slavica Topić and Jovana Jankovski from the Centre for Democracy and Transitional Justice, and to Božica Živković-Rajilić and the Association of War Victims *Republika Srpska* for facilitating the research. The contributions of the following professionals must also be acknowledged: Dr Devla Baraković, a psychologist in Brčko District; Zemina Kadirić, the director of the Centre for Social Work in Sanski Most; Edita Alijagić, a social worker from the Centre for Social Work in Bihać and Azra Karabašić, a psychologist from the non-governmental organisation *Udruženje Prijedorčanki Izvor*.

In Colombia, the project had crucial on-the-ground support from the following organisations: *Profamilia, Ruta Pacífica de las Mujeres*, the *Red de Mujeres* xii Acknowledgements

Victímas y Profesionales, El Meta con Mirada de Mujer and *Colombia Diversa*. I wish to personally thank the following people: Marcela Sanchez, Rosio Murad, Luz Janeth Forero, Juan Carlos Rivillas and Marta Royo (from *Profamilia*); Marina Gallego, Teresa Aristizabal, Dunia Leon, Amanda Lucia Camila and Shima Pardo (from *Ruta Pacífica de las Mujeres*); Pilar Rueda and Angela Escobar (from the *Red de Mujeres Victímas y Profesionales*); Nancy Gómez Ramos (from *El Meta con Mirada de Mujer*) and Daniela Díaz (from *Colombia Diversa*). I further extend my deep appreciation to Dr Luz Maria Londoño, a psychologist in Medellín.

The organisation Facilitation for Peace and Development (FAPAD), based in Lira, facilitated the fieldwork in northern Uganda. I especially wish to thank Grace Achot, Babra Otuku and Salome Adit. The Justice and Reconciliation Project (JRP) in Gulu also supported some of the early fieldwork and I am grateful to Okwir Isaac Odiya. The Lango elders Vincent Oling of Minakulu in Oyam district and Angelina Atyam in Lira offered valuable advice and wisdom during parts of the project. The Prime Minister of the Ker Kal Kwaro Acholi (Acholi Cultural Institution), Ladit Ambrose Olaa, and the then Prime Minister of the Lango Cultural Foundation, Awitong Dr Richard Nam, also shared many important insights.

The Dr Denis Mukwege Foundation organised three workshops in 2021, which made it possible to share some of the research findings with members of SEMA – The Global Network of Victims and Survivors to End Wartime Sexual Violence. Thank you in particular to Dr Malini Laxminarayan and Camila Fernandes Thomaz, and to the women from SEMA who took part in the workshops.

Several people provided crucial research assistance. Dušica Štilić in BiH, Estefany Largo in Colombia, Grace Acan and Peace Acheng in Uganda and Dr Hebe Powell transcribed and/or translated the interviews. Peace Acheng, a clinical psychologist, also took notes during the reflections workshops in 2021 and followed up with some of the participants. Dr Philip Jefferies analysed the quantitative data, and Dr Adrian Bromage, Dr Sarah Foley and Dr Kristin Hadfield were also involved in the process at various stages. Dr Thomas Stocks coded some of the interviews, and both he and Bryony Pike gave invaluable administrative support. I learned how to use NVivo thanks to Ben Meehan from QDA Training, a wonderful and extremely patient teacher who never tired of answering my questions.

The members of the project's International Advisory Board were on hand to give guidance and were an important sounding board. Thank you to Professor Michael Ungar, Professor Helen A. Neville, Professor Rashida Manjoo and Professor Juan E. Méndez.

At the start of the project, I established an eight-member independent Ethics Board to monitor the many complex ethics issues that the research raised. Thank you to Professor Jennie E. Burnett (chair of the Board), Professor Suzanne Buckley-Zistel, Dr Tereza Capelos, Professor Sabina Čehajić-Clancy, Dr Elizabeth Dartnall, Professor Rosie Harding, Professor Inger Skjelsbaek and Professor Stefan Wolff for their insights. In northern Uganda, Dr Martin Ogwang and Moses Odongkara from the Lacor Hospital Institutional Ethics Committee reviewed the multiple study tools and provided guidance on doing research in a complex post-conflict context, and the Ugandan National Council for Science and Technology reviewed and approved the study. The Sarajevo School of Science and Technology and the Research Ethics Committee at Rosario University in Colombia reviewed the study protocols and ethics procedures relating to BiH and Colombia respectively. Thank you also to the Humanities and Social Sciences Ethical Review Committee at the University of Birmingham (the host institution) and to the European Research Council Executive Agency.

Finally, I would like to thank my Mother, Marion Jane Clark, for always being positive, for lifting my spirits and for encouraging me every time that I doubted myself.

Abbreviations

AAR – Agreement on Accountability and Reconciliation
ABiH – Army of Bosnia-Herzegovina
ARM – Adult Resilience Measure
ARV – Antiretroviral
AUC – United Self-Defence Forces of Colombia
BiH – Bosnia-Herzegovina
CAS – Complex adaptive systems
CNMH – National Centre for Historical Memory
COR – Conservation of Resources theory
CRSV – Conflict-related sexual violence
CYRM – Child and Youth Resilience Measure
DRC – Democratic Republic of Congo
EC – European Commission
EC – European Community
ELN – National Liberation Army
ELP – Popular Liberation Army
FAPAD – Facilitation for Peace and Development
FARC – Revolutionary Armed Forces of Colombia
FCO – Foreign and Commonwealth Office
HDZ – Croatian Democratic Union
HIV – Human immunodeficiency virus
HOS – Croatian Defence Forces
HRW – Human Rights Watch
HSMF – Holy Spirit Mobile Force
HVO – Croatian Defence Council
ICC – International Criminal Court
ICMP – International Commission on Missing Persons
ICRC – International Committee of the Red Cross
ICTY – International Criminal Tribunal for the former Yugoslavia
ILO – International Labour Organization
JEP – Special Jurisdiction for Peace
JNA – Yugoslav National Army

JRP – Justice and Reconciliation Project
LC1 – Local Council 1
LGBT – Lesbian, gay, bisexual, transgender
LRA – Lord's Resistance Army
NATO – North Atlantic Treaty Organization
NGO – Non-governmental organisation(s)
NRA – National Resistance Army
OMC – Observatory of Memory and Conflict
OSRSG-SVC – Office of the Special Representative of the Secretary-General on Sexual Violence in Conflict
OTP-ICC – Office of the Prosecutor of the International Criminal Court
PFRJR – Protective Factors for Reducing Juvenile Reoffending
PTG – Post-traumatic growth
RCT – Relational-Cultural Theory
RS – *Republika Srpska*
SDA – Party of Democratic Action
SDS – Serbian Democratic Party
SES – Social-ecological systems
SFRY – Socialist Federal Republic of Yugoslavia
SGBV – Sexual and gender-based violence
SOC – Sense of Coherence
SPSS – Statistical Package for the Social Sciences
TEC – Traumatic Events Checklist
UN – United Nations
UNHCR – United Nations Refugee Agency
UNICEF – United Nations International Children's Emergency Fund
UNLA – Ugandan National Liberation Army
UPDA – Ugandan People's Defence Army
UPDF – Uganda People's Defence Forces
US – United States
VRS – Army of *Republika Srpska*
VSLA – Village Saving and Loan Association(s)
WHO – World Health Organization
ŽŽR – *Žena Žrtva Rata*

Figures

3.1	TEC results by country	74
3.2	Ethnic profile of research participants	77
3.3	Participants by age	77

Tables

3.1 Basic demographic profile of the 63 interviewees   79

Note on Diacritics

The book uses all necessary diacritics (e.g., Karadžić, Medellín). In cases where authors' names are published without diacritics, this book similarly omits them.

Introduction
Resilience, Conflict-Related Sexual Violence and Transitional Justice

I first met Džana (not her real name) in 2014. It was a cold, murky day in November. She was waiting for me at the bus stop when I arrived in her town in Bosnia-Herzegovina (BiH). We made the short walk to her house. I recall that en route, she invited me to stay with her and her family that night as there were no accommodation options in the town. We were almost the same age and the conversation flowed easily. Džana and I did an interview that afternoon, as part of a research project that I was working on at the time, focused on the long-term consequences of conflict-related sexual violence (CRSV; see Clark, 2017).

Three things particularly stayed with me from that first visit. First, Džana revealed that she rarely went out. She spent most of her time indoors doing household chores, and I remember her washing the dishes in cold water and telling me that it made her hands hurt. Second, the warm and welcoming atmosphere in her home stood out. The family were living in poor conditions – the roof leaked, there was condensation on the windows, the bathroom was barely fit for purpose – but there was a great deal of love and happiness within those four walls. I enjoyed spending time with the family and getting to know them. Third, Džana had been a teenager when the Bosnian war started in 1992. She was raped multiple times while detained in a camp. The war put an end to her education and her dreams of entering the medical profession. What struck me about her, however, was her fierce determination to get on with life and to make it as good as it could be, for her own sake but above all for that of her children.

I returned to Tuzla the next day, where I was based, but I remained in contact with Džana and continued to regularly visit her during the year that I spent in BiH – and during subsequent trips to the country. Over time, I observed her grow and change. She tirelessly sought out resources to give her children a safe and comfortable home; she set up her own local non-governmental organisation (NGO); she used her creativity (making soaps, jewellery, bags) to generate income; and she started to socialise more and to make new friends.

I distinctly remember where I was when the idea for the research that underpins this book began to take shape and to crystallise. It was the summer of 2015.

DOI: 10.4324/9781003323532-1

2 Introduction

I was sitting outside the premises of the Bosnian NGO *Snaga Žene* in Tuzla. My aforementioned fieldwork in BiH, which the NGO had facilitated, was coming to an end and I was thinking about what I would do next. In Bosnian, the word *inat* does not have a direct English equivalent, but it can roughly be translated as 'spite' – in the sense of stubbornness or defiance (Horigan, 2021: 37). Džana exhibited *inat*; she was defying the men who violated and beat her by moving forward with her life and focusing on the future. So too were many of the other women and men who fundamentally contributed to my research by sharing their stories. Yet, it was more than just *inat*. It suddenly struck me that there was something missing from existing research on the use of CRSV[1] during the Bosnian war – and from the various trauma-centred narratives that I had frequently heard from NGOs. What was missing was any significant discussion or acknowledgement of resilience.

Over the following months, I began to explore the vast corpus of extant scholarship on resilience, which spans multiple disciplinary perspectives (see, e.g., Adger, 2000; Bourbeau and Ryan, 2018; Coaffee and Lee, 2016; McEwen et al., 2015; Rutter, 1987; Ungar, 2021). As I did so, something else caught my attention. Bonanno et al. (2015: 139) point out that 'Interest in the human capacity for resilience in the face of aversive life events has grown exponentially. . . . The last decade, in particular, has witnessed a surge of research and theory about psychologically resilient functioning'. Broadly, however, this interest has not carried over to existing literature on CRSV (and beyond just BiH).

There are a small number of exceptions. Zraly et al.'s research (2013), based on 16 months of ethnographic fieldwork in Rwanda and focused on women who were raped during the 1994 genocide, has explored the relationship between motherhood and resilience. Koos' (2018: 196) work on CRSV during the civil war in Sierra Leone (1991–2002) 'adds to the growing discourse on resilience by providing evidence that individuals, households, and communities in postconflict settings are able to absorb certain shocks and distress'. In the context of northern Uganda, Edström et al. (2016: 5) have found – albeit while leaving the term resilience undefined – that 'despite pervasive discrimination, groups of male survivors [of CRSV] have been able to develop resilience and mutual support through collective action'.

In general, however, scholars working on CRSV have addressed resilience only indirectly or peripherally (i.e., without explicitly referring to it). Oliveira and Baines (2022: 753) have explored some of the ways that formerly abducted Acholi women in northern Uganda who returned from the bush with children are actively engaged in 'repairing systems of relatedness'; and Coulter's (2009: 123) work has discussed some of the everyday 'strategies of survival' of women and girls who became 'bush wives' to rebel commanders during the aforementioned Sierra Leonean civil war. Relatedly, some scholars have examined various ways that individuals who have suffered CRSV demonstrate agency, including through social activism, the pursuit of legal justice and caring practices (Berry, 2018; Crosby and Lykes, 2019; Kreft, 2019; Krystalli and Schulz, 2022; Touquet and Schulz, 2021; Zulver, 2022).

The crucial point is that, to date, there are no major studies – and certainly no comparative studies – of resilience and CRSV. At the same time, resilience scholars have given very little attention to CRSV. As Liebenberg and Moore (2018: 4) highlight, 'most resilience research has focused on the experiences of children and adolescents'. This interdisciplinary book, which is based on a five-year research project funded by the European Research Council (2017–2022), constitutes the first large-scale study of resilience with a specific focus on victims-/survivors[2] of CRSV. It is, however, necessary to stress that the women and men who took part in the research were much more than just victims-/survivors of CRSV, in the sense that they had all experienced multiple forms of violence. The book adopts a comparative focus. Drawing on extensive field-work data from BiH, Colombia and Uganda – three countries that have faced high levels (and very different types) of CRSV – it offers a unique conceptual and empirical analysis of resilience.

Resilience Controversies and Clarifications

It is important to acknowledge at the outset that resilience is not an uncontentious concept. Some scholars maintain that it has become a catch-all term and a 'quasi-universal answer' to a wide range of contemporary issues, from climate change to terrorism (Aradau, 2014: 73; see also Diprose, 2015: 44; Hanisch, 2016: 2). Some also insist that resilience discourse places a heavy and unequal burden on particular individuals and communities to positively adapt to adversities that are not of their own making (see, e.g., Barrios, 2016: 31; Jordan, 2019: 167). Viewed in this way, resilience policies do not necessarily offer new solutions and can simply entrench the status quo (Cretney, 2014: 636). Relatedly, individuals' circumstances may force them to be resilient due to lack of alternatives. For example, 'one can be very poor and unwell, but very resilient' (Béné et al., 2012: 14).

Linked to the aforementioned arguments, one of the main critiques of resilience is that it forms part of a wider neoliberal agenda that effectively 'redistributes responsibilities – and possibilities of blame' away from governments (Dunn Cavelty et al., 2015: 7). Complex problems are consequently depoliticised as the onus is placed on individuals to 'brace themselves, build-up strength, and bounce-back from so-called exogenous shocks and stresses' (Sharma, 2021: 1082). Individuals thereby take part in their own depoliticisation (Evans and Reid, 2015: 156), becoming 'implementers' of global resilience policies that they have few opportunities to resist (Bargués-Pedreny and Martin de Almagro, 2020: 343).

These trenchant criticisms of resilience may help to explain why the concept has received so little direct attention within extant scholarship on CRSV. In particular, if resilience is viewed through a neoliberal lens, any discussion of it in the context of CRSV could be construed as promoting a laissez-faire approach that leaves victims-/survivors to 'withstand and adapt to stress' (Diprose, 2015: 44). Such a framing makes the idea of resilience appear ontologically out of place in a field of scholarship and policymaking that places a strong emphasis on supporting victims-/survivors, their needs and priorities – as exemplified by the rhetoric of a 'survivor-centred approach' (Clark, 2021).

Neoliberal critiques of resilience, however, have themselves met with criticism. According to Bourbeau (2018: 22), 'scholars have been busy documenting neoliberal expressions of resilience without paying much attention to expressions of resilience not dictated by neoliberalism'. There are also important issues regarding the meaning of neoliberalism. Particularly apposite in this regard is Gamble's (2019: 985) argument – albeit not made specifically in relation to resilience – that neoliberalism has become a very broad term and 'has often been used indiscriminately to refer to all policies pursued by western governments since the 1980s'.

It is imperative to make clear from the start that this book does not embrace a neoliberal approach to resilience. In particular, it is not putting the onus on individuals to *be* resilient, and nor is it making a normative argument that victims-/survivors of CRSV 'ought to be "resilient"' (MacKinnon and Derickson, 2013: 262). It is grounded in, and contributes to, a body of scholarship – which neoliberal arguments and criticisms do not sufficiently reflect or engage with – that conceptualises resilience as an interactive process between individuals and their social ecologies (Masten, 2016; Moletsane and Theron, 2017; Oldfield and Ainsfield, 2022; Suarez et al., 2021; Theron, 2016; Ungar, 2015). These social ecologies, which Ungar (2013: 256) refers to as 'formal and informal social networks', essentially encapsulate everything that individuals have around them – including emotionally, physically, spiritually, practically – from families and communities to land, NGOs and state institutions. The essential point about social-ecological approaches to resilience is that they do not leave individuals to simply 'deal with' adversity. What they emphasise is the importance of 'Creating and sustaining facilitative environments' that enable and foster resilience (Ungar et al., 2013: 351), reflecting the fact that people are not resilient in isolation (van Breda and Theron, 2018: 238).

To return to the example of Džana, this is a Bosnian woman who has arguably demonstrated considerable resilience. She has done so, however, with crucial support from and interactions with her wider social ecology, including her husband and family, the various NGOs that have provided her with resources to develop into income-generating activities (such as bee keeping) and the local mayor who made available to her free of charge the office from which she runs her own NGO. Resilience, in other words, is 'co-facilitated by individuals and the systems of which individuals are part' (Theron et al., 2021: 361). This book specifically defines it as *a relational and dynamic process between individuals and their social ecologies in response to past and/or ongoing shocks and stressors.*

Introduction   5

The research examines some of the ways that the social ecologies of victims-/survivors of CRSV in three very different countries foster, or hinder, resilience. Seeking to demonstrate that resilience offers a multi-systemic framework for thinking about how best to support victims-/survivors and, relatedly, their wider social ecologies, it develops its own social-ecological conceptual framework. It uses this to analyse the empirical data, and specifically the qualitative interview data that form the central core of the book. Ultimately, the wider significance of the research for transitional justice theory and practice is explored and discussed. Indeed, the three key elements of the book that make it highly original are its conceptual approach, its empirical analyses and its proposed social-ecological framing of transitional justice. The following sections discuss these elements.

Thinking About Resilience Through Connectivity: A Novel Conceptual Framework

Social-ecological approaches to resilience are highly relational. They accentuate the resources that social ecologies make available, as well as individuals' capacities to navigate and negotiate access to those resources (Ungar, 2010: 6). More broadly, the concept of social-ecological systems (SES), which refers to 'integrated systems of people . . . set within their natural environments' (Gardner and Dekens, 2007: 318), foregrounds cross-scale interactions, feedbacks and relationships. For example,

> each breath of a human being is an event, that is, a set of processes experienced by the human being. In this event, many other processes come together – the production of oxygen by surrounding trees, the extraction of such oxygen by our lungs, etc.
>
> (Hertz et al., 2020: 332)

As my analysis of the empirical data progressed, it became clear that there was a larger story to be told about resilience through relationships and the stories embedded within those relationships. This book develops a narrative about resilience through a focus on connectivities – a term that better captures some of the emotional and affective dimensions of relationships than the more utilitarian-sounding term 'resources'. It explores the many connectivities between individuals and their social ecologies, and the stories of those connectivities (in different socio-cultural contexts) in the sense, inter alia, of what they do, what happens to them and how they change.

Connectivity has been discussed in many different contexts, including neuroscience (Santarnecchi and Rossi, 2016), terrorism (Desouza and Hensgen, 2007) and disability studies (Gibson, 2014). This book's use of the concept specifically draws on and has its roots in ecology scholarship, which underscores the critical significance of connectivity for the healthy functioning of complex

6 Introduction

ecosystems, such as wetlands, coral reefs and mangroves. To cite McRae et al. (2008: 2712), 'Connectivity among habitats and populations is considered a critical factor determining a wide range of ecological phenomena', including seed dispersal, maintenance of biodiversity and gene flow.

The significance of ecology in the development of research on resilience – reflected particularly in Holling's (1973, 1996) pioneering work – cannot be overstated. An important example of this, Ungar (2018) points out that 'As researchers come to understand ecological resilience better, a growing number of ecologists are shifting their focus to the resilience of social-ecological systems'. Some scholars, however, have problematised the application of ecological ideas to social systems. As Adger (2000: 350) highlights,

> Simply taking the concept of resilience from the ecological sciences and applying it to social systems assumes that there are no essential differences in behaviour and structure between socialized institutions and ecological systems. This is clearly contested in the social sciences.

One of this book's aims is precisely to demonstrate that an idea taken from the field of ecology, connectivity, has relevance and utility within a social science context, as a novel social-ecological way of thinking about and exploring resilience. Denoting movement within and between ecosystems, and the 'dispersal or movement routes of organisms' (Dickson et al., 2019: 240), connectivity offers a particularly suitable framework for analysing resilience, which itself 'is not a static concept' (Berbés-Blázquez and Scott, 2017: 10). Connectivity does not simply give a snapshot of what resilience is or looks like at a particular moment in time, and hence it allows the concept to 'move'. Relatedly, what the book's overall framework enables is a dynamic approach to resilience that captures the fluid and multi-storied connectivities between individuals and their social ecologies.

To operationalise the social-ecological synthesis that is central to its analysis, the research utilises several concepts from ecology-based literature on connectivity and repurposes them to create the core elements of its connectivity framework. The development of this framework involved what Simpson (2016: 141) has neatly termed 'iterative dialogic exchanges' between my reflections on connectivity, based on engagement with the literature, and my early explorations of the empirical data – and specifically the qualitative data (see the next section). As Chapter 2 discusses the framework in depth, it is sufficient here to briefly outline it.

First, two important concepts within ecological research on connectivity, and in particular landscape connectivity, are structural connectivity and functional connectivity. The former refers to 'the adjacency or proximity of patches within a landscape and is a measure of the degree to which patches are connected' (Van Looy et al., 2014: 228). In other words, it is about physical connectivity. Functional connectivity, in contrast, is a more behavioural concept encompassing how organisms use connectivity. It follows, therefore, that 'the functional connectivity of a landscape is likely to be both species and context-dependent' (Bélisle, 2005: 1989). There were important synergies and resonances between these ideas and the many relational connectivities that the women and men who took part in this research talked about. They spoke about crucial connectivities (including with their faith, their children and in some cases with other victims-/survivors of CRSV) that were helping them to deal with everything that they had gone through and to move forward with their lives (structural connectivity). They also discussed some of the ways that they actively utilised and drew on these connectivities (functional connectivity). This research thus incorporates the concepts of structural and functional connectivity through an in-depth analysis of the supportive and sustaining connectivities – and their contextual dimensions – that were such a prominent overarching theme within the data.

Second, McRae et al. (2008: 2712) point out that the preservation and restoration of connectivity have become a critical conservation priority, thereby indirectly illuminating the issue of fragmentation and the serious challenges that it poses. In short, 'As habitat is lost, landscapes become more fragmented and less connected, usually with negative effects on biodiversity' (Auffret et al., 2015: 51). Within the interview data, the idea of fragmentation was also present, in the sense that interviewees in all three countries spoke about the impact of their experiences – and of war and armed conflict more broadly – on some of their relationships with different parts of their social ecologies. This research uses and adapts the concept of fragmentation through its exploration of the various broken and ruptured connectivities within the data.

Third, there is a growing recognition within ecology scholarship that connectivity is dynamic. Ruiz et al.'s (2014: 515) research on playas ('inherently dynamic wetlands'), for example, underscores the importance of exploring connectivity as 'a dynamic landscape property'. What also makes connectivity dynamic is the fact that organisms themselves can create it (McCauley et al., 2012: 1711). In the interview data, it was prominent that some of the interviewees were actively engaged in building new connectivities with their social ecologies, including, in some cases, by giving back to these ecologies. This book's conceptual framework integrates the concept of dynamic connectivity by exploring these new connectivities within the data.

To summarise, this research uses a distinctive conceptual framework to analyse resilience, unpacking the relationships between individuals and their social ecologies through a focus on broken and ruptured connectivities, supportive and sustaining connectivities and new connectivities (the order in which they are discussed and examined). It demonstrates the utility of this framework, in turn, by applying it to the interview data from BiH, Colombia and Uganda. In so doing, it develops a unique set of connectivity stories about resilience. These stories capture some of the similarities and differences in how connectivities cluster and behave in varied socio-cultural contexts, and thus they make a significant contribution to both extant resilience research and scholarship on CRSV.

Applying the Conceptual Framework: The Empirical Data and Analyses

CRSV is a well-researched issue, as evidenced by a rich corpus of scholarship (see, e.g., Baaz and Stern, 2013; Boesten, 2014; Brownmiller, 1975; Engle, 2020; Kirby, 2013; Leatherman, 2011: Wood, 2009; Zalewski, 2022). BiH, Colombia and Uganda, and the use of sexual violence during these countries' respective conflicts, have also been extensively researched (see, e.g., Baines, 2014; Helms, 2014; Kreft, 2020; Porter, 2017; Sachseder, 2020; Schulz, 2021; Simić, 2018; Skjelsbaek, 2012; Stallone, 2021; Stiglymayer, 1994; Touquet, 2022). What this book uniquely provides, however, is the first in-depth comparative study of BiH, Colombia and Uganda, with a specific focus on CRSV and resilience.

The rationale for the particular choice of case studies is discussed in detail in Chapter 3. On the broader issue of the book's comparative design, which Chapter 3 also addresses, two points should be highlighted. The first is that notwithstanding the volume of extant scholarship on CRSV, there are few comparative studies. Indeed, Leiby's (2009: 447) observation that there exists 'a pressing need to add to the comparative literature on wartime sexual violence' remains highly pertinent today.

The second point is that the book's comparative approach is important from a cultural perspective. As Ungar (2008: 221) points out, 'We must understand the context in which the resources to nurture resilience are found in order to avoid hegemony in how we characterize successful development and good coping strategies'. In focusing on three heterogeneous case studies from different continents, this book seeks to capture some of the ways that cultural context shapes possibilities for resilience, what it 'looks' like and how it is expressed. Fundamentally, thinking in social-ecological ways about resilience necessarily requires sensitivity to cultural elements that are an integral part of individuals' social ecologies.

It is also necessary to acknowledge, however, that the decision to adopt a comparative approach made this research extremely challenging, from planning and organising fieldwork in multiple sites in three countries to analysing a very large amount of data, rich in cultural nuances, and making difficult decisions about what to include and what to leave out. It is also important to note in this context that I carried out the fieldwork in BiH, while two postdoctoral researchers completed the fieldwork in Colombia and Uganda respectively (all fieldwork was undertaken in the relevant local languages without interpreters).[3] This, in turn, meant that I did not have the same relationship with the Colombian and Ugandan data that I had with the Bosnian data.

Borbasi et al. (2005: 495) note that for feminist researchers, 'relationships are characterized by intimacy, self-disclosure, reciprocity and caring'. I was not able to directly develop these relationships in Colombia and Uganda. Moreover, while I can still clearly picture many of the Bosnian women and

Introduction 9

men who took part in this research – how they sat, their body language, how they interacted with me – I do not have any direct research memories to draw on in relation to the Colombian and Ugandan data (although I did make short scoping visits to both countries with the two postdoctoral researchers in 2018). Nevertheless, part of the richness of comparative working across datasets is that 'it soon sheds light on the ways in which data are embedded in the contexts in which they are produced' (Irwin et al., 2012: 68). Ultimately, I achieved 'closeness' with all three datasets (which include post-interview notes) through a process of immersion and working intensively with them for more than two years.

As Chapter 3 discusses, this research used a mixed methods approach to explore some of the complexities of resilience, and in total 449 victims-/survivors of CRSV in BiH, Colombia and Uganda took part in the study by completing a questionnaire. This book's analyses and arguments, however, are primarily based on the qualitative data, and in particular 63 semi-structured interviews (21 in each of the three countries). The data reflect the complexity and multiple layers of the interviewees' stories, but also the immense efforts that were made to capture and convey some of the diversity of victims-/survivors of CRSV and their experiences in each country. Discussions about and research on the use of sexual violence during the Bosnian war, for example, have overwhelmingly focused on Bosniak women. Helms (2014: 623) notes that it is 'beyond doubt that the majority of those raped were women (although men are often forgotten as victims of sexualized abuse) targeted for being Bosniaks, and that such atrocities were committed by far on the largest scale by Serb forces'. This does not mean, however, that acts of sexual violence committed by Bosniak and Croat forces, or the victims-/survivors of such violence, should be overlooked or treated as less important (Berry, 2017: 843). In this research, therefore, one of the priorities was to reach victims-/survivors from all three main ethnic groups in BiH, including men.

With regards to Colombia, the armed conflict has had a disproportionate impact on Indigenous and Afro-Colombian women (Acosta et al., 2018: 109; Sachseder, 2020: 165), which is linked to and reflects the wider historical context of their communities' marginalisation (Guzman-Tordecilla et al., 2022: 211). It was especially important, therefore, to ensure that both the quantitative and qualitative samples captured some of the experiences of these women. Turning to Uganda, while various scholars have undertaken extensive research on the use of sexual violence during the war between the government and Joseph Kony's Lord's Resistance Army (LRA; see, e.g., Baines, 2017; Porter, 2017; Schulz, 2021), they have predominantly concentrated on Acholi victims-/survivors. In this way, according to Apio (2016: 24), they 're-imagine the region as settled by just one language group – the Acholi, downplaying the significance of the war on other neighbouring groups', including the Langi. This research captures some of the experiences and stories of both Acholi and Lango women and men.

As the conceptual framework took shape, some of the central themes within the data started to emerge more clearly. The three aforementioned components of the framework – broken and ruptured connectivities, supportive and sustaining connectivities and new connectivities – are used to structure the three empirical chapters; and the eight core themes developed from the data are linked, in turn, to these three components. In this way, the book demonstrates both the analytical utility and the cross-cultural application of its connectivity framework.

The empirical chapters also draw on the data from several in-country reflections workshops that took place in 2021, two years after the main fieldwork was completed. The fact that these workshops were organised in the context of a global pandemic meant that they had to be on a much smaller scale than I had planned when I designed the study in 2016. It was important, however, that they went ahead – with all necessary safety measures in place – because they were a valuable opportunity to share and discuss with some of the participants key findings from the research. Valdovinos and Moreno Sandoval (2021) use the analogy of a spider weaving its web to discuss their journey as Indigenous scholars. In the reflections workshops, the analogy of a spider and its web was used to present the concepts of connectivity and social ecologies, and to explore with participants – using illustrative examples from all three countries – the significance of the many relational 'threads' (positive and negative, strong, broken, new) that they had/have in their lives.

While the Ugandans engaged most with the analogy, participants in each country frequently found it useful to learn something about the lives and experiences of victims-/survivors of CRSV in the other two countries. It was always one of the aims of this research to indirectly 'connect' people and to foster a sense of solidarity through dissemination of comparative research findings. At the close of the reflections workshops, participants were invited to write or to verbally express any messages of support that they would like to share with other victims-/survivors of CRSV. These messages appear at the end of the book.

Wider Implications for Transitional Justice: Developing the Field in New Social-Ecological Directions

The United Nations (UN, 2010: 2) has defined transitional justice as 'the full range of processes and mechanisms associated with a society's attempt to come to terms with a legacy of large-scale past abuses, in order to ensure accountability, serve justice and achieve reconciliation'. These judicial and non-judicial processes and mechanisms include criminal trials, truth commissions, reparations, institutional reforms and memorials. There have been important transitional justice developments, past and ongoing, in and relating to BiH, Colombia and Uganda (see, e.g., Allen, 2008; Baines, 2010; Fairey and Kerr, 2020; Flórez et al., 2022; Stahn et al., 2020; Theidon, 2007). These developments, however,

Introduction   11

are not the particular focus of this book's reflections about transitional justice. Resilience and social ecologies are.

Just as existing literature on CRSV has largely overlooked the concept of resilience, the latter is similarly noticeably absent from the wealth of research and scholarship on transitional justice (see, however, Ainley and Kersten, 2020; Clark and Ungar, 2021; Kastner, 2020; Wiebelhaus-Brahm, 2017). This is surprising as there are many linkages between the two. Kastner (2020: 371), for example, notes that 'Both transitional justice and resilience are concepts that are employed in the context of seemingly intractable problems that are encountered and that need to be dealt with, managed or adapted to'. Moreover, fostering resilience is, implicitly at least, an important part of transitional justice work. As one illustration, transitional justice processes effectively help to 'build and strengthen the adaptive capacity of multiple institutions' (Arnold and Gunderson, 2013: 10431) through capacity-building, institutional reforms and vetting. Additionally, there are synergies between resilience and relational goals of transitional justice, such as reconciliation. For instance, the extent to which transitional environments 'make available and accessible the resources that promote well-being' (Ungar, 2013: 258) will almost certainly shape and influence everyday relationships on the ground.

Instead of directly focusing on the multiple nexuses between resilience and transitional justice, however, this book does something more original. It demonstrates that its conceptual framework and social-ecological approach to resilience reflected within that framework have wider implications for transitional justice. De Greiff (2012: 34) has commented on the 'thickness' of the 'web of interrelationships that binds . . . different transitional justice measures'. This research underscores that transitional justice processes unfold within thick webs of inter-relationships, illustrating the many connectivities between individuals and their social ecologies. It uses the book's connectivity framework, in turn, to develop the argument that social ecologies fundamentally matter for transitional justice theory and practice. More specifically, it examines how the three core elements of its connectivity framework potentially translate into new social-ecological ways of thinking about and doing transitional justice.

First, the frequency with which interviewees in BiH, Colombia and Uganda spoke about broken and ruptured connectivities in their lives highlights the issue of harm. Miller (2009: 508) notes that 'How one conceptualizes harm is ultimately determined by the guiding conception of the self that an account employs'. That transitional justice has its roots in Western liberalism (Sharp, 2014: 75), reflected in 'the liberal end goals of transition' (Bell and O'Rourke, 2007: 37), means that it prioritises harms that violate individual autonomy. This book not only problematises (neo)liberal approaches to resilience, but it also challenges liberal framings of transitional justice. It does so by arguing the case for relational approaches to harm within transitional justice theory and practice, to ensure that some of the wider social-ecological legacies and reverberations of individual human rights violations are properly recognised.

12 Introduction

In short, it links the broken and ruptured connectivities element of its connectivity framework to the concepts of harm and relationality, and it posits a correlation between thinking relationally about harm and developing the field of transitional justice in new social-ecological directions.

It points to the significance of posthumanism (Braidotti, 2013; Haraway, 2008) as a potential framework for developing and eventually operationalising relational understandings of harm that capture social-ecological connectivities. While the field of transitional justice has largely overlooked it, posthumanism 'is rooted in a relational ontology' (Zapata et al., 2018: 479). What the book primarily underlines, however – and in this regard it makes another linkage between resilience and transitional justice – is a reconceptualisation of societies that have suffered armed conflict, large-scale violence and systematic rights abuses as SES. This would constitute a major epistemic shift, in the sense of relocating individualist conceptualisations of harm within a systemic framework and, thus, recognising the interconnectedness between individuals, their wellbeing and their social ecologies (Armitage et al., 2012).

Second, deficits – including unmet needs and expectations (see, e.g., Millar, 2010: 492; Weber, 2020: 18) – are a common theme in discussions about transitional justice (and also CRSV). The interviewees in this research, however, spoke not only about deficits, but also about what they *had* in their lives, in the sense of supportive and sustaining connectivities. The book associates this particular component of its connectivity framework with adaptive capacity, a key concept in research on resilience and, relatedly, SES (Dapilah et al., 2020; Folke et al., 2002). It argues that the prominence within the data of individuals' supportive and sustaining connectivities highlights that there is important adaptive capacity within societies like BiH, Colombia and Uganda; and it links this, in turn, to the fact that societies – as SES – are also complex adaptive systems (Holland, 1992). It further posits, therefore, that viewed within a social-ecological framework, transitional justice has a pivotal part to play in fostering this adaptive capacity, by strengthening and investing in the connectivities that support and sustain victims-/survivors of CRSV and other forms of violence in rebuilding their lives and moving forward.

Third, this book couples the remaining element of its connectivity framework – new connectivities – with mutuality, which is also an important idea within SES research (Renaud et al., 2011: 7). That many of the interviewees, in various ways, were actively building new connectivities in their lives illustrates the mutualities between them and their social ecologies. Some of them, moreover, were actively giving back to their social ecologies, for example by helping other victims-/survivors of violence. This research argues, thus, that another aspect of developing transitional justice in new social-ecological directions means exploring how it can support and encourage mutuality (thereby further investing in adaptive capacity), including, inter alia, by creating opportunities for victims-/survivors of CRSV and/or any other form of violence to forge new connectivities in their lives through story-telling and 'story-sharing'

Introduction   13

with each other. It also accentuates in this regard a conceptualisation of reparations not only as reparative but as enabling – an idea that strongly emerged from the interview data – and, thus, an important way of supporting those victims-/survivors who want to make a difference within their social ecologies.

The book's contributions to transitional justice scholarship are primarily conceptual. However, it does also make several practical suggestions, and its arguments are informed by the empirical data. What it aims to show is that its social-ecological approach to resilience, centred on connectivity, provides the basis for a social-ecological framing of transitional justice that brings resilience and transitional justice scholarship into significant dialogue with each other.

Outline of the Book

This book consists of eight chapters. The first chapter is one of two chapters that lays the conceptual foundations on which the subsequent chapters build. It gives a broad overview of resilience scholarship and of how it has developed since some of the earliest research on 'resilient children'. It explores both psychological and ecological approaches to resilience, and it particularly focuses on the shift from ecological understandings of resilience to much broader social-ecological framings concerned with the dynamics and inter-dependencies between social and ecological systems. The chapter situates the book's own conceptualisation of resilience in the larger context of this shift and demonstrates its originality by discussing some social-ecological examples of studying and analysing resilience within extant scholarship. To make it clear that the book is not adopting an uncritical approach to resilience, the chapter concludes by examining some of the main criticisms of resilience, including arguments that problematise the application of ecological ideas to the study of social systems.

The second chapter further expands on and develops the social-ecological approach to resilience adopted in this research, by introducing and detailing the book's conceptual framework based on connectivity. While connectivity, like resilience, has been discussed in many different contexts, the chapter discusses the rationale for this book's particular ecology-grounded approach to connectivity, underlining that the research reflects a social-ecological fusion that brings something fresh to both existing resilience literature and scholarship on CRSV. It outlines the core concepts that it takes from ecology-based discussions of connectivity – namely, structural and functional connectivity, fragmentation and dynamic connectivity – and explains how it adapts them to form the three key elements of its conceptual framework.

The third chapter provides important background information about the study that underpins this book. It explains the study design, focusing on the rationale for using a comparative case study approach and mixed methods. It also discusses the quantitative and qualitative parts of the study, including sampling criteria, data coding and the reflections workshops that took place in

2021. The chapter additionally reflects on some of the many ethics issues that the research raised. In so doing, it addresses two key questions: Is it ethical to seek information directly from victims-/survivors of CRSV? What about the risks of retraumatising research participants?

The fourth chapter acts as an important bridge to the empirical chapters. It outlines the background to the Bosnian war (1992–1995), the more than five decades of armed conflict in Colombia (which largely persists despite the signing of a historic peace agreement in 2016) and the two-decade-long war in northern Uganda (from the mid-1980s onwards) between government forces and the LRA. It discusses the dynamics of these conflicts and their key actors. It also gives a detailed overview of the prevalence, uses and patterns of sexual violence in these conflicts.

The fifth, sixth and seventh chapters constitute the book's empirical chapters, focused on BiH, Colombia and Uganda respectively. Collectively, they deliver a broad story about resilience through the core themes developed from the interview data (while also drawing on some of the quantitative data and on material from the reflections workshops), centred around the three elements of the book's connectivity framework. Individually, they tell very contextual stories of multiple connectivities, how they cluster and what they do in diverse socio-cultural contexts. Each of the chapters begins with a section called 'Contextualising Experiences of Violence', which discusses and unpacks the many forms of violence that the interviewees (and indeed all the participants in this research) had experienced. This is important for making clear that these women and men were not *only* victims-/survivors of CRSV. It also accentuates that the significance and implications of this research, its analyses and arguments are broader than and extend beyond CRSV.

The final chapter brings the different elements of the book together by situating and thinking about them in relation to transitional justice. It begins by examining some of the ways that interviewees in BiH, Colombia and Uganda spoke about transitional justice and their experiences (if any) of it, and it draws attention to the fact that there were some implicit social-ecological ideas about transitional justice embedded within the data. What the chapter fundamentally aims to demonstrate is that the concept of social ecologies that is so central to the book's framing and analyses of resilience is also relevant to transitional justice theory and practice. It argues that there is substantial scope for developing the field of transitional justice in new social-ecological directions, and it uses the three overarching connectivities that run through the entire book to outline a social-ecological framing of transitional justice. To do so, it links broken and ruptured connectivities, supportive and sustaining connectivities and new connectivities to the concepts, respectively, of harm and relationality, adaptive capacity and mutuality; and it translates these concepts into social-ecological avenues for exploration within transitional justice theory and practice.

The conclusion, inter alia, gives a broad summary of the book and makes some suggestions for further research relating to CRSV, resilience and transitional

Introduction   15

justice. It also presents messages from those who took part in the reflections workshops in 2021. These are messages of support that the participants wanted to communicate to other victims-/survivors of CRSV.

Notes

1 This book understands the term CRSV as referring to 'rape, sexual slavery, forced prostitution, forced pregnancy, forced abortion, enforced sterilization, forced marriage and any other form of sexual violence of comparable gravity perpetrated against women, men, girls or boys that is directly or indirectly linked to a conflict' (UN Secretary-General, 2020: 3).
2 This book uses the terminology of victims-/survivors, to reflect the fact that some of the women and men who took part in the research regarded themselves mainly as victims, some considered themselves first and foremost as survivors and some saw themselves as both victims (because of what they had gone through) and survivors (because of what they had overcome).
3 The main fieldwork was completed before the start of the global COVID-19 pandemic.

References

Acosta M, Casteñeda A, García D, Hernández F, Muelas D and Santamaria A (2018) The Colombian transitional process: Comparative perspectives on violence against Indigenous women. *International Journal of Transitional Justice* 12(1): 108–125.

Adger WN (2000) Social and ecological resilience: Are they related? *Progress in Human Geography* 24(3): 347–364.

Ainley K and Kersten M (2020) Resilience and the impacts of hybrid courts. *Leiden Journal of International Law* 33(4): 969–974.

Allen T (2008) *Trial Justice: The International Criminal Court and the Lord's Resistance Army.* London: Zed Books.

Apio EO (2016) Children born of war in northern Uganda: Kinship, marriage and the politics of post-conflict reintegration in Lango society. PhD thesis, University of Birmingham. Available at: https://etheses.bham.ac.uk/id/eprint/6926/ (accessed 4 January 2022).

Aradau C (2014) The promise of security: Resilience, surprise and epistemic politics. *Resilience* 2(2): 73–87.

Armitage D, Béné C, Charles AT, Johnson D and Allison EH (2012) The interplay of well-being and resilience in applying a social-ecological perspective. *Ecology and Society* 17(4): 15.

Arnold CA and Gunderson LH (2013) Adaptive law and resilience. *Environmental Law Reporter* 43: 10426–10443.

Auffret AG, Plue J and Cousins SAO (2015) The spatial and temporal components of functional connectivity in fragmented landscapes. *Ambio* 44: 51–59.

Baaz ME and Stern M (2013) *Sexual Violence as a Weapon of War? Perceptions, Prescriptions, Problems in the Congo and Beyond.* London: Zed Books.

Baines E (2010) Spirits and social reconstruction after mass violence: Rethinking transitional justice. *African Affairs* 109(436): 409–430.

Baines E (2014) Forced marriage as a political project: Sexual rules and relations in the Lord's Resistance Army. *Journal of Peace Research* 51(3): 405–417.

Baines E (2017) *Buried in the Heart: Women, Complex Victimhood and the War in Northern Uganda.* Cambridge: Cambridge University Press.

Bargués-Pedreny P and Martin de Almagro M (2020) Prevention from afar: Gendering resilience and sustaining hope in post-UNMIL Liberia. *Journal of Intervention and Statebuilding* 14(3): 327–348.

Barrios RE (2016) Resilience: A commentary from the vantage point of anthropology. *Annals of Anthropological Practice* 40(1): 28–38.

Bélisle M (2005) Measuring landscape connectivity: The challenge of behavioral landscape ecology. *Ecology* 86(8): 1988–1995.

Bell C and O'Rourke C (2007) Does feminism need a theory of transitional justice? An introductory essay. *International Journal of Transitional Justice* 1(1): 23–44.

Béné C, Godfrey Wood R, Newsham A and Davies M (2012) Resilience: New utopia or new tyranny? Reflection about the potentials and limits of the concept of resilience in relation to vulnerability reduction programmes. *IDS Working Papers* 404: 1–61.

Berbés-Blázquez M and Scott D (2017) The development of resilience thinking. In: Butler RW (ed.), *Tourism and Resilience*. Wallingford: CAB International, pp. 9–22.

Berry ME (2017) Barriers to women's progress after atrocity: Evidence from Rwanda and Bosnia-Herzegovina. *Gender and Society* 31(6): 830–853.

Berry ME (2018) *Women, War and Power: From Violence to Mobilization in Rwanda and Bosnia-Herzegovina*. Cambridge: Cambridge University Press.

Boesten J (2014) *Sexual Violence during War and Peace: Gender, Power, and Post-Conflict Justice in Peru*. New York, NY: Palgrave Macmillan.

Bonanno GA, Romero SA and Klein SI (2015) The temporal elements of psychological resilience: An integrative framework for the study of individuals, families and communities. *Psychology Inquiry* 26(2): 139–169.

Borbasi S, Jackson D and Wilkes L (2005) Fieldwork in nursing research: Positionality, practicalities and predicaments. *Journal of Advanced Nursing* 51(5): 493–501.

Bourbeau P (2018) A genealogy of resilience. *International Political Sociology* 12(1): 19–35.

Bourbeau P and Ryan C (2018) Resilience, resistance, infrapolitics and enmeshment. *European Journal of International Relations* 24(1): 221–239.

Braidotti R (2013) *The Posthuman*. Cambridge: Polity Press.

Brownmiller S (1975) *Against Our Will: Men, Women and Rape*. New York, NY: Fawcett Columbine.

Clark JN (2017) *Rape, Sexual Violence and Transitional Justice Challenges: Lessons from Bosnia-Herzegovina*. Abingdon: Routledge.

Clark JN (2021) Beyond a 'survivor-centred approach' to conflict-related sexual violence? *International Affairs* 97(4): 1067–1084.

Clark JN and Ungar M (eds.) (2021) *Resilience, Adaptive Peacebuilding and Transitional Justice: How Societies Recover after Collective Violence*. Cambridge: Cambridge University Press.

Coaffee J and Lee P (2016) *Urban Resilience: Planning for Risk, Crisis and Uncertainty*. London: Palgrave.

Coulter C (2009) *Bush Wives and Girl Soldiers: Women's Lives through War and Peace in Sierra Leone*. Ithaca, NY: Cornell University Press.

Cretney R (2014) Resilience for whom? Emerging critical geographies of socio-ecological resilience: Resilience of what, for whom? *Geography Compass* 8(9): 627–640.

Crosby A and Lykes MB (2019) *Beyond Repair? Mayan Women's Protagonism in the Aftermath of Genocidal Harm*. New Brunswick, NJ: Rutgers University Press.

Dapilah F, Nielsen JØ and Friis C (2020) The role of social networks in building adaptive capacity and resilience to climate change: A case study from northern Ghana. *Climate and Development* 12(1): 42–56.

De Greiff P (2012) Theorizing transitional justice. *NOMOS: American Society for Political and Legal Philosophy* 51: 31–77.

Desouza KC and Hensgen T (2007) Connectivity among terrorist groups: A two models business maturity approach. *Studies in Conflict & Terrorism* 30(7): 593–613.

Dickson BG, Albano CM, Anantharaman R, Beier P, Fargione J, Graves TA, Gray ME, Hall KR, Lawler JJ, Leonard PB, Littlefield CE, McClure ML, Novembre J, Schloss CA, Schumaker NH, Shah VB and Theobald DM (2019) Circuit-theory applications to connectivity science and conservation. *Conservation Biology* 33(2): 239–249.

Diprose K (2015) Resilience is futile. *Soundings* 58: 44–56.

Dunn Cavelty M, Kaufmann M and Søby Kristensen K (2015) Resilience and (in)security: Practices, subjects, temporalities. *Security Dialogue* 46(1): 3–14.

Edström J, Dolan C and Shahrokh T, with David O (2016) Therapeutic activism: Men of Hope refugee association Uganda breaking the silence over male rape in conflict-related sexual violence. IDS Evidence Report 182.

Engle K (2020) *The Grip of Sexual Violence in Conflict: Feminist Interventions in International Law.* Stanford, CA: Stanford University Press.

Evans B and Reid J (2015) Exhausted by resilience: Response to the commentaries. *Resilience* 3(2): 154–159.

Fairey T and Kerr R (2020) What works? Creative approaches to transitional justice in Bosnia and Herzegovina. *International Journal of Transitional Justice* 14(1): 142–164.

Flórez MCC, Parada AFM and Hoyos JFS (2022) Punishment and pardon: The use of international humanitarian law by the Special Jurisdiction for Peace in Colombia. *International Review of the Red Cross* 104(919): 1199–1221.

Folke C, Carpenter S, Elmqvist T, Gunderson L, Holling CS and Walker B (2002) Resilience and sustainable development: Building adaptive capacity in a world of transformations. *Ambio* 31(5): 437–440.

Gamble A (2019) Why is neo-liberalism so resilient? *Critical Sociology* 45(7–8): 983–994.

Gardner JS and Dekens J (2007) Mountain hazards and the resilience of social-ecological systems: Lessons learned in India and Canada. *Natural Hazards* 41: 317–336.

Gibson BE (2014) Parallels and problems of normalization in rehabilitation and universal design: Enabling connectivities. *Disability and Rehabilitation* 36(16): 1328–1333.

Guzman-Tordecilla DN, Lucumi D and Peña M (2022) Using an intervention mapping approach to develop a program for preventing high blood pressure in a marginalized Afro-Colombian population: A community-based participatory research. *Journal of Prevention* 43: 209–224.

Hanisch M (2016) What is resilience? Ambiguities of a key term. *Federal Academy for Security Policy.* Security Policy Working Paper No. 19/2016: 1–4.

Haraway DJ (2008) *When Species Meet.* Minneapolis, MN: University of Minnesota Press.

Helms E (2014) Rejecting Angelina: Bosnian war rape survivors and the ambiguities of sex in war. *Slavic Review* 73(3): 612–634.

Hertz T, Garcia MM and Schlüter M (2020) From nouns to verbs: How process ontologies enhance our understanding of social-ecological systems understood as complex adaptive systems. *People and Nature* 2(2): 328–338.

Holland JH (1992) Complex adaptive systems. *Daedalus* 121(1): 17–30.

Holling CS (1973) Resilience and stability of ecological systems. *Annual Review of Ecology and Systematics* 4: 1–23.

Holling CS (1996) Engineering resilience versus ecological resilience. In: Schulze P (ed.), *Engineering Within Ecological Constraints.* Washington, DC: National Academy Press, pp. 31–44.

Horigan KP (2021) Signs of the vanished: Commemoration in contexts of precarity. *Journal of Folklore Research* 58(3): 29–51.

Irwin S, Bornat J and Winterton M (2012) Timescapes secondary analysis: Comparison, context and working across data sets. *Qualitative Research* 12(1): 66–80.

Jordan JC (2019) Deconstructing resilience: Why gender and power matter in responding to climate stress in Bangladesh. *Climate and Development* 11(2): 167–179.

Kastner P (2020) A resilience approach to transitional justice? *Journal of Intervention and State-building* 14(3): 368–388.

Kirby P (2013) How is rape a weapon of war? Feminist international relations, modes of critical explanation and the study of wartime sexual violence. *European Journal of International Relations* 19(4): 787–821.

Koos C (2018) Decay or resilience? The long-term social consequences of conflict-related sexual violence in Sierra Leone. *World Politics* 70(2): 194–238.

Kreft AK (2019) Responding to sexual violence: Women's mobilization in war. *Journal of Peace Research* 56(2): 220–233.

Kreft AK (2020) Civil society perspectives on sexual violence in conflict: Patriarchy and war strategy in Colombia. *International Affairs* 96(2): 457–478.

Krystalli R and Schulz P (2022) Taking love and care seriously: An emergent research agenda for remaking worlds in the wake of violence. *International Studies Review* 24(1). https://doi.org/10.1093/isr/viac003.

Leatherman JL (2011) *Sexual Violence and Armed Conflict*. Cambridge: Polity Press.

Leiby ML (2009) Wartime sexual violence in Guatemala and Peru. *International Studies Quarterly* 53(2): 445–468.

Liebenberg L and Moore JC (2018) A social ecological measure of resilience for adults: The RRC-ARM. *Social Indicators Research* 136 (2019): 1–19.

MacKinnon D and Derickson KD (2013) From resilience to resourcefulness: A critique of resilience policy and activism. *Progress in Human Geography* 37(2): 253–270.

Masten AS (2016) Resilience in developing systems: The promise of integrated approaches. *European Journal of Developmental Psychology* 13(3): 297–312.

McCauley DJ, Young HS, Dunbar RB, Estes JA, Semmens BX and Micheli F (2012) Assessing the effects of large mobile predators on ecosystem connectivity. *Ecological Applications* 22(6): 1711–1717.

McEwen BS, Gray JD and Nasca C (2015) Recognizing resilience: Learning from the effects of stress on the brain. *Neurobiology of Stress* 1: 1–11.

McRae BH, Dickson BG, Keitt TH and Shah VB (2008) Using circuit theory to model connectivity in ecology, evolution and conservation. *Ecology* 89(10): 2712–2724.

Millar G (2010) Assessing local experiences of truth-telling in Sierra Leone: Getting to 'why' through a qualitative case study analysis. *International Journal of Transitional Justice* 4(3): 477–496.

Miller SC (2009) Moral injury and relational harm: Analyzing rape in Darfur. *Journal of Social Philosophy* 40(4): 504–523.

Moletsane R and Theron L (2017) Transforming social ecologies to enable resilience among girls and young women in the context of sexual violence. *Agenda* 31(2): 3–9.

Oldfield J and Ainsfield S (2022) Decentring the 'resilient teacher': Exploring interactions between individuals and their social ecologies. *Cambridge Journal of Education* 52(4): 409–430.

Oliveira C and Baines E (2022) 'It's like giving birth to this girl again': Social repair and motherhood after conflict-related sexual violence. *Social Politics* 29(2): 750–770.

Porter H (2017) *After Rape: Violence, Justice and Social Harmony in Uganda*. Cambridge: Cambridge University Press.

Renaud FG, Dun O, Warner K and Bogardi J (2011) A decision framework for environmentally induced migration. *International Migration* 49(1): 5–29.

Ruiz L, Parikh N, Heintzman LJ, Collins SD, Starr SM, Wright CK, Henebry GM, vanGestel N and McIntrye ME (2014) Dynamic connectivity of temporary wetlands in the southern Great Plains. *Landscape Ecology* 29: 507–516.

Rutter M (1987) Psychosocial resilience and protective mechanisms. *American Journal of Orthopsychiatry* 57(3): 316–331.

Sachseder J (2020) Cleared for investment? The intersections of transnational capital, gender and race in the production of sexual violence and internal displacement in Colombia's armed conflict. *International Feminist Journal of Politics* 22(2): 162–186.

Santarnecchi E and Rossi S (2016) Advances in the neuroscience of intelligence: From brain connectivity to brain perturbation. *The Spanish Journal of Psychology* 19: E94.

Schulz P (2021) *Male Survivors of Wartime Sexual Violence: Perspectives from Northern Uganda*. Oakland, CA: University of California Press.

Sharma SE (2021) Reactive, individualistic and disciplinary: The urban resilience project in Dhaka. *New Political Economy* 26(6): 1078–1091.

Sharp DN (2014) Addressing dilemmas of the global and the local in transitional justice. *Emory International Law Review* 29(1): 71–118.

Simić O (2018) *Silenced Victims of Wartime Sexual Violence*. Abingdon: Routledge.

Simpson A (2016) Designing pedagogic strategies for dialogic learning in higher education. *Technology, Pedagogy and Education* 25(2): 135–151.

Skjelsbaek I (2012) *The Political Psychology of War Rape: Studies from Bosnia and Herzegovina*. Abingdon: Routledge.

Stahn C, Agius C, Brammertz S and Rohan C (eds.) (2020) *Legacies of the International Criminal Tribunal for the Former Yugoslavia: A Multidisciplinary Approach*. Oxford: Oxford University Press.

Stallone K (2021) Strategic submission to rape is not consent: Sexual violence in the Colombian armed conflict. *Violence Against Women*. https://doi.org/10.1177/10778012211054872.

Stiglymayer A (ed.) (1994) *Mass Rape: The War against Women in Bosnia-Herzegovina*. Lincoln, NE: University of Nebraska Press.

Suarez EB, Logie C, Arocha JF, Sanchez H and Shokirova T (2021) Contesting everyday violence: Resilience pathways of gay and transgender youth in Peru. *Global Public Health* 16(5): 706–728.

Theidon K (2007) Transitional subjects: The disarmament, demobilization and reintegration of former combatants in Colombia. *International Journal of Transitional Justice* 1(1): 66–90.

Theron LC (2016) The everyday ways that school ecologies facilitate resilience: Implications for school psychologists. *School Psychology International* 37(2): 87–103.

Theron LC, Levine D and Ungar M (2021) African emerging adult resilience: Insights from a sample of township youth. *Emerging Adulthood* 9(4): 360–371.

Touquet H (2022) Silent or inaudible? Male survivor stories in Bosnia-Herzegovina. *Social Politics* 29(2): 706–728.

Touquet H and Schulz P (2021) Navigating vulnerabilities and masculinities: How gendered contexts shape the agency of male sexual violence survivors. *Security Dialogue* 52(3): 213–230.

UN (2010) Guidance note of the Secretary-General: United Nations approach to transitional justice. Available at: www.un.org/ruleoflaw/files/TJ_Guidance_Note_March_2010FINAL.pdf (accessed 21 March 2021).

20 Introduction

UN Secretary-General (2020) Conflict-related sexual violence: Report of the United Nations Secretary-General. Available at: www.un.org/sexualviolenceinconflict/wp-content/uploads/2020/07/report/conflict-related-sexual-violence-report-of-the-united-nations-secretary-general/2019-SG-Report.pdf (accessed 19 June 2021).

Ungar M (2008) Resilience across cultures. *The British Journal of Social Work* 38(2): 218–235.

Ungar M (2010) What is resilience across cultures and contexts? Advances to the theory of positive development among individuals and families under stress. *Journal of Family Psychotherapy* 21(1): 1–16.

Ungar M (2013) Resilience, trauma, context and culture. *Trauma, Violence & Abuse* 14(3): 255–266.

Ungar M (ed.) (2015) *The Social Ecology of Resilience: A Handbook of Theory and Practice*. New York, NY: Springer.

Ungar M (2018) Systemic resilience: Principles and processes for a science of change in contexts of adversity. *Ecology and Society* 23(4): 34.

Ungar M (2021) *Multisystemic Resilience: Adaptation and Transformation in Contexts of Change*. New York, NY: Oxford University Press.

Ungar M, Ghazinour M and Richter J (2013) Annual research review: What is resilience within the social ecology of development? *The Journal of Child Psychology and Psychiatry* 54(4): 348–366.

Valdovinos MG and Moreno Sandoval CD (2021) Cihuãtocameh (spiderwomen) weaving twenty years of transformative justice work in higher education. *Educational Studies* 57(5): 524–543.

van Breda A and Theron LC (2018) A critical review of South African child and youth resilience studies, 2009–2017. *Children and Youth Services Review* 91 (2018): 237–247.

Van Looy, Piffady J, Cavillon C, Tormos T, Landry P and Souchon Y (2014) Integrated modelling of functional and structural connectivity of river corridors for European otter recovery. *Ecological Modelling* 273: 228–235.

Weber S (2020) Trapped between promise and reality in Colombia's Victims' Law: Reflections on reparations, development and social justice. *Bulletin of Latin American Research* 39(1): 5–21.

Wiebelhaus-Brahm E (2017) After shocks: Exploring the relationships between transitional justice and resilience in post-conflict societies. In: Duthie R and Seils P (eds.), *Justice Mosaics: How Context Shapes Transitional Justice in Fractured Societies*. New York, NY: International Center for Transitional Justice, pp. 140–165.

Wood E (2009) Armed groups and sexual violence: When is wartime rape rare? *Politics & Society* 37(1): 131–161.

Zalewski M (2022) Theorising sexual violence in global politics: Improvising with feminist theory. *Review of International Studies* 48(1): 129–148.

Zapata A, Kuby CR and Thiel JJ (2018) Encounters with writing: Becoming-with posthumanist ethics. *Journal of Literary Research* 50(4): 478–501.

Zraly M, Rubin SE and Mukamana D (2013) Resilience and motherhood among Rwandan genocide-rape survivors. *Ethos* 41(4): 411–439.

Zulver JM (2022) *High-Risk Feminism in Colombia: Women's Mobilization in Violent Context*. New Brunswick, NJ: Rutgers University Press.

Chapter 1

Thinking About Resilience as a Social-Ecological Concept

Resilience, according to Duffield (2012: 480), is distinguished 'by its effortless ability to move across the natural, social and psychological sciences', making it 'multidisciplinary in a radical sense of the term'. Illustrating this, scholars have discussed and analysed the concept from fields as diverse as neuroscience (Hunter et al., 2018), law (Garmestani et al., 2019), education (Jennings et al., 2011), conservation (Fischer et al., 2009) and security studies (Coaffee and Fussey, 2015). Xue et al. (2018: 487), moreover, note that the number of publications addressing resilience increased six-fold between 1995 and 2004, with the 'prosperous stage' accelerating sharply after 2005.

It is therefore striking that in some areas of research, resilience has attracted relatively little attention. Studies and analyses of resilience in the context of war and armed conflict, for example, remain limited (see, e.g., De Luca and Verpoorten, 2015; Kimhi and Eshel, 2009; Winter et al., 2016). Additionally, they often approach the topic from a psychological angle and adopt a specific focus on children (Ager and Metzler, 2017; Betancourt, 2012; Fernando and Ferrari, 2015). For the purposes of this research, and as discussed in the Introduction, it is particularly significant that scholarship on conflict-related sexual violence (CRSV) has not substantively engaged with resilience. Addressing this gap, this book demonstrates why the concept is relevant to CRSV and, relatedly, transitional justice – and how it can foster important interdisciplinary dialogue (Brand and Jax, 2007).

The primary aim of this first chapter is to contextualise the research and its social-ecological approach to resilience within a wider corpus of literature. It begins by giving an overview of how resilience research has developed, focusing on a psychological 'strand' and an ecological 'strand'. The second section highlights a significant shift within the literature from ecological to much broader – and looser – social-ecological framings of resilience, and relatedly it explores the concept of social-ecological systems. The third section discusses various examples of social-ecological approaches to studying and analysing resilience, and in so doing it sets out the originality of the book's own approach (which Chapter 2 develops more fully). The fourth section examines some of the core criticisms of resilience – including those that problematise the application

DOI: 10.4324/9781003323532-2

22 Thinking About Resilience as a Social-Ecological Concept

of ecological principles to social systems – and the final section gives its own responses to these criticisms.

Development of the Resilience Field

While noting that there is still some disagreement about the origins of resilience research, Manyena (2006: 433) points out that 'Most of the literature . . . states that the study of resilience evolved from the disciplines of psychology and psychiatry in the 1940s'. During the 1970s, Holling's work advanced the study of resilience within the field of ecology. This section focuses on these two strands of scholarship – the psychological and the ecological. That the study of resilience has taken shape within very different disciplines can help to explain why the concept has been described, inter alia, as 'messy' (Ziervogel et al., 2017: 123), 'opaque' (Panter-Brick, 2014: 432) and 'imprecise' (Hassler and Kohler, 2014: 119). Both of the aforementioned strands, however, have significantly evolved. This has brought them closer together, through a common emphasis on the relationships between individuals and their broader environments.

Psychological Strand

Reviewing some of the early work on resilience (see, e.g., Cowen, 1994; Rutter et al., 1979; Werner and Smith, 1982), Ungar has identified three different meanings of the term. In his words:

> First, it [resilience] may be a description of a constellation of characteristics children have when, despite being born and raised in disadvantaged circumstances, they grow up successfully. In this sense resilience refers to better than expected developmental outcomes. Second, resilience may refer to competence when under stress. Resilient children may show competence dealing with threats to their well-being. And third, resilience may be positive functioning indicating recovery from trauma.
>
> (Ungar, 2008: 220)

The notion of competence was particularly prominent in the work of the psychologist Garmezy, one of the most influential early writers on resilience. During the 1940s and 1950s, Garmezy's research focused on competence in psychiatric patients – and in particular on the adaptive and maladaptive behaviours of adult schizophrenia patients. This progressed into an interest in how children at risk of psychopathology, including schizophrenia, were developing successfully and doing well, a topic which, according to Garmezy (1987: 164), had been 'inexplicably neglected'. During the 1970s, he accordingly established Project Competence aimed at addressing this gap (Garmezy et al., 1984: 97).

Garmezy did not, however, romanticise the concept of resilience. In particular, he stressed that it was not intended to present 'a heroic image' of children who continued to thrive despite adversity, or to thereby set them apart from other children who fared less well (Garmezy, 1991: 459). For him, rather, it was 'designed to reflect the capacity for recovery and maintained adaptive behavior that may follow initial retreat or incapacity upon initiating a stressful event' (Garmezy, 1991: 459). His work thus represented a departure from some of the other early research on resilience, which 'was dominated by a strong cultural ethos in the United States that glorified rugged individualism – that Horatio Alger ability to "pick oneself up by one's own bootstraps" and succeed solely through one's own efforts' (O'Dougherty Wright et al., 2013: 16). Within this context, children who functioned well despite challenging life circumstances were regarded as 'invulnerable' to stress (Anthony, 1974; Anthony and Cohler, 1987; Cowen and Work, 1988), as a result of their inner strength or protective 'character armor' (O'Dougherty Wright et al., 2013: 16).

As research continued to evolve, the focus expanded beyond the individual traits and characteristics of 'resilient children' (Masten and Garmezy, 1985; Werner and Smith, 1992). Increasingly, 'resilience came to be viewed in terms of an interplay of multiple risk and protective processes over time, involving individual, family, and larger sociocultural influences' (Walsh, 2003: 2). In other words, contextual factors became much more salient, highlighting the expansion of resilience from a primarily psychological idea to a wider psychosocial concept. As Rutter (1987: 317) underlined, 'If circumstances change, resilience alters'. This book, therefore, does not describe any of the women and men who took part in this research *as* resilient, as if resilience were an innate or fixed quality. What it gives salience to, rather, are some of the ways that they *demonstrated* resilience in their daily lives.

The growing emphasis on context further challenged the idea that there is something 'exceptional' about individuals who demonstrate resilience. To cite Masten (2001: 235), 'What began as a quest to understand the extraordinary has revealed the power of the ordinary'. Scholars have variously described resilience as 'a dynamic process encompassing positive adaptation within the context of significant adversity' (Luthar et al., 2000: 543); 'the capacity to do well despite adverse experience' (Gilligan, 2000: 37); 'a dynamic process of maintaining positive adaptation and effective coping strategies in the face of adversity' (Allen et al., 2011: 1); and the ability to 'maintain relatively stable, healthy levels of psychological and physical functioning' (Bonanno, 2004: 20). The key point is that resilience involves basic human adaptational systems that need be supported and cared for (Masten, 2001: 235).

On one hand, the accent on ordinariness can leave the boundaries of resilience very broad and loose; potentially almost anything can be framed as an expression of everyday resilience. Moreover, terms such as 'positive adaptation' and 'doing well' are rather vague. On the other hand, ideas of ordinariness and the everyday draw attention to 'the processes rather than the traits of resilience'

24   Thinking About Resilience as a Social-Ecological Concept

(Lenette et al., 2013: 639), and to the relevance of wider socio-cultural factors in shaping what resilience 'looks' like (Atari-Khan et al., 2021; Nguyen-Gillham et al., 2008; Ryan, 2015; Simonin, 2015).

Ecological Strand

The ecological strand of resilience research focused not on individual behaviour but on system behaviour, and it 'emerged directly out of dissatisfaction with models of ecosystem dynamics in ecological science in the 1970s' (Cote and Nightingale, 2012: 476). Central to this dissatisfaction was the premise – drawn from mathematical sciences – that ecological systems tend toward a single equilibrium state within a single domain of attraction, thus exhibiting a stable and reasonably predictable form of behaviour (Davidson, 2010: 1137). The late Holling (1996: 33) referred to this idea as 'engineering resilience' and underscored its limitations. According to him, 'The present concerns for pollution and endangered species are specific signals that the well-being of the world is not adequately described by concentrating on equilibria and conditions near them' (Holling, 1973: 2). For Holling, the reality of multiple disturbances within highly transient ecological systems, including human-made disturbances, necessitated a different and more dynamic framing of how these systems function and behave.

He contrasted engineering resilience with what he called ecological resilience, thereby emphasising 'conditions far from any equilibrium steady state, where instabilities can flip a system into another regime of behavior – that is, to another stability domain' (Holling, 1996: 33). According to this framing, resilience is not about an ecological system's post-disturbance return to an earlier state of equilibrium, precisely because there is no such equilibrium to return to (Holling, 1973: 9). Indeed, Walker (2020) insists that viewing resilience as a process of 'bouncing back' – which is actually closest to the original Latin term *resilare*, meaning a 'leap backwards' (Cretney, 2014: 629) – is perhaps 'the most common misinterpretation of resilience'.[1] Resilience, he argues, 'is largely about learning how to change in order not to be changed' (Walker, 2020). A resilient system, thus, is not one that does not change at all, but, rather, one that knows *how much* to change.

Illustrating this change dynamic, Holling (1973: 14; 1996: 33) defined ecological resilience as a 'measure of the persistence of systems and of their ability to absorb change and disturbance and still maintain the same relationships between populations or state variables'. Holling used the example of spruce budworm, a forest defoliator that damages fir trees. Budworm outbreaks are favourable to spruce and birch, which are far less vulnerable to budworm attack. The interim period between outbreaks, however, appears to favour the fir. 'This interplay with the budworm', according to Holling (1973: 14), 'maintains the spruce and birch which otherwise would be excluded through competition. The fir persists because of its regenerative powers and the interplay of forest growth rates and climatic conditions that determine the timing of budworm outbreaks'. What is crucial in this example is that high levels of instability and resilience can co-exist (Holling, 1973: 15). Rather than returning to a state of equilibrium (stability), the forest budworm community absorbs change and disturbance, and hence its very instability (fluctuations) enables its resilience.

The broader point is that the two views of resilience that Holling put forward are not incompatible. The key difference between them, as Gunderson (2010) underlines, is 'whether the system of interest returns to a prior state or reconfigures into something very different'. In this regard, the significance of Holling's work is that it offered a novel way of conceptualising the behaviour of complex ecological systems and their responses to instability and shocks – not as exceptions but as 'disturbance events, such as fire, that are essential to renew the ecosystem before another cycle of growth and development can proceed' (Berkes and Ross, 2013: 7). In the context of ecological systems, thus, the concept of adaptation has a very clear meaning, referring to the 'patterns and processes of behaviour that engage change to maintain a system within the parameters of critical thresholds' (Cretney, 2014: 630). Adaptation can be contrasted with transformation, the latter entailing a more radical shift that moves a system into another basin of attraction (Folke et al., 2005: 457). In short, 'deliberate transformation involves breaking down the resilience of the old and building the resilience of the new' (Folke et al., 2010).

Ecological systems, however, do not exist in isolation. Adger et al. (2005: 23), for example, have examined how human activities such as chronic over-fishing near coral reefs have made these complex ecosystems more vulnerable to threats such as global warming (see also Folke et al., 2010). Holling (1973: 2) himself discussed human influence on ecological systems, recognising that ecosystems and social systems need to be viewed together (Walker and Salt, 2006: 80). Resilience scholarship, therefore, has increasingly shifted to a focus on combined social and ecological systems.

Social-Ecological Systems

The concept of social–ecological systems (SES) accentuates 'humans–in–nature' (Berkes et al., 2003: 3) and, more broadly, 'the connections and feedbacks between social and environmental interactions in real-world systems' (de Vos et al., 2019; see also Cretney and Bond, 2017: 11). In other words, it highlights the limitations of any discussions about resilience and adaptive responses to shocks and stressors that do not address the relationships and dynamics between coupled social and ecological systems. Focusing on only one to the detriment of the other cannot give the full picture. For example, a society may appear to be coping well with change, such as enhancing irrigation technologies or investing more in agricultural subsidies. However, 'an evaluation of overall resilience must also include the sustainability of the adaptation from an ecological

26 Thinking About Resilience as a Social-Ecological Concept

perspective (e.g., the ecological impacts of increased farming and groundwater pumping)' (Nelson et al., 2007: 399; see also Folke et al., 2005: 443–44).

SES constitute complex adaptive systems (Holland, 1992), meaning that they consist of myriad inter-related parts and sub-systems. If the study of SES thus reflects a multi-systemic approach to resilience, the many interactions that occur within these systems reinforce the idea that resilience is highly dynamic (Masten, 2021: 2). A crucial part of SES resilience is these systems' adaptive capacity, in the sense of their ability to respond and adjust to shocks and perturbations while remaining within the same stability domain and not fundamentally changing (Folke et al., 2010; see also Folke et al., 2005: 427). This adaptive capacity is itself dynamic, as the heuristic of the adaptive cycle illustrates (Holling, 1986, 2001).

This cycle consists of four phases, although they can occur in any order. The first two phases of the cycle, namely a growth and exploitation phase (r) and a conservation phase (K), 'comprise a slow, cumulative forward loop of the cycle, during which the dynamics of the system are reasonably predictable' (Walker et al., 2004). However, as more resources are accumulated and stored in the K phase, the system becomes increasingly less flexible and less able to respond to external shocks – an 'accident waiting to happen' (Holling, 2001: 394). This inevitably leads to a chaotic collapse and release phase (Ω), which rapidly develops into a reorganisation and renewal phase (α). These latter two phases comprise an unpredictable and uncertain back loop, with different potential outcomes (Davidson, 2010: 1138). In summary, 'The sequence of gradual change is followed by a sequence of rapid change, triggered by disturbance', which underscores the broader point that both stabilities and instabilities organise the behaviour of SES (Folke, 2006: 258; Holling, 2001: 395).

Further evidencing the complexity of SES, different adaptive cycles simultaneously occur within them at different scales, which means that these systems cannot be studied or understood at only one scale (Walker et al., 2004). SES research thus necessitates multi-scalar analysis, and crucial in this regard is the concept of panarchy – referring to 'hierarchies across scales' (Gunderson and Holling, 2002: 5).[2] According to Allen et al. (2014: 578), panarchy 'provides a framework that characterizes complex systems of people and nature as dynamically organized and structured within and across scales of space and time'. It is the multi-scale interactions and feedbacks that occur within SES that further shape and influence the resilience of these systems (Walker et al., 2006).

The omega (Ω) and K phases of the adaptive cycle, for example, have been referred to respectively as 'revolt' and 'remember'. 'Revolt' essentially captures upward dynamics, illustrating how disturbances at a lower level can move up the system. Folke (2006: 259) uses the example of

> a small ground fire that spreads to the crown of a tree, then to a patch in the forest and then to a whole stand of trees. Each step in that cascade of events moves the disturbance to a larger and slower level.

Other examples might include economic crises, wars, pandemics and localised protests that develop into large-scale revolutions.

'Remember', in contrast, reflects a downward dynamic and it has a stabilising function. It refers to the cumulative knowledge, experience and stored capital of a system that it can utilise. For instance, 'a coral reef hit by a storm draws on its own legacies and the memory of the seascape of which it is a part' (Holling, 2001: 398). Accordingly, the 'memory' within this 'remembering' is ecological memory – the legacies of systemic adaptations to past shocks and disturbances (Johnstone et al., 2016: 371). It is interesting to think about this idea in relation to transitional justice – an important element of this book. Transitional justice processes, which can be seen as part of societies' 'reorganisation' phase of the adaptive cycle, place a strong emphasis on memory and remembering (Manning, 2017: 5; Shaw, 2007: 193). Little attention, however, has been given to cross-scale memory dynamics (in the sense, for example, of memory 'resources' being co-opted in the design of transitional justice interventions); or to the potential uses of accumulated memory across these scales as resources for building systems that are more resilient to future shocks and disturbances (Clark, 2020).

Analyses of SES have taken the field of resilience research in exciting new directions. They also offer an important illustration of Masten's (2001: 234–235) argument that:

> The new frontier for resilience research is understanding . . . [adaptive] processes at multiple levels, from genes to relationships, and investigating how the individual as a complex living system interacts effectively and ineffectively over time with the systems in which it is embedded.
>
> (see also Ungar, 2021a; Walsh, 2007)

Some of the ideas that this section has outlined, moreover, can be applied in many different contexts. The adaptive cycle heuristic, for example, has been discussed, inter alia, in relation to addiction interventions and research (Randle et al., 2015), the development of community-based tourism in Taiwan (Tsao and Ni, 2016) and the dynamics of urban centres on Mexico's Caribbean coast (Pelling and Manuel-Navarrete, 2011). Xu and Kajikawa (2018: 247), for their part, maintain that the adaptive cycle can help to explain how individuals deal with trauma and why some 'recover' more quickly than others.

Nevertheless, it can be hard to pin down exactly what these systems are. As Walsh-Dilley and Wolford (2015: 175) underline, the concept links social and ecological systems 'across scales from the most miniscule to the global and even cosmic levels . . . making system limits difficult to define'. The immense complexity of these systems, moreover, including their cross-scale dynamics, creates further challenges in the sense of how to study them and what to focus on. Reflecting on the concept of panarchy, for example, Karkkainen (2005: 65) has argued that it 'conjures up not only intricate layers of impenetrable and seemingly unmanageable complexity, but also a sense of futility, coupled with less clarity and optimism about how to respond'.

This book is not about SES in the broad sense of systemic behaviour and dynamics, and it is not about relationships between people and nature. It is, however, about relationships between people – and specifically the female and male victims-/survivors of CRSV in BiH, Colombia and Uganda who took part in this research – and their wider environments. In this regard, it adopts a social-ecological approach to resilience, both conceptually and analytically. The next section gives some examples of social-ecological approaches to resilience within extant scholarship, before delineating the book's own (and novel) approach.

Resilience as a Social-Ecological Concept

While resilience is increasingly discussed as a social-ecological concept, there are different interpretations of what this means, reflected in different types of social-ecological approaches within the literature. Adger, for example, has explored the linkages between social and ecological resilience through a focus on communities' dependence on ecosystems. According to him, communities' direct dependence 'is an influence on their social resilience and ability to cope with shocks, particularly in the context of food security and coping with hazards' (Adger, 2000: 354). Hence, anything that affects ecosystem resilience will also have an impact on communities' resilience. Adger illustrates this using the example of mangrove conversion in northern Vietnam. The privatisation and market liberalisation of these mangroves has reduced their resilience and, by extension, the social resilience of communities who rely on these coastal ecosystems for their livelihoods (Adger, 2000: 359). In other words, 'The interaction of the management of the coastal resources with the social system forms a direct coevolving link between ecological and social resilience' (Adger, 2000: 360).

Folke et al.'s (2010) research has explored the impact of human behaviour on surrounding ecosystems. Using the example of the Goulburn-Broken catchment in the Murray Darling Basin, Australia, they showed that the area appeared to be thriving, as evidenced by its significant contribution (25 per cent) to export earnings within the State of Victoria. Adding a social-ecological lens, however, gave a very different perspective. According to the authors, 'Widespread clearing of native vegetation and high levels of water use for irrigation have resulted in rising water tables, creating severe salinization problems; so severe that the region faces serious social-ecological thresholds with possible knock-on effects between them' (Folke et al., 2010). A social-ecological approach to resilience can therefore offer important insights into how human actions potentially harm or threaten ecological resilience, in turn underscoring that 'social change is essential for SES resilience' (Folke et al., 2010).

Taking the ecological part of SES as referring to the environment, ecosystems and natural resources, Garmestani et al.'s discussion is less about nature-society relationships per se and more about how laws and legal systems deal with them. In defining resilience as 'the amount of disturbance a linked social-ecological system can absorb before reorganizing into a new state characterized by a different set of processes and structures' (Garmestani et al., 2014: 6), they examine how the interactions between social and ecological systems may create change dynamics that inherently challenge how the law works – and some of the assumptions that it makes about stability. In their words,

> Although the change-slowing effect of law helps society to absorb shocks and disturbances up to a point, law can be brittle and maladaptive if it cannot keep up with the pace, scale, and direction of social-ecological change, such as drought and flooding patterns and their effects.
> (Garmestani et al., 2014: 3)

What their analysis illuminates, thus, is the need for legal decision-making that is sensitive to the underlying ecological and social context. Relatedly, it supports the case for 'an adaptive legal system' which, through its processes and structures, itself builds 'the resilience and adaptive capacity of both nature and society' (Garmestani et al., 2014: 8).

Other scholars conceptualise the 'ecological' as referring more broadly to an individual's general environment – including family, friends, teachers, institutions and recreational spaces. Discussing resilience in relation to children, for example, Ungar (2011: 12) maintains that 'Under stress, a child's social and physical ecology is likely to account for more of the variance in developmental pathways than that accounted for by personal factors'. For him, therefore, a social-ecological approach to resilience means putting context before individuals (Ungar, 2011: 4, 12; see also Ungar, 2005: 429).

A social-ecological approach thus framed, however, does not imply a one-way dynamic of environments shaping and influencing individual outcomes. Pointing to the importance of two key processes, namely navigation and negotiation, Ungar et al. (2008: 168) insist that individuals must be able to navigate their way to crucial resources, but also to negotiate for these resources to be provided in culturally meaningful ways (see also Ungar, 2008: 225). Inherent in this navigation and negotiation is a crucial dialectic between individuals and their environments, reflecting the bigger point that 'The personal agency of individuals to navigate and negotiate for what they need is dependent upon the capacity and willingness of people's social ecologies to meet those needs' (Ungar, 2013: 256).

Similarly, Theron et al. (2014: 254) stress that resilience processes 'are embedded in reciprocal collaborations' – at different levels – between individuals and their social ecologies (see also Theron and Malindi, 2010: 718). In their research on the resilience of Black youths in South Africa, they explore the significance of reciprocity in the relationships between young people and their teachers in schools. They underline the importance not

30 Thinking About Resilience as a Social-Ecological Concept

just of supportive school environments for young people, but also of 'rights-based school environments' that value 'youths' right to freedom of expression (including being able to request support and behave agentically) and opportunities for youths to develop optimally and responsibly' (Theron et al., 2014: 260).

In their study of the social-ecological resilience resources of adults who, as children, experienced clerical institutional abuse in Ireland, Liebenberg and Moore do not specifically define what they mean by social ecology. However, they accent 'the quality of physical and relational resources located in the social ecology that support resilience processes' (Liebenberg and Moore, 2018: 2). 'Ecology' thereby refers to a person's environment in a broad sense – and to what the different layers of this environment offer. More specifically, the authors' exploratory factor analysis on the Adult Resilience Measure (ARM; Resilience Research Centre, 2016) – a measurement tool discussed in Chapter 3 of this book – led them to identify five protective factors operating within the research participants' social ecologies. These factors were social/community inclusion, family attachment and supports, spirituality, national and cultural identity and personal competencies (Liebenberg and Moore, 2018: 8).

This book adopts its own novel social-ecological approach to resilience. Emphasising the idea of connectivity, which it borrows from the field of ecology (as discussed in the next chapter), it explores resilience through a focus on the relational connectivities between individuals and their social and physical ecologies – including families, communities, local organisations and natural resources. These connectivities and connectivity clusters variously support resilience, frustrate it and contextually shape it. They are dynamic, reflecting the 'changing environments' in which individuals live and grow (Bronfenbrenner, 1977: 513). Hence, they are significant in their own right. Resilience literature focuses on the feedbacks within SES as they respond to disturbances, but it neglects the impact that disturbances themselves have on these feedbacks and interactions. Resilience, thus, is partly a story of connectivities – what they do, what happens to them, how they change. This research, as set out in the Introduction, defines it as a relational and dynamic process between individuals and their social ecologies in response to past and/or ongoing shocks and stressors.

Conceptually and empirically, this book makes an original contribution to existing literature on resilience – and CRSV. As Bourbeau (2015: 390) points out, however, 'If the emergence of resilience in the social sciences is hard to miss these days, so too are the polarizing remarks that the prominence of resilience has provoked'. The next section of this chapter explores some of the main criticisms of resilience (and SES). These include arguments that specifically problematise the 'migration' of resilience from the field of ecology and physical sciences into the social sciences and policy sphere (MacKinnon and Derickson, 2013: 253).

Some Critical Views of Resilience

The concept of SES assumes the existence of strong synergies between social and ecological systems in how they behave and react to disturbance. The adaptive cycle concept previously discussed is one illustration of this. According to Barrios (2016: 29), however, the use of the term resilience reflects a number of assumptions that simply do not work when applied to people and social systems. He particularly takes issues with what he terms an assumption of stability or of return to a pre-disturbance state. For him,

> the idea that resilience is the capacity to return to a precatastrophe state of affairs, where the 'prestate' was a stable condition, is a fundamentally inadequate model for understanding what human communities are, and how they may respond to disasters.
>
> (Barrios, 2016: 30)

Karkkainen, for his part, expresses concerns about the potential meaning of the adaptive cycle and panarchy concepts from a human perspective. If we are all 'just along for the ride on the "Double Loop [a reference to the forward and back loops of the adaptive cycle] Panarchy Express"', he argues, the implications of this appear 'pretty scary' (Karkkainen, 2005: 64–65). For him,

> It is a bit like being trapped on a twenty-first century, high-tech version of a double-looping carnival ride, armed with the capacity to fiddle with the precise trajectory but only in ultimately unpredictable ways, and never able to change the basic pattern of our interminable trip: forward, up, around, down, back loop, down, around, up, forward again, and the more we try to adjust course, the more the pattern stays the same.
>
> (Karkkainen, 2005: 65)

Both of these arguments, however, simplify how complex SES work. Most importantly, and as this chapter has discussed, there is no single equilibrium to which these systems 'bounce back', thereby returning to a pre-disturbance stability. Rather, as complex adaptive systems, they have 'multiple states or domains of attraction and multiple equilibria' (Berkes et al., 2003: 15). Their complexity and related non-linearity, moreover, mean that these systems are far more dynamic than Karkkainen's interpretation suggests. To cite Berkes and Ross (2013: 7), SES are 'unpredictable systems, subject to cycles of continuous change and renewal'.

MacKinnon and Derickson signal a different problem with utilising ecological principles to study and explain social dynamics. According to them, 'Both the ontological nature of "the system" and its normative desirability escape critical scrutiny. As a result, the existence of social divisions and inequalities tends to be glossed over when resilience thinking is extended to society' (MacKinnon

32 Thinking About Resilience as a Social-Ecological Concept

and Derickson, 2013: 258). Cote and Nightingale (2012: 479), similarly, point to the risks of 'a kind of social analysis that hides the possibility to ask important questions about the role of power and culture in adaptive capacity, or to unpack normative questions such as "resilience of what?" and "for whom?" when applied to the social realm' (see also Vale, 2014: 191; Ziervogel et al., 2017: 126). This section explores some of the key criticisms of resilience with specific reference to these two important questions.

Resilience of What?

Resilience is specifically a response to adversity. In short, it 'only exists where there has been a perturbation that is unusual and stressful for one or more interdependent systems' (Ungar, 2021b: 10; see also Masten and Powell, 2003: 2; Rutter, 2012: 336). However, scholars have drawn attention to how adversities and shocks may be unequally distributed, reflecting deeper power dynamics, and place a disproportionate burden on particular groups to 'adapt'. In her discussion of climate change in Oceania, for example, McDowell (2020: 69) frames resilience as a 'morally-loaded discourse' that places the responsibility for dealing with disasters on individuals and communities, while simultaneously removing responsibility from the very actors – states and the 'global international community of polluters' – that are predominantly contributing to climate change. For her, 'The most effective way of ensuring the resilience of people in Oceania to the threats posed by climate change and disaster is to stop global carbon emissions' (McDowell, 2020: 69). Making a similar argument in a different context, Barrios (2016: 31) notes that:

> In the Gulf of Mexico Coast of Southeastern Louisiana . . . there are a number of federally unrecognized Native American communities such as Isle de Jean Charles that are facing the need to resettle due to coastal erosion and rising sea levels.

The crucial point – illuminating what Chandler (2020: 210) has called ' "artificial" or "coercive" forms of adaption' – is that these communities have *had* to adapt to climate-related stressors for which they themselves are not responsible. Coastal erosion, Barrios underlines, is the result of petrochemical companies and the United States Army Corps of Engineers altering the natural environment though channel-building efforts and the construction of levees along the banks of the Mississippi River. This, for him, raises the pivotal question of what exactly resilience building means in this case. If it refers to the capacity of Indigenous coastal communities to adapt to the destructive environmental practices and legacies of capitalist industrialisation, 'the concept of resilience does not mitigate disasters but serves as a mechanism for the maintenance of the "system" that creates them' (Barrios, 2016: 31). More specifically, it legitimises a global political economy that preserves and serves the interests of the

Thinking About Resilience as a Social-Ecological Concept   33

powerful (Barrios, 2016: 32; see also Cannon and Muller-Mahn, 2010: 633; Chandler, 2020: 10; Cretney and Bond, 2017: 11).

The asymmetrical distribution of threats and adversities evidences, in turn, deeper structural inequalities (Jordan, 2019: 168; MacKinnon and Derickson, 2013: 254), and some scholars have particularly foregrounded gender inequalities. Sultana (2010: 46), for example, comments that 'In general, gender relations and social norms often reinforce women's vulnerabilities to floods and disasters'; and Smyth and Sweetman (2015: 410) point out that 'Women living in poverty in contexts threatened by complex crises are required each day to be resilient and withstand stresses and shocks which threaten the wellbeing – and sometimes the very lives – of themselves and their dependents'. These inequalities have important intersectional dimensions (Ajibade et al., 2013: 1723; Carr and Thompson, 2014: 187) and may be linked to wider cultural norms (Jordan, 2019: 175). They also affect how individuals (and in particular women) adapt to adversity – and the resources that they can access (Agarwal, 1992: 137; Kiewisch, 2015: 500; Nelson and Stathers, 2009: 82). Drawing on their research in nine countries in West and East Africa, including Senegal, Ethiopia and Uganda, Perez et al. (2015: 105–106) reflect that 'The real challenge for women . . . is not accessing outside institutions in general but specifically overcoming tremendous anti-women biases by public and private agencies that foster agriculture and livestock production'. These biases, they add, render female-headed households vulnerable to food insecurity and increase the challenges of adapting livelihood practices to economic and climate-based risks (Perez et al., 2015: 105–106).

If resilience creates unequal burdens, which themselves tell a much bigger story, it also entails trade-offs. Fundamentally, resilience at one level 'may be at odds with resilience at other levels' (Berkes and Ross, 2016: 191). In rural Bolivia, for example, market-dominated shifts in the international price of quinoa positively contributed to the wellbeing of quinoa farmers, but they undermined rural resilience more broadly (Chelleri et al., 2015: 190). Relatedly, because resilience can exist at any scale within a panarchy, there may be significant variations within a system that is resilient overall (Allen and Holling, 2010: 3; Vale, 2014: 195). What some scholars have specifically underlined, however, is that 'power operates in and through socio-environmental systems' (Cote and Nightingale, 2012: 481). Hence, power is necessarily imbricated in resilience trade-offs and in decisions about which trade-offs are 'acceptable'. According to Béné et al. (2014: 608), 'experience has taught us that already-marginalised households are likely to be amongst the "new" losers' (see also McDowell, 2020: 68).

For Davoudi (2012: 306), therefore, we cannot talk about resilience – and its desirability – in a social context without also discussing 'issues of justice and fairness' relating to decision-making processes and the spread of benefits and burdens. This further reinforces the importance of asking whose resilience are we talking about – and, relatedly, for whose/what purpose (Cinner and Barnes,

2019: 55; Leach et al., 2010: 371; Olsson et al., 2015: 6). Using the example of post-Katrina New Orleans, Vale (2014: 197) asks, inter alia: 'Is "New Orleans" resilient even if some of its component neighbourhoods remain half-empty? Is "the city" resilient even if many of its poorest former citizens have not been able to return?' In short, 'Whose New Orleans matters?' (Vale, 2014: 197). More generally, who decides what does and does not constitute resilience (Lenette et al., 2013: 640)?

Finally, some scholars have articulated concerns that in SES research, attention to structures deflects from issues of agency and decision-making – which are themselves unequally distributed (Davidson, 2010: 1143). Béné et al. (2012: 12), for example, assert that in many discussions about resilience and SES, the focus is on 'the ability of the "system" to recover from shocks . . . rather than the choices exercised by individuals within the system, who may, or may not, exert control over the processes by which resilience is shaped'. One of the consequences, critics argue, is the common idea within resilience policies that communities need to be 'acted upon'. If such policies thus privilege some forms of agency over others, they also, by extension, disregard local sources of knowledge (McDowell, 2020: 60; Nelson and Stathers, 2009: 89).

Resilience for Whom?

A broad set of criticisms within extant scholarship centres on the idea that resilience serves a wider political agenda – and specifically a neoliberal agenda (Chandler, 2012; De Lint and Chazal, 2013; Evans and Reid, 2013). Joseph (2013: 40), for example, maintains that resilience 'has been plucked from the ecology literature and used in a fairly instrumental way to justify particular forms of governance which emphasise responsible conduct'. 'Responsible', in this regard, means that individuals are expected 'to govern themselves in appropriate ways' (Joseph, 2013: 41), to 'cope with uncertainty' (Howell and Voronka, 2012: 4) and to manage risks (O'Malley, 2010: 505). More broadly, the practice of 'responsibilising' entails diminishing the state's responsibilities towards its citizens and 'increasingly putting the onus for preventing and preparing for disruptive challenge – in all its guises – on to institutions, professions, communities and individuals' (Coaffee, 2013: 248).

Scholars such as Duffield have expressed particular concerns about the use of resilience policies vis-à-vis developing countries. According to him, 'The debased political subject of resilience is not expected to demand state protection or unrealistically insist that threats are effectively dealt with' (Duffield, 2016: 154). For him, moreover, the operationalisation of resilience policies through a 'neoliberal stripping away', particularly in the areas of social and economic welfare, points to the emergence of a new biopolitics which frames disasters and disturbances as necessary (Duffield, 2012: 481; see also Welsh, 2014: 248). What this means is that individuals are expected to show resilience in the face of risks with minimal state support and interventions (Coaffee, 2013: 248).

Neoliberal agendas legitimise state rollbacks, but so too, according to some scholars, do the very dynamics of SES. Their complexity and non-linearity create a justification – in the context of the need for perpetual adaptability to uncertainties that are beyond our control (Walker and Cooper, 2011: 156) – for 'the neoliberal belief in the necessity of risk as a private good' (Joseph, 2016: 374). The wider implications of this, according to Chandler (2014: 58), are that resilience thinking denotes 'a rationality of governing which removes the modernist understanding of government as instrumentally acting in a world potentially amenable to cause-and-effect understandings of policy-making'. An emphasis on systemic properties, however, deflects from the fact that policy-making can itself be part of the problem. Policies aimed at promoting societal resilience, for example, can result in 'forced' resilience that 'cascades' problems through the system by increasing anthropogenic dependencies and weakening ecosystemic sources of resilience (Chandler, 2020: 199). Hence, governance practices and interventions can themselves generate significant shocks and disturbances that reduce systemic resilience.

Reflecting Critically on the Criticisms

The trenchant arguments discussed in the previous section make it clear that resilience is by no means a straightforward concept, and this book does not treat it as such. At the same time, however, it is not uncritical of some of the critiques developed in the literature. First and foremost, it maintains that many of the claims focused around neoliberalism and governmentality offer a reductionist view of resilience. As Bourbeau (2015: 375) maintains, 'although resilience may be in some instances a neoliberal device for governance, it has a wider range of meanings as well. Reducing resilience to a neoliberal product limits more than it reveals in the context of international politics' (see also Bourbeau, 2018; Corry, 2015; Juncos, 2018; Schmidt, 2015). The accent that neoliberal arguments place on the purported agenda underpinning resilience, moreover, gives little insights into what exactly resilience *is* (Bourbeau, 2015: 379) or how it manifests in diverse socio-cultural environments. As Brassett and Vaughan-Williams (2015: 39) point out, it is important to reflect on what resilience does and means in different contexts.

As an illustration of this, Bourbeau and Ryan have analysed the interconnections between resilience and resistance in relation to the Palestinian national liberation struggle. According to them,

> The forms of Palestinian resilience interact with and shape the forms of resistance that are possible, and, in turn, Palestinian resistance and refusal to acquiesce makes resilience necessary because (overt) Palestinian resistance is almost invariably met with an Israeli response that makes daily life more difficult.
>
> (Bourbeau and Ryan, 2018: 234; see also Ryan, 2015)

36 Thinking About Resilience as a Social-Ecological Concept

This example powerfully challenges Reid's (2012: 76) assertion that 'To be resilient is to forego the very power of resistance'. Indeed, one of Juncos' (2018: 560) criticisms of neoliberal conceptualisations of resilience is precisely that they 'neglect the possibility of contestation and agency'. The Palestinian example also counters and complexifies the idea of 'responsibilisation' and its emphasis on the responsibilities that neoliberal agendas *require* of individuals, neglecting the responsibilities that individuals may themselves *choose* to take on. For Howell (2015: 68), moreover, responsibilisation arguments betray 'a nostalgia for the welfare state', which, she underlines, is 'perhaps not shared by those who have chronicled how women, queers, racialised people, those institutionalised in psychiatric facilities, and indigenous peoples in settler societies have had vexed relations with the welfare state'.

For the purposes of this research, neoliberal governmentality critiques of resilience raise two particular issues. First, they overwhelmingly treat resilience as a policy (see, e.g., Duffield, 2012; Joseph and Juncos, 2019), with a frequent focus on the United Kingdom (Anderson and Adey, 2012; Welsh, 2014: 19; Zebrowski, 2009). This book, to be clear, is not approaching resilience as a policy. It analyses some of the ways that victims-/survivors of CRSV in three different countries, and through their relationships with their social ecologies, express and demonstrate resilience. In discussing the wider significance of the research and its connectivity framework for transitional justice, the book posits a linkage between the latter and resilience. However, its argument is not that resilience should be a policy of transitional justice processes, which are themselves policies. Rather, its focus is on why social ecologies matter for transitional justice; and in unpacking this, it draws out some important and largely unexplored ways that judicial and non-judicial processes of dealing with past human rights violations might themselves potentially contribute to resilience.

Second, arguments about responsibilisation and state rollbacks are quintessentially discordant with the aims of this research. The book is not advocating a laissez-faire approach to individuals and communities affected by large-scale violence, conflict and human rights abuses. In focusing on the stories of men and women who have found different ways to get on with and start to rebuild their lives, it locates everyday expressions of resilience in the interactions and connectivities between individuals and their social ecologies. What it seeks to demonstrate, thus, is that exploring resilience can usefully inform policy in the sense of illustrating why social ecologies matter, including in the sense of what they lack (deficits) and what they provide (resources). Doing so is not about leaving individuals to govern themselves (Joseph, 2013: 41). It is about drawing attention to, and seeking to address, the reality that 'adaptive responses are not equal in terms of the sustainability of resource use, energy intensity, reduction of vulnerability, or in the distribution of their benefits' (Adger et al., 2011: 757).

Turning to some of the normative critiques (focused on issues of power and inequalities) discussed in the previous section, and to which Adger et al.'s aforementioned argument is itself linked, these are very significant. In particular, they underline the importance of 'critically thinking through resilience for whom, what, when, where, and why' (Meerow and Newell, 2019: 310). They also make it clear that resilience is not always something positive. Ruhl et al. (2021: 514) point out that 'If, for example, a legal system is highly resilient in the engineering sense, but it is producing outcomes that are no longer normatively acceptable to society, its resilience is a problem, not a virtue'. Similarly, while they are not desirable, poverty cycles in inner-city areas (Berkes and Ross, 2013: 16), pathogenic viruses (Hassler and Kohler, 2014: 127) and dictatorships (Walker, 2020) can all be highly resilient. In this regard, it is essential to reiterate that this book is not suggesting that victims-/survivors of CRSV *should* demonstrate resilience in dealing with their experiences of adversity, which in many cases have cross-temporal dimensions (i.e., they are not only confined to periods of war and armed conflict). The fundamental point is that very little attention to date has been given to some of the different and contextually specific ways that many of these men and women actually *do* manifest resilience.

What some of the normative criticisms of resilience usefully bring to the foreground is the relationship between the social and the ecological within SES. A mechanical or too literal transposition of broad ecological systems theory to complex social systems can marginalise important 'human' dimensions of resilience. It is precisely to bring out these dimensions that some scholars specifically refer to social resilience. Adger (2000: 347), for example, defines this as 'the ability of groups or communities to cope with external stresses and disturbances as a result of social, political, and environmental change'; and Herman (2015: 103) uses the term to mean 'the way in which individuals, communities and societies adapt, transform, and potentially become stronger when faced with environmental, social, economic or political challenges'. These examples illustrate that the concept of social resilience has a strong actor-oriented focus (Keck and Sakdapolrak, 2013: 14). Certainly, it is imperative that research on SES does not minimise the fundamental importance of social actors and agency. At the same time, however, there is considerable merit in Davidson's (2010: 1141) argument that 'Prospects for moving toward a conceptual framework that integrates . . . social and ecological systems also appear to be strong'. Folke (2006: 260), moreover, has commented that efforts to understand SES are still in a relatively early stage, meaning that there is ample opportunity 'for creative approaches and perspectives'. This book's own social-ecological approach to resilience utilises that opportunity.

★★★

This chapter has provided an overview of existing scholarship on resilience. The purpose was not to give a detailed genealogy of resilience (Bourbeau, 2018). The aim, rather, was to broadly map out how this field of research has developed – and in particular how it has evolved from an early focus on the 'invulnerability' of children facing adversity to complex multi-disciplinary and multi-systemic studies of SES and the relationships between individuals and their social ecologies. The chapter has thus clearly located this research and its

38 Thinking About Resilience as a Social-Ecological Concept

own social-ecological approach to resilience within a larger body of scholarship. The next chapter further elaborates on the book's approach to resilience and develops its conceptual framework, focused on connectivity.

Notes

1 My own work has also challenged the association of resilience with 'bouncing back' (see Clark, 2021).
2 Holling (2001: 396) explained that:

> Because the word 'hierarchy' is so burdened by the rigid, top-down nature of its common meaning, we decided to look for another term that would capture the adaptive and evolutionary nature of adaptive cycles that are nested one within each other across space and time scales. . . . We therefore melded the image of the Greek god Pan as the epitoma of unpredictable change with the notion of hierarchies across scales to invent a new term that could represent structures that sustain experiment, test its results, and allow adaptive evolution. Hence, 'panarchy'.

References

Adger WN (2000) Social and ecological resilience: Are they related? *Progress in Human Geography* 24(3): 347–364.

Adger WN, Brown K, Nelson DR, Berkes F, Eakin H, Folke C, Galvin K, Gunderson L, Goulden M, O'Brien K, Ruitenbeek J and Tompkins EL (2011) Resilience implications of policy responses to climate change. *WIREs Climate Change* 2(5): 757–766.

Adger WN, Hughes TP, Folke C, Carpenter SR and Rockström J (2005) Social-ecological resilience to coastal disasters. *Science* 309(5737): 1036–1039.

Agarwal B (1992) The gender and environment debate: Lessons from India. *Feminist Studies* 18(1): 119–158.

Ager A and Metzler J (2017) Where there is no intervention: Insights into processes of resilience supporting war-affected children. *Peace and Conflict* 23(1): 67–75.

Ajibade I, McBean G and Bezner-Kerr R (2013) Urban flooding in Lagos, Nigeria: Patterns of vulnerability and resilience among women. *Global Environmental Change* 23(6): 1714–1725.

Allen CR and Holling CS (2010) Novelty, adaptive capacity and resilience. *Ecology and Society* 15(3): 24.

Allen CR, Angeler DG, Garmestani AS, Gunderson LH and Holling CS (2014) Panarchy: Theory and application. *Ecosystems* 17: 578–589.

Allen RS, Haley PH, Harris GM, Fowler SN and Pruthi R (2011) Resilience: Definitions, ambiguities and applications. In: Resnick B, Gwyther L and Roberto K (eds.), *Resilience in Ageing*. New York, NY: Springer, pp. 1–13.

Anderson B and Adey P (2012) Governing events and life: 'Emergency' in UK civil contingencies. *Political Geography* 31(1): 24–33.

Anthony EJ (1974) The syndrome of the psychologically invulnerable child. In: Anthony EJ and Koupernik C (eds.), *The Child in His Family: Children at Psychiatric Risk*. New York, NY: Wiley, pp. 529–545.

Anthony EJ and Cohler BJ (eds.) (1987) *The Invulnerable Child*. New York, NY: Guilford Press.

Atari-Khan R, Covington AH, Gerstein LH, Al Herz H, Varner BR, Brasfield C, Shurigar B, Hinnenkamp SF, Devia M, Barrera S and Deogracias-Schleich A (2021) Concepts of resilience among trauma-exposed Syrian refugees. *The Counselling Psychologist* 49(2): 233–268.

Barrios RE (2016) Resilience: A commentary from the vantage point of anthropology. *Annals of Anthropological Practice* 40(1): 28–38.

Béné C, Newsham A, Davies M, Ulrichs M and Godfrey Wood R (2014) Resilience, poverty and development. *Journal of International Development* 26(5): 598–623.

Béné C, Wood RG, Newsham A and Davies M (2012) Resilience: New utopia or new tyranny? Reflection about the potentials and limits of the concept of resilience in relation to vulnerability reduction programmes. *IDS Working Papers* 404: 1–61.

Berkes F and Ross H (2013) Community resilience: Toward an integrated approach. *Society & Natural Resources* 26(1): 5–20.

Berkes F and Ross H (2016) Panarchy and community resilience: Sustainability science and policy implications. *Environmental Science & Policy* 61: 185–193.

Berkes F, Colding J and Folke C (2003) Introduction. In: Berkes F, Colding J and Folke C (eds.), *Navigating Social-Ecological Systems: Building Resilience for Complexity and Change.* Cambridge: Cambridge University Press, pp. 1–29.

Betancourt TS (2012) The social ecology of resilience in war-affected youth: A longitudinal study from Sierra Leone. In: Ungar M (ed.), *The Social Ecology of Resilience.* New York, NY: Springer, pp. 347–356.

Bonanno GA (2004) Loss, trauma and human resilience: Have we underestimated the human capacity to thrive after extremely aversive events? *American Psychologist* 59(1): 20–28.

Bourbeau P (2015) Resilience and international politics: Premises, debates, agenda. *International Studies Review* 17(3): 374–395.

Bourbeau P (2018) A genealogy of resilience. *International Political Sociology* 12(1): 19–35.

Bourbeau P and Ryan C (2018) Resilience, resistance, infrapolitics and enmeshment. *European Journal of International Relations* 24(1): 221–239.

Brand FS and Jax K (2007) Focusing the meaning(s) of resilience: Resilience as a descriptive concept and a boundary object. *Ecology and Society* 12(1): 23.

Brassett J and Vaughan-Williams N (2015) Security and the performative politics of resilience: Critical infrastructure protection and humanitarian emergency preparedness. *Security Dialogue* 46(1): 32–50.

Bronfenbrenner U (1977) Toward an experimental ecology of human development. *American Psychologist* 32(7): 513–531.

Cannon T and Muller-Mahn D (2010) Vulnerability, resilience and development discourses in the context of climate change. *Natural Hazards* 55(3): 621–635.

Carr ER and Thompson MC (2014) Gender and climate change adaptation in agrarian settings: Current thinking, new directions and research frontiers. *Geography Compass* 8(3): 182–197.

Chandler D (2012) Resilience and human security: The post-interventionist paradigm. *Security Dialogue* 43(3): 213–229.

Chandler D (2014) Beyond neoliberalism: Resilience, the new art of governing complexity. *Resilience* 2(1): 47–63.

Chandler D (2020) Security through societal resilience: Contemporary challenges in the Anthropocene. *Contemporary Security Policy* 41(2): 195–214.

Chelleri L, Waters JJ, Olazabal M and Minucci G (2015) Resilience trade-offs: Addressing multiple scales and temporal aspects of urban resilience. *Environment and Urbanization* 27(1): 181–198.

40 Thinking About Resilience as a Social-Ecological Concept

Cinner JE and Barnes ML (2019) Social dimensions of resilience in social-ecological systems. *One Earth* 1(1): 51–56.

Clark JN (2020) Re-thinking memory and transitional justice: A novel application of ecological memory. *Memory Studies* 14(4): 695–712.

Clark JN (2021) Beyond 'bouncing': Resilience as an expansion-contraction dynamic within a holonic frame. *International Studies Review* 23(3): 556–579.

Coaffee J (2013) Rescaling and responsibilising the politics of urban resilience: From national security to local place-making. *Politics* 33(4): 240–252.

Coaffee J and Fussey P (2015) Constructing resilience through security and surveillance: The policies, practices and tensions of security-driven resilience. *Security Dialogue* 46(1): 86–105.

Corry O (2015) From defense to resilience: Environmental security beyond neo-liberalism. *International Political Sociology* 8(3): 256–274.

Cote M and Nightingale AJ (2012) Resilience thinking meets social theory: Situating social change in social-ecological systems (SES) research. *Progress in Human Geography* 36(4): 475–489.

Cowen EL (1994) The enhancement of psychological wellness: Challenges and opportunities. *American Journal of Community Psychology* 22(2): 149–180.

Cowen EL and Work WC (1988) Resilient children, psychological wellness and primary prevention. *American Journal of Community Psychology* 16: 591–607.

Cretney R (2014) Resilience for whom? Emerging critical geographies of socio-ecological resilience: Resilience of what, for whom? *Geography Compass* 8(9): 627–640.

Cretney RM and Bond S (2017) Shifting relationships to place: A relational place-based perspective on SES resilience. *Urban Geography* 38(1): 8–24.

Davidson DJ (2010) The applicability of the concept of resilience to social systems: Some sources of optimism and nagging doubts. *Society and Natural Resources* 23(12): 1135–1149.

Davoudi S (2012) Resilience: A bridging concept or a dead end? *Planning Theory and Practice* 13(2): 299–333.

De Lint W and Chazal N (2013) Resilience and criminal justice: Unsafe at low altitude. *Critical Criminology* 21: 157–176.

De Luca G and Verpoorten M (2015) Civil war, social capital and resilience in Uganda. *Oxford Economic Papers* 67(3): 661–686.

de Vos A, Biggs R and Preiser R (2019) Methods for understanding social-ecological systems: A review of place-based studies. *Ecology and Society* 24(4): 16.

Duffield M (2012) Challenging environments: Danger, resilience and the aid industry. *Security Dialogue* 43(5): 475–492.

Duffield M (2016) The resilience of the ruins: Towards a critique of digital humanitarianism. *Resilience* 4(3): 147–165.

Evans B and Reid J (2013) Dangerously exposed: The life and death of the resilient subject. *Resilience* 1(2): 1–16.

Fernando C and Ferrari M (eds.) (2015) *Handbook of Resilience in Children of War*. New York, NY: Springer.

Fischer J, Peterson GD, Gardner TA, Gordon LJ, Fazey I, Elmqvist T, Felton A, Folke C and Dovers S (2009) Integrating resilience thinking and optimisation for conservation. *Trends in Ecology & Evolution* 24(10): 549–554.

Folke C (2006) Resilience: The emergence of a perspective for social-ecological systems analyses. *Global Environmental Change* 16(3): 253–267.

Folke C, Carpenter SR, Walker B, Scheffer B, Chapin T and Rockström J (2010) Resilience thinking: Integrating resilience, adaptability and transformability. *Ecology and Society* 15(4): 20.

Folke C, Hahn T, Olsson P and Norberg J (2005) Adaptive governance of social-ecological systems. *Annual Review of Environment and Resources* 30: 441–473.

Garmestani A, Ruhl JB, Chaffin BC, Craig RK, van Rijswick HFMW, Angeler DG, Folke C, Gunderson L, Twidwell D and Allen CR (2019) Untapped capacity for resilience in environmental law. *PNAS: Proceedings of the National Academy of Sciences of the United States of America* 116(40): 19899–19904.

Garmestani AS, Allen CR, Arnold CA and Gunderson LH (2014) Introduction: Social-ecological resilience and law. In: Garmestani AS and Allen CR (eds.), *Social-Ecological Resilience and Law*. New York, NY: Columbia University Press, pp. 1–14.

Garmezy N (1987) Stress, competence and development: Continuities in the study of schizophrenic adults, children vulnerable to psychopathology and the search for stress-resistant children. *American Journal of Orthopsychiatry* 57(2): 159–174.

Garmezy N (1991) Resilience in children's adaptation to negative life events and stressed environments. *Pediatrics* 20(9): 459–466.

Garmezy N, Masten AS and Tellegen A (1984) The study of stress and competence in children: A building block for developmental psychopathology. *Child Development* 55(1): 97–111.

Gilligan R (2000) Adversity, resilience and young people: The protective value of positive school and spare time experiences. *Children and Society* 14(1): 37–47.

Gunderson LH (2010) Ecological and human community resilience in response to natural disasters. *Ecology and Society* 15(2): 18.

Gunderson LH and Holling CS (eds.) (2002) *Panarchy. Understanding Transformations in Human and Natural Systems*. Washington, DC: Island Press.

Hassler U and Kohler N (2014) Resilience in the built environment. *Building Research & Information* 42(2): 119–129.

Herman A (2015) Enchanting resilience: Relations of care and people-place connections in agriculture. *Journal of Rural Studies* 42: 102–111.

Holland JH (1992) Complex adaptive systems. *Daedalus* 121(1): 17–30.

Holling CS (1973) Resilience and stability of ecological systems. *Annual Review of Ecology and Systematics* 4: 1–23.

Holling CS (1986) The resilience of terrestrial ecosystems: Local surprise and local change. In: Clark WC and Munn RE (eds.), *Sustainable Development of the Biosphere*. Cambridge: Cambridge University Press, pp. 292–317.

Holling CS (1996) Engineering resilience versus ecological resilience. In: Schulze P (ed.), *Engineering Within Ecological Constraints*. Washington, DC: National Academy Press, pp. 31–44.

Holling CS (2001) Understanding the complexity of economic, ecological and social systems. *Ecosystems* 4: 390–405.

Howell A (2015) Resilience as enhancement: Governmentality and political economy beyond 'responsibilisation'. *Politics* 35(1): 67–71.

Howell A and Voronka J (2012) Introduction: The politics of resilience and recovery in mental health care. *Studies in Social Justice* 6(1): 1–7.

Hunter RG, Gray JD and McEwen BS (2018) The neuroscience of resilience. *Journal of the Society for Social Work and Research* 9(2): 305–339.

Jennings PA, Snowberg KE, Coccia MA and Greenberg MT (2011) Improving classroom learning environments by cultivating awareness and resilience in education (CARE): Results of two pilot studies. *The Journal of Classroom Interaction* 46(1): 37–48.

Johnstone JF, Allen CD, Franklin JF, Frelich LE, Harvey BJ, Higuera PE, Mack MC, Meentemeyer RK, Metz MR, Perry GLW, Schoenaggel T and Turner MG (2016) Changing disturbance regimes, ecological memory and forest resilience. *Frontiers in Ecology and the Environment* 14(7): 369–378.

Jordan JC (2019) Deconstructing resilience: Why gender and power matter in responding to climate stress in Bangladesh. *Climate and Development* 11(2): 167–179.

Joseph J (2013) Resilience as embedded neoliberalism: A governmentality approach. *Resilience* 1(1): 38–52.

Joseph J (2016) Governing through failure and denial: The new resilience agenda. *Millennium* 44(3): 370–390.

Joseph J and Juncos AE (2019) Resilience as an emergent European project? The EU's place in the resilience turn. *Journal of Common Market Studies* 57(5): 995–1011.

Juncos AE (2018) Resilience in peacebuilding: Contesting uncertainty ambiguity, and complexity. *Contemporary Security Policy* 39(4): 559–574.

Karkkainen BC (2005) Panarchy and adaptive change: Around the loop and back again. *Minnesota Journal of Law, Science & Technology* 7: 59–78.

Keck M and Sakdapolrak P (2013) What is social resilience? Lessons learned and ways forward. *Erkunde* 67(1): 5–19.

Kiewisch E (2015) Looking within the household: A study on gender, food security and resilience in cocoa-growing communities. *Gender & Development* 23(3): 497–513.

Kimhi S and Eshel Y (2009) Individual and public resilience and coping with long-term outcomes of war. *Journal of Applied Biobehavioral Research* 14(2): 70–89.

Leach M, Scoones I and Stirling A (2010) Governing epidemics in an age of complexity: Narratives, politics and pathways to sustainability. *Global Environmental Change* 20(2): 369–377.

Lenette C, Brough M and Cox L (2013) Everyday resilience: Narratives of single refugee women with children. *Qualitative Social Work* 12(5): 637–653.

Liebenberg L and Moore JC (2018) A social ecological measure of resilience for adults: The RRC-ARM. *Social Indicators Research* 136: 1–19.

Luthar SS, Cicchetti D and Becker B (2000) The construct of resilience: A critical evaluation and guidelines for future work. *Child Development* 71(3): 543–562.

MacKinnon D and Derickson KD (2013) From resilience to resourcefulness: A critique of resilience policy and activism. *Progress in Human Geography* 37(2): 253–270.

Manning P (2017) *Transitional Justice and Memory in Cambodia: Beyond the Extraordinary Chambers*. Abingdon: Routledge.

Manyena SB (2006) The concept of resilience revisited. *Disasters* 30(4): 434–450.

Masten AS (2001) Ordinary magic: Resilience processes in development. *American Psychologist* 56(3): 227–238.

Masten AS (2021) Resilience of children in disasters: A multisystem perspective. *International Journal of Psychology* 56(1): 1–11.

Masten AS and Garmezy N (1985) Risk, vulnerability and protective factors in developmental psychopathology. In: Lahey B and Kazdin A (eds.), *Advances in Clinical Child Psychology*, Vol. 8. New York, NY: Plenum Press, pp. 1–52.

Masten AS and Powell JL (2003) A resilience framework for research, policy and practice. In: Luthar SS (ed.), *Resilience and Vulnerability: Adaptation in the Context of Childhood Adversities*. New York, NY: Cambridge University Press, pp. 1–28.

McDowell S (2020) Other dark sides of resilience: Politics and power in community-based efforts to strengthen resilience. *Anthropological Forum* 30 (1–2): 55–72.

Meerow S and Newell JP (2019) Urban resilience for whom, what, when, where, and why? *Urban Geography* 40(3): 309–329.

Nelson DR, Adger WN and Brown K (2007) Adaptation to environmental change: Contribution of a resilience framework. *Annual Review of Environment and Resources* 32: 395–419.

Nelson V and Stathers T (2009) Resilience, power, culture and climate: A case study from semi-arid Tanzania and new research directions. *Gender & Development* 17(1): 81–94.

Nguyen-Gillham V, Giacaman R, Naser G and Boyce W (2008) Normalising the abnormal: Palestinian youth and contradictions of youth in protracted conflict. *Health and Social Care in the Community* 16(3): 291–298.

O'Dougherty Wright M, Masten AS and Narayan AJ (2013) Resilience processes in development: Four waves of research on positive adaptation in the context of adversity. In: Goldstein S and Brookes R (eds.), *Handbook of Resilience in Children*. Boston, MA: Springer, pp. 15–37.

O'Malley P (2010) Resilient subjects: Uncertainty, warfare and liberalism. *Economy and Society* 39(4): 488–509.

Olsson L, Jerneck A, Thoren H, Persson J and O'Byrne D (2015) Why resilience is unappealing to social science: Theoretical and empirical investigations of the scientific use of resilience. *Science Advances* 1(4): e1400217.

Panter-Brick C (2014) Health, risk and resilience: Interdisciplinary concepts and applications. *Annual Review of Anthropology* 43: 431–448.

Pelling M and Manuel-Navarrete D (2011) From resilience to transformation: The adaptive cycle in two Mexican urban centers. *Ecology and Society* 16(2): 11.

Perez C, Jones EM, Kristjanson P, Cramer L, Thornton PK, Förch W and Barahona C (2015) How resilient are farming households and communities to a changing climate in Africa? A gender-based perspective. *Global Environmental Change* 34: 95–107.

Randle JM, Stroink ML and Nelson CH (2015) Addiction and the adaptive cycle: A new focus. *Addition Research and Theory* 23(1): 81–88.

Reid J (2012) The disastrous and politically debased subject of resilience. *Development Dialogue* 58: 67–79.

Resilience Research Centre (2016) The Resilience Research Centre Adult Resilience Measure (RRC-ARM): User's manual. Available at: https://cyrm.resilienceresearch.org/files/ArchivedMaterials.zip (accessed 9 October 2021).

Ruhl JB, Cosens B and Soininen N (2021) Resilience of legal systems: Toward adaptive governance. In: Ungar M (ed.), *Multisystemic Resilience: Adaptation and Transformation in Contexts of Change*. New York, NY: Oxford University Press, pp. 509–529.

Rutter M (1987) Psychosocial resilience and protective mechanisms. *American Journal of Orthopsychiatry* 57(3): 316–331.

Rutter M (2012) Resilience as a dynamic concept. *Development and Psychopathology* 24: 335–344.

Rutter M, Maughan B, Mortimore P and Ouston J (1979) *Fifteen Thousand Hours: Secondary Schools and their Effects on Children*. Cambridge, MA: Harvard University Press.

Ryan C (2015) Everyday resilience as resistance: Palestinian women practising *sumud*. *International Political Sociology* 9(4): 299–315.

Schmidt J (2015) Intuitively neoliberal? Towards a critical understanding of resilience governance. *European Journal of International Relations* 21(2): 402–426.

Shaw R (2007) Memory frictions: Localizing the truth and reconciliation commission in Sierra Leone. *International Journal of Transitional Justice* 1(2): 183–207.

Simonin PW (2015) From sea to spirit: Resilience conceptions in coastal communities of Kaledupa, Indonesia. *Resilience* 3(3): 199–206.

Smyth I and Sweetman C (2015) Introduction: Gender and resilience. *Gender & Development* 23(3): 405–414.

Sultana F (2010) Living in hazardous waterscapes: Gendered vulnerabilities and experiences of floods and disasters. *Environmental Hazards* 9(1): 43–53.

Theron LC and Malindi MJ (2010) Resilient street youth: A qualitative South African study. *Journal of Youth Studies* 13(6): 717–736.

Theron LC, Liebenberg L and Malindi MJ (2014) When schooling experiences are respectful of children's rights: A pathway to resilience. *School Psychology International* 35(3): 253–265.

Tsao CY and Ni CC (2016) Vulnerability, resilience and the adaptive cycle in a crisis-prone tourism community. *Tourism Geographies* 18(1): 80–105.

Ungar M (2005) Pathways to resilience among children in child welfare, corrections, mental health and educational settings: Navigation and negotiation. *Child and Youth Care Forum* 34(6): 423–444

Ungar M (2008) Resilience across cultures. *The British Journal of Social Work* 38(2): 218–235.

Ungar M (2011) The social ecology of resilience: Assessing contextual and cultural ambiguity of a nascent construct. *American Journal of Orthopsychiatry* 81(1): 1–17.

Ungar M (2013) Resilience, trauma, context and culture. *Trauma, Violence & Abuse* 14(3): 255–266.

Ungar M (ed.) (2021a) *Multisystemic Resilience: Adaptation and Transformation in Contexts of Change.* New York, NY: Oxford University Press, pp. 6–31.

Ungar M (2021b) Modeling multisystemic resilience: Connecting biological, psychological, social and ecological adaptation in contexts of adversity. In: Ungar M (ed.), *Multisystemic Resilience: Adaptation and Transformation in Contexts of Change.* New York, NY: Oxford University Press, pp. 6–31.

Ungar M, Liebenberg L, Boothroyd R, Kwong WM, Lee TY, Leblanc J, Duque L and Makhnach A (2008) The study of youth resilience across cultures: Lessons from a pilot study of measurement development. *Research in Human Development* 5(3): 166–180.

Vale LJ (2014) The politics of resilient cities: Whose resilience and whose city? *Building Research & Information* 42(2): 191–201.

Walker BH (2020) Resilience: What it *is* and is not. *Ecology and Society* 25(2): 11.

Walker BH and Salt D (2006) *Resilience Thinking: Sustaining Ecosystems and People in a Changing World.* Washington, DC: Island Press.

Walker BH, Gunderson L, Kinzig A, Folke C, Carpenter S and Schultz L (2006) A handful of heuristics and some propositions for understanding resilience in social-ecological systems. *Ecology and Society* 11(1): 13.

Walker BH, Holling CS, Carpenter SR and Kinzig A (2004) Resilience, adaptability and transformability in social-ecological systems. *Ecology and Society* 9(2): 5.

Walker J and Cooper M (2011) Genealogies of resilience: From systems ecology to the political economy of crisis adaptation. *Security Dialogue* 42(2): 143–160.

Walsh F (2003) Family resilience: A framework for clinical practice. *Family Process* 41(2): 1–18.

Walsh F (2007) Traumatic loss and major disasters: Strengthening family and community resilience. *Family Process* 46(2): 207–227.

Walsh-Dilley M and Wolford W (2015) (Un)Defining resilience: Subjective understandings of 'resilience' from the field. *Resilience* 3(3): 173–182.

Welsh M (2014) Resilience and responsibility: Governing uncertainty in a complex world. *The Geographical Journal* 180(1): 15–26.

Werner EE and Smith RS (1982) *Vulnerable but Invincible: A Longitudinal Study of Resilient Children and Youth*. New York, NY: McGraw-Hill.

Werner EE and Smith RS (eds.) (1992) *Overcoming the Odds: High Risk Children from Birth to Adulthood*. Ithaca, NY: Cornell University Press.

Winter DA, Brown R, Goins S and Mason C (2016) *Trauma, Survival and Resilience in War Zones: The Psychological Impact of War in Sierra Leone and Beyond*. Abingdon: Routledge.

Xu L and Kajikawa Y (2018) An integrated framework for resilience research: A systematic review based on citation network analysis. *Sustainability Science* 13: 235–254.

Xue X, Wang L and Yang RJ (2018) Exploring the science of resilience: Critical review and bibliometric analysis. *Natural Hazards* 90: 477–510.

Zebrowski C (2009) Governing the network society: A biopolitical critique of resilience. *Political Perspectives* 3(1).

Ziervogel G, Pelling M, Cartwright A, Chu E, Deshpande T, Harris L, Hyams K, Kaunda J, Klaus B, Michael K, Pasquini L, Pharoah R, Rodina L, Scott D and Zweig P (2017) Inserting rights and justice into urban resilience: A focus on everyday risk. *Environment and Urbanization* 29(1): 123–138.

Chapter 2

Analysing Resilience Through Connectivity

This chapter develops the conceptual framework that informs the book's particular social-ecological approach to resilience, as well as its empirical analyses and, ultimately, its arguments about transitional justice. The framework is based on connectivity, a concept that is widely discussed in many different disciplines and contexts. In urban design, for example, connectivity refers to street networks and residents' walking behaviours (Koohsari et al., 2014). In neuroscience, connectivity is about large-scale networks and complex connections within the brain (Zalesky et al., 2012: 1055). According to Kaufmann (2013: 53), moreover, 'connectivity seems to have become an essential quality of modern societies'. We are interconnected, inter alia, through technologies, communication, health, trade and global economies.

Drawing on ecology scholarship, which broadly discusses connectivity as referring to interactions and movement within and between ecosystems (Dakos et al., 2015: 80), this book explores resilience through a focus on the multi-layered and dynamic connectivities between individuals and their social ecologies – and the stories encapsulated within those connectivities. Embracing the argument that 'the phenomenon of connectivity and how it matters should be studied as contextually situated and experienced' (Cecez-Kecmanovic et al., 2014), it examines different manifestations and clusters of connectivity within the interview data from Bosnia-Herzegovina (BiH), Colombia and Uganda. It demonstrates how they affect experiences and legacies of conflict-related sexual violence (CRSV), and how they variously shape, support or hinder resilience.

It is important to stress from the outset that connectivity, like resilience, is not necessarily beneficial or desirable. It can exacerbate the effects and impact of financial crises, particularly on local livelihoods (Adger et al., 2009: 156), and facilitate the spread of disease and pest outbreaks (Dakos et al., 2015: 89). Relatedly, Crooks and Suarez (2006: 452–453) highlight the issue of 'hyper-connectivity', which they define as increased connections resulting from anthropogenic activities that create opportunities for widespread species invasions.[1] While this research therefore adopts a nuanced approach to connectivity, in order to capture both its positive and negative aspects, its focus is not on the quantitative question – which is arguably implicit in the concept of

DOI: 10.4324/9781003323532-3

Analysing Resilience Through Connectivity   47

hyperconnectivity – of 'how much connectivity is right?' If this, according to Walker (2020), is 'one of those tricky Goldilocks questions', it also detracts from the important point that 'the "connectivity of what-to-what" and "how connectivity changes" are as important as the fact that connectivity increases or decreases' (Freeman et al., 2017: 84).

The chapter begins by elaborating on the rationale for the book's particular use of connectivity as its conceptual framework. The second section gives an overview of some of the ways that other scholars have linked resilience and connectivity in their own work, directly or indirectly. The third, fourth and fifth sections outline the three dimensions of connectivity that constitute the book's conceptual (and applied) framework – namely, supportive and sustaining connectivities, broken and ruptured connectivities and new connectivities. That these connectivities are multi-systemic, moreover, is significant in the wider context of 'a growing recognition that resilience is multidimensional and multidetermined, and can best be understood as the product of transactions within and between multiple systemic levels over time' (Waller, 2001: 294).

Why Connectivity

The idea of connectivity, loosely defined, is present in extant literature on sexual and gender-based violence (SGBV) in various ways. Some scholars, for example, have expressed concerns that a heavy focus on CRSV detracts from 'the continuum of violence which connects multiple forms of SGBV across both war and peace' (Gray, 2019: 190).[2] On this point, Boesten (2017: 507) maintains that global policies that effectively exceptionalise CRSV critically omit 'to address what makes such violence possible' (see also Baaz and Stern, 2018; Boesten, 2014; Crawford, 2013; Davies and True, 2015; Kirby and Shepherd, 2016; Meger, 2016: Motlafi, 2018). Scholarship has also examined some of the ways that CRSV can damage connectivities (without specifically using this terminology) – and in particular connections and relationships with others (see, e.g., Di Lellio et al., 2019; Mukamana and Brysiewicz, 2008; Schulz, 2018). Additionally, the concept of intersectionality, which is frequently discussed in feminist research on SGBV, is about connectivity in the sense of multiple and interconnected dimensions of identity – including gender, race, class, caste and sexuality – that converge to explain discrimination, oppression and exclusion (Crenshaw, 1989, 1991; MacKinnon, 2013; Salem, 2018).

This research specifically utilises connectivity – 'the complex phenomenon of being connected, making and maintaining that connection' (Angelopulo, 2014: 210) – to build a narrative about resilience. During the process (discussed in more detail in Chapter 3) of analysing the interview data that are central to this book, one of the ideas that started to strongly emerge was relational connectivities. Illustrating that 'life is always lived in relationship with others' (Rose, 2017: 496; see also Jordan and Walker, 2004: 2), interviewees in BiH, Colombia and Uganda all spoke about important connections in their lives – cultural, emotional, physical, spiritual – that were helping them to deal with their experiences. As the process of identifying and developing core themes from the data advanced, the idea of connectivity progressively became more prominent. Nevertheless, there were other possible conceptual frameworks that this research might have used instead.

Most obviously, perhaps, it could have adopted a feminist framework, to recognise 'feminist expertise in deploying relationality as a critical theoretical and methodological tool' (Zalewski, 2019: 616) – and to reflect the richness of feminist research on relational concepts such as care (de la Bellacasa, 2012; Nelson and Power, 2018; Tronto, 1998). It could, alternatively, have developed a framework around social network theory and analysis, to disaggregate and explore the significance of individuals' many social networks – such as friendship networks and advice networks (Prell, 2012: 7) – and the role of these networks in fostering 'the capacity to buffer, adapt to, and shape change' (Rockenbauch and Sakdapolrak, 2017). Another possibility would have been to use Relational-Cultural Theory (RCT), which also foregrounds relationships (Hartling, 2008; Jordan, 2008) and shares much in common with this book's emphasis on connectivity. RCT constitutes a theory about 'our basic interconnectedness' and growth 'through and toward connection' (Jordan, 2017: 231).

This book, however, has a specific rationale for using connectivity as its conceptual framework and for drawing on connectivity research within the field of ecology. This rationale is fundamentally linked to the discussion of social-ecological systems (SES) in the previous chapter. To reiterate, there is a need for further research – and greater clarity – on how the social and ecological parts of these systems fit together and interact. Bodin and Tengö (2012: 430), for example, argue that there has been limited 'methodological and theoretical progress on how to, in detail, quantitatively study these social-ecological interdependencies'; and Janssen et al. (2006) insist that 'Studies on the resilience of social-ecological systems lack the guidance of a clear framework'. Illustrating this point, Binder et al. (2013) have identified 16 potential frameworks for studying SES, ten of which they explore in depth. According to them, 'Our analysis has shown that frameworks used to analyze social-ecological systems vary significantly as to their theoretical and disciplinary origin, their purpose, and the way they conceptualize the social and the ecological systems, their interaction and dynamics' (Binder et al., 2013).

One of the aims of this research was precisely to develop its own framework. By adapting a concept from the field of ecology and repurposing it within a social science context, what the book contributes to existing scholarship is a novel social-ecological approach to resilience and way of thinking about the 'linkages and feedbacks' within SES (Cinner and Barnes, 2019: 55). It explores the connectivities between victims-/survivors of CRSV and their wider social ecologies, and how these connectivities – in different ways – shape resilience. It is also significant that in the field of ecology, connectivity – to reiterate – is largely about movement; it is what allows 'materials or organisms to move between or influence habitats, populations or assemblages that are intermittently isolated in space or time' (Sheaves, 2009: 108). In other words, application of the book's connectivity framework fosters a 'moving' narrative of resilience, focused on the changing and multiple connectivities between individuals and their social ecologies.

Cecez-Kecmanovic et al. (2014) refer to 'stories about living connectivity'. The use of the word 'living' reinforces the idea that connectivity is dynamic and fluid. As one illustration, while resilience is a response to adversity and disturbances (Ungar, 2021a: 6), these same stressors can greatly impact – positively or negatively – on connectivities themselves. In Finland, for example,

> A shock to the system, in the form of a major flood in 2005, forced improved communication between local, regional, and higher-level agencies, whereas in the past, institutional barriers between the leaders and bureaucrats in Helsinki limited the coordination of emergency response.
> (Garmestani et al., 2014: 372)

To take a different example, climate disturbances can affect connectivity within ocean ecosystems. According to Gerber et al. (2014: 11), 'Ocean warming and acidification may alter the spatial scale of connectivity, potentially increasing connectivity among nearby habitats and reducing connectivity among already distant habitats'. What this book underlines, therefore, is that connectivities, and the interactions between connectivities, tell their own stories, including of what they do and of how they change in reaction to shocks and stresses such as war and armed conflict.

A final important point to accentuate regarding connectivity is that it is a multi-systemic concept. It can be defined at different levels (Bani et al., 2019: 111), and the connectivities (and the stories of those connectivities) that this book explores occur and evolve at multiple social-ecological levels. They extend from the micro-system level, which Bronfenbrenner (1977: 514) defined as referring to an individual's 'immediate setting' (such as home or workplace), to the macro-system level and 'overarching institutional patterns of the culture or subculture, such as the economic, social, educational, legal, and political systems' (Bronfenbrenner, 1977: 515). The book's analysis of connectivities, thus, both strongly resonates with and contributes to important and developing multi-systemic theorisations of resilience (see, e.g., Masten, 2021; Theron and van Breda, 2021; Ungar, 2021b).

As discussed in the previous chapter, some scholars have problematised an 'overemphasis on the similarities between social and ecological dynamics in resilience thinking' (Cote and Nightingale, 2012: 480; see also Barrios, 2016: 29; Duit et al., 2010: 365). While this book's approach to connectivity specifically draws on ecology scholarship, its aim, to be clear, is not to make simplistic comparisons between social and ecological dynamics. What it seeks to demonstrate is the utility of 'interdisciplinary borrowing' (Byford and Tileagă, 2014:

361), by developing a framework that reflects and enables a dynamic approach to resilience.

It is additionally important to stress that the book's interdisciplinary approach and use of ecology scholarship should not be construed in any way as detracting from the stories of the individual women and men in BiH, Colombia and Uganda who participated in this research. Indeed, application of its connectivity framework provides new and multi-dimensional insights into their lives – as the three empirical chapters demonstrate. This is significant because one of the book's arguments is that supporting victims-/survivors of CRSV also means supporting, as much as possible, their social ecologies – and the resources within those ecologies. Contrary to critical arguments (discussed in the previous chapter) that associate resilience with 'a neoliberal governance agenda' (Leitner et al., 2018: 1277) and individual responsibility, this research conceptualises resilience as a 'co-construction' (Haysom, 2017: 1).

The empirical chapters, moreover, do not focus just on CRSV. They additionally give attention to and discuss the complex and interlocking experiences of violence – connected across time and space – that many of the research participants had gone through. Swaine (2015: 759) points out that:

> Rarely is it acknowledged in this talk of strategic rape[3] that women [and men] may experience *wider* and *variant* harms alongside, and as part of, that act of rape, and that it may occur on multiple occasions from a multiple range of assailants at multiple sites.
> (emphasis in the original; see also Gray, 2019: 191)

Exploring these wider and variant harms, and their 'multiple' elements, this research also draws attention to social-ecological harms and harms done to connectivities themselves.

This section has explained the rationale for the book's use of connectivity. The research, however, is not the first to link resilience and connectivity. The next section, therefore, gives a brief overview of some of the ways that other scholars have done so. This is important for demonstrating the relevance of connectivity for resilience research and for further evidencing the originality of this book's own approach.

Resilience and Connectivity

While there is recognition within extant scholarship that connectivity can be problematic and is not always advantageous, in general it is positively associated with resilience. One obvious example is that being connected to someone or something – such as friends, family, community, places – can foster resilience (Jordan, 2004; Landau, 2007; Madsen and O'Mullan, 2016). This idea is central to the aforementioned RCT, which underlines that 'relationships are a primary source of one's ability to be resilient in the face of personal and social

Analysing Resilience Through Connectivity   51

hardships or trauma' (Hartling, 2008: 54). Connections with others, underscoring the interactional dynamics of resilience (Kent, 2012: 111; see also Heliwell and Putnam, 2004: 1437), potentially help to 'cushion' and mitigate the effects of one-off or ongoing adversities. Interesting in this regard, therefore, is Rew et al.'s (2001) study of homeless youth, which found an inverse relationship between social connectedness and resilience. According to the authors, 'Despite their reasons for leaving home and being socially disconnected from family and friends, many of these youth were highly resilient and lonely. Many felt hopeless and engaged in life-threatening behavior, including attempting suicide' (Rew et al., 2001: 38). Their research thus draws attention to the important point that whether or not resilience is something positive heavily depends on the particular context and circumstances.

Looking at connectivity in a broader sense than just connections with others, Cassidy and Barnes' (2012) research, focused on a rural community in Botswana, has found that more resilient households (i.e., those less vulnerable to livelihood shocks, such as drought) are more connected in the sense of their social networks. However, the research also points to important gendered dimensions of resilience and connectivity. For example, 'gender may influence the ability to engage in certain livelihood strategies', in turn creating varying levels of resilience (and opportunities to build connectivities) within a single household. Relatedly, poorer, female-headed households are commonly 'on the edges of a community's social networks' (Cassidy and Barnes, 2012).

Indeed, the previous chapter noted that resilience has attracted some strong gender-based criticisms (see, e.g., Hirani et al., 2016; Kawarazuka et al., 2017; Smyth and Sweetman, 2015). However, scholars have also given examples (sometimes indirectly) of positive gendered linkages between connectivity and resilience. In their research with women anti-mining activists in Andean Peru and Ecuador, Jenkins and Rondón (2015: 420) comment on the perils of thinking uncritically about resilience, insisting that 'an approach to resilience which emphasises uncovering and challenging unequal power relations is crucial'. Their aim, however, is not to portray the women simply as 'vulnerable victims of powerful mining corporations', but also to acknowledge their resilience – and resistance – to the challenges they face (Jenkins and Rondón, 2015: 421). Significantly, the authors note that 'The women situate their persistence and determination in terms of a strong sense of identity, particularly rooted in a strong connection to the environment and to their local landscape' (Jenkins and Rondón, 2015: 423).

This example thus reveals an important gendered connectivity – linked to everyday activities of cultivating the land (Mertens and Pardy, 2017: 969) – that the women were able to draw on in their fight against the mining corporations, as well as deeper trans-corporeal 'connections and interchanges between bodies and environments' (Alaimo, 2012: 480). Moreover, the women's connections to activists in other parts of Latin America, and their visits to other communities affected by mining, had further contributed to their resilience and resistance by fostering stronger solidarities (what this book refers to as experiential solidarity). In the authors' words, 'Women who undertook such visits reported a renewed sense of commitment which in turn contributed to sustaining both groups' [in Peru and Ecuador] determination to oppose mining developments over the long term' (Jenkins and Rondón, 2015: 424).

Exploring related themes, Feitosa and Yamaoka's (2020) research on agroecological projects in Brazil makes clear that women and their networks cannot be viewed only or primarily as victims of climate change and the many risks that it poses. Fundamentally, they must be seen as 'change agents and protagonists of paths that build climate resilience' (Feitosa and Yamaoka, 2020: 474). If the reference to networks evokes a nexus between resilience and connectivity, the authors further link social network connectivity to a broader environmental connectivity. According to them, any initiatives that encourage people to value the land they live on can make social groups stronger and deepen 'understanding of the benefits of connecting with the natural environment' (Feitosa and Yamaoka, 2020: 474).

In her work on India, Agarwal has similarly focused on more than just women's vulnerability to climate change. While acknowledging this vulnerability, she has also stressed that through their 'everyday interactions with nature', peasant and tribal women 'acquire a special knowledge of species varieties and the processes of natural regeneration' (Agarwal, 1992: 126). Her work does not promote an essentialised conception of women and their relationship with nature – one of the frequent criticisms directed at ecofeminism.[4] Indeed, she has explicitly distanced herself from ecofeminism (Agarwal, 1992: 127; see also Agarwal, 2000: 189). What is important for the purposes of this discussion is that Agarwal's arguments, while not actually mentioning resilience, bring to the forefront knowledge-based social-ecological connectivities that can potentiate resilience as an adaptive response to climate change.

Her research has also demonstrated (albeit more implicitly than Jenkins and Rondón's aforementioned work) that connectivity – in this case meaning 'complex networks of informal cooperation among women within neighbourhood clusters, work clusters, or at the village level' (Agarwal, 2000: 293) – can foster resilience in the sense of resistance to environmental degradation. She notes, for example, that during a field visit to the Uttar Pradesh hills in northwest India in 1993, 'I found that cooperation around forest protection through forming patrol groups was strengthened by the multiple intersecting connections that grew out of women's other group activities [such as sewing classes]' (Agarwal, 2000: 293).

These examples illuminate some of the different ways that connectivity is relevant to resilience. The heuristic of the adaptive cycle (Gunderson and Holling, 2002), discussed in the previous chapter, is a more direct example of how resilience and connectivity are inter-linked. The crucial point is that just as resilience varies through the different phases of the cycle, so too, by extension, do the connections within and between systems (Burkhard et al., 2011: 2879). It will be recalled that the cycle consists of four phases: a growth and exploitation phase (r), a conservation phase (K), a chaotic collapse and release phase (Ω) and a reorganisation and renewal phase (α). What is noteworthy is that connectivity is associated with high resilience only up to the point where a system enters the K phase of the cycle. Once it does so, it can fall into a rigidity trap and lose flexibility as its different parts become overly connected (Haider et al., 2018: 314).

In their work on drug addiction, for example, Randle et al. (2015: 82) argue that a rigidity trap occurs when the various behaviours that help to maintain an addiction become increasingly connected, with the result that 'the system essentially becomes "stuck" in a recurrent and unchanging pattern of behaviour'. The addiction is thus sustained during the conservation phase of the adaptive cycle (Randle et al., 2015: 84). In other words, connectivity can make a system less resilient in the sense of its ability to absorb and respond to shocks. Another example, although it does not specifically refer to the adaptive cycle, is Perz et al.'s (2013) study of rural households in the south-western Amazon. The authors found that being connected to markets resulted in decreased livelihood diversity and thus reduced households' resilience – meaning their ability to sustain and support themselves in response to uncertainty or sudden change (Perz et al., 2013: 499).

The adaptive cycle can itself be viewed, in part, as a story about connectivity – in the sense of what happens to connections during the different phases of the cycle. A disturbance that exceeds a system's resilience 'breaks apart its web of reinforcing interactions' (Walker and Salt, 2006: 77) and the system enters the collapse and release phase (Ω). This is a phase of loose and ruptured connections, creating maximum flexibility and new possibilities, thereby ultimately allowing the system to move into the reorganisation and renewal phase (α).

It should, however, be noted that high connectivity (interconnectedness) within a system is not universally associated with low or decreased resilience. Discussing the earthquakes that struck Christchurch, New Zealand, in 2010 and 2011, for example, Huck et al. (2020) insist on the need for cross-institutional connectivity in building urban resilience. Unpacking three different types of connectivity – which they term vertical, horizontal and territorial – and how they operate within and across institutions and governance structures, they point out that 'Enhancing institutional connectivity is often described as the main way of achieving resilient cities and infrastructures' (Huck et al., 2020). For his part, Ungar (2021a: 22) asserts that 'Resilient systems are connected systems' (see also Cefai, 2021: 222). While acknowledging some of the previously mentioned downsides of connectivity, which can create or expose vulnerabilities within complex systems (Ungar, 2018), he maintains that 'The better connected systems are, the more likely they are to provide access to the resources systems need to overcome disruption when the system's own resources become overwhelmed' (Ungar, 2021a: 22).

Arguably a more nuanced perspective is one that recognises and disaggregates the differential impact of high connectivity at different levels. On this point, Scheffer et al. (2012: 344–345) argue that 'Strong connectivity promotes local resilience, because effects of local perturbations are eliminated quickly through subsidiary inputs from the broader system'. However, this local resilience comes at the expense of wider systemic resilience; 'the repeated recovery from small-scale perturbations can give a false impression of resilience, masking the fact that the system may actually be approaching a tipping point for a systemic shift' (Scheffer et al., 2012: 345). The reality of such trade-offs reinforces the significance of social-ecological and multi-systemic analyses of resilience that can give a much fuller picture, including of structural disadvantage and 'the absence of obvious systemic enablers' for particular groups or communities (Jones et al., 2021).

Some of the most extensive research on connectivity, and on the relationships between resilience and connectivity, has taken place within the field of ecology. This scholarship has addressed, inter alia, some of the ways that connectivity between different ecosystems can foster resilience in response to climate change and other environmental stressors (Krosby et al., 2010; Nuñez et al., 2013). Relatedly, it has explored important issues regarding the genesis of connectivity (Folke, 2006), in the sense of who or what creates it (and maintains it), and the active use of connectivity in contributing to resilience. Mumby and Hastings' research, for instance, demonstrates that connectivity between two ecosystems – mangroves and coral reefs – enables fish to graze on the reefs. This grazing influences macroalgae cover on reefs, which competes with corals. By keeping macroalgae at a low level, therefore, both the fish and the connectivity that they and their grazing reflect enhance the resilience of coral reefs to disturbances (Mumby and Hastings, 2008: 861).

Ecology scholarship also makes it very clear that connectivity is inherently contextual. The aforementioned linkage between connectivity and movement, for example, is not a given. Whether and to what extent connectivity facilitates movement depends on what is trying to move (Crooks and Sanjayan, 2006: 4) – and how. The contextuality of connectivity is particularly relevant to this research and its comparative approach. The empirical chapters analyse how context shapes multi-layered connectivities, their dynamics and the stories that they tell, as well as the relationship(s) between connectivity and 'movement' – in the sense of how individual victims-/survivors of CRSV in BiH, Colombia and Uganda have moved/are moving forward with their lives.

While scholars in diverse fields have discussed connectivity, the flexibility of the concept is also a potential downside. In his book *The Ecological Thought*, Morton (2010: 28) notes that 'Since everything is interconnected, there is no definite background and therefore no definite foreground'. One of the issues with connectivity, thus, is knowing exactly what to focus on. Morton (2010: 15) theorises interconnectedness through his concept of 'the mesh', underlining that 'The mesh of interconnected things is vast, perhaps immeasurably so'. This 'vastness' further accentuates the difficulties of operationalising connectivity and making it workable. If the mesh 'consists of infinite connections'

Analysing Resilience Through Connectivity   55

and if we cannot 'rigidly specify anything as irrelevant', then 'where are we?' (Morton, 2010: 30).

This research adopts a particular approach to operationalising connectivity, and in so doing it brings something new – conceptually and empirically – to existing scholarship on resilience (and especially resilience and connectivity). It specifically borrows from ecology scholarship the concepts of structural and functional connectivity, fragmentation and dynamic connectivity, and it adapts them to construct 'the mesh' that constitutes its own social-ecological framework for analysing resilience. The chapter's remaining sections detail this framework.

Supportive and Sustaining Connectivities (Structural and Functional Connectivity)

Structural connectivity and functional connectivity are two concepts that are widely discussed within existing literature on connectivity. In the field of neuroscience, structural connectivity refers to 'the anatomical connections between brain regions' (Damoiseaux and Greicius, 2009: 526), and functional connectivity 'reflects neuronal synchronization between brain regions, which presumably requires some form of structural connectivity' (Straathoff et al., 2019: 190). In ecology scholarship, from which this research directly draws, structural and functional connectivity are concepts commonly used in relation to landscape connectivity (Merriam, 1984). A connected landscape is one that allows movement between different resource patches (Galvin, 2008: 370). In this context, thus, structural connectivity refers to the structural features of a landscape that enable such movement. It is important to note, however – reiterating the earlier point that connectivity is intrinsically contextual – that 'the same landscape will have different connectivities for different organisms' (Tischendorf and Fahrig, 2000: 8). In other words, structural connectivity is only a physical characteristic.

Functional connectivity, in contrast, refers to the practical usage of structural connectivity and to whether and how 'landscape patches function as connected from the perspective of the organism' (LaPoint et al., 2015: 869). This means that structural connectivity can exist without functional connectivity; the existence of a structural corridor does not mean that a species will necessarily be able to use it to reach another landscape patch (Galvin, 2008: 370–371). By itself, therefore, structural connectivity tells only part of the story. According to Weins (2006: 24), 'It is the stage on which the dramas of ecology and evolution are played'. Yet, in the absence of the players, 'it is sterile and uninformative' (Weins, 2006: 24). It is the players – how they access and use connectivity, how they adapt it to their needs, how they make structural connectivity into something functional – that bring the 'stage' to life.

This research takes the concepts of structural and functional connectivity and adapts them to form the first element of its connectivity framework, *supportive and sustaining connectivities.* Interviewees in all three countries talked about multi-layered connectivities – including children and family, women's (and women-led) organisations and spirituality – that were personally important to them in dealing with adversity and rebuilding their lives. This research examines these various connectivities (structural connectivity) in different socio-cultural contexts, and it also studies how the interviewees were actively drawing on and using these connectivities (functional connectivity). This is significant as regards the issue of agency, which is discussed in the final section.

It is also essential to take note, however, that connectivity is not necessarily supportive. Outside of ecology, for example, structural connectivity should also be understood, inter alia, as referring to 'structural dimensions in the wider political context of victims' lives in order to understand how violence functions at multiple (macro, meso, and micro) levels' (Kostovicova et al., 2020: 253–254).[5] Furthermore, while connectivity in ecology is an 'entirely scale and target dependent phenomenon' (Crooks and Sanjayan, 2006: 3), the larger point is that there are contextual dimensions of scale – including gendered and intersectional dimensions – that shape which connectivities individuals can access and use (Drolet et al., 2015: 438; Truelove, 2011: 148).

In their research on fisheries in Zambia, for example, Cole et al. (2018) examine how post-harvest fish losses have primarily affected women. A key reason for this is the existence of gender constraints that affect women's abilities to process fish and sustain only minimal losses. As a summary of the problem,

> Fish that remains too long in gill nets while waiting to be harvested can begin to spoil. Predation by animals and theft by humans lead to losses for people sun drying their fish unattended in the open. Women who process while also carrying out household duties can overprocess their fish. This results in immediate or future breakages for women when storing or transporting fish.
>
> (Cole et al., 2018)

Specifically addressing the issue of movement, the authors underline that in the Barotse Floodplain, women's domestic and care-giving responsibilities restrict them from travelling long distances, which in turn means that they are unable to access better-quality fish further afield (Cole et al., 2018). In other words, the fish are a structural connectivity, as a particular resource that the women – the principal processors and traders of dried fish in the Barotse Floodplain fishery – can utilise to support themselves and their families. Yet, broader gender and cultural factors intervene to shape how they are able to functionally use this particular connectivity.

To take a very different example, Nightingale's (2011: 156) research on Hindu women in Mugu District in Nepal discusses how the 'intersectionality of caste, gender, age, space and material practice' effectively limits and constrains women's access to and use of structural connectivity (including water and crops) when they are menstruating or have recently experienced childbirth. According to her, these women are regarded as 'highly polluting', and hence they are not permitted to enter people's homes or to move around freely in public spaces (Nightingale, 2011: 156). This further illuminates some of the wider socio-cultural dynamics of structural and functional connectivity, reinforcing the book's argument that exploring connectivity potentially provides many rich insights into individuals' social ecologies.

Even if connectivity is not always something positive, in ecology it is often discussed as a way of dealing with fragmentation – and the threats that the latter poses to ecosystems and their adaptability. This idea of fragmentation was also present in the qualitative data; interviewees in BiH, Colombia and Uganda spoke not only about supportive and sustaining connectivities in their lives, but also about those that had become damaged or broken.

Broken and Ruptured Connectivities (Fragmentation)

The existence and active use of connectivity can enable species to move to new areas and find new habitats, as a way of responding and adapting to the stressors of climate change (Costanza et al., 2020; Krosby et al., 2010). Hence, increasing and fostering connectivity requires actions 'to reverse some of the effects of fragmentation – to reconnect small, isolated populations and restore their ability to function as larger, more resilient populations' (Doerr et al., 2014). In ecology, fragmentation therefore refers to fundamental disconnects that undermine healthy ecosystemic functioning, leaving particular species potentially more vulnerable to extinction (Baguette et al., 2013: 311; Crooks and Sanjayan, 2006: 7).

Utilising this idea of fragmentation, and underlining what Kolb (2008: 128) refers to as 'an underlying duality of "connects" and "disconnects"', the second element of this book's connectivity framework is *broken and ruptured connectivities*. What happens to connectivities themselves – a crucial dimension of the stories that they tell – is a pivotal part of analysing resilience. Splits and breakages affect interactions between individuals and their social ecologies – and, relatedly, the availability and use of supportive and sustaining connectivities as protective resources. Jordan (2004: 28), for example, argues that when individuals 'move . . . into disconnection, they are often beset by a damaging sense of immobilization and isolation'. It is also the case, however, that just as there is variation in 'the effects of fragmentation in different landscapes' (Erős and Campbell Grant, 2015: 1488), this also applies to the effects of broken and ruptured connectivities in different socio-cultural 'landscapes'.

More broadly, broken and ruptured connectivities highlight the important issue of legacy, which is also very relevant to resilience. Transitional justice processes are about dealing with the legacy (or, more accurately, legacies) of past human rights abuses (Haldemann, 2008: 676; Niezen, 2016: 920). However, there is little critical engagement with the notion of 'legacy' or what exactly it encompasses (Clark, 2020a: 143). Moreover, in divided societies that have experienced major systemic

58 Analysing Resilience Through Connectivity

shocks and perturbations related to war and armed conflict, 'legacy' is often a contentious concept and one whose boundaries and meaning necessarily have a crucial perspectival dimension. Lundy (2011: 96), for example, has remarked on 'the contested nature of memory and disputed interpretations of the past in Northern Ireland'; and Kent (2011: 444) asserts that 'all local memory practices involve political contestation at some level and bring to the fore competing viewpoints about which events should be remembered and how'.

Without specifically using social-ecological terminology, scholars have discussed some of the wider effects and legacies of CRSV – including on the families and communities of direct victims-/survivors (see, e.g., Bouvier, 2014; Christian et al., 2011; Mukamana and Brysiewicz, 2008), and on victims-/survivors' relationships (see, e.g., Albutt et al., 2017; Denov and Kahn, 2019; Mertens and Pardy, 2017; Traunmüller et al., 2019). Thinking about these themes in terms of multi-systemic and multi-dimensional broken and ruptured connectivities offers a more comprehensive approach to disaggregating the legacies of CRSV and other co-occurring forms of violence.

In their work on environmental peacebuilding, Yoshida and Céspedes-Báez (2021: 24) insist that 'Considering women and men as connected to and living actively in their ecosystems helps to enrich understanding of the implications of armed conflict for their lives and for their communities'. That these implications further extend to issues such as environmental sustainability and preservation (Yoshida and Céspedes-Báez, 2021: 24) also accentuates the need for more relational approaches to harm in transitional justice contexts (Clark, 2020b), as explored more fully in Chapter 8. This is not in any way to diminish the seriousness of individual harms, but simply to spotlight that they are entangled with, and influenced by, wider sets of harms. Fundamentally, within a connectivity framework, 'it is impossible to think of harm accruing to one being or set of beings in isolation' (Mitchell, 2014: 7; see also Alaimo, 2010: 31). War and armed conflict, for example, had displaced some of the interviewees, particularly those in Colombia and in BiH. This physical displacement – one of the many broken and ruptured connectivities within the data – had not only harmed these individuals, including emotionally and economically, but also their land, what they grew on that land and their animals.

New Connectivities (Dynamic Connectivity)

The previous chapter discussed the heuristic of the adaptive cycle, to which this chapter has also referred. The three elements of this book's connectivity framework can themselves also be likened to a cycle. They do not occur in a specific order, just as the four phases of the adaptive cycle do not always follow the same pattern. The point is that the three elements are deeply interconnected. An important example of this is that broken and ruptured connectivities need not remain permanently severed.

The final key concept that this research draws from ecology scholarship is dynamic connectivity, which encapsulates variations in levels and degrees of connectivity within ecosystems. Hooke (2003: 80), for example, points out that 'fluvial systems are dynamic and that the degree of connectivity can change over time'; and Xie et al.'s (2020) research highlights dynamic hydrological connectivity in the Yellow River Delta in China due to complex tidal channel networks. Connectivity is also dynamic, however, in the sense that connections can be weakened and strengthened, reformed and reshaped or created anew. As one illustration, McCauley et al.'s study (2012) examines how large predators in a Pacific tropical marine ecosystem forge cross-system linkages through their mobile foraging practices. More broadly, because SES are complex adaptive systems, as discussed in the previous chapter, they are self-organising; and through this self-organisation, they can rebuild connectivity (as the adaptive cycle illustrates) following shocks and disturbances (Abel et al., 2006).

This research integrates the concept of dynamic connectivity into its conceptual framework by looking at some of the ways that victims-/survivors of CRSV in BiH, Colombia and Uganda were actively building *new connectivities* with and within their social ecologies. This is significant because like the aforementioned idea of functional connectivity, it gives salience to issues of agency; and one of the common criticisms of SES research – and more broadly of using ecological principles to study resilience in a social context – is that it minimises agency through its accent on structure (see, e.g., Mulrennan and Bussières, 2018; Stone-Jovicich, 2015). Indeed, Davidson (2010: 1145) contends that 'human agency is the most contentious wrinkle in the application of an ecological framework to social systems'.[6]

Joining or establishing an organisation/association that brings victims-/survivors together is an important example of forging new connectivities – and of what Haraway (1988: 584) has referred to as 'the possibility of webs of connections called solidarity'. Mukamana and Brysiewicz (2008: 382) describe a basket-making project in post-genocide Rwanda that enabled women to come together and to share their pain. They point out that while the 1994 genocide fundamentally destroyed support networks (an example of broken and ruptured connectivities), 'bringing rape survivors together in an association like AVEGA [Association of Widows of the Genocide] allowed them to recreate a community for themselves' (Mukamana and Brysiewicz, 2008: 383). Similarly, in his research with male victims-/survivors of CRSV in northern Uganda, Schulz (2018: 598) has demonstrated that:

> Groups enable survivors to connect with others who share a lived reality and to collectively demand recognition of their otherwise marginalized and silenced experiences by wider society, the state and their communities. For survivors themselves, this is important to break the silence surrounding crimes of male rape, and for them to be able to escape social exclusion and isolation.

Efforts to establish and build new connectivities can be an important expression of resilience. Part of the significance of new connectivities in this regard is that they

60 Analysing Resilience Through Connectivity

illustrate what Masten (2001: 230) calls 'the bidirectional nature of influence in living systems'. Interviewees' lives were shaped by their social ecologies, but some of them were also shaping dynamics within these ecologies, with the aim of bringing about systemic change. It is also essential to note, however, that opportunities to create these new connectivities may be limited by contextual and systemic factors.

A study of gender relations in a small island fishing community (Grand Manan) on Canada's east coast, for example, found that developments such as new technologies and new market conditions linked to globalisation had fundamentally altered 'The nature of connectivity, how connections are made, sustained and are perceived' (Marshall, 2001: 392). Whereas previously both the community and local fishery were key sites of social connectivity for women living on the island, economic restructuring had resulted in them needing to find ways of building new social connectivities. Women who moved away from the island had opportunities for 'expanded levels of connectivity' (Marshall, 2001: 407), whereas those who stayed on the island were more restricted, including by a patriarchal culture and by men spending more time at home (Marshall, 2001: 407).

★★★

Through its approach to connectivity, this chapter has sought to respond to Janssen et al.'s (2006) argument that 'there is no clear indication of how connectivity is related to resilience, in contrast to the adaptive cycle proposed by Holling'. It has introduced and developed the book's conceptual framework – and its three key elements of supportive and sustaining connectivities, broken and ruptured connectivities and new connectivities – as a new social-ecological approach to thinking about and analysing resilience. In so doing, it has underlined that resilience 'is dependent upon context or environment, including our relationships' (Kent, 2012: 111). The significance of connectivity in this regard is that it tells a story about these relationships, and it thereby reflects and captures the fact that resilience is something highly dynamic.

The utility of the book's connectivity framework is not only conceptual. It also has a significant practical application. In the three empirical chapters, focused on BiH, Colombia and Uganda, respectively, the framework is used to explore the empirical data and to draw out similarities and differences between the three case studies. As important background to these chapters, the next chapter discusses the fieldwork on which this research is based and key issues relating to methodology and ethics.

Notes

1   The idea of hyperconnectivity has also been discussed in other contexts (see, e.g., Edwards et al., 2021: 2).
2   Some scholars have problematised what they regard as an over-focus on CRSV on other/additional grounds. Using the example of the Democratic Republic of Congo (DRC), Meger (2016: 155) asserts that:

the exclusive focus on sexual violence . . . encouraged Congolese women to exploit conflict-related sexual violence as a commodity fetish as a survival strategy. There are now reports of women who claim to have been raped in order to have access to the health, social, and judicial care that has been exclusively earmarked for victims of sexual violence.

Also focused on the DRC, Autesserre (2012: 205) has argued that 'Interveners have singled out for support one category of victims, sexually injured women and girls, at the expense of others, notably those tortured in a non-sexual manner, child soldiers, and the families of those killed'.

3 Swaine (2015: 759) notes that international policy and legal discourse on CRSV primarily focuses on strategic rape. In using the term 'strategic', she means 'violence that is part of organized group violence by armed conflict actors and that satisfies the international law requirements for wartime sexualized violence' (Swaine, 2015: 757).

4 Ecofeminism seeks to 'connect feminist and ecological perspectives, thought and movements' (Plumwood, 2004: 43) and it explores the domination of women and the domination of nature as 'intimately connected and mutually reinforcing' (King, 1989: 18). Alaimo and Heckman (2008: 4), however, note that 'The mainstream of feminist theory . . . has, more often than not, relegated ecofeminism to the backwoods, fearing that any alliance between feminism and environmentalism could only be founded upon a naïve, romantic account of reality' (see, e.g., Moore, 2008: 283).

5 Discussing resilience and Indigenous girls in Canada, for example, de Finney (2017: 11) asks: 'How do we move past narrow, individualised, depoliticised psycho-social understandings of resilience that ignore the ways the Canadian state has, for centuries, deliberately and systematically attacked and committed genocide against Indigenous communities?'

6 Despite such criticisms, it is not the case that SES research overlooks agency (see, e.g., Barnes et al., 2017; Janssen et al., 2006).

References

Abel N, Cumming DHN and Anderies JHN (2006) Collapse and reorganization in social-ecological systems: Questions, some ideas and policy implications. *Ecology and Society* 11(1): 17.

Adger WN, Eakin H and Winkles A (2009) Nested and teleconnected vulnerabilities to environmental change. *Frontiers in Ecology and the Environment* 7(3): 150–1157.

Agarwal B (1992) The gender and environment debate: Lessons from India. *Feminist Studies* 18(1): 119–158.

Agarwal B (2000) Conceptualising environmental collective action: Why gender matters. *Cambridge Journal of Economics* 24(3): 283–310.

Alaimo S (2010) The naked world: The trans-corporeal ethics of the protecting body. *Women and Performance* 20(1): 15–36.

Alaimo S (2012) States of suspension: Trans-corporeality at sea. *Interdisciplinary Studies in Literature and Environment* 19(3): 476–493.

Alaimo S and Heckman S (2008) Introduction: Emerging models of materiality in feminist theory. In: Alaimo S and Heckman S (eds.), *Material Feminisms*. Bloomington, IN: Indiana University Press, pp. 1–20.

Albutt K, Kelly J, Kabanga J and VanRooyen M (2017) Stigmatisation and rejection of survivors of sexual violence in eastern Democratic Republic of Congo. *Disasters* 41(2): 211–227.

Angelopulo G (2014) Connectivity. *Communicatio* 40(3): 209–222.

Autesserre S (2012) Dangerous tales: Dominant narratives on the Congo and their unintended consequences. *African Affairs* 111(443): 202–222.

Baaz ME and Stern M (2018) Curious erasures: The sexual in wartime sexual violence. *International Feminist Journal of Politics* 20(3): 295–314.

Baguette M, Blanchet S, Legrand D, Stevens VM and Turlure C (2013) Individual dispersal, landscape connectivity, and ecological networks. *Biological Reviews* 88 (2): 310–326.

Bani R, Fortin MJ, Daigle RM and Guichard F (2019) Dispersal traits interact with dynamic connectivity to affect metapopulation growth and stability. *Theoretical Ecology* 12: 111–127.

Barnes ML, Bodin Ö, Guerrero AM, McAllister RRJ, Alexander SM and Robins G (2017) The social structural foundations of adaptation and transformation in social-ecological systems. *Ecology and Society* 22(4): 16.

Barrios RE (2016) Resilience: A commentary from the vantage point of anthropology. *Annals of Anthropological Practice* 40(1): 28–38.

Binder CR, Hinkel J, Bots PWG and Pahl-Wostl C (2013) Comparison of frameworks for analyzing social-ecological systems. *Ecology and Society* 18(4): 26.

Bodin Ö and Tengö M (2012) Disentangling intangible social-ecological systems. *Global Environmental Change* 22(2): 430–439.

Boesten J (2014) *Sexual Violence during War and Peace: Gender, Power, and Post-Conflict Justice in Peru.* New York, NY: Palgrave Macmillan.

Boesten J (2017) Of exceptions and continuities: Theory and methodology in research on conflict-related sexual violence. *International Feminist Journal of Politics* 19(4): 506–519.

Bouvier P (2014) Sexual violence, health and humanitarian ethics: Towards a holistic, person-centred approach. *International Review of the Red Cross* 96(894): 565–584.

Bronfenbrenner U (1977) Toward an experimental psychology of human development. *American Psychologist* 32(7): 513–531.

Burkhard B, Fath BD and Müller F (2011) Adapting the adaptive cycle: Hypotheses on the development of ecosystem properties and services. *Ecological Modelling* 222(16): 2878–2890.

Byford J and Tileagă C (2014) Social psychology, history and the study of the Holocaust: The perils of interdisciplinary borrowing. *Peace and Conflict* 20(4): 349–364.

Cassidy L and Barnes GD (2012) Understanding household connectivity and resilience in marginal rural communities through social network analysis in the village of Habu, Botswana. *Ecology and Society* 17(4): 11.

Cecez-Kecmanovic D, Boell S and Campbell J (2014) Materiality of connectivity in the networked society: A sociomaterial perspective. 25th Australasian conference on information systems, 8–10 December 2014, Auckland, New Zealand. Available at: https://openresearch-repository.anu.edu.au/bitstream/1885/154074/2/01_Cecez-Kecmanovic_Materiality_of_connectivity_in_2014.pdf (accessed 5 March 2021).

Cefai C (2021) A transactional, whole-school approach to resilience. In: Ungar M (ed.), *Multisystemic Resilience: Adaptation and Transformation in Contexts of Change.* New York, NY: Oxford University Press, pp. 220–231.

Christian M, Safari O, Ramazani P, Burnham G and Glass N (2011) Sexual and gender based violence against men in the Democratic Republic of Congo: Effects on survivors, their family and the community. *Medicine, Conflict and Survival* 27(4): 227–246.

Cinner JE and Barnes ML (2019) Social dimensions of resilience in social-ecological systems. *One Earth* 1(1): 51–56.

Clark JN (2020a) Emotional legacies, transitional justice and alethic truth: A novel basis for exploring reconciliation. *Journal of International Criminal Justice* 18(1): 141–165.

Clark JN (2020b) The COVID-19 pandemic and ecological connectivity: Implications for international criminal law and transitional justice. *Journal of International Criminal Justice* 18(5): 1045–1068.

Cole SM, McDougall, Kaminski AM, Kefi AS, Chilala A and Chisule G (2018) Postharvest fish loss and unequal gender relations: Drivers of the social-ecological trap in the Barotse Floodplain fishery, Zambia. *Ecology and Society* 23(2): 18.

Costanza JK, Watling J, Sutherland R, Belyea C, Dilkina B, Cayton H, Bucklin D, Romañach SS and Haddad NM (2020) Preserving connectivity under climate and land-use change: No one-size-fits-all approach for focal species in similar habitats. *Biological Conservation* 248: 109678.

Cote M and Nightingale AJ (2012) Resilience thinking meets social theory: Situating social change in social-ecological systems (SES) research. *Progress in Human Geography* 36(4): 475–489.

Crawford KF (2013) From spoils to weapons: Framing wartime sexual violence. *Gender & Development* 21(3): 505–517.

Crenshaw K (1989) Demarginalizing the intersection of race and sex: Black feminist critique of antidiscrimination doctrine, feminist theory and antiracist politics. *University of Chicago Legal Forum* 1989: 139–168.

Crenshaw K (1991) Mapping the margins: Intersectionality, identity politics, and violence against women of color. *Stanford Law Review* 43(6): 1241–1300.

Crooks JA and Suarez AV (2006) Hyperconnectivity, invasive species and the breakdown of barriers to dispersal. In: Crooks KR and Sanjayan M (eds.), *Connectivity Conservation*. Cambridge: Cambridge University Press, pp. 451–478.

Crooks KR and Sanjayan M (2006) Connectivity conservation: Maintaining connections for nature. In: Crooks KR and Sanjayan M (eds.), *Connectivity Conservation*. Cambridge: Cambridge University Press, pp. 1–20.

Dakos V, Quinlan A, Baggio JA, Bennett E, Bodin Ö and Burn Silver S (2015) Principle 2 – Manage connectivity. In: Biggs R, Schlüter M and Schoon ML (eds.), *Principles for Building Resilience: Sustaining Ecosystem Services in Social-Ecological Systems*. Cambridge: Cambridge University Press, pp. 80–104.

Damoiseaux J and Greicius MD (2009) Greater than the sum of its parts: A review of studies combining structural connectivity and resting-state functional connectivity. *Brain Structure and Function* 213: 525–533.

Davidson DJ (2010) The applicability of the concept of resilience to social systems: Some sources of optimism and nagging doubts. *Society and Natural Resources* 23(12): 1135–1149.

Davies SE and True J (2015) Reframing conflict-related sexual and gender-based violence: Bringing gender analysis back in. *Security Dialogue* 46(6): 495–512.

de Finney S (2017) Indigenous girls' resilience in settler states: Honouring body and land sovereignty. *Agenda* 31(2): 10–21.

de la Bellacasa MP (2012) 'Nothing comes without its world': Thinking with care. *The Sociological Review* 60(2): 197–216.

Denov M and Kahn S (2019) 'They should see us as a symbol of reconciliation': Youth born of genocidal rape in Rwanda and the implications for transitional justice. *Journal of Human Rights Practice* 11(1): 151–170.

Di Lellio A, Rushiti F and Tahiraj K (2019) 'Thinking of you' in Kosovo: Art activism against the stigma of sexual violence. *Violence Against Women* 25(13): 1543–1557.

Doerr ED, Doerr VAJ, Davies MJ and McGinness HM (2014) Does structural connectivity facilitate movement of native species in Australia's fragmented landscapes? A systematic review protocol. *Environmental Evidence* 3: 9.

Drolet J, Dominelli N, Alston M, Ersing R, Mathbor G and Wu H (2015) Women rebuilding lives post-disaster: Innovative community practices for building resilience and promoting sustainable development. *Gender & Development* 23(3): 433–448.

64 Analysing Resilience Through Connectivity

Duit A, Galaz V and Eckerberg K (2010) Governance, complexity and resilience. *Global Environmental Change* 20(3): 363–368.

Edwards A, Webb H, Housley W, Beneito-Montagut R, Procter R and Jirotka M (2021) Forecasting the governance of harmful social media communications: Findings from the digital wildfire policy Delphi. *Policing and Society* 31(3): 1–19.

Erős T and Campbell Grant EH (2015) Unifying research on the fragmentation of terrestrial and aquatic habitats: Patches, connectivity and the matrix in riverscapes. *Freshwater* 60(8): 1487–1501.

Feitosa C and Yamaoka M (2020) Strengthening climate resilience and women's networks: Brazilian inspiration from agroecology. *Gender & Development* 28(3): 459–478.

Folke C (2006) Resilience: The emergence of a perspective for social-ecological systems analyses. *Global Environmental Change* 16(3): 253–267.

Freeman J, Hard RJ and Mauldin RP (2017) A theory of regime change on the Texas coastal plain. *Quaternary International* 446: 83–94.

Galvin KA (2008) Responses of pastoralists to land fragmentation: Social capital, connectivity and resilience. In: Galvin KA, Reid RS, Behnke Jr. RH and Hobbs NT (eds.), *Fragmentation in Semi-Arid and Arid Landscapes: Consequences for Human and Natural Systems.* Dordrecht: Springer, pp. 369–389.

Garmestani AS, Allen CR, Ruhl JB and Holling CS (2014) The integration of social-ecological resilience and law. In: Garmestani AS and Allen CR (eds.), *Social-Ecological Resilience and Law.* New York, NY: Columbia University Press, pp. 365–382.

Gerber LR, Del Mar Mancha-Cisneros M, O'Connor MI and Selig ER (2014) Climate change impacts on connectivity in the ocean: Implications for conservation. *Ecosphere* 5(3): 1–18.

Gray H (2019) The 'war'/'not-war' divide: Domestic violence in the Preventing Sexual Violence Initiative. *British Journal of Politics and International Relations* 21(1): 189–206.

Gunderson LH and Holling CS (eds.) (2002) *Panarchy: Understanding Transformations in Human and Natural Systems.* Washington, DC: Island Press.

Haider LJ, Boonstra WJ, Peterson GD and Schlüter M (2018) Traps and sustainable development in rural areas: A review. *World Development* 101: 311–321.

Haldemann F (2008) Another kind of justice: Transitional justice as recognition. *Cornell International Law Journal* 41(3): 675–738.

Haraway D (1988) Situated knowledges: The science question in feminism and the privilege of partial perspective. *Feminist Studies* 14(3): 575–599.

Hartling LM (2008) Strengthening resilience in a risky world: It's all about relationships. *Women & Therapy* 31(2–4): 51–70.

Haysom L (2017) Moving the social ecology to the centre: Resilience in the context of gender violence. *Agenda* 31(2): 1–2.

Heliwell JF and Putnam RD (2004) The social context of well-being. *Philosophical Transactions of the Royal Society* 359: 1435–1446.

Hirani S, Lasiuk G and Hegadoren K (2016) The intersection of gender and resilience. *Journal of Psychiatric and Mental Health Nursing* 23: 455–467.

Hooke J (2003) Coarse sediment connectivity in river channel systems: A conceptual framework and methodology. *Geomorphology* 56(1–2): 79–94.

Huck A, Monstadt J and Driessen P (2020) Building urban and infrastructure resilience through connectivity: An institutional perspective on disaster risk management in Christchurch, New Zealand. *Cities* 98: 102573.

Janssen MA, Bodin Ö, Anderies JM, Elmqvist T, Ernstson H, McAllister RRJ, Olsson P and Ryan P (2006) Toward a network perspective of the study of resilience in social-ecological systems. *Ecology and Society* 7(1): 15.

Jenkins K and Rondón G (2015) 'Eventually the mine will come': Women anti-mining activists' everyday resilience in opposing resource extraction in the Andes. *Gender & Development* 23(3): 415–431.

Jones N, Pincock K, Emirie G, Gebeyehu Y and Yadete W (2021) Supporting resilience among young people at risk of child abuse in Ethiopia: The role of social system alignment. *Child Abuse & Neglect* 111(2): 105137.

Jordan JV (2004) Relational resilience. In: Jordan JV, Walker M and Hartling LM (eds.), *The Complexity of Connection: Writings from the Stone Center's Jean Baker Miller Training Institute*. New York, NY: The Guildford Press, pp. 28–46.

Jordan JV (2008) Recent developments in relational-cultural theory. *Women & Therapy* 31(2–4): 1–4.

Jordan JV (2017) Relational-cultural theory: The power of connection to transform our lives. *The Journal of Humanistic Counseling* 56(3): 228–243.

Jordan JV and Walker M (2004) Introduction. In: Jordan JV, Walker M and Hartling LM (eds.), *The Complexity of Connection: Writings from the Stone Center's Jean Baker Miller Training Institute*. New York, NY: The Guildford Press, pp. 1–8.

Kaufmann M (2013) Emergent self-organisation in emergencies: Resilience rationales in interconnected societies. *Resilience* 1(1): 53–68.

Kawarazuka N, Locke C, McDougall C, Kantor P and Morgan M (2017) Bringing analysis of gender and social-ecological resilience together in small-scale fisheries research: Challenges and opportunities. *Ambio* 46: 201–213.

Kent L (2011) Local memory practices in East Timor: Disrupting transitional justice narratives. *International Journal of Transitional Justice* 5(3): 434–455.

Kent M (2012) From neuron to social context: Restoring resilience as a capacity for good survival. In: Ungar M (ed.), *The Social Ecology of Resilience: A Handbook of Theory and Practice*. New York, NY: Springer, pp. 111–126.

King Y (1989) The ecology of feminism and the feminism of ecology. In: Plant J (ed.), *Healing the Wounds: The Promise of Ecofeminism*. Basingstoke: Green Print, pp. 19–28.

Kirby P and Shepherd LJ (2016) The futures past of the women, peace and security agenda. *International Affairs* 92(2): 373–392.

Kolb DG (2008) Exploring the metaphor of connectivity: Attributes, dimensions and duality. *Organization Studies* 29(1): 127–144.

Koohsari MJ, Sugiyama T, Lamb KE, Villanueva K and Owen N (2014) Street connectivity and walking for transport: Role of neighborhood destinations. *Preventive Medicine* 66: 118–122.

Kostovicova D, Bojicic-Dzelilovic V and Henry M (2020) Drawing on the continuum: A war and post-war political economy of gender-based violence in Bosnia and Herzegovina. *International Feminist Journal of Politics* 22(2): 250–272.

Krosby M, Tewksbury J, Haddad NM and Hoekstra J (2010) Ecological connectivity for a changing climate. *Conservation Biology* 24(6): 1686–1689.

Landau J (2007) Enhancing resilience: Families and communities as agents for change. *Family Process* 46(3): 351–365.

LaPoint S, Balkenhol N, Hale J, Sadler J and van der Ree R (2015) Ecological connectivity research in urban areas. *Functional Ecology* 29(7): 868–878.

Leitner H, Sheppard E, Webber S and Colven E (2018) Globalizing urban resilience. *Urban Geography* 39(8): 1276–1284.

Lundy P (2011) Paradoxes and challenges of transitional justice at the 'local' level: Historical enquiries in Northern Ireland. *Contemporary Social Science* 6(1): 89–105.

MacKinnon CA (2013) Intersectionality as method: A note. *Signs* 38(4): 1019–1030.

Madsen W and O'Mullan C (2016) Perceptions of community resilience after natural disaster in a rural Australian town. *Journal of Community Psychology* 44(3): 277–292.

Marshall J (2001) Connectivity and restructuring: Identity and gender relations in a fishing community. *Gender, Place and Culture* 8(4): 391–409.

Masten AS (2001) Ordinary magic: Resilience processes in development. *American Psychologist* 56(3): 227–238.

Masten AS (2021) Resilience of children in disasters: A multisystem perspective. *International Journal of Psychology* 56(1): 1–11.

McCauley DJ, Young HS, Dunbar RB, Estes JA, Semmens BX and Micheli F (2012) Assessing the effects of large mobile predators on ecosystem connectivity. *Ecological Applications* 22(6): 1711–1717.

Meger S (2016) The fetishization of sexual violence in international security. *International Studies Quarterly* 60(1): 149–159.

Merriam G (1984) Connectivity: A fundamental ecological characteristic of landscape pattern. In: Brandt J and Agger P (eds.), *Proceedings of the 1st International Seminar on Methodology in Landscape Ecological Research and Planning*. Roskilde: Roskilde University, pp. 5–15.

Mertens C and Pardy M (2017) 'Sexurity' and its effects in eastern Democratic Republic of Congo. *Third World Quarterly* 38(4): 956–979.

Mitchell A (2014) Only human? A worldly approach to security. *Security Dialogue* 45(1): 5–21.

Moore N (2008) Eco/feminism, non-violence and the future of feminism. *International Feminist Journal of Politics* 10(3): 282–298.

Morton T (2010) *The Ecological Thought*. Cambridge, MA: Harvard University Press.

Motlafi N (2018) The coloniality of the gaze on sexual violence: A stalled attempt at a South Africa – Rwanda dialogue. *International Journal of Feminist Politics* 20(1): 9–23.

Mukamana D and Brysiewicz P (2008) The lived experience of genocide rape survivors in Rwanda. *Journal of Nursing Scholarship* 40(4): 379–384.

Mulrennan ME and Bussières V (2018) Social-ecological resilience in indigenous coastal edge contexts. *Ecology and Society* 23(3): 18.

Mumby PJ and Hastings A (2008) The impact of ecosystem connectivity on coral reef resilience. *Journal of Applied Ecology* 45(3): 854–862.

Nelson JA and Power M (2018) Ecology, sustainability and care: Developments in the field. *Feminist Economics* 24(3): 80–88.

Niezen R (2016) Templates and exclusions: Victim centrism in Canada's truth and reconciliation commission on Indian residential schools. *Journal of the Royal Anthropological Institute* 22(4): 920–938.

Nightingale AJ (2011) Bounding difference: Intersectionality and the material production of gender, caste, class and environment in Nepal. *Geoforum* 42(2): 153–162.

Nuñez TA, Lawler JA, McRae BH, Pierce DJ, Krosby MB, Kavanagh DM, Singleton PH and Tewksbury JJ (2013) Connectivity planning to address climate change. *Conservation Biology* 27 (2): 407–416.

Perz SG, Rosero M, Leite FL, Carvalho LA, Castillo J and Mejia CV (2013) Regional integration and household resilience: Infrastructure connectivity and livelihood diversity in the southwestern Amazon. *Human Ecology* 41: 497–511.

Plumwood V (2004) Gender, eco-feminism and the environment. In: White R (ed.), *Controversies in Environmental Sociology*. Cambridge: Cambridge University Press, pp. 43–60.

Prell C (2012) *Social Network Analysis: History, Theory and Methodology*. London: SAGE.

Randle JM, Stroink ML and Nelson CH (2015) Addiction and the adaptive cycle: A new focus. *Addition Research and Theory* 23(1): 81–88.

Rew L, Taylor-Seehafer M, Thomas NY and Yockey RD (2001) Correlates of resilience in homeless adolescents. *Journal of Nursing Scholarship* 33(1): 33–40.

Rockenbauch T and Sakdapolrak P (2017) Social networks and the resilience of rural communities in the Global South: A critical review and conceptual reflections. *Ecology and Society* 22(1): 10.

Rose DB (2017) Connectivity thinking, animism, and the pursuit of liveliness. *Educational Theory* 67(4): 491–508.

Salem S (2018) Intersectionality and its discontents: Intersectionality as traveling theory. *European Journal of Women's Studies* 25(4): 403–418.

Scheffer M, Carpenter SR, Lenton TM, Bascompte J, Brock W, Dakos V, van de Koppel J, van de Leemput IA, Levin SA, van Nes EH, Pascual M and Vandermeer J (2012) Anticipating critical transitions. *Science* 338(6105): 344–348.

Schulz P (2018) The 'ethical loneliness' of male sexual violence survivors in northern Uganda: Gendered reflections on silencing. *International Feminist Journal of Politics* 20(4): 583–601.

Sheaves M (2009) Consequences of ecological connectivity: The coastal ecosystem mosaic. *Marine Ecology Progress Series* 391: 107–115.

Smyth I and Sweetman C (2015) Introduction: Gender and resilience. *Gender & Development* 23(3): 405–414.

Stone-Jovicich S (2015) Probing the interfaces between the social sciences and social-ecological resilience: Insights from integrative and hybrid perspectives in the social sciences. *Ecology and Society* 20(2): 25.

Straathoff M, Sinke MRT, Dijkhuizen RM and Otte WM (2019) A systemic review on the quantitative relationship between structural and functional network connectivity strength in mammalian brains. *Journal of Cerebral Blood Flow & Metabolism* 39(2): 189–209.

Swaine A (2015) Beyond strategic rape and between the public and private: Violence against women in armed conflict. *Human Rights Quarterly* 37(3): 755–786.

Theron L and van Breda A (2021) Multisystemic enablers of sub-Saharan child and youth resilience to maltreatment. *Child Abuse & Neglect* 111(2): 105083.

Tischendorf L and Fahrig L (2000) On the usage and measurement of landscape connectivity. *OIKOS* 90(1): 7–19.

Traunmüller R, Kiwejski S and Freitag M (2019) The silent victims of sexual violence during war: Evidence from a list experiment in Sri Lanka. *Journal of Conflict Resolution* 63(9): 2015–2042.

Tronto J (1998) An ethic of care. *Generations* 22(3): 15–20.

Truelove Y (2011) (Re-)Conceptualizing water inequality in Delhi, India through a feminist political ecology framework. *Geoforum* 42(2): 143–152.

Ungar M (2018) Systemic resilience. *Ecology and Society* 23(4): 34.

Ungar M (2021a) Modeling multisystemic resilience: Connecting biological, psychological, social and ecological adaptation in contexts of adversity. In: Ungar M (ed.), *Multisystemic Resilience: Adaptation and Transformation in Contexts of Change*. New York, NY: Oxford University Press, pp. 6–31.

Ungar M (2021b) *Multisystemic Resilience: Adaptation and Transformation in Contexts of Change*. New York, NY: Oxford University Press.

Walker BH (2020) Resilience: What it *is* and is not. *Ecology and Society* 25(2): 11.

Walker BH and Salt D (2006) *Resilience Thinking: Sustaining Ecosystems and People in a Changing World*. Washington, DC: Island Press.

Waller MA (2001) Resilience in ecosystemic context: Evolution of the concept. *American Journal of Orthopsychiatry* 71(3): 290–297.

Weins JA (2006) Introduction: Connectivity research – What are the issues? In: Crooks KR and Sanjayan M (eds.), *Connectivity Conservation*. Cambridge: Cambridge University Press, pp. 23–28.

Xie C, Cui B, Xie T, Yu S, Liu Z, Chen C, Ning Z, Wang Q, Zou Y and Shao X (2020) Hydrological connectivity dynamics of tidal flat systems impacted by severe reclamation in the Yellow River Delta. *Science of the Total Environment* 739: 139860.

Yoshida K and Céspedes-Báez LM (2021) The nature of women, peace and security: A Colombian perspective. *International Affairs* 97(1): 17–34.

Zalesky A, Cocchi L, Fornito A, Murray MM and Bullmore E (2012) Connectivity differences in brain networks. *NeuroImage* 60(2): 1055–1062.

Zalewski M (2019) Forget(ting) feminism? Investigating relationality in international relations. *Cambridge Review of International Affairs* 32(5): 615–635.

Chapter 3

Research Design, Methodology and Ethics

Central to this book are the stories and experiences of female and male victims-/survivors of conflict-related sexual violence (CRSV) in Bosnia-Herzegovina (BiH), Colombia and Uganda. The three empirical chapters focus primarily on the data from 63 semi-structured interviews. The interviews, however, took place in the context of a larger mixed methods study, in which more than 400 men and women participated. This chapter provides important background information about the underpinning research and fieldwork that constitute the book's foundations.

The chapter begins by discussing the study design. The second section focuses on the quantitative part of the research and issues relating to sampling. The third section centres on the qualitative part of the study and the semi-structured interviews. It provides information about the interviewees in each country and explains how they were selected from the quantitative dataset. It also outlines the reflections workshops that took place in 2021 as a way of sharing with participants some of the key research findings. The fourth section explains how the data were analysed, and the final section reflects on some of the important ethics issues that the research raised.

The Research Design

This section discusses and elaborates on two particular aspects of the research design, namely its comparative case study approach and use of mixed methods.

A Comparative Case Study Approach

Scholars writing about CRSV most often use single case studies (see, e.g., Baaz and Stern, 2013; Boesten, 2014; Davies and True, 2017; Kreft, 2019; Mookherjee, 2015; Porter, 2017; Schulz, 2018; Skjelsbaek, 2012). Beyond what Boesten (2017: 516) has referred to as 'the trend in political science to analyze patterns in conflict-related sexual violence via quantitative causal analysis of comparative data sets' (see, e.g., Cohen and Nordås, 2014; Nagel and

DOI: 10.4324/9781003323532-4

70 Research Design, Methodology and Ethics

Doctor, 2020), comparative research on CRSV – and, more specifically, comparative case study-based qualitative research – is rare.

This book's novel use of a comparative approach is not simply about addressing a gap within existing scholarship. Its focus on three case studies is also linked to and is a logical extension of its conceptual approach to resilience. Specifically, the emphasis that the book places on the interactions and relationships between individuals and their social ecologies creates a strong rationale for exploring these connectivities – and the stories of these connectivities – in different countries and contexts. The research accordingly uses a diverse cross-case method to achieve 'maximum variance along relevant dimensions' (Seawright and Gerring, 2008: 300), including historical, political, social and cultural dimensions. Significant differences between the three case studies as regards, inter alia, the nature and dynamics of the conflicts, the actors involved, conflict duration and uses/patterns of CRSV – discussed in detail in the next chapter – further facilitate a maximal application of the book's social-ecological approach to resilience.

Various combinations of countries, however, could have achieved these high levels of diversity. The specific focus on BiH, Colombia and Uganda, and their individual importance to the research, thus requires explanation. BiH was an obvious choice of case study. It is a country that I have extensively researched and written about for more than a decade and I have a deep professional and personal attachment to it. In previous research (2014–2015), I spent a year in BiH doing fieldwork and speaking to female and male victims-/survivors of CRSV, with the aim of exploring some of the long-term legacies of sexual violence crimes committed during the 1992–1995 Bosnian war (Clark, 2017). It was a natural step and progression to further build on that research, taking it in a new direction using a resilience lens. It is also significant that the Bosnian war strongly contributed to what Kreft (2019: 223) has referred to as 'a skyrocketing international involvement around CRSV'; and, relatedly, it led to major developments in the international prosecution of such violence (Askin, 2003; Brammertz and Jarvis, 2016; Buss, 2002; Sellers, 2008). These factors additionally contributed to the decision to include BiH as one of the three case studies.

Turning to Colombia, the use of sexual violence has been widespread during more than five decades of armed conflict. According to a report by ABColombia et al. (2013: 1), for example,

> Women's groups collating and analysing data on conflict-related sexual violence agree with the conclusions of the Colombian Constitutional Court [in 2008] that this is a crime perpetrated by all armed actors and that it is 'an habitual, extensive, systematic and invisible practice'.[1]

Colombian non-governmental organisations (NGOs) and women's associations have carried out important research on the topic. Academic research (at least in English) on CRSV in Colombia, however, remains limited (see, e.g., Kreft, 2019; Stallone, 2021; Valiñas, 2020; Zalesne, 2019). It is also very relevant in the context of this research that notwithstanding the signing of a peace agreement between the government and the Revolutionary Armed Forces of Colombia (FARC) in 2016, 'it is increasingly apparent that the country's armed conflict is reconfiguring rather than abating' (Zulver, 2021: 441). In other words, the country is not so much transitioning from conflict to 'peace' as transitioning from one form of conflict to another. This made it an extremely interesting case study for thinking about both resilience and transitional justice.

The use of CRSV in Uganda, as in BiH, has been extensively researched (see, e.g., Baines, 2014; Edström and Dolan, 2019; Porter, 2019; Schulz, 2021a). Existing scholarship, however, has focused heavily – although not exclusively – on sexual violence committed by members of Joseph Kony's Lord's Resistance Army (LRA). Selecting Uganda as a case study was an opportunity to explore different uses and patterns of sexual violence by different actors – including government forces and cattle rustlers from the Karamoja region – and how these contextual dynamics might affect and shape resilience and its expression. It was also potentially an opportunity to influence transitional justice developments in the country, particularly relating to the National Transitional Justice Policy which the Ugandan Cabinet approved in June 2019 (Kasande, 2019); and, in this context, to elicit feedback on the basic idea of a social-ecological framing of transitional justice that this research proposes (see Chapter 8).

A Mixed Methods Approach

Creswell (2009: 98) has noted that 'Many fields are adopting and using mixed methods'. Certainly, studies of resilience frequently combine quantitative and qualitative methods (see, e.g., Boardman et al., 2011; Cairns-Nagi and Bambra, 2013; Farewell et al., 2020). For the purposes of this research, which thus builds on a broader trend, the use of mixed methods was considered an optimal approach to explore and capture some of the richness and complexity of resilience discussed in the two previous chapters. To cite Johnson et al. (2007: 113), 'Mixed methods research is, generally speaking, an approach to knowledge (theory and practice) that attempts to consider multiple viewpoints, perspectives, positions, and standpoints (always including the standpoints of qualitative and quantitative research)'.

A mixed methods design was additionally appropriate for achieving both breadth and depth of analysis. In all three case study countries, for example, particular groups of victims-/survivors of CRSV have been significantly overlooked, as discussed in the next section. Incorporating a quantitative component within the research design was an opportunity to create samples that both included these neglected groups and, more broadly, reflected some of the diverse demographic profiles of victims-/survivors in all three countries. Complementing the quantitative part of the study, semi-structured interviews provided crucial insights into participants' social ecologies in ways

72 Research Design, Methodology and Ethics

that the questionnaire data alone could not. By extension, they brought into focus the cultural context within which the participants were rebuilding their lives and managing everyday challenges. This is important because resilience research increasingly 'foregrounds deeper understandings of the complex nuances of culture and how these promote thriving under adversity' (Theron et al., 2011: 801).

Leech and Onwuegbuzie's (2009: 267–268) three-dimensional typology of mixed methods designs is based on (a) the level of mixing ('on a continuum from not mixed . . . to fully mixed methods'); (b) time orientation (concurrent or sequential); and (c) emphasis of approaches (equal status or dominant status). Using these three dimensions, the authors have proposed eight types of mixed methods designs, and this research largely used what they refer to as a partially mixed sequential dominant status design (Leech and Onwuegbuzie, 2009: 268).

First, the different components of the study's mixed methods approach – questionnaires, semi-structured interviews and reflections workshops – were undertaken sequentially rather than concurrently. The intention was that each stage would build on the next in a systematic way. As Ivankova et al. (2006: 4) point out, however, 'Despite its popularity and straightforwardness, this mixed-methods design is not easy to implement'. In this research, analysis of the questionnaire data took considerably longer than expected, due to the need to outsource the work[2] and to engage different people to do different parts of it (reflecting their particular areas of expertise and/or limited time commitments). Hence, the study only partly followed a sequential research design. While the data collection process itself proceeded sequentially, most of the actual analysis of the questionnaire data occurred at the same data as the qualitative data were being coded and analysed.

Second, the research design gives greater prominence to the qualitative data over the quantitative data. While both are important in different ways, it is the qualitative data that enable the 'thick description' (Geertz, 2008) and fine-grained analysis that a complex comparative study of resilience demands. In focusing primarily on the qualitative part of the research, one of the aims of this book is precisely to demonstrate 'the substantial contribution qualitative research can make to how resilience-related phenomena are studied and understood' (Ungar, 2003: 86).

Third, while there are multiple ways of integrating quantitative and qualitative data, it is also important to keep in mind Uprichard and Dawney's (2019: 20) argument that there exists 'a fundamental paradox at the heart of mixed methods research'. Mixed methods, they point out, 'are assumed to be useful because of the complexity of the social world', yet at the same time there also exists an assumption that it is 'both possible and desirable to integrate data relating to the study of complex, messy social objects' (Uprichard and Dawney, 2019: 20). This research involved a partial but not full mixing of methods. The data were integrated in two main ways.

The first is what Fetters et al. (2013: 2139) refer to as 'integration through connecting'. The purpose of such integration is 'to link the two data types through sampling' (Fetters and Molina-Azorin, 2017: 300). In this research, interviewees were selected from a larger sample of participants (N = 449), all of whom had completed a study questionnaire. The key reason for this selection strategy was to ensure that the interview samples for each country captured both the demographic diversity of participants and the spread of resilience scores – based on a quantitative measure (discussed in the next section) – within the overall study sample.

The second type of integration occurred through the analysis itself. Both the questionnaire data and the interview transcripts were uploaded into NVivo – a computer software programme for qualitative and mixed methods research. Once the codebook had been developed and all of the interviews coded, multiple mixed methods queries were run to explore the relations between individual parts of the questionnaire – and in particular participants' resilience scores – and codes and emergent themes from the qualitative data. This is one of the two 'major routes to integration' through data handling that Bazeley (2006: 66) identifies.

The Quantitative Phase of the Research

The Study Questionnaire

The quantitative phase of the research involved the development and application of a questionnaire. As Walker and Salt (2012: 67) underline, 'resilience is not a single number or a result'. However, it was part of the research design to explore whether and how participants' resilience scores from a quantitative measure might translate into the qualitative data, and whether the latter could help to explain variance in these scores.

Van Rensburg et al. (2019: 93) note that 'various resilience scales have been developed over the years'. These include the Resilience Scale (Wagnild and Young, 1993), the Resilience Scale for Adults (Hjemdal et al., 2001), the Connor-Davidson Resilience Scale (Connor and Davidson, 2003) and the Brief Resilience Scale (Smith et al., 2008). This research opted to use the Adult Resilience Measure (ARM) – a 28-item scale developed by Ungar and colleagues at the Resilience Research Centre (2016) at Dalhousie University in Canada. The first reason is that the ARM measures a person's protective resources across individual, relational and contextual sub-scales. It thus reflects a social-ecological understanding of resilience – consistent with this book's own approach – in a way that some of the other scales do not. The aforementioned Brief Resilience Scale, for example, focuses on an individual's ability to 'bounce back'[3] from adversity rather than on the extent to which social ecologies themselves – and specifically the protective resources within them – support resilience. The six items in the scale, which are very narrowly framed, include 'I tend to bounce back quickly after hard times' and 'it does not take me long to recover from a stressful event' (Smith et al., 2008: 196).

The second reason for choosing the ARM over other resilience scales is that it had significant potential to be easily understood in BiH, Colombia and Uganda, including by participants with little or no education. It is important to note that the ARM is an extension of the earlier Child and Youth Resilience Measure (CYRM), the development of which involved mixed methods research across 14 sites in 11 different countries – including Colombia, Russia, Tanzania and India (see Ungar and Liebenberg, 2011: 128). In their research on Irish survivors of clerical institutional abuse, moreover, Liebenberg and Moore (2018: 13) found that 'in contrast to some longer and more complex measures of resilience, the RRC [Resilience Research Centre]-ARM may be a good fit for vulnerable adult populations'.

The questionnaire additionally included a Traumatic Events Checklist (TEC), specifically developed to provide important background information about (potentially) traumatic events[4] that participants had experienced in the context of war/armed conflict. As Figure 3.1 illustrates, the adversities and stressors that these women and men had faced were multiple. Another section of the questionnaire was about current problems (including economic insecurity/ poverty, land issues and abuse/bullying from community members), and respondents' answers showed that many of them continued to face significant everyday challenges.

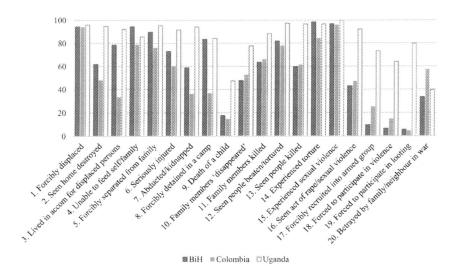

Figure 3.1 TEC results by country

Note: The bars on the graph are given as a percentage of each country sample.

The study questionnaire was translated into the relevant local languages (Bosnian/Croatian/Serbian, Spanish and the Acholi and Lango dialects of the Luo language) and piloted during field visits to BiH, Colombia and Uganda between January and April 2018.[5] Application of the final version of the questionnaire took place between May and December 2018. In total, 449 victims-/survivors of CRSV – 126 in BiH, 171 in Colombia and 152 in Uganda[6] – completed a study questionnaire. Due to the sensitive nature of the research, a self-administered questionnaire would not have been appropriate. Hence, a personal, face-to-face approach was adopted; the three members of the research team (the author and two postdoctoral researchers), the various in-country organisations that supported the research[7] and three psychologists in BiH and Colombia were all involved in applying the questionnaire.

Sampling Challenges, Limitations and Priorities

The challenges of finding and establishing contact with victims-/survivors of CRSV in BiH, Colombia and Uganda meant that this study relied heavily on convenience sampling and on the aforementioned in-country organisations that facilitated the fieldwork. The contacts that these organisations had, whether with victims-/survivors directly or with other organisations that worked with them, fundamentally shaped who ultimately participated in this research. The limitations of this sampling strategy must be acknowledged, and one potential criticism is that the very central role played by the organisations in identifying and facilitating access to research participants might have created a resilience bias.

On this point, it is important to emphasise that some of the participants were merely known to the organisations and were not in regular contact with them or in receipt of any direct support. Indeed, many of them had not received any help, particularly those living in remote areas of northern Uganda. What unquestionably did create a potential resilience bias within the sample, however, is the fact that some of the Colombian participants were social leaders and activists (linked to the training and support that they had received from organisations like *Ruta Pacífica de las Mujeres*) and also led their own organisations. This is discussed more in Chapter 6.

Alongside convenience sampling, purposive sampling was used as much as possible to ensure that the overall sample conveyed some of the heterogeneity and diversity of victims-/survivors of CRSV in each country. There were two particular priorities in this regard. The first was to include male victims-/survivors. Increasingly, there is more research being done on CRSV against men (see, e.g., Chynoweth et al., 2017; Edström and Dolan, 2019; Njoku and Dery, 2021; Njoku et al., 2022; Schulz, 2021a; Sivakumaran, 2007; Zalewski et al., 2018). Schulz and Touquet (2020: 1175), however, maintain that the issue 'remains underexplored in scholarship and policymaking alike'. The use of CRSV against men in Colombia is particularly neglected (Flisi, 2019: 253).

76 Research Design, Methodology and Ethics

Unfortunately, one of the limitations of this research is precisely the very small number of male participants. Of the 449 individuals who completed a study questionnaire in 2018, just 27 were men (12 in BiH, five in Colombia and ten in Uganda). Dolan et al. (2020: 1155) make the important point that 'Reaching survivors for research on violence through groups and services from which they have already sought and received support, and with which they have established relationships of trust, facilitates their sense of safety in sharing their experiences'. Particularly in BiH and Colombia, however, few men who have suffered CRSV receive such support,[8] and the in-country organisations that facilitated the fieldwork predominantly (and in some cases exclusively) focused their attention on women. Further adding to the challenges of making contact with male victims-/survivors, 'Men often find it very difficult to acknowledge and express their ordeal, using words such as "abuse" or "torture"' (Solangon and Patel, 2012: 422).

A second priority was to include victims-/survivors of CRSV from different ethnic groups in each country. This was important not only for exploring whether any significant relationships would emerge between resilience and ethnicity, but also for addressing the previously mentioned fact that some victims-/survivors have received little attention – or less attention than others. Scholarship and reports on the use of CRSV during the Bosnian war, for example, have overwhelmingly focused on Bosniak women. Such one-sided coverage, as Simić (2016: 103) points out, 'has made it difficult to acknowledge the complexity of Serb and other women's [and men's] wartime experiences'. Practical factors have also played a part. There are more NGOs in the BiH Federation working with victims-/survivors of CRSV than there are in *Republika Srpska* (RS), which makes it easier to establish contact with Bosniak women.[9] That the country remains deeply divided, moreover, means that trying to work with organisations in both the BiH Federation and RS is extremely difficult. During her own fieldwork in BiH, for example, Močnik (2019: 461) found that 'some groups refused to collaborate with me because I had previously collaborated with other groups or individuals they were hostile to'.

In Colombia, the longevity and complexity of the armed conflict, extending over more than five decades, made it important to capture a variety of conflict experiences – and some of the specific challenges that certain groups have faced. A particular imperative in this regard was to reach Indigenous and Afro-Colombian women, who have historically faced significant marginalisation and structural violence – and often continue to do so (see, e.g., Acosta et al., 2018: 115; Barragan, 2017: 58; Zulver, 2018). Regarding Uganda, existing research on CRSV during the war in the north between government forces and the LRA has mainly focused on ethnic Acholi victims-/survivors (see, e.g., Baines, 2017; Porter, 2017). This reflects the fact that '"Acholiland" . . . was the epicentre of the war' (Blackmore, 2020: 685). One of the priorities of this study was to extend the focus beyond just one ethnic group, and the total Ugandan sample included an equal number of Acholi and Lango participants.

Research Design, Methodology and Ethics 77

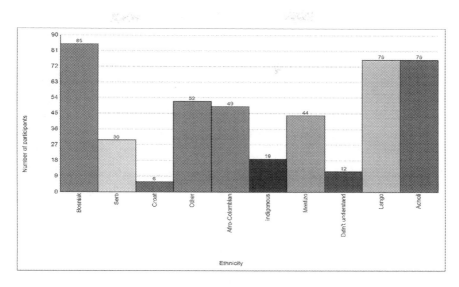

Figure 3.2 Ethnic profile of research participants
Note: The 'other' column combines respondents from BiH (5) and Colombia (47).

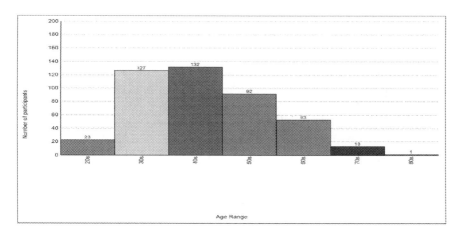

Figure 3.3 Participants by age
Note: Data missing for eight participants.

Figure 3.2 shows the breakdown of research participants (those who completed a questionnaire) by ethnicity in each country. Figure 3.3 shows the breakdown of participants by age. The majority were in their 30s and 40s. On average, participants from BiH were older overall (M = 55), compared to those in Colombia (M = 42) and Uganda (M = 40). Part of the explanation for these age variations lies in the conflicts themselves. Many of the Bosnian participants

78 Research Design, Methodology and Ethics

suffered sexual violence during the first year of the Bosnian war (i.e., 1992). In contrast, the very protracted nature of the armed conflict in Colombia meant that Colombian participants' experiences of sexual violence had a much greater temporal spread. In Uganda, some of the participants were very young when they suffered CRSV, reflecting the fact that they were abducted as children and forcibly recruited into the LRA.

The Qualitative Phase of the Research

Selecting the Interviewees

Once the questionnaire data were inputted into SPSS (Statistical Package for the Social Sciences), mean ARM scores were calculated – 111.77 for BiH, 107.33 for Colombia and 107.97 for Uganda – and participants in each country were grouped into quartiles based on their total ARM scores.[10] In the qualitative phase of the research, interviewees were selected from across the quartiles. There are obvious limitations in compressing something as complex and multifaceted as resilience into a numerical form. However, using ARM scores to inform the choice of interviewees was not only a useful way of combining the quantitative and qualitative parts of the study, but it also created opportunities to explore whether these numbers told a bigger story – and specifically whether and how they correlated with codes and themes in the qualitative data (discussed in the next section).

Each member of the research team chose five interviewees from each set of country quartiles, ensuring that all selection decisions reflected, as much as possible, the diversity within the quartiles – and in particular gender, ethnic and age diversity. Selection choices were always discussed, to ensure that the researchers were applying the same criteria, and although reserve lists were prepared, the number of participants who declined to take part in an interview was very small. A bigger issue was that, in many cases, there was a considerable time lag (of up to nine months) between participants completing a questionnaire and taking part in an interview. Some of them had moved or changed telephone numbers in the interim (this was especially an issue in Colombia), making it very difficult or impossible to contact them.

In addition to the five interviewees selected from each set of country quartiles, for different reasons each member of the research team ultimately conducted one additional interview. In total, therefore, 63 women and men (21 in each country) participated in the interview stage of the research. The interviews took place between January and July 2019. Table 3.1 gives a broad overview of the interviewees' demographic profiles, highlighting particular variables that were considered from the outset to be potentially relevant for explaining resilience. The empirical chapters – each of which focuses on one of the three countries – specifically refer to interviewees' gender and ethnicity, for the reasons discussed in the previous section, and they mention other demographic characteristics (such

Research Design, Methodology and Ethics   79

Table 3.1 Basic demographic profile of the 63 interviewees

	BiH	*Colombia*	*Uganda*
Gender	Female – 16	Female – 19	Female – 17
	Male – 5	Male – 2	Male – 4
Ethnicity	Bosniak – 11	Afro-Colombian – 4	Acholi – 11
	Croat – 3	Indigenous – 3	Lango – 10
	Serb – 6	Mestizo – 5	
	Other – 1	Other – 7	
		Did not understand – 2	
Age range*	30s – 1	20s – 1	20s – 1
	40s – 6	30s – 6	30s – 10
	50s – 8	40s – 5	40s – 3
	60s – 6	50s – 7	50s – 4
		60s – 2	60s – 1
			70s – 1
Education**	Primary – 7	Primary – 8	Primary – 8
	Secondary – 12	Secondary – 5	Secondary – 1
	University – 2	*Tecnica profesional*† – 3	No education/did
		Profesional†† – 2	not complete
			primary
			education – 12
Marital	Single – 3	Single – 8	Single – 6
status	Married – 14	Married – 5	Married – 7
	Divorced/	Divorced/separated – 1	Divorced/
	separated – 2	Cohabiting – 4	separated – 2
	Cohabiting – 1	Widowed – 3	Cohabiting – 1
	Widowed – 1		Widowed – 5
Children	Yes – 17	Yes – 19	Yes – 20
	No – 4	No – 2	No – 1

Notes
* Data missing for one of the Ugandan interviewees.
** Data missing for three of the Colombian interviewees.
† *Tecnica profesional* refers to short vocational training courses covering, inter alia, hairdressing, information technology or road safety.
†† *Profesional* refers to a university degree.

as age) where relevant. However, the interview sample sizes for each country were not large enough to systematically explore the potential significance of demographic variables. Furthermore, there was very little variation within some of these variables (e.g., whether interviewees had children).

The Interviews

To capture the spread of CRSV in each country, and to reach particular ethnic groups, interviews took place in multiple research sites. In BiH, I conducted interviews in five of the ten cantons within the BiH Federation, including Tuzla Canton, Central Bosnia Canton and Una-Sana Canton, as well as in several locations in RS and in Brčko District (a self-governing administrative

80 Research Design, Methodology and Ethics

unit bordering Croatia). Interviews in Colombia were organised in ten of the country's 32 departments, including Antioquia in the Andean region, Bolívar in the Caribbean region and Putumayo in the Amazon region. In Uganda, interviewees were located in eight different districts, including Gulu, Lira, Oyam and Pader. The in-country organisations continued to be a valuable source of support during the qualitative part of the research. When necessary, for example, they provided a safe and secure space within their premises where the interviews could take place. This was especially important in those cases where it was not possible to visit the interviewees in their homes, whether for security, privacy and/or practical reasons.

On average, interviews lasted approximately one hour, although some were considerably longer. All of them were conducted by the researchers in the local language/s and were recorded (with the interviewees' informed consent) using fully encrypted digital voice recorders. Detailed post-interview notes were also made (and coded). In some cases, the researchers had already met the interviewees during the quantitative part of the research, which often helped to create a more relaxed atmosphere. In other cases, however (namely, when the three independent psychologists in BiH and Colombia or individuals from the in-country organisations had themselves administered the study questionnaire), the researchers were meeting the interviewees for the first time.

All interviews involved the use of an interview guide (see Appendix 1). Boesten and Henry (2018: 582–583) emphasise that anyone doing research on CRSV should think carefully about the questions they pose and ask themselves 'what data are already available and what is missing?' The general lack of cross-fertilisation to date between resilience scholarship and scholarship on CRSV meant that the questions asked in this study were primarily about addressing 'missing' data. Specifically, the interview guide was designed to provide important insights into some of the similar and contextually specific ways that interviewees in all three countries were demonstrating resilience, as well as to draw out some of the key resources and factors that were both helping and hindering resilience. Questions included the following: What resources do you have that help you to deal with challenges (e.g., your own inner resources, services within your community, government institutions)? Who or what are the sources of support in your life? After everything that you have gone through, what are the factors that have been most important in helping you to rebuild/ start to rebuild your life? What are the factors that have made it difficult for you to rebuild/start to rebuild your life?

Another priority when designing the interview guide was to keep the narrative space open, by giving interviewees the opportunity to share and speak about different aspects of their lives. This was the rationale for such questions as: If you were to tell the story of your life, what title would you give it? Can you think about the last time that you experienced something very stressful that you feel comfortable sharing; how did you deal with that experience and who did you turn to? Are there parts of your story which are important to you and

Research Design, Methodology and Ethics   81

which you are never asked about? Additionally, and to facilitate intersectional analyses, the interview guide included questions about the significance, if any, of interviewees' gender, ethnicity and place of birth (or current place of residence, if different) for how they have dealt with challenges and adversity in life.

Some of the questions in the interview guide directly built on parts of the questionnaire (e.g., current problems), and some issues were only asked about in the questionnaire yet also emerged during the interviews. While the questionnaire, for example, asked participants to rate their general state of health on a scale of 1 ('poor') to 5 ('excellent'), the interview guide itself did not include any specific health-related questions. Nevertheless, health was a recurring thematic within the interviews (and is discussed in all three empirical chapters). Moreover, interviewees talked about aspects of health that may not have emerged had specific questions been asked, including the health of their environment. Some of the Ugandan interviewees, as one illustration, spoke about the problem of drought and its impact.

The Reflections Workshops

Two years after the qualitative interviews were completed, reflections workshops took place in each country. The aim was to share and discuss some of the key research findings with research participants and to give them the opportunity to comment and ask questions. The ongoing COVID-19 pandemic meant that the original (pre-pandemic) plans for these workshops needed to be significantly revised and downsized. To allow social distancing, no more than eight people took part in each workshop. There were two reflections workshops in BiH (led by the NGO *Snaga Žene*), three in Colombia (organised by *Ruta Pacifica de las Mujeres* and *Profamila* respectively) and four in Uganda (undertaken by the in-country researcher and a research assistant). All of the workshops took place in 2021.

Some of the participants had been involved in only the quantitative phase of the project, and some of them had completed a questionnaire and taken part in an interview. Not only was their feedback on the research extremely valuable, but the workshop discussions also yielded important new data. The empirical chapters accordingly draw on some of the material from these discussions, and particularly those that took place in Uganda.

Analysing the Data, Coding and Theme Development

The Quantitative Data

The questionnaire data are not the main focus of this book and have been analysed elsewhere (see Clark et al., 2021, 2022).[11] It is, however, necessary to comment on the relationship between the ARM and the interview data. To reiterate, one of the aims was to examine whether the interview data might elucidate variations in ARM scores and, relatedly, whether ARM quartiles would correlate in any way with particular codes and themes. Multiple queries were run in NVivo to explore these possible relations, yet they yielded few significant results. Indeed, in their development of the CYRM, Ungar and Liebenberg (2011: 142) acknowledged that 'we are disappointed that at no point in the process were we able to demonstrate convergence between our qualitative and quantitative findings'.

It is important to point out that the decision to use the ARM was made prior to the development of the conceptual framework that ultimately guided the qualitative analysis, and this may help to explain why the anticipated synergies between ARM scores and the interview data were largely absent. While Liebenberg et al. (2012: 219) underscore that 'resilience is not a static state', which highlights the importance of longitudinal research, by itself what the ARM effectively conveys is a 'snapshot' of an individual's protective resources at a particular moment in time. Qualitative data necessarily paint a more complex picture. In this research, the themes developed from the qualitative data not only provide insights into the interviewees' protective resources. They also tell a larger and more temporally expansive story about those resources, including lost resources (broken and ruptured connectivities). In other words, individuals' ARM scores were only a small part of a much larger narrative. Hence, with a few exceptions, the empirical chapters do not refer specifically to interviewees' ARM scores.

The Qualitative Data

Deterding and Waters (2021: 712) note that 'Coding is the most laborious and time-consuming part of interview research. Yet it is granted little space in published academic articles and books'. My aim here is to give it 'sufficient' space, in the sense of enabling the reader to understand how the coding process was undertaken and how it developed, but without discussing every detail and minutiae of it. While I disagree with Saldaña (2013: 38) that coding is 'a behind-the-scenes matter', it is important to find the right balance between too much and too little information.

All interviews were transcribed verbatim (in accordance with the study's transcription protocol) and translated into English (by a combination of the researchers and professional translators). As the interviews were translated, I started to read the full transcripts and to make notes of possible codes and recurring ideas, thus 'immersing' myself in the data. According to Green et al. (2007: 547), 'Data immersion . . . lays the foundation for connecting disjointed elements into a clearer picture of the issue being investigated'. Once all interviews were translated, the transcripts – together with the detailed post-interview notes and an Excel spreadsheet containing the questionnaire data – were uploaded into NVivo.

Research Design, Methodology and Ethics   83

I started the process of developing the codebook by reading through a selection of transcripts from each country and inputting broad data-driven code names into the nascent codebook. At this very early stage, I simply used descriptive coding, 'which summarizes in a word or short phrase – most often as a noun – the basic topic of a passage of qualitative data' (Saldaña, 2013: 88). This process generated 159 codes, some of which consisted of words or phrases that interviewees themselves had used. The codes included 'fighting', 'humiliation', 'intimacy', 'intrusion of the past', 'new skills/learning', 'not alone/not the only one', 'pain as a reminder', 'spiritual resources' and 'wound that cannot heal'. It quickly became clear that if I continued working through the data at this rudimentary level, the result would be an overwhelming number of codes from which it would be very difficult to identify core themes and to tell an overall 'story' about the data.

Weston et al. (2001: 397) liken the coding process 'to continually zooming in and out'. In their words, 'One begins with the big picture, an overall conception of the phenomenon, moves in to focus on details through coding, and moves out again to see how the details might have changed the way we interpret the larger picture' (Weston et al., 2001: 397). Part of the process of 'zooming out' was to focus not just on the individual codes, but on broader categories that linked these codes together. As I read more of the transcripts and revisited the initial codes, I started to group them. The resultant categories, which were extremely broad, included 'environmental stressors', 'learning, growth and renewal' and 'resource clusters and support systems'.

Once I had a first draft of the codebook that I was happy with, including detailed descriptions for each of the codes, I discussed it with the other coders (one of the postdoctoral researchers and a research assistant) and we began by jointly coding an interview from each country. This was a way for them to practically familiarise themselves with the codebook and for all of us to see how the codes were working, which codes were missing and so on. Over the next five months, we coded the 63 interviews. As we went along, I continued to amend and refine the codebook by adding, combining or removing codes, and in some cases tweaking the code names. The vast majority of the interviews were coded by two people, to ensure consistency of coding (I coded all except six of the interviews), and inter-coder agreement was generally high. Weekly meetings were held to discuss coding and to reconcile any coding disagreements.

Once the first cycle of coding was completed, I undertook a second cycle, to check that everything had been correctly coded and to further refine some of the categories and clusters of codes. At this point, I had 17 categories, including 'breakage, rupture and loss', 'children', 'dealing and living with the past' and 'repair, regeneration and growth'. I also ran numerous queries in NVivo, including matrix queries, comparison diagrams and visualisations, to explore some of the patterns and relationships within the data. Throughout the entire coding process, I wrote more than 300 pages of detailed analytic memos, to

84 Research Design, Methodology and Ethics

keep a note of new reflections about the data and to record the progression of my ideas. I also created several concept and mind maps in NVivo to help visualise my thoughts.

As I began to think more laterally across the entire dataset, rather than simply focusing on bits of it, I moved more directly into thematic analysis, which Braun and Clarke (2012: 57) define as 'a method for systematically identifying, organizing, and offering insight into patterns of meaning (themes) across a data set'. They identify six phases of thematic analysis (see Braun and Clarke, 2012: 60–69). The process, however, is not a linear one; there is a 'constant moving back and forward' between the different phases (Nowell et al., 2017: 4). Moreover, doing thematic analysis, and doing it well, is challenging. Braun and Clarke (2019: 594) underline that:

> Themes do not passively emerge from either data or coding; they are not 'in' the data, waiting to be identified. . . . Themes are creative and interpretive stories about the data, produced at the intersection of the researcher's theoretical assumptions, their analytic resources and skill, and the data themselves.

What increasingly struck me as I worked backwards and forwards through the data was the significance of relationships. Interviewees frequently spoke about the different relationships in their lives – including with family, with children, with local organisations, with God, with land – from which they drew strength to move forward and deal with ongoing challenges. Resilience scholars often use terms such as 'protective resources', 'protective factors' or 'protective processes' to broadly refer to different things, people or environments in an individual's life that potentially help to 'cushion' some of the impact of shocks and adversities (Betancourt and Khan, 2008; Hjemdal et al., 2006; Ungar, 2019). One of the limitations of such terminology, however, is that it does not capture or convey the particular emotions, feelings and attachments that may be integral to something or someone having a 'protective' function. Hence, rather than simply thinking about the relationships that interviewees talked about in terms of protective resources/factors/processes, I conceptualised them as connectivities – to emphasise the sense of deep connection and connectedness between individuals and different parts of their social ecologies.

As the idea of relational connectivity began to take shape as a theme, it also became clear that there was a bigger story to tell within the data about connectivity – and about the relationships between connectivity and resilience. A limitation of the ARM, and indeed of many scales that seek to measure and quantify resilience, is that they only tell part of a larger story, primarily by focusing on the 'resources' that an individual *has* in his/her life. As Quinlan et al. (2016: 679) underline, however, 'Resilience assessment involves a process of identifying how resilience is created, maintained or broken down'; and this,

Research Design, Methodology and Ethics 85

fundamentally, is largely the story that this research seeks to tell, through its focus on different dimensions and trajectories of connectivity.

I developed eight core connectivity themes. As I worked on them, I also immersed myself within extant literature on connectivity, particularly within the field of ecology (see Chapter 2). It was through this process that I started to see important synergies between ecological discussions of connectivity and the data. The eight core themes – each of which includes a direct quote from the interview data – are the following: 1. *'I am all that I've lived': Connectivities of violence;* 2. *'It isn't there anymore': Connectivities lost;* 3. *'The problem of ill health is there': Health connectivities and everyday stressors;* 4. *'With them I get through it': Relational connectivities;* 5. *'Why did this have to be': Making connections and finding meaning;* 6. *'We have to live': Reconnecting with life;* 7. *'I want to achieve more': (Re)Building connections and making a difference;* 8. *'It didn't change anything': Justice that connects/ makes a difference.* These themes are discussed and developed in the empirical chapters (and in Chapter 8, in the case of the final theme). Each of the themes is linked, in turn, to one of the three core elements of the book's conceptual framework discussed in the previous chapter (i.e., supportive and sustaining connectivities, broken and ruptured connectivities and new connectivities).

Ethics Issues and Reflections

This research received ethics approval from the Humanities and Social Sciences Ethical Review Committee at the University of Birmingham, the European Research Council and relevant authorities in BiH, Colombia and Uganda (including the Ugandan National Council for Science and Technology). During the many months that it took to secure the necessary approvals, some of the key ethics issues that had to be explained and addressed included the following: informed consent, confidentiality, protection of personal data, data storage, data transfer, incidental findings, possible stigmatisation of research participants within their communities and fair benefit sharing. The thoroughness of the entire process meant that it was never at risk of becoming what Connor et al. (2018: 408) have called 'a tick-a-box exercise with little reflection'. Rather than discuss all of the complex ethics issues, some of which I have written about elsewhere (see, e.g., Clark et al., 2021), I will focus on two important and inter-related questions which arise from them.

Is it Ethical to Seek Information Directly From Victims-/Survivors of CRSV?

In a recent article about the politics of sexual violence statistics in the Democratic Republic of Congo, Lewis (2022: 58) notes that 'For ethical reasons, this study did not include interviews with survivors'. The idea that it is 'unethical' to interview victims-/survivors is unhelpful, however, especially without further discussion. Of course, there are unethical ways of interviewing victims-/survivors

86 Research Design, Methodology and Ethics

of CRSV (and indeed any research participants). Examples include making empty promises or falsely raising expectations (e.g., about the outcomes and 'rewards' of participating in the research); asking extremely intrusive or insensitive questions (such as questions that imply judgement or blame); rushing through the interview questions rather than allowing the interviewee to set the pace; and not taking the time to put the interviewee at ease (as much as possible) or to really listen to her/his answers.

How we interview victims-/survivors of CRSV, however, is separate from (albeit related to) the bigger issue of *whether* we should even seek to interview them. Arguably one important justification for interviewing victims-/survivors is that they themselves, directly or indirectly, can potentially contribute in very valuable ways to the development of good practices in the field, by expressing what they want and need from the interview process. Campbell et al.'s (2009) research with victims-/survivors of sexual violence in the United States is an excellent example of this, as is Foster and Minwalla's (2018) research with Yazidi women to explore the latter's views on journalistic practices of reporting sexual violence by Islamic State militants.

In the development of what she calls a Gender Justice Methodology, Campbell (2018: 480) explains her own decision 'not to use sexual violence survivors as key respondents', on the grounds that 'these victims have become "over-researched"'. While the problem of 'over-research' is not specific to the issue of CRSV (see, e.g., Clark, 2008; Omata, 2020; Sukarieh and Tannock, 2013), it is essential to ask *which* victims-/survivors have been over-researched. BiH, for example, might be broadly described as 'over-researched' (Boesten and Henry, 2018: 579). Nevertheless, when it comes to CRSV, the overwhelming focus, as previously noted, has been on the experiences of Bosniak women (Berry, 2017: 841). In other words, it is important to unpack claims about over-researched populations and communities.

The recent Murad Code – officially known as the Global Code of Conduct for Gathering and Using Information about Systematic and Conflict-Related Sexual Violence – states that wherever possible, information about CRSV should be sought 'from sources other than survivors (such as fact-pattern witnesses and expert reports) to reduce pressure on survivors' (Nadia's Initiative et al., 2022). Similarly, the World Health Organization's (WHO, 2007: 12) Ethical and Safety Recommendations for Researching, Documenting and Monitoring Sexual Violence in Emergencies stipulate that 'Individuals who have been or may be survivors of sexual violence should not be interviewed unless the required information cannot be obtained in any other way'. The Recommendations add that:

> The case for direct interviewing must thus demonstrate: that the desired outcome cannot be achieved without gathering information in this way, that the information is needed and is not otherwise available, that information cannot be obtained in a less invasive manner (e.g. by using other

Research Design, Methodology and Ethics 87

methods, or by involving a different community, in a different time, or a different context with lower risk), and that the welfare of respondents can be properly protected.

(WHO, 2007: 10)

While I will address the issue of respondents' welfare separately, these conditions were arguably met in the context of this research. First, the general lack of attention to and discussion about resilience within extant scholarship on CRSV created a strong justification for working directly with victims-/survivors in BiH, Colombia and Uganda. Interviews were necessary to explore some of the ways that these women and men were dealing with their experiences, which resources and connectivities they were drawing on in the process and how they were expressing and manifesting everyday resilience in different cultural and social-ecological contexts. The policy implications of this research, moreover, particularly for transitional justice, demonstrate that such information 'is needed'.

Second, this research could have been done in a 'less invasive manner'. For example, interviews could have been conducted with NGOs that work with victims-/survivors of CRSV, including some of the organisations that supported the fieldwork. However, I fundamentally take issue with giving anyone the right to speak *on behalf of* these women and men – a practice that I have frequently observed in BiH (Clark, 2019).[12] As one of the Colombian interviewees from the Indigenous Pastos people powerfully emphasised: 'the memories we have inside us, that's . . . that's our own voice, it doesn't belong to anyone else' (interview, Colombia, 4 February 2019). Of course, not everyone will want to talk about or to share these memories. For some of the interviewees, however, having reached the point where they were able to talk about their experiences was an important achievement and step forward. In the words of another female interviewee, who identified as Afro-Colombian:

I mean, when everything was all bottled up, I felt like this [she demonstrates how she felt by shrugging her shoulders and clasping her hands between her legs]. 'What's wrong with you?' – 'Nothing' – 'Why are you like that?' – 'No reason' – 'What's going on with you?' – 'Nothing'. Now, on the other hand, I've started to talk about it all and I cry at the time, I feel sad at the time, but afterwards, hey, I emerge. That's the difference. I'm not the same sad woman I was before, in those days when what happened to me happened. I feel different now.

(interview, Colombia, 30 March 2019)

What About the Risks of Retraumatising Research Participants?

As a final question, interviewees were asked to comment on the interview process and how they had experienced it. The answers they gave were overwhelmingly positive. In BiH, for example, one of the three Croat interviewees

88 Research Design, Methodology and Ethics

described the interview as 'useful' and commented specifically on the question about what title she would give her life story. She reflected:

> I have never thought about my life story. What would I call it? Today, through this conversation, this was something – I don't want to say forced, but produced. I have never thought like that, and this was a sort of a challenge . . . as if I recognised my life.
>
> (interview, BiH, 30 January 2019)

Notwithstanding claims about over-research, some interviewees did not feel that they had previously had many opportunities to talk and be listened to; and in this sense, the interview experience gave them something that they wanted and appreciated. As an illustration, a female interviewee in Colombia and member of the Indigenous Nasa people explained:

> You know what I want, I'd like to meet the lady who has organised all this [referring to the research] and go over there, to her country, to say thank you and ask for God to keep her and bless her for allowing us to tell our stories.
>
> (interview, Colombia, 6 March 2019)

Some of the Ugandans, moreover, viewed the interview process in very practical terms. An Acholi woman, for example, revealed to the interviewer: 'Our talk went well. I also picked some good lessons from it'. She further added that 'All of the questions were moments of learning between us' (interview, Uganda, 15 April 2019), thereby highlighting that the interview was a shared knowledge experience. The larger point, as some scholars have underlined (see, e.g., Schulz, 2021b; Thapar-Björkert and Henry, 2004), is that the relationship between researcher and research participant is not necessarily as one-sided as it is sometimes portrayed.

These positive examples do not in any way detract from the fact that the interview experience (or the process of answering the questions in the study questionnaire) was almost certainly not easy for any of the participants. Some of them, for example, revealed that they felt nervous beforehand, wondering what they might be asked. Some of them, moreover, did get upset, although they did so for different reasons and not always or only when talking about their experiences of CRSV. A Bosniak interviewee, for example, started to cry when speaking about her family situation. She was the breadwinner, worked long hours as a cleaner and was also responsible for caring for her disabled brother and infirm mother. Sometimes she found everything too much. In her words,

> I am focused when I'm at work, but there are moments when my brain is at home, wondering if my mother is alive, what I will prepare for them

Research Design, Methodology and Ethics 89

[her mother, brother and two grown-up sons], if I have anything to prepare, if I have money to buy medicines.

(interview, BiH, 2 June 2019)

In Colombia, some of the participants became upset when answering the ARM section of the questionnaire, and specifically questions about family. These questions were a painful reminder of what the armed conflict had done to their families. That some of the participants cried does not mean, however, that the research was retraumatising. Discussing trauma-focused research, Legerski and Bunnell (2010: 440) argue that:

> The evidence does not suggest that participation in and of itself can be retraumatizing. Furthermore, although there is a risk for some individuals to experience varying levels of distress during or immediately following participation, these reactions do not appear to be lasting.

In their research with Yazidi women, Foster and Minwalla (2018: 60) maintain that their findings 'call into question liberal feminist notions that survivors of mass rape and genocide are inevitably revictimized and re-traumatized in the retelling of traumatic experiences'. Draucker (1999: 161), moreover, has argued that 'Reflecting on traumatic experiences in a research context may be a positive cathartic experience, an initial step in seeking mental health services, or an empowering opportunity to help other victims'.

On this latter point, some of the interviewees stressed that they wanted their stories to be known, in the hope that others would not have to experience what they themselves went through. In the words of one of the Bosnian inter-viewees who identified as 'other' (reflecting the fact that her father was an ethnic Albanian),

> I love, I love that at least someone is fighting to carry out this research. For people to know what happened, for the world to know, for everyone to hear, so that, if at all possible, it does not happen to anyone ever again.
>
> (interview, BiH, 20 March 2019)

The very sensitive nature of the research, however, did inevitably carry some risks, and various steps were taken to minimise them as much as possible. The partici-pants' welfare was the foremost priority, and it was imperative to ensure that none of them were left feeling alone or used. According to the WHO's guidelines on researching violence against women, which this research closely followed: 'At a minimum . . . researchers have an ethical obligation to provide a respondent with information or services that can help her situation' (Ellsberg and Heise, 2005: 40). All participants in the study, regardless of which part of it they were involved in, were given an information booklet with names and contact details of relevant local organisations and potential sources of support. Additionally, every participant

90 Research Design, Methodology and Ethics

received at least one follow-up telephone call, in many cases from a psychologist from the nearest in-country organisation, to check on their wellbeing. Those who needed it were offered support by the organisation or, in some cases, were put in contact with local NGOs for the first time.

Some were also referred to organisations outside the project's support network. Several of the Ugandan participants with health issues, for example, were referred – with their consent – to a local NGO for medical treatment. Unfortunately, funding for this programme dried up and the organisation was unable to offer any help. However, a benefactor from Belgium subsequently came forward and medical treatment was secured for seven of the female research participants. One of them had a hysterectomy. Another had surgery to repair a uterine prolapse.

★★★

This chapter has discussed the research design, the quantitative and qualitative phases of the study, the research participants and ethics-related issues. Although all of these could have been covered in the book's Introduction, albeit much more briefly, their importance meant that they merited their own chapter. The aim was not simply to give a 'nuts and bolts' account of what was done, but also to explain how and why. The richness of the chapter lays solid foundations for the empirical chapters. So too does the next chapter, but in a different way. It provides crucial background and contextual information about the conflicts in BiH, Colombia and Uganda, and about the use of CRSV in each country.

Notes

1 This is a reference to the Auto 092, in which 'the Constitutional Court highlighted the disproportionate impact of violence on women and called on the state to prevent gender-based – especially sexual – violence against women in conflict and during or after forced displacement' (Meertens, 2010: 155).

2 I am not a quantitative researcher, and neither were the two postdoctoral researchers employed on the study.

3 This terminology is itself problematic. The idea of individuals 'bouncing back' after experiencing major shocks and adversities is unrealistic and it does not take account of the fact that changes within their social ecologies – such as the destruction of their homes or villages – can make it physically impossible to 'bounce back' to what was (see Clark, 2021).

4 I use the word 'potentially' because as Edkins (2003: 40) argues, 'Trauma is not experienced as such – as an experience – when it occurs'. Rather, it is an individual's reaction to the event and the meaning – if any – that s/he attaches to it that are crucially determinative of its impact (Ganzevoort, 2008: 20).

5 Thirty-two women and men in BH, Colombia and Uganda took part in the piloting of the questionnaire.

6 The aim was to have 150 completed questionnaires in each country. However, logistical challenges and different levels of on-the-ground support and 'manpower' in each country meant that ultimately the samples were unbalanced.

7 These organisations were the following: *Snaga Žene* and the Centre for Democracy and Transitional Justice in BiH; *Ruta Pacifica de las Mujeres*, *Profamilia* and *Colombia Diversa*

Research Design, Methodology and Ethics 91

in Colombia; and Facilitation for Peace and Development (FAPAD) and the Justice and Reconciliation Project (JRP) in Uganda. All except one of these organisations are NGOs.

8 The NGO *Colombia Diversa*, which supports members of the LGBT (lesbian, gay, bisexual, transgender) community in Colombia, is in contact with male victims-/survivors of CRSV. It administered a small number of study questionnaires and two of the male participants were LGBT. In BiH, several of the male participants had received (mainly economic) support from the organisation *Snaga Žene*, but there are no NGOs specifically helping male victims-/survivors. In Uganda, some male victims-/survivors have received valuable support from the Refugee Law Project (Dolan et al., 2020: 1154–1155) and have organised to form their own support groups (Edström et al., 2016; Edström and Dolan, 2019; Schulz, 2019).

9 Skjelsbaek (2006: 378) explains that her own research on CRSV in BiH drew on interviews with Bosniak women for 'pragmatic reasons'. In her words,

> Though many of the local organizations I contacted aim to be multiethnic, there are simply more Bosniak women members of such organizations than members from other nationalities. It was therefore easier to get in touch with Bosniak women who were willing to talk than to contact similar women from other nationalities.
> (Skjelsbaek, 2006: 378)

10 While the ARM is divided into individual, relational and contextual sub-scales, it was participants' total scores on the ARM (i.e., combining the three sub-scale scores) that were used to create the quartiles from which interviewee selections were subsequently made.

11 Using confirmatory factor analysis, the research found, for example, that the factor structure of the ARM did not work equally well across BiH, Colombia and Uganda (Clark et al., 2021). Similarly, research on the aforementioned CYRM has found differences between the New Zealand and Canadian factor structures and the South African factor structure. Van Rensburg et al. (2019: 99) point out, however, that this does not invalidate the scale, but instead 'supports more recent contentions that resilience processes are likely to manifest differently across cultures and contexts and that generalized explanations need to be tested for goodness of fit within a specific sample'. In this research, subsequent exploratory factor analysis of the data from BiH, Colombia and Uganda resulted in the identification of separate factor structures for each country (Clark et al., 2021).

12 Reflecting on her own fieldwork in BiH, Močnik (2019: 467) remarks on 'a general tendency of strong leadership' in these organisations. She notes, for example, that 'it often happens that in the first meeting with a group of 10–15 survivors, the representative of the organisation – the "director" – talks in the name and presence of everyone else, while the others mostly nod and agree' (Močnik, 2019: 467). Commenting on the leader of one particular NGO, however, Helms (2013: 215) points out that 'After frustrating reactions from survivors when she testified at the ICTY [International Criminal Tribunal for the former Yugoslavia], Vive žene's Jasna Zejčević decided it was not her or the other activists' place to speak for victims because, she said, "I don't know what they really feel"'.

References

ABColombia, Sisma Mujer and US Office on Colombia (2013) Colombia: Women, conflict-related sexual violence and the peace process. Available at: https://reliefweb.int/sites/reliefweb.int/files/resources/ABColombia_Conflict_related_sexual_violence_report.pdf (accessed 7 May 2021).

92 Research Design, Methodology and Ethics

Acosta M, Castañeda A, García D, Hernández F, Muelas D and Santamaria D (2018) The Colombian transitional process: Comparative perspectives on violence against Indigenous women. *International Journal of Transitional Justice* 12(1): 108–125.

Askin KD (2003) Prosecuting wartime rape and other gender-related crimes under international law: Extraordinary advances, enduring obstacles. *Berkeley Journal of International Law* 21(2): 288–349.

Baaz ME and Stern M (2013) *Sexual Violence as a Weapon of War? Perceptions, Prescriptions, Problems in the Congo and Beyond*. London: Zed Books.

Baines E (2014) Forced marriage as a political project: Sexual rules and relations in the Lord's Resistance Army. *Journal of Peace Research* 51(3): 405–417.

Baines E (2017) *Buried in the Heart: Women, Complex Victimhood and the War in Northern Uganda*. Cambridge: Cambridge University Press.

Barragan Y (2017) To end 500 years of great terror. *NACLA Report on the Americas* 49(1): 56–63.

Bazeley P (2006) The contribution of computer software to integrating qualitative and quantitative data analyses. *Research in the Schools* 13(1): 64–74.

Berry ME (2017) Barriers to women's progress after atrocity: Evidence from Rwanda and Bosnia-Herzegovina. *Gender & Society* 31(6): 830–853.

Betancourt TS and Khan KT (2008) The mental health of children affected by armed conflict: Protective processes and pathways to resilience. *International Review of Psychiatry* 20(3): 317–328.

Blackmore K (2020) Humanitarian remains: Erasure and the everyday of camp life in northern Uganda. *Journal of Refugee Studies* 33(4): 684–705.

Boardman F, Griffiths F, Kokanovic R, Potiriadis M, Dowrick C and Gunn J (2011) Resilience as a response to the stigma of depression: A mixed methods analysis. *Journal of Affective Disorders* 135 (1–3): 267–276.

Boesten J (2014) *Sexual Violence during War and Peace: Gender, Power, and Post-Conflict Justice in Peru*. New York, NY: Palgrave Macmillan.

Boesten J (2017) Of exceptions and continuities: Theory and methodology in research on conflict-related sexual violence. *International Feminist Journal of Politics* 19(4): 506–519.

Boesten J and Henry M (2018) Between fatigue and silence: The challenges of conducting research on sexual violence in conflict. *Social Politics* 25(4): 568–588.

Brammertz S and Jarvis M (2016) *Prosecuting Conflict-Related Sexual Violence at the ICTY*. Oxford: Oxford University Press.

Braun V and Clarke V (2012) Thematic analysis. In: Cooper H, Camic PM, Long DL, Panter AT, Rindskopf D and Sher KJ (eds.), *APA Handbook of Research Methods in Psychology, Vol. 2 Research Designs: Quantitative, Qualitative, Neuropsychological and Biological*. Washington, DC: American Psychological Association, pp. 57–71.

Braun V and Clarke V (2019) Reflecting on reflexive thematic analysis. *Qualitative Research in Sport, Exercise and Health* 11(4): 589–597.

Buss D (2002) Prosecuting mass rape: *Prosecutor v. Dragoljub Kunarac, Radomir Kovac and Zoran Vukovic. Feminist Legal Studies* 10: 91–99.

Cairns-Nagi JM and Bambra C (2013) Defying the odds: A mixed-methods study of health resilience in deprived areas of England. *Social Science & Medicine* 91: 229–237.

Campbell K (2018) Producing knowledge in the field of sexual violence in armed conflict research: Objects, methods, politics, and gender justice methodology. *Social Politics* 25(4): 469–495.

Campbell R, Adams AE, Wasco SM, Ahrens CE and Sefl T (2009) Training interviewers for research on sexual violence: A qualitative study of rape survivors' recommendations for interview practice. *Violence Against Women* 15(5): 595–617.

Chynoweth SK, Freccero J and Touquet H (2017) Sexual violence against men and boys in conflict and forced displacement: Implications for the health sector. *Reproductive Health Matters* 25(51): 90–94.

Clark JN (2017) *Rape, Sexual Violence and Transitional Justice Challenges: Lessons from Bosnia-Herzegovina.* Abingdon: Routledge.

Clark JN (2019) Helping or harming? NGOs and victims-/survivors of conflict-related sexual violence in Bosnia-Herzegovina. *Journal of Human Rights* 18(2): 246–265.

Clark JN (2021) Beyond 'bouncing': Resilience as an expansion-contraction dynamic within a holonic frame. *International Studies Review* 23(3): 556–579.

Clark JN, Jefferies P, Foley S and Ungar M (2021) Measuring resilience in the context of conflict-related sexual violence: A novel application of the Adult Resilience Measure (ARM). *Journal of Interpersonal Violence.* https://doi.org/10.1177/08862605211028323.

Clark JN, Jefferies P and Ungar M (2022) Event centrality and conflict-related sexual violence: A new application of the Centrality of Event Scale (CES). *International Review of Victimology.* https://doi.org/10.1177/02697580221116125.

Clark T (2008) 'We're over-researched here!': Exploring accounts of research fatigue within qualitative research engagements. *Sociology* 42(5): 953–970

Cohen DK and Nordås R (2014) Sexual violence in armed conflicts: Introducing the SVAC dataset, 1989–2009. *Journal of Peace Research* 51(3): 418–428.

Connor J, Copland S and Owen J (2018) The infantilized researcher and research subject: Ethics, consent and risk. *Qualitative Research* 18(4): 400–415.

Connor KM and Davidson JRT (2003) Development of a new resilience scale: The Connor-Davidson Resilience Scale (CD-RISC). *Depression & Anxiety* 18(2): 76–82.

Creswell JW (2009) Editorial: Mapping the field of mixed methods research. *Journal of Mixed Methods Research* 3(2): 95–108.

Davies SE and True J (2017) The politics of counting and reporting conflict-related and gender-based violence: The case of Myanmar. *International Feminist Journal of Politics* 19(1): 4–21.

Deterding NM and Waters MC (2021) Flexible coding of in-depth interviews: A twenty-first-century approach. *Sociological Methods & Research* 50(2): 708–739.

Dolan C, Baaz ME and Stern M (2020) What is sexual about conflict-related sexual violence? Stories from men and women survivors. *International Affairs* 96(5): 1151–1168.

Draucker CB (1999) The emotional impact of sexual violence research on participants. *Archives of Psychiatric Nursing* 13(4): 161–169.

Edkins JE (2003) *Trauma and the Memory of Politics.* Cambridge: Cambridge University Press.

Edström J and Dolan C (2019) Breaking the spell of silence: Collective healing as activism amongst refugee male survivors of sexual violence in Uganda. *Journal of Refugee Studies* 32(2): 175–196.

Edström J, Dolan C and Shahrokh T, with David O (2016) Therapeutic activism: Men of Hope refugee association Uganda breaking the silence over male rape in conflict-related sexual violence. IDS Evidence Report 182.

Ellsberg M and Heise L (2005) *Researching Violence against Women: A Practical Guide for Researchers and Activists.* Washington, DC: WHO, PATH. Available at: http://apps.who.int/iris/bitstream/handle/10665/42966/9241546476_eng.pdf;jsessionid=BA3BE35932D79BAD9C2C42E726FA6BFD?sequence=1 (accessed 3 March 2020).

94 Research Design, Methodology and Ethics

Farewell CV, Jewell J, Walls J and Leiferman JA (2020) A mixed-methods pilot study of perinatal risk and resilience during COVID-19. *Journal of Primary Care & Community Health* 11: 1–8.

Fetters MD, Curry LA and Creswell JW (2013) Achieving integration in mixed methods designs – Principles and practices. *Health Services Research* 48(6): 2134–2156.

Fetters MD and Molina-Azorin AF (2017) The *Journal of Mixed Methods Research* starts a new decade: The mixed methods research integration trilogy and its dimensions. *Journal of Mixed Methods Research* 11(3): 291–307.

Flisi I (2019) Engendering the understanding of wartime sexual violence in Colombia: Hyper-masculinities and sexual violence against men. In: Danielsson SK (ed.), *War and Sexual Violence: New Perspectives in a New Era*. Leiden: Brill, pp. 243–275.

Foster JE and Minwalla S (2018) Voices of Yazidi women: Perceptions of journalistic practices in the reporting on ISIS sexual violence. *Women's Studies International Forum* 67: 53–64.

Ganzevoort R (2008) Scars and stigmata: Trauma, identity and theology. *Practical Theology* 1(1): 19–31.

Geertz C (2008) Thick description: Toward an interpretative theory of culture. In: Oakes TS and Price PL (eds.), *The Cultural Geography Reader*. Abingdon: Routledge, pp. 29–39.

Green J, Willis K, Hughes E, Small R, Welch N, Gibbs L and Daly J (2007) Generating best evidence from qualitative research: The role of data analysis. *Australian and New Zealand Journal of Public Health* 31(6): 545–550.

Helms E (2013) *Innocence and Victimhood: Gender, Nation, and Women's Activism in Postwar Bosnia-Herzegovina*. Madison, WI: University of Wisconsin Press.

Hjemdal O, Friborg O, Martinussen M and Rosenvinge JH (2001) Preliminary results from the development and validation of a Norwegian scale for measuring adult resilience. *Journal of the Norwegian Psychological Association* 38(4): 310–317.

Hjemdal O, Friborg O, Stiles TC, Martinussen M and Rosenvinge JH (2006) A new scale for adolescent resilience: Grasping the central protective resources behind healthy development. *Measurement and Evaluation in Counseling and Development* 39(2): 84–96.

Ivankova NV, Creswell JW and Stick SL (2006) Using mixed-methods sequential exploratory design: From theory to practice. *Field Methods* 18(1): 3–20.

Johnson RB, Onwuegbuzie AJ and Turner LA (2007) Toward a definition of mixed methods research. *Journal of Mixed Methods Research* 1(2): 112–133.

Kasande SK (2019) Beyond symbolism: Translating Uganda's transitional justice policy into real changes in the lives of victims. Available at: www.ictj.org/news/beyond-symbolism-translating-uganda%E2%80%99s-transitional-justice-policy-real-changes-lives-victims (accessed 9 July 2021).

Kreft AK (2019) Responding to sexual violence: Women's mobilization in war. *Journal of Peace Research* 56(2): 220–233.

Leech NL and Onwuegbuzie AJ (2009) A typology of mixed methods research designs. *Quality and Quantity* 43: 265–275.

Legerski JP and Bunnell SL (2010) The risks, benefits, and ethics of trauma-focused research participation. *Ethics & Behavior* 20(6): 429–442.

Lewis C (2022) The making and re-making of the 'rape capital of the world': On colonial durabilities and the politics of sexual violence statistics in DRC. *Critical African Studies* 14(1): 55–72.

Liebenberg L and Moore JC (2018) A social ecological measure of resilience for adults: The RRC-ARM. *Social Indicators Research* 136: 1–19.

Liebenberg L, Ungar M and Van de Vijver F (2012) Validation of the Child and Youth Resilience Measure-28 (CYRM-28) among Canadian youth. *Research on Social Work Practice* 22(2): 219–226.

Meertens D (2010) Forced displacement and women's security in Colombia. *Disasters* 34(2): 147–164.

Močnik N (2019) Collective victimhood of individual survivors: Reflecting the uses and impacts of two academic narratives two decades after the war-rapes in Bosnia-Herzegovina. *East European Politics* 35(4): 457–473.

Mookherjee N (2015) *The Spectral Wound: Sexual Violence, Public Memories and the Bangladesh War of 1971*. Durham, NC: Duke University Press.

Nadia's Initiative, International Institute for Criminal Investigations and the Preventing Sexual Violence in Conflict Initiative (2022) Global code of conduct for gathering and using information about systematic and conflict-related sexual violence (Murad Code). Available at: www.muradcode.com/murad-code (accessed 24 April 2022).

Nagel RU and Doctor AC (2020) Conflict-related sexual violence and rebel group fragmentation. *Journal of Conflict Resolution* 64(7–8): 1226–1253.

Njoku ET and Dery I (2021) Spiritual security: An explanatory framework for conflict-related sexual violence against men. *International Affairs* 97(6): 1785–1803.

Njoku ET, Akintayo J and Dery I (2022) Sex trafficking and sex-for-food/money: Terrorism and conflict-related sexual violence against men in the Lake Chad region. *Conflict, Security & Development* 22(1): 79–95.

Nowell LS, Norris JM, White DE and Moules NJ (2017) Thematic analysis: Striving to meet the trustworthiness criteria. *International Journal of Qualitative Methods* 16(1): 1–13.

Omata N (2020) 'Over-researched' and 'under-researched' refugee groups: Exploring the phenomena, causes and consequences. *Journal of Human Rights Practice* 12(3): 681–695.

Porter H (2017) *After Rape: Violence, Justice and Social Harmony in Uganda*. Cambridge: Cambridge University Press.

Porter H (2019) Moral spaces and sexual transgression: Understanding rape in war and post conflict. *Development and Change* 50(4): 1009–1032.

Quinlan AE, Berbés-Blázquez M, Haider LJ and Peterson GD (2016) Measuring and assessing resilience: Broadening understanding through multiple disciplinary perspectives. *Journal of Applied Ecology* 53(3): 677–687.

Resilience Research Centre (2016) The Resilience Research Centre Adult Resilience Measure (RRC-ARM): User's manual. Available at: https://cyrm.resilienceresearch.org/files/ArchivedMaterials.zip (accessed 9 October 2021).

Saldaña J (2013) *The Coding Manual for Qualitative Researchers*. 2nd ed. London: SAGE.

Schulz P (2018) Displacement from gendered personhood: Sexual violence and masculinities in northern Uganda. *International Affairs* 94(5): 1101–1119.

Schulz P (2019) 'To me, justice means to be in a group': Survivors' groups as a pathway to justice in northern Uganda. *Journal of Human Rights Practice* 11(1): 171–189.

Schulz P (2021a) *Male Survivors of Wartime Sexual Violence: Perspectives from Northern Uganda*. Oakland, CA: University of California Press.

Schulz P (2021b) Recognizing research participants' fluid positionalities in (post-)conflict zones. *Qualitative Research* 21(4): 550–567.

Schulz P and Touquet H (2020) Queering explanatory frameworks for wartime sexual violence against men. *International Affairs* 96(5): 1169–1187.

96 Research Design, Methodology and Ethics

Seawright J and Gerring J (2008) Case selection techniques in case study research: A menu of qualitative and quantitative options. *Political Research Quarterly* 61(2): 294–308.

Sellers PV (2008) Sexual torture as crime under international criminal and humanitarian law. *New York City Law Review* 11(2): 339–352.

Simić O (2016) Rape, silence and denial. In: Fischer M and Simić O (eds.), *Transitional Justice and Reconciliation: Lessons from the Balkans*. Abingdon: Routledge, pp. 102–120.

Sivakumaran S (2007) Sexual violence against men in armed conflict. *European Journal of International Law* 18(2): 253–276.

Skjelsbaek I (2006) Victim and survivor: Narrated social identities of women who experienced rape during the war in Bosnia-Herzegovina. *Feminism & Psychology* 16(4): 373–403.

Skjelsbaek I (2012) *The Political Psychology of War Rape: Studies from Bosnia and Herzegovina*. Abingdon: Routledge.

Smith BW, Dalen J, Wiggins K, Tooley E, Christopher P and Bernard J (2008) The Brief Resilience Scale: Assessing the ability to bounce back. *International Journal of Behavioral Medicine* 15: 194–200.

Solangon S and Patel P (2012) Sexual violence against men in countries affected by armed conflict. *Conflict, Security & Development* 12(4): 417–442.

Stallone K (2021) Strategic submission to rape is not consent: Sexual violence in the Colombian armed conflict. *Violence Against Women*, https://doi.org/10.1177/10778012211054872.

Sukarieh M and Tannock S (2013) On the problem of over-researched communities: The case of the Shatila Palestinian refugee camp in Lebanon. *Sociology* 47(3): 494–508.

Thapar-Björkert S and Henry M (2004) Reassessing the research relationship: Location, position and power in fieldwork accounts. *International Journal of Social Research Methodology* 7(5): 363–381.

Theron L, Cameron CA, Didkowsky N, Lau C, Liebenberg L and Ungar M (2011) A 'day in the lives' of four resilient youths: Cultural roots of resilience. *Youth & Society* 43(3): 799–818.

Ungar M (2003) Qualitative contributions to resilience research. *Qualitative Social Work* 2(1): 85–102.

Ungar M (2019) Designing resilience research: Using multiple methods to investigate risk exposure, promotive and protective processes, and contextually relevant outcomes for children and youth. *Child Abuse & Neglect* 96: 104098.

Ungar M and Liebenberg L (2011) Assessing resilience across cultures using mixed methods: Construction of the Child and Youth Resilience Measure. *Journal of Mixed Methods Research* 5(2): 126–149.

Uprichard E and Dawney L (2019) Data diffraction: Challenging data integration in mixed methods research. *Journal of Mixed Methods Research* 13(1): 19–32.

Valiñas M (2020) The Colombian Special Jurisdiction for Peace: A few issues for consideration when investigating and adjudicating sexual and gender-based crimes. *Journal of International Criminal Justice* 18(2): 449–467.

Van Rensburg AC, Theron L and Ungar M (2019) Using the CYRM-28 with South African young people: A factor structure analysis. *Research on Social Work Practice* 29(1): 93–102.

Wagnild G and Young H (1993) Development and psychometric evaluation of the Resilience Scale. *Journal of Nursing Measurement* 1(2): 165–178.

Walker BH and Salt D (2012) *Resilience Practice: Building Capacity to Absorb Disturbance and Maintain Function*. Washington, DC: Island Press.

Weston C, Gandell T, Beauchamp J, McAlpine L, Wiseman C and Beauchamp C (2001) Analyzing interview data: The development and evolution of a coding system. *Qualitative Sociology* 4: 381–400.

WHO (2007) WHO ethical and safety recommendations for researching, documenting and monitoring sexual violence in emergencies. Available at: www.who.int/reproductive-health/publications/violence/9789241595681/en/ (accessed 15 June 2020).

Zalesne D (2019) Making rights a reality: Access to health care for Afro-Colombian survivors of conflict-related sexual violence. *Columbia Human Rights Law Review* 51(2): 668–722.

Zalewski M, Drumond P, Prügl E and Stern M (eds.) (2018) *Sexual Violence against Men in Global Politics*. Abingdon: Routledge.

Zulver JM (2018) Colectiva Matamba resists. *NACLA Report on the Americas* 50(4): 377–380.

Zulver JM (2021) The endurance of women's mobilization during 'patriarchal backlash': A case from Colombia's reconfiguring armed conflict. *International Feminist Journal of Politics* 23(3): 440–462.

Chapter 4

The Conflicts and Use of Sexual Violence in Bosnia-Herzegovina, Colombia and Uganda

This chapter has an important contextual function and broadly sets the scene for the empirical chapters that follow. It provides an overview of the conflicts in Bosnia-Herzegovina (BiH), Colombia and Uganda, seeking to convey some of their complexity while also distilling core facts and details to deliver a succinct account of events. The chapter additionally discusses the use of sexual violence in each of the conflicts, including some of the patterns that such violence followed and some of the purposes that it served. I bring in some of my own personal insights when writing about BiH, reflecting the fact that I have spent many years doing research in the country. The first two sections focus on BiH, the second two on Colombia and the final two on Uganda.

The Bosnian War

'Much ink has been spilled', as Andreas (2004: 33) notes, 'trying to explain the war in Bosnia' – and, by extension, the disintegration of Yugoslavia that preceded it (see, e.g., Burg and Shoup, 2000; Cohen and Dragović-Soso, 2008; Glenny, 1996; Ramet, 2002; Vulliamy, 1994; Woodward, 1995). Yet, any attempt at explanation necessarily involves 'issues of interpretation and representation' (Campbell, 1998: 263). What follows, therefore, is itself an interpretative summary (which is the case for all of the conflict summaries in this chapter) that draws on secondary literature, some of the judgements of the International Criminal Tribunal for the former Yugoslavia (ICTY) – established by the United Nations (UN) Security Council in 1993 – and my own reading of events.

The Break-up of Yugoslavia

BiH was one of the six republics that constituted the Socialist Federal Republic of Yugoslavia (SFRY), established in the aftermath of World War II – 'a time of particularly bitter strife . . . with accusations of atrocities emanating from all quarters' (Prosecutor v. Mladić, 2017: vol. IV, para. 3581). In this context of internecine violence, the very fact that President Josip Broz Tito was able to

DOI: 10.4324/9781003323532-5

create a unified SFRY has been described as 'possibly the most miraculous' of all his achievements (Campbell, 1980: 1050). Nevertheless, Yugoslavia was in many ways a fragile construction, albeit not the 'house of cards' that scholars such as Hoare (2013: 2) have claimed it was. According to Calić (2019: 329), 'even if Tito had been granted immortality, he could not have held back the internal erosion of the Yugoslav system'.

Myriad factors contributed to this erosion. Mounting economic problems during the 1980s resulted in growing rivalry and tensions between the republics (Hammel et al., 2010: 1127). Furthermore, developments in the SFRY's largest republic, Serbia – and specifically President Slobodan Milošević's efforts 'to increase Serbian dominance within Yugoslavia' (Bieber, 2002: 101) – caused increasing unease within the other republics. In January 1990, the Slovene delegation – followed by the Croatian delegation – walked out of the 14th Special Congress of the League of Communists of Yugoslavia, effectively marking the latter's end. Strongly supported by Germany and Austria (Calić, 2019: 298), both Croatia and Slovenia subsequently declared independence from the SFRY on 25 June 1991, triggering full-scale war.

The war in Slovenia was brief. After just ten days, the Yugoslav National Army (JNA) – one of the largest armies in Europe – withdrew (Niebuhr, 2006: 512). Crucially, there were very few Serbs living in Slovenia. In contrast, Serbs constituted 12.2 per cent of Croatia's population in 1991 (Sokolić, 2017: 791). The war in Croatia involved significant fighting, loss of life and destruction (Cigar, 1993; Tanner, 2010) and ended with a UN-negotiated ceasefire in January 1992. Amidst these developments, BiH's own future looked increasingly precarious.

How BiH Moved Closer to War

Multi-party elections had taken place in November 1990 and the three main nationalist parties – the Party of Democratic Action (SDA), the Serbian Democratic Party (SDS) and the Croatian Democratic Union (HDZ) – secured the largest number of votes. Although these parties formed a coalition, which broke down less than a year later in October 1991, they had very different visions for BiH – Yugoslavia's most ethnically diverse republic.[1] The SDS wanted BiH to remain within what was left of Yugoslavia and made it clear that it would never accept the republic's secession; Serbs would be a minority in an independent BiH (Meier, 1999: 191). In a plebiscite organised in early November 1991, moreover, the majority of Serbs in BiH voted to remain part of Yugoslavia. The SDA and HDZ, however, increasingly favoured the option of independence (Prosecutor v. Mucić et al., 1998: para. 99).

BiH faced a very difficult choice; 'Remain in the (by then) Serb-dominated rump Yugoslavia, with all the prospects of permanent inequality . . . or opt for independence and face the probability of military confrontation with Serbia' (Banac, 2009: 467–468). In a referendum held on 29 February and

100 Use of Sexual Violence in Bosnia-Herzegovina, Colombia, Uganda

1 March 1992, the population of BiH – with the exception of Serbs who boycotted it – voted for independence (Prosecutor v. Karadžić, 2016: para. 54). BiH subsequently declared independence on 1 March 1992. Just two months earlier, on 9 January 1992, Serbs had proclaimed the Republic of Serbian People of BiH, which later became *Republika Srpska* (RS).

War was not, however, a foregone conclusion (Toal and Dahlman, 2011: 99; for an alternative interpretation, see Hayden, 1996: 741). It was also not driven by 'ancient ethnic hatreds' and 'seething enmities' (Zimmermann, 1994: 75) – a facile and reductionist argument that said more about *Realpolitik* and the interests of those who favoured a policy of non-intervention than it did about the complex dynamics of the conflict. Mixed marriages were relatively common (Kaufman and Williams, 2004: 428) and few Bosnians believed that BiH would descend into bloodshed, even as the situation escalated in neighbouring Slovenia and Croatia (Meier, 1999: 198). BiH's ethnic diversity, however, can be likened to marbles delicately balanced on sticks, as in the children's game of *Ker Plunk*. Once political leaders started to interfere with the sticks and to remove some of them, everything came tumbling down.

Issues of Blame and the War's Changing Dynamics

A huge share of the responsibility and blame for the Bosnian war lies with the then Bosnian Serb leadership (and with the Milošević regime in Belgrade). Fundamentally, its territorial ambitions were incompatible with a multi-ethnic BiH. According to the Mladić Trial Chamber judgement at the ICTY, for example, the Bosnian Serb leadership took the view that '"the Serbian people" had a historical right to territory in which Serbs constituted a majority of the population, as well as territory in Bosnia-Herzegovina in which Serbs constituted a majority before World War II' (Prosecutor v. Mladić, 2017: vol. IV, para. 3590). At the same time, however, blaming only Serbs for everything that happened dilutes the complexity of the conflict. Many media reports were particularly one-sided, presenting a black and white narrative of 'good guys' and 'bad guys' (see, e.g., Ruigrok's [2008] analysis of Dutch media). The reality is that all sides in the war committed crimes, albeit to different degrees (Helms, 2013: 54).

Frequent emphasis on the Bosnian Serbs' quest for a so-called 'Greater Serbia' (see, e.g., Gutman, 1994: xi; MacKinnon, 1994a: 8; Snyder et al., 2006: 190), moreover, should not detract from the oft-overlooked territorial ambitions of the Bosnian Croat leadership (Prosecutor v. Prlić et al., 2013: vol. IV, para. 24), backed by Zagreb. On 18 November 1991, the Bosnian Croat leader, Mate Boban, proclaimed the creation of the Croatian Community of Herceg-Bosna (later renamed the Croatian Republic of Herceg-Bosna) as a 'political, cultural, economic and territorial entity' that covered 30 municipalities within BiH (Prosecutor v. Prlić et al., 2013: vol. I, paras. 421, 425).

This development, and the Bosnian Croat leadership's subsequent declaration in July 1992 of Herceg-Bosna as an independent state, further added to the complexity of the Bosnian war.

The alliance between the Army of BiH (ABiH) and the Croatian Defence Council (HVO) broke down, and bitter fighting between the two armies ensued – with serious human rights abuses on both sides (Shrader, 2003). In 1994, the signing of the Washington Accords ended the conflict between the ABiH and HVO. This resulted in renewed military cooperation between them and reversed some of the early territorial gains (which were aided by a UN-imposed arms embargo in September 1991) made by the Army of RS (VRS). The launch of NATO airstrikes, following the genocide that unfolded in Srebrenica in July 1995,[2] further squeezed VRS positions.

With the tide of war now turning, the Bosnian Serb leader Radovan Karadžić had little option but to accept a modified version of a peace plan that he had rejected just a year earlier (Hoare, 2011: 91). On 21 November 1995, Presidents Milošević, Tudjman and Izetbegović, in peace talks brokered by the United States (US), reached an agreement in Dayton, Ohio. The Dayton Accords (officially known as the General Framework for Peace in Bosnia and Herzegovina) were signed in Paris a few weeks later. The peace agreement formally ended a three-year war in which more than 100,000 people were killed, tens of thousands disappeared and over 2 million were displaced (International Committee of the Red Cross [ICRC], 2019; ICTY, 2011).

The Use of Sexual Violence in the Bosnian War

One aspect of the Bosnian war (although not unique to it) that attracted significant international attention was the widespread use of sexual violence, and much has been written on this topic (see, e.g., Allen, 1996; Askin, 1997; Bassiouni and McCormick, 1996; Engle, 2005; Hansen, 2000; Helms, 2014; Olujić, 1998; Simić, 2018; Skjelsbaek, 2012; Stiglmayer, 1994; Žarkov, 2007). It is widely stated that between 20,000 and 50,000 women were raped, and the Bosnian Ministry of the Interior has used the higher figure (Olujić, 1998: 40). However, there has been little, if any, discussion about the origin of these statistics (see Appendix 2).

My point is not in any way to question or to minimise the fact that large numbers of women and men suffered sexual violence during the Bosnian war. Nor is it my intention to suggest that commonly cited figures are necessarily wrong or too high. As Amnesty International (2009: 5) has underlined, 'The real number of those who were raped during the 1992–1995 armed conflict will probably never be established'. What I do want to emphasise is that an uncritical and unreflective use of statistics has contributed to promoting a particular narrative – of large-scale rapes committed by only one side in the conflict – that conceals a more nuanced reality (Skjelsbaek, 2012: 64).

Claims of Genocidal Rape

Hansen (2000: 57) has identified three representations of the rapes committed during the Bosnian war, namely 'rape as normal/Balkan warfare', 'rape as exceptional/Serbian warfare' and 'Balkan patriarchy'. The second and third of these interpretations were pivotal to the divides that developed between feminists in the former Yugoslavia. Some of them embraced 'the global feminist position taken by some US feminists in particular' (Helms, 2013: 61); they stressed the significance of gender and the vulnerability of all women, regardless of ethnicity. Helms (2013: 61) notes, however, that 'With the increasing international publicity around wartime rape . . . some feminist and women's groups in Zagreb began to object to the focus on gender: yes, women were the victims but it was only happening to *certain* women' (emphasis in the original). The narrative began to take shape, thus, that what was happening in BiH was a very particular type of rape – genocidal rape committed by Serbs against Bosniak women (see, e.g., Diken and Laustsen, 2005: 115; Fisher, 1996: 120; Salzman, 1998: 366).

Some US feminist scholars, such as Beverley Allen and Catharine MacKinnon, also played a central role in developing and promoting this particular interpretation. Many of the arguments they put forward, however, are flawed and based on very limited sources. Allen's (1996: 4) book, for example, relies heavily on what her 'informants' – among them 'an American woman of Croatian heritage' – told her. It makes sweeping claims and generalisations,[3] and appears to reduce the multi-causal dimensions of war rape in BiH to the 'belief' of the 'Chetnik[4] or Serb soldier' that in raping women, he is 'creating "little Chetniks" or "Serb soldier-heroes"' (Allen, 1996: 96). While helpfully pointing out to readers the 'logical glitch' of the 'Serb genocidal policy' in this regard, Allen (1996: 96) goes on to make the further unsupported claim that 'One of the most tragic psychological results of this policy is that the victims, if they survive, often do so believing the Serb illogic'.

Some of MacKinnon's claims about conflict-related sexual violence (CRSV) in BiH are similarly problematic. One example is her argument that 'In the West, the sexual atrocities have been discussed largely as rape or as genocide, not as what they are, which is rape as genocide, rape directed toward women because they are Muslim or Croatian' (MacKinnon, 1994a: 9). Aside from MacKinnon's narrow fixation on rapes committed only by Serbs (Kesić, 1994: 276), the other issue is that rape does not become 'genocidal' simply because it has an ethnic dimension. What is crucial to establishing the crime of genocide in law is the *intent* of the perpetrators, but MacKinnon – a legal scholar – does not systematically address this. She emphasises the sexual pleasure that 'Serbs' derived from their crimes (MacKinnon, 1994a: 14) and posits a direct causal linkage between rape and pornography (and in so doing makes a series of unsupported assertions).[5] This is highly reductionist (Kesić, 1994: 276). In Chinkin's (1994: 328–329) measured words,

Use of Sexual Violence in Bosnia-Herzegovina, Colombia, Uganda 103

The connection between pornographic projections of women and the use as war propaganda of these and other media images can be readily accepted; but to identify these as the sole, or even major cause of the abuse of women throughout that area [BiH and the former Yugoslavia] is simplistic and misleading.

More broadly, claims of genocidal rape have contributed to the construction and maintenance of victim hierarchies (Berry, 2018: 129), in the sense of downplaying and detracting from other ('non-genocidal') cases of rape. As the late Copelon (1994: 246) underscored, labelling rape as genocidal 'significantly increases the likelihood that condemnation will be limited to this seemingly exceptional case'. Unfounded assertions about rape being 'worse' for Bosniak women than it was for anyone else in BiH (see, e.g., Carmichael, 2015: 161; Gutman, 1994: x) have further fed into these hierarchies of victimhood. Such arguments are based on generalisations and assumptions that do not capture the heterogeneity of victims-/survivors or the nuances of their individual lives and relationships with their social ecologies. Helms (2013: 66), for example, points out that 'not all rape survivors came from conservative rural communities, nor were they all religious or religious in the same ways'. During her own extensive research in BiH, moreover, she found 'no indication that Bosniac women experienced rape any differently from women of other ethnic or religious backgrounds' (Helms, 2013: 67; see also Clark, 2017: 67).

Causal Complexity and Sexual Violence by All Sides

Mono-dimensional explanations do not do justice to the multiple and diverse reasons why CRSV was committed in BiH (or, indeed, in any conflict). An analysis of relevant ICTY judgements illuminates this causal complexity. In some cases, CRSV in BiH was the result of individuals in positions of authority abusing their power for their own ends. According to the Kvočka et al. Trial Chamber judgement, for example – which details myriad human rights violations and depravities committed in the Serb-run Omarska camp in 1992 – one of the defendants, Mlađo Radić (a guard shift leader in the camp), 'grossly abused his position and took advantage of the vulnerability of the detainees' (Prosecutor v. Kvočka et al., 2001: para. 548). The judgement goes on to describe how, on one occasion, Radić 'called Witness J into his office and told her that he could help her if she had sexual intercourse with him' (Prosecutor v. Kvočka et al., 2001: para. 548).

CRSV also often occurred alongside interrogation and/or as a means of extracting information. The ICTY's sentencing judgement against Miroslav Bralo, for example, describes how 'on or about 15 May 1993, members of the "Jokers" [the anti-terrorist platoon of the 4th Military Police Battalion of the HVO] took a Bosnian Muslim woman ("Witness A") to the "bungalow" [the headquarters of the "Jokers"] where she was interrogated' (Prosecutor v. Bralo, 2005: para. 15). During the time that she was detained, Witness A 'was repeatedly raped and sexually assaulted' by the defendant (Prosecutor v. Bralo, 2005: para. 15; see also Prosecutor v. Furundžija, 1998: especially paras. 40–41, 83).

The Mucić et al. case focused on human rights abuses committed against Serbs in the Čelebići camp near Konjic, including the rape of two Serb women – Milojka Antić and Grozdana Ćećez – by Hazim Delić, a Bosniak deputy commander of the camp and subsequently the commander. According to the judgement, one of the purposes of the rapes committed by Delić was to obtain information from the women – including 'information about the whereabouts of Ms. Ćećez's husband who was considered an armed rebel' (Prosecutor v. Mucić et al., 1998: para. 941; see also para. 963). The judgement additionally notes that the violence suffered by both women was inflicted on them *because* they are women (Prosecutor v. Mucić et al., 1998: paras. 941, 963).

When men were specifically targeted for acts of sexual violence, humiliation was arguably one of the key motives (although not exclusively in cases involving male victims-/survivors; see, e.g., Prosecutor v. Prlić et al., 2013: vol. II, para. 272). For example, Ranko Češić – a member of the Bosnian Serb Police Reserve Unit at the Brčko police station – admitted that around 11 May 1992, he forced two Bosniak brothers to perform fellatio on each other and left the office door open to allow several camp guards to watch and laugh (Prosecutor v. Češić, 2004: para. 14). His sentencing judgement underlines that 'The family relationship and the fact that they [the brothers] were watched by others make the offence of humiliating and degrading treatment particularly serious' (Prosecutor v. Češić, 2004: para. 35).

As these examples illuminate, various forms of sexual violence were committed by all sides in the conflict (Berry, 2018; Clark, 2017; Simić, 2018; Skjelsbaek, 2012). However, it is also important to underline that there were fundamental differences – qualitative and quantitative. The UN Commission of Experts (1994: para. 228),[6] for example, referred to HVO camps where grave breaches of the Geneva Conventions occurred, including rape. It also commented that it had 'not been able to detect any particular pattern or policy in operating these camps' (UN Commission of Experts, 1994: para. 228). This was in contrast to the use of sexual violence by Serb forces, which, the Commission opined, seemed:

> to be a part of an overall pattern whose characteristics include: similarities among practices in non-contiguous geographic areas; simultaneous commission of other international humanitarian law violations; simultaneous military activity; simultaneous activity to displace civilian populations; common elements in the commission of rape, maximizing shame and humiliation to not only the victim, but also the victim's community; and the timing of rapes.
>
> (UN Commission of Experts, 1994: para. 252)

The widespread abuse of Bosniak women in Foča, a town and municipality in eastern BiH, is just one example of the very organised and systematic way that some acts of sexual violence were committed by Serb forces (Buss, 2002: 94). However, the crimes in Foča – successfully prosecuted as crimes against humanity and violations of the laws or customs of war in the ICTY case of Prosecutor v. Kunarac et al. (2001) – were not charged as genocide. This is significant in the context of previously discussed claims that Serbs were committing genocidal rape.

It is also noteworthy that the Bosnian Serb leader, Karadžić, was charged with two counts of genocide – the second relating to Srebrenica and the first to crimes committed in various municipalities in BiH, including Foča and Prijedor (where the infamous Omarska camp, among others, was established). These crimes included, inter alia, 'the causing of serious bodily or mental harm to thousands of Bosnian Muslims and Bosnian Croats . . . during their confinement in detention facilities where they were subjected to cruel or inhumane treatment, including torture, physical and psychological abuse, rape, other acts of sexual violence, and beatings' (Prosecutor v. Karadžić, 2016: para. 537). The Chamber was satisfied, for the purpose of Article 4(2)(b) of the ICTY's Statute – addressing the different forms of *actus rei* (actions) that the crime of genocide may take – that 'members of the Bosnian Muslim and Bosnian Croat groups were subjected to serious bodily or mental harm in the Count 1 Municipalities' (Prosecutor v. Karadžić, 2016: para. 2582).[7] Ultimately, however, it was 'not satisfied beyond reasonable doubt that the acts under Article 4(2) . . . in the Count 1 Municipalities were committed with genocidal intent' (Prosecutor v. Karadžić, 2016: para. 2626) – meaning with 'the intent to destroy, in part, the Bosnian Muslim and the Bosnian Croat groups as such' (Prosecutor v. Karadžić, 2016: para. 2591).

In an article written several years before the ICTY Trial Chamber delivered its verdict against Karadžić, the Bosnian scholar Bećirević (2010: 483) asserts that 'There are inherent problems with using the verdicts of international courts to establish which historical cases of mass violence are genocide and which are not'. Certainly, the ICTY faced 'many questions of interpretation' (Tournaye, 2003: 461) as regards the issue of genocidal intent. However, there is also a strong case for arguing, contra Bećirević, that such courts *are* best placed to decide, based on the totality of evidence before them, whether the existence of genocidal *mens rea* (guilty mind) is established. The fact that some Serb soldiers reportedly made comments that the women they raped would give birth to Serb babies (Snyder et al., 2006: 190; UN Commission of Experts, 1994: para. 248) hardly constitutes sufficient evidence of such intent (Helms, 2013: 70–71).

The bigger point about courts is that criminal prosecutions have been an important part of transitional justice work relating to BiH. The ICTY, which completed its mandate at the end of 2017, indicted 161 individuals and sentenced 91 – some of them on charges linked to CRSV (ICTY, 2016). The Tribunal's capacity-building work with courts in BiH (and the former Yugoslavia more broadly), moreover, made a fundamental contribution to local justice efforts. Ferizović and Mlinarević (2020: 326) note that while there are

The Armed Conflict in Colombia

Pinzón (2016: 3) notes that 'Every [Colombian] president since 1982 has attempted some sort of peace accord with the Revolutionary Armed Forces of Colombia', the leftist guerrilla group more commonly known by its Spanish acronym FARC. On 24 August 2016, after four years of negotiations, the then Colombian President, Juan Manuel Santos, concluded a historic peace agreement with the FARC. However, it needed the endorsement of the Colombian people to come into force. On 2 October 2016, voters went to the polls. A victory for the 'yes' campaign had been expected, but in a shock result a narrow majority (50.2 per cent) of voters rejected the peace agreement (BBC, 2016). Following the referendum, further negotiations took place between the government and the FARC. On 24 November 2016, a revised peace agreement – containing 50 changes to the original agreement – was signed and subsequently approved by the National Congress.

The peace agreement officially ended the FARC's more than 50 years of armed struggle against the Colombian state. Six years after the agreement was signed, however, levels of violence and insecurity in the country remain high (Zulver, 2020). More than 400 social leaders have been killed since 2016 (Human Rights Watch [HRW], 2021a), and children in some areas 'are afraid to return to school, out of fear of armed clashes and mines on the way to class' (Norwegian Refugee Council, 2022). The FARC's withdrawal from its former strongholds, moreover, has created dangerous power vacuums in which rival armed groups fight for control of land and natural resources, thereby exacerbating 'the structural problems of inequality, exclusion and poverty that affect the majority of the campesino [rural/farming] population and Afro-descendant and Indigenous communities' (Amnesty International, 2020: 12). Cases of sexual violence also remain high (UN Secretary-General, 2021: para. 24), as will be discussed in the next section.

To unpack some of the complexity of a conflict in which thousands of people have been killed[8] and forcibly disappeared (International Commission on Missing Persons [ICMP], 2021), and more than 8.2 million people have been displaced from their homes and land (HRW, 2021b), a crucial starting point is the period of *La Violencia*.

La Violencia *and the Emergence of the Guerrillas*

La Violencia was a civil war between Liberals and Conservatives that was primarily fought in rural areas of Colombia and it has been described as 'one of the world's most extensive and complex internal wars' of the twentieth century (Ramsey, 1973: 3). The assassination on 9 April 1948 of the Liberal politician Jorge Eliécer Gaitán gave rise to large-scale riots in the capital, Bogotá, and was a catalyst for the bloodshed that followed. As violence seeped into the countryside, large sections of the liberal peasantry organised themselves into armed groups to fight against the Conservative-led government (Norman, 2018: 640). Thousands of people were killed during *La Violencia* (Uribe, 2004: 83), and significant violence was also directed at women (Meertens, 2001: 133).

La Violencia, which was not the first period of conflict between Liberals and Conservatives, represented 'an explosive expression of peasant grievances and local conflict' (LeoGrande and Sharpe, 2000: 3). However, the National Front power-sharing agreement – in force from 1958 until 1974 – that brought *La Violencia* to an end left multiple grievances unresolved, such as failed land reform and rural poverty. The agreement thus 'directly contributed to the formation of the FARC' (Norman, 2018: 640) and other guerrilla organisations, including the National Liberation Army (ELN).[9]

The FARC was formed in 1964, developing out of rural self-defence groups established by the Colombian Communist Party during *La Violencia*. Led by Manuel Marulanda, the FARC strongly championed agrarian reform and land rights (Kaplan, 2017: 65). It is significant to note in this regard that Colombia has one of the highest degrees of land concentration in the world (Aviles, 2008: 417). According to Faguet et al. (2020), 'The total area of Colombia is 110 million hectares, of which 60 million ha are registered private property'. Having achieved a national presence by 1982 (Kaplan, 2017: 65),[10] the FARC had an estimated 16,000–18,000 combatants by 2001, making it one of the largest guerrilla organisations in the world.

Narcotics played a fundamental part in the FARC's growth. Colombia is the world's single biggest exporter of cocaine (Saab and Taylor, 2009: 455), and the huge demand for cocaine in the US during the early 1990s 'transformed the FARC into a formidable military opponent with control over large swaths of national territory' (Norman, 2018: 640). Indeed, according to estimates in 1985, the FARC had been able to generate $99 million in a single year by taxing cocaine production and the cultivation of coca bushes (Guáqueta, 2007: 422). Some of its victims – including members of the Indigenous Awá community living in coca-rich areas in the Department of Nariño – paid the ultimate price for getting in the way of its fight to control lucrative drug routes (Inter-American Commission of Human Rights, 2009: 345).

Initially at least, the ELN was less involved in the drugs trade than the FARC (Fisher and Meitus, 2017: 791). Established in 1964 by students who supported the values of the Cuban Revolution, the ELN has primarily focused its efforts on the oil industry, 'blowing up pipelines and kidnapping oil executives for ransom' (LeoGrande and Sharpe, 2000: 4). Indeed, kidnappings have been a large part of both the FARC's and the ELN's 'repertoires of violence' (Wood, 2010: 125) over the years. According to an interim report by the Office of the

Prosecutor of the International Criminal Court (OTP-ICC, 2012: para. 41), these two guerrilla groups have carried out the largest number of hostage-takings in Colombia.

Notwithstanding the 2016 peace agreement and the FARC's formal demobilisation, dissident groups have emerged that continue to engage in violence (HRW, 2022). There have also been regular attacks on former members of the FARC (UN, 2021). The ELN was not a party to the peace agreement and remains active. It has stated that it wants, inter alia, an 'open debate' regarding the use of Colombia's resources, especially oil (Griffin, 2021).

The Paramilitaries

As the guerrillas became more powerful, they posed an increased threat to the state – and to the country's landowners (Jonsson et al., 2016: 549). In response to this situation, various right-wing paramilitary groups were established, particularly in areas where the guerrillas were strongest. Founded in 1997 and led by Carlos Castaño, the United Self-Defence Forces of Colombia (AUC) brought the different independent paramilitary organisations together under a single umbrella. According to Saab and Taylor (2009: 461), 'By 2001, most sources suggest the AUC had between 8,000 and 10,000 armed combatants with a presence in approximately 40 percent of Colombia's municipalities'.

There are documented linkages between the AUC and the Colombian state (Tate, 2001: 171), although the relationship between the two has also been described as 'ambivalent' (Holmes et al., 2021: 195). In the Department of Antioquia, which experienced high levels of AUC violence, Wienand and Tremaria (2017: 26) argue that paramilitaries 'exerted a status quo-oriented violence to ensure both the established political power structures and the achievement of their private economic interests'. In areas under their control, paramilitaries also sought to establish 'law and order'. Operation *Limpieza* (Social Cleansing), as one illustration, targeted, inter alia, prostitutes, drug users, members of the LGBT (lesbian, gay, bisexual, transgender) community and petty thieves, and involved gross and systematic human rights violations (Sanford, 2003: 76).

Paramilitary violence was especially brutal, and the infamous 'chopping houses' (*casa de pique*) are just one example. Paramilitaries took some of their victims to these houses, often situated in highly populated areas, and proceeded to dismember them with tools such as machetes and chainsaws (McGee, 2017: 177, n41; see also Theidon, 2007: 83). Paramilitaries have also been most responsible for the huge numbers of internally displaced people in Colombia (Tovar-Restrepo and Irazábal, 2014: 45–46), for many of the massacres committed (Arvelo, 2006: 425) and for the largest number of sexual violence crimes (Kreft, 2020: 476).

In 1999, peace negotiations commenced between President Andrés Pastrana (1998–2002) and the FARC, then at the height of its military strength.

According to Jonsson et al. (2016: 549), these negotiations 'were doomed from their inception, since arguably neither FARC nor the government was honestly pursuing a negotiated settlement at the time'. Following his own inauguration in 2002, President Uribe – who always denied the existence of Colombia's armed conflict – showed little interest in negotiating with the FARC (Lozano and Machado, 2012: 59–60). In a context where more and more Colombians were demanding peace (Theidon, 2007: 72), however, his government commenced negotiations with the paramilitaries in August 2002. Almost a year later, in July 2003, the AUC became a signatory to the Santa Fe de Ralito Accord (followed by a second agreement in May 2004). The terms of this 'included the demobilization of all combatants by the end of 2005, and obligated the AUC to suspend its lethal activities, maintain a unilateral cease-fire, and aid the government in its anti-drug trafficking efforts' (Theidon, 2016: 52).

By 2006, 31,671 combatants from 37 different paramilitary *bloques* had demobilised (García-Godos and Lid, 2010: 504). Under the provisions of the 2005 Justice and Peace Law (Law 975), paramilitaries who did not confess to having committed any crimes and who did not have any pending criminal charges against them were given immunity, whereas those (known as *postulados*) who admitted their involvement in the perpetration of acts of violence faced criminal prosecution. García-Godos and Lid (2010: 504) point out that 'In regular criminal prosecutions the aforementioned crimes are punishable with sentences of between 20 and 60 years in prison. Under the framework of Law 975 these sentences can be reduced to prison terms of between five and eight years'. These reduced sentences – which contributed to the popular perception of Uribe as a president who was sympathetic to the paramilitaries (Guáqueta, 2007: 445) – were one of the controversies surrounding the Justice and Peace Law (Nussio, 2011: 88). Despite the AUC's demobilisation, moreover, paramilitary violence has continued in Colombia, particularly in areas of weak state presence (Holmes et al., 2021: 207).

The Use of Sexual Violence in Colombia's Armed Conflict

The Wider Context

In discussing the use of CRSV in BiH, this chapter problematised the uncritical use of statistics. In any war or conflict situation, obtaining precise figures is necessarily difficult, if not impossible. In Colombia, multiple factors have enhanced the challenges in this regard – including the longevity of the conflict (Oxfam, 2009: 12) and the wider socio-cultural context, in which 'violence is viewed as normal and women are expected to remain silent' (Jolin, 2016: 380).

Research carried out by several Colombian women's organisations between 2001 and 2009 and spanning 407 municipalities found that there were 489,687 victims of CRSV during this nine-year period. As the authors note, 'This is an average of 54,410 women per year, 149 per day, or 6 women every hour suffering sexual violence' (Sanchez et al., 2011: 7). However, research was only conducted in 15 of the 407 municipalities and only 2,693 women completed a survey (Sanchez et al., 2011: 11–12). According to a report by the National Centre for Historical Memory (CNMH, 2017: 25), covering a considerably longer period and based on data from the Observatory of Memory and Conflict (OMC), 15,076 crimes against freedom and sexual integrity[11] took place between 1985 and 2017. The figures used by Colombia's Victims' Unit are substantially higher.[12] According to its website (at the time of writing in 2022), there are 35,429 victims of crimes against freedom and sexual integrity (Victims' Unit, 2022).

By themselves, however, figures do not give the bigger picture. Significant in this regard is the Colombian Constitutional Court's landmark ruling in 2008 (known as Auto 092), which described sexual violence as 'a habitual, extensive, systematic and invisible practice in the context of the Colombian armed conflict' (Kravetz, 2017: 723, n62). Echoing this, a report by ABColombia et al. (2013: 2) has underlined that 'analysis of sexual violence committed by all armed actors from the Cartagena Ombudsman's Office, the Constitutional Court and the ICC lead to the conclusion that conflict-related sexual violence is a systematic and generalised practice'. Emphasis on the systematic use of sexual violence during the armed conflict highlights the wider socio-cultural context and deeper layers of violence, partly linked to the legacies of colonialism (Viveros-Vigoya, 2016: 230). According to Linda Cabrera, director of the non-governmental organisation (NGO) *Sisma Mujer*, 'Sexual violence against women and girls is a kind of discrimination that comes from long-existing structures' (cited in Stallone and Janetsky, 2021; see also Ruta Pacífica de las Mujeres et al., 2015: 160).

These structures, in turn, help to explain why Afro-Colombian and Indigenous women – who have historically suffered 'multi-faceted discrimination' (Inter-American Commission of Human Rights, 2009: 517) and often continue to face 'colorism' (Koopman, 2021: 63) – have been particularly exposed to CRSV (Davies and True, 2015: 505–506; Oxfam, 2009: 3; Svallfors, 2021). Those who live in resource-rich areas, moreover, have been at higher risk of forced displacement (Goldscheid, 2020: 258; Tovar-Restrepo and Irazábal, 2014: 43), which further increases their vulnerability to sexual violence (Sachseder, 2020: 168) – and, relatedly, their economic vulnerability (Amnesty International, 2020: 12).

Cultural and racist stereotypes about Black women's bodies have been an additional contributing factor. Zalesne (2020: 680), for example, points out that 'Black women are often stereotyped as "'naturally' voracious" and more likely to have consented to sex than white women' (see also Goldscheid, 2020: 258). These stereotypes, which help to foster blame, themselves have deep roots and can be traced back to the colonial period, when women 'were racialized as Black or Indigenous and portrayed as grotesquely hypersexual and constantly willing' (Sachseder, 2020: 169).

Use of Sexual Violence in Bosnia-Herzegovina, Colombia, Uganda   111

Women's experiences of sexual and gender-based violence (SGBV) – which are not confined to Afro-Colombian and Indigenous women – also extend beyond the framework of the armed conflict. There exist high levels of domestic violence and femicide in Colombia (Moloney, 2015), further exacerbated by the COVID-19 global pandemic (Alsema, 2020). Cultural factors specific to particular groups can also contribute to and fuel SGBV. Discussing the Indigenous Emberá people in the Chocó region, for example, Acosta et al. (2018: 123) stress that women's bodies and sexuality are under the control of men within Emberá culture – and the continued practice of clitoral ablation is just one illustration of this.

While this discussion has focused on women, Colombian men have also suffered acts of sexual violence in the armed conflict. The UN Secretary-General (2021: para. 24), for example, has noted that 'In 2020, the National Victims' Unit recorded 239 cases of conflict-related sexual violence. Of these, 197 were committed against women, 15 against girls, 13 against men and 6 against boys'. Unfortunately, however, there is very little data regarding cases of CRSV against men; and according to Flisi (2019: 253), 'as is the case in many other contexts, the problem has not been recognized and addressed sufficiently'. Sexual violence has also been used against the LGBT community (Thylin, 2020: 448) – including within the ranks of armed groups themselves, as will be discussed more next.

Armed Groups, Sexual Violence and an Enduring Continuum of Violence

As in BiH, all armed groups in Colombia have used sexual violence (OTP-ICC, 2012: para. 78; UN Secretary-General, 2021: para. 24). The paramilitaries have been the main perpetrators, followed by the guerrillas (CNMH, 2018: 45). State agents, such as members of the police and the army, have also committed CRSV. A report by ABColombia et al. (2013: 11) has made the important point that:

> When sexual violence is committed by the Security Forces (Army and Police) the civilian population are left with no authority to whom they can turn for justice; as those responsible for enforcing justice are the very authorities that are violating their rights.

Sexual violence has served several different purposes in Colombia (CNMH, 2017: 26–27; OTP-ICC, 2012: para. 79; Svallfors, 2021), just as it did during the Bosnian war. It has been a method – which all armed groups have employed – for forcibly expelling communities from resource-rich lands and thereby securing economic gains. As the UN Secretary-General (2013: para. 9) has observed, 'In Colombia, illegal armed groups have used sexual violence to forcibly displace populations from lucrative mining or agricultural zones and from areas of strategic importance for drug trafficking'. Once armed groups secure control of these areas, moreover, they can halt the return of displaced populations or control the income of returnees (Davies and True, 2015: 506).

Sexual violence has additionally been used as a form of 'punishment', including against women believed to be collaborating with an enemy group (OTP-ICC, 2012: para. 79) or accused of having a relationship with a member of the guerrillas (CNMH, 2017: 26). Indeed, some of the Colombian interviewees had themselves suffered this punitive sexual violence. Individuals who challenge the authority of armed actors, such as women activists and human rights leaders, have also been at high risk of sexual violence (Amnesty International, 2004: 22). According to Zulver (2020), 'The logic of militarized masculinity that guides these armed groups does not look kindly on women who transgress traditional gender roles'. Crucially, paramilitary efforts to impose social control have extended to the control of women's bodies and behaviours (Sachseder, 2020: 963).

Sexual violence against members of the LGBT community (Thylin, 2020: 448) – who have reported increasing violence and discrimination (Bartell, 2020) – is also often about punishment, as well as humiliation. Payne recounts the story given by a former paramilitary, Roberto, about how his commander rounded up homosexual men in the town of Caucasia in northern Antioquia. In Payne's (2016: 336) words:

> In a public ritual in the main square they would have their heads shaved, be stripped, tied up and beaten in front of the townpeople and then told to leave the region. He [Roberto] said that the public humiliation was meant to serve as a lesson for the civilian population regarding acceptable behaviour and that those who did not leave were often later found dead.

In some cases, moreover, armed groups committed sexual violence against their own members. Thylin (2020: 450) notes that such violence was used within the AUC to punish individuals who deviated from the organisation's heterosexual norms. Payne (2016: 337) discusses an incident – as described by one of his interviewees – in which a paramilitary commander found two male members of his organisation having sex. The man who was penetrated was subsequently raped, tortured and ultimately killed. This, Payne (2016: 337) argues, 'casts the "passive" sexual role as more transgressive of normative expectations and suggests a link between the oppression of women and extreme violence against sexual minorities in a context marked by misogyny and patriarchy'.

The FARC and other guerrillas have similarly used sexual violence against their own members (Vivanco, 2016). For example, the FARC employed sexual violence to forcibly recruit girls and as a form of 'payment' for protecting other members of their family (ABColombia et al., 2013: 1). According to Herrera and Porch (2008: 210), moreover, 'A former US special forces colonel with long experience in Colombia agreed that the female guerrillas were "just passed around" among their male colleagues'. In addition, there was enforced use of contraception and forced abortion for female combatants within the FARC

(Hernández and Romero, 2003: 32); and Bates (2022: 159) has described the organisation as 'a harsh perpetrator of gender violence against bodies considered unintelligible due to their non-conformity with normative sexual practices and/or binary gender'.

Notwithstanding the 2016 peace agreement, sexual violence persists in Colombia (UN Secretary-General, 2021: para. 24), further evidencing the fact that it forms part of a broader continuum of violence (Viveros-Vigoya, 2016: 233). Indeed, Kreft (2020: 471–472) maintains that 'In terms of prevalence, everyday sexual violence [rather than specifically CRSV] is more common in Colombia'. Anti-government protests in 2021 created new opportunities for sexual violence or threats of such violence (UN Secretary-General, 2022: para. 24). According to Amnesty International (2021), there were various reports of sexual abuse committed by Colombia's security forces against protesters. The fact, moreover, that many armed groups and criminal gangs are still active – which also reflects the involvement in the conflict of external actors such as transnational corporations (Sachseder, 2020: 165) – means that the risk of sexual violence remains high. This is particularly the case in areas where armed groups and gangs continue to fight for control of territory (UN Secretary-General, 2021: para. 25).

To conclude this section on a more positive note, there have been some notable transitional justice developments in the country. Indeed, 'Colombia has been recognized as a pioneer in the design and implementation of ambitious TJ mechanisms' (de Waardt and Weber, 2019: 215). These include the aforementioned 2005 Justice and Peace Law, the 2011 Victims and Land Restitution Law – 'which is particularly recognized for advancing the rights and protections of displaced victims' (Summers, 2012: 227) – and, most recently, the establishment of the Special Jurisdiction for Peace (JEP). Created under the provisions of the 2016 peace agreement, the JEP's mandate is to investigate and prosecute the most serious crimes and human rights violations committed by the FARC and Colombia's armed forces prior to 1 December 2016. Significantly, acts of sexual violence are 'clearly excluded from amnesty, pardon or special treatment' (Valiñas, 2020: 455). Especially relevant for the purposes of this research, there are now some important examples from Colombia (see, e.g., Huneeus and Rueda Sáiz, 2021: 210–211; Yoshida and Céspedes-Báez, 2021: 32–33) of what it might mean to take transitional justice in new social-ecological directions – the focus of the book's final chapter.

The War in Northern Uganda

Untangling the Roots of the War

Uganda became a protectorate of the British Empire in 1894, finally achieving independence in 1962. During this period of colonial rule, British policies created divisions between the north and south of the country and the latter

114 Use of Sexual Violence in Bosnia-Herzegovina, Colombia, Uganda

was favoured politically (Jackson, 2002: 36). This differential treatment also extended to the economic sphere (Baines, 2007: 99; Doom and Vlassenroot, 1999: 8). After independence, the colonial division of labour did not substantially change, 'except that the military dominance of the north was reinforced under the presidencies of Milton Obote (1962–1971 and 1980–1985) and Idi Amin (1971–1979), both from the northern military elite' (Baines, 2007: 99).

In 1981, Yoweri Museveni – Uganda's longest-serving president who remains in power to this day – established the National Resistance Army (NRA) and launched a guerrilla campaign against Obote's government and the Acholi-dominated Ugandan National Liberation Army (UNLA). It is important to note that 'Museveni waged his guerrilla campaign with support from his own region in the southwest, and also from the central south of the country, where there was widespread aversion to what was perceived as northern domination' (Prosecutor v. Ongwen, 2021: para. 2). In 1986, following a bloody and protracted battle between the UNLA and the NRA in the Luwero Triangle – an area north-west of the capital Kampala – Museveni became the new President of Uganda. In a coup d'état, he overthrew General Tito Akello, an Acholi from the north who had briefly replaced Obote (Akhavan, 2005: 406).

Museveni and the NRA proceeded to unleash violence against civilians in the north, as a way of curbing any potential rebellion against the new government (Baines, 2014: 408). Human rights abuses, including killings and rape, 'became the order of the day in Acholiland' (Finnström, 2006: 203). Museveni's efforts to suppress the north, however, dismally failed and instead stoked the very rebellion against the government that the NRA had feared (Branch, 2010: 34). In response to the NRA's crimes in the north, disaffected Acholi formed the Ugandan People's Defence Army (UPDA) in 1986, with the aim of ousting Museveni. A series of military defeats, however, brought the UPDA to the negotiating table. Baines (2007: 99) remarks that 'While some UPDA members eventually returned home peacefully, the NRA hunted down and killed anyone who appeared to be reluctant to accept the outcomes of the negotiations, refuelling fear among the Acholi population'. By the mid-1980s, there were a number of groups opposed to Museveni and the NRA (Jackson, 2002: 30).

The Holy Spirit Mobile Force and the Lord's Resistance Army

Alice Auma (also known as Alice Lakwena) was a young Acholi woman who claimed to be possessed by several spirits (Behrend, 2000: 1) – and in particular the spirit of an elderly Italian soldier (Lakwena) who died during World War I. Auma established the Holy Spirit Mobile Force (HSMF, also known as the Holy Spirit Movement) and led a holy war against the NRA. Doom and Vlassenroot (1999: 18) have described the HSMF as 'a political manifestation of an Acholi society driven into a corner after Museveni's assumption of national power'. According to the spirits that spoke through Auma, however, the fault

Use of Sexual Violence in Bosnia-Herzegovina, Colombia, Uganda   115

also partly lay with the Acholi themselves, who therefore needed to be 'purified' and rid of their sins (Allen, 1991: 378).

The HSMF attracted substantial support, and not only among Acholi (Behrend, 2000: 174). Indeed, Allen (2008: 35) has described it as 'extraordinarily effective'. Nevertheless, after some initial successes, the HSMF was defeated in 1987 and Auma herself fled to Kenya. At this stage, according to Prunier (2004: 366), 'the movement almost collapsed. But Joseph Kony, a nephew or a cousin of Alice, also declared that he had had visions and laid claim to the rebellious prophet's mantle'. Different opinions exist regarding the exact relationship between the HSMF and the Lord's Resistance Army (LRA) – and the extent to which the latter was a continuation of the former (see, e.g., Allen, 2008: 36; Dunn, 2004: 104; Jackson, 2002: 38). The bigger point is that both Auma and Kony emerged as leaders in the context of systematic violence and brutality by Museveni's NRA (which in 1995 became the Uganda People's Defence Forces [UPDF]) against the Acholi people in northern Uganda (Apuuli, 2006: 181). The paradox is that the LRA itself became infamous for its use of extreme violence – including against fellow Acholi, as discussed below.

Scholars have accordingly questioned what exactly the LRA was seeking to achieve in northern Uganda. According to Akhavan (2005: 407), for example, 'the LRA has had no coherent ideology, rational political agenda, or popular support'; and Van Acker (2004: 336) opined that 'The rebels' vision of an alternative society is poorly articulated, to put it mildly'. Words such as 'rational' and 'poorly articulated', however, raise the question: from whose perspective? The LRA (and more specifically Kony) did have objectives, regardless of how others viewed them. One of these was to establish a government based on the Ten Commandments (Nkabala, 2017: 91), an illustration of how the spiritual and political dimensions of the LRA were 'intimately entangled' (Baines, 2014: 406). Another of its objectives was to overthrow Museveni's government (Schulz, 2021: 53).[13]

It is also the case, however, that the LRA changed and evolved over time, and so too did the levels of violence that it used. A significant factor in this regard was the failure of the 1993 peace talks between the government and the LRA, after which Kony's position hardened. He became very critical of the Acholi people, accusing them of siding with the government, and he particularly directed his wrath at Acholi elders whom he perceived as having betrayed him (Baines, 2017: 34–35). From this point onwards, the LRA became especially violent. This caused it to lose popular support (Finnström, 2001: 253), which further fuelled its brutal methods. These included cutting off lips, noses, ears and legs (Kramer, 2012: 23; Vinci, 2005: 370). According to a report by Amnesty International (1997: 6), extreme violence was 'a deliberate tool used to terrorize civilians into providing support or newly abducted persons into staying with their captors, and as punishment for not following edicts laid down by LRA commanders'.

Loss of support also helped to explain the LRA's 'signature strategy of recruitment' (Baines, 2014: 405) – namely, the mass abduction of children.[14] Pham et al. (2008: 173) have conservatively estimated that the LRA abducted 25,000–38,000 children between 1986 and 2006. The risk of being abducted was particularly high at night, when the LRA carried out many of its raids on villages and camps. The LRA also targeted schools. In 1996, for example, it abducted 139 girls ('the Aboke girls') from St. Mary's College, a Catholic boarding school in Aboke (Temmerman, 2009). Due to the courageous efforts of the school's deputy head teacher, the LRA subsequently released 109 of the girls, and five of the remaining 30 died in captivity (McDonnell and Akallo, 2007: 24).

A second crucial factor in the LRA's development was the wider regional context – and in particular the role of Sudan. In response to the Ugandan government's support for the rebel Sudan People's Liberation Movement, from the early 1990s the Sudanese government began supporting the LRA, and the latter relocated its bases to southern Sudan. According to Dunn (2010: 49), 'Sudanese support effectively helped transform a rag-tag group of rebels into a coherent, well-supplied military force, largely through training, sharing of logistics, and the introduction of more powerful and sophisticated weaponry such as land mines and rocket-propelled grenades' (see also Jackson, 2002: 30). Uganda and Sudan subsequently signed a peace agreement, and in 2002 the UPDF launched Operation Iron Fist with the aim of destroying LRA bases in Sudan. The LRA consequently re-entered Uganda and, in so doing, pushed further into the country (Dunn, 2010: 49). This resulted, inter alia, in increased internal displacement, which, according to Baines (2007: 101), 'more than tripled from 500,000 people to 1.7 million, and abductions doubled to an estimated total of 30,000 Acholi children and youth'.

After the 9/11 terrorist attacks, however, the international context critically changed. In December 2001, the US added the LRA to its Terrorist Exclusion List and increasingly supported Uganda in its own 'war on terror', through military funding and assistance (Branch, 2009: 482; Demmers and Gould, 2018: 371). Such support greatly strengthened the UPDF, resulting in several military victories against the LRA. The Juba peace talks – brokered by Sudan – between the government and the LRA commenced in July 2006. The final peace agreement negotiated between the two sides was never actually signed. Kony refused to sign it unless the ICC suspended its indictments and arrest warrants – unsealed by the Court's then Prosecutor, Luis Moreno Ocampo, in 2005 – against him and four other high-ranking members of the LRA. In 2006, the LRA withdrew from Uganda and moved into neighbouring countries – namely the Democratic Republic of Congo, the Central African Republic and South Sudan – where it has continued to use violence against civilians (UN Security Council, 2016; Victor and Porter, 2017: 593).

'Protected Villages' and Mass Displacement

It is important to emphasise that while the LRA caused immense suffering in northern Uganda, it was not alone in this regard (Jeffrey, 2011: 84). Government forces, for example, also committed sexual violence (Schulz, 2021), as will be discussed in the next section – and so too did cattle rustlers from the Karamoja region.[15] The government also forcibly moved huge numbers of people into camps, supposedly to protect them from LRA attacks. In reality, these so-called 'protected villages' were 'tragically unprotected' (Branch, 2009: 481) and were more about controlling the Acholi people and other displaced communities than keeping them safe (Allen et al., 2020: 666). Above all, the camps were ultimately about weakening the LRA; they were part of a '"scorched earth" counter insurgency policy to deny the rebels resources, cover, and intelligence' (Amone P'Olak, 2007: 643).

Poverty, over-crowding, disease and vulnerability to attacks defined living conditions in the camps (Okello and Hovil, 2007: 439). In late 2005, more than 1.5 million people in northern Uganda were internally displaced (Finnström, 2006: 203) and living in these 'rural prisons' (Porter, 2019: 1013). Indeed, Dolan (2009: 1) maintains that what happened in northern Uganda was not an internal war between the government and the LRA, but 'a form of mass torture'. More specifically, he describes the so-called 'protected villages' as 'Social Torture, as evidenced in widespread violation, dread, disorientation, dependency, debilitation and humiliation, all of which are tactics and symptoms typical of torture, but perpetrated on a mass rather than individual scale' (Dolan, 2009: 1). Compared to direct violence committed by the LRA, the camps killed a larger number of people and additionally destroyed many livelihoods (Macdonald, 2019: 231).

Unfortunately, there has been little accountability to date for the immense suffering inflicted by both sides in the conflict. The aforementioned Juba peace talks did produce an Agreement on Accountability and Reconciliation (AAR) and led to the establishment of a Transitional Justice Working Group. However, progress has been limited[16] and 'justice remains elusive for the vast majority of people who suffered during the conflict' (Macdonald, 2019: 226). A crucial issue in this regard is the fact that Uganda has not undergone a political transition; Museveni has been in power for more than three decades and has made life very difficult for anyone who has stood against him in presidential elections – most recently the former musician Bobi Wine (BBC, 2021). That the political establishment in Uganda has not been in a hurry to move forward with transitional justice is hardly surprising, particularly given the government's own human rights record during the war – which, for political reasons, the Office of the Prosecutor at the ICC has largely overlooked (Nouwen and Werner, 2011: 951). In June 2019, the Ugandan Cabinet approved a National Transitional Justice Policy, more than ten years after both the government and the LRA signed the aforementioned AAR. It remains to be seen whether, when and how the policy will be implemented in practice.

On 4 February 2021, Trial Chamber IX of the ICC found Dominic Ongwen – the former commander of the Sinia Brigade of the LRA – guilty of 61 counts of war crimes and crimes against humanity in northern Uganda (Prosecutor v. Ongwen, 2021). His trial attracted huge international attention, not only because he was the first member of the LRA to be prosecuted at the ICC, but also because he was 'the first known person to be charged with the war crimes of which he is also a victim' (Baines, 2009: 163–164). Ongwen was abducted by the LRA when he was around nine years old, while on his way to school. His case – while far from unique in this regard – thus 'complicates the simplistic narrative of the victim as "pure" and "innocent", and the perpetrator as "evil" and "guilty"' (Kan, 2018: 75) and illustrates how complex conflicts can destabilise victim/perpetrator binaries. On 6 May 2021, Ongwen was sentenced to 25 years' imprisonment and his case is currently on appeal.

The Use of Sexual Violence in the War in Northern Uganda

Forced Marriage in the LRA

In the Ongwen trial at the ICC, witness P-0351 told the court:

> In the bush women and girls have no choice. You cannot choose who your husband is. It is only after you have been given to someone that you realise it has happened. Most of the girls in the bush were given to men as wives.
> (Prosecutor v. Ongwen, 2021: para. 2204)

Witness P-0264 testified that one of the LRA's rules was that 'a mature woman, one deemed to be mature enough to be able to have sex with a man should be assigned to a husband' (Prosecutor v. Ongwen, 2021: para. 2224). Based on the evidence presented to it, the Trial Chamber was left in no doubt that the sexual violence that took place between LRA fighters and their 'wives' occurred through force or threat of force. It further found that fighters used the fact that women and girls 'were held captive and under oppressive control and coercion' to make them submit to sex, in so doing relying on the LRA's own rules (Prosecutor v. Ongwen, 2021: para. 2270). Ultimately, the Court adjudged that 'the abuse of women and girls in the LRA, including forced marriage and sexual violence, were truly systemic and institutional' (Prosecutor v. Ongwen, 2021: para. 2109).

The treatment of women and girls in the LRA cannot be decoupled from the wider patriarchal context in northern Uganda and gendered socio-cultural norms. Illustrating this, a report by Amnesty International (1997: 19) underlined that 'The power inherent in the ownership of girl-children and women by male LRA soldiers is a twisted and extended form of that which exists in more familiar social settings'. Moreover, 'wives' within the LRA were expected to perform the duties that Acholi culture and tradition prescribed for them (Carlson and Mazurana, 2008: 15). To cite Porter (2017: 81), 'An Acholi wife's primary duties involve satisfying the physical needs of her husband, including feeding him and having sex with him – and consequently, producing and feeding the children that result from their relationship'. To view forced marriage within the LRA simply as a reflection (or a more extreme form) of wider social practices, however, is problematic and detracts from the purposes that it served within the organisation.

It has been argued that forced marriage was a way of boosting fighters' morale (Carlson and Mazurana, 2008: 15). Relatedly, Kramer (2012: 28) maintains that 'wives' were effectively allocated to men as compensation and markers of status in the context of an army that had few material resources. Forced marriage may additionally have helped to create bonds between fighters and foster dependency on the LRA, thereby strengthening the group's effectiveness (Kramer, 2012: 28). According to Baines (2014: 408), forced marriage became an institutionalised practice only when support from Khartoum enabled the LRA to set up military bases in Sudan and, by extension, to establish a more 'settled life'. She also argues that the institutionalisation of forced marriage reflected important changes within the organisation and served larger aims. In the context of the failed 1993 peace talks, which, as previously discussed, had a critical impact on the LRA leader's perceptions of the Acholi people, 'Kony and his men began to talk of Acholi *manyen*, or the new Acholi' (Baines, 2014: 410). Factors such as moral behaviour and respect for cultural practices distinguished the new Acholi from the old Acholi; and, hence, the LRA's rules – dictated by the spirits – sought to limit contact and interactions between those within the organisation and those outside it (Baines, 2014: 410).

For Baines (2014: 210), the crucial point is that 'The vision of the "new Acholi" was operationalised through the institution of forced marriage and recreation of the familial unit'. Hence, 'marriage' within the LRA was not simply about controlling the sexuality of women and girls (Prosecutor v. Ongwen, 2021: para. 2281). More fundamentally, it was linked to the wider political vision of the LRA (Baines, 2014: 414). In this context, 'Women's bodies, central to the reproduction of the nation, became sites upon which this vision was forged' (Baines, 2014: 415). Women's worth within the LRA therefore increased when they became mothers (Baines, 2017: 49).[17]

The LRA's rules regarding sex and marriage were strictly enforced, and anyone caught violating them was severely punished (Annan et al., 2011: 883). To further protect the purity of the Acholi *manyen*, rape was forbidden (see, e.g., Kramer, 2012: 30), although it still happened in some cases. Young girls who were not yet ready to be 'given' to a man, for example, had the role of domestic servants or *ting ting*, but there were cases of commanders raping *ting ting* (Baines, 2014: 412), sometimes as a way of forcing them into 'marriage' (Aijazi and Baines, 2017: 475). According to the Ongwen judgement, 'The men to whom girls were "distributed" as *ting tings* relied on the very same detention and coercion of the *ting tings* to force them into sexual intercourse' (Prosecutor v. Ongwen, 2021: para. 2274).

While this discussion has focused on women and girls, it is important to acknowledge that the institutionalised practice of forced marriage also constrained the choices that some men within the LRA (excluding commanders) themselves could make. While senior commanders could choose the 'wives' they wanted (and physical attractiveness and level of education[18] were important in this regard), the remaining women and girls were allocated to lower-ranking fighters in the LRA hierarchy (Carlson and Mazurana, 2008: 20). The latter's relationships with senior commanders fundamentally shaped whether they could refuse a particular woman (Aijazi and Baines, 2017: 477). Furthermore, even though male fighters certainly had greater power to negotiate than women, 'their commanders nevertheless maintained the power to remove their wives and children altogether, or force them to be with someone they did not desire' (Aijazi and Baines, 2017: 477). Yet, some men did grow close to their wives (Aijazi and Baines, 2017: 477). Similarly, and notwithstanding the coercive context of their relationships, some women appear to have developed bonds with their 'husbands'. Gustavsson et al.'s (2017) research, for example, involved 16 women (aged 19–28) formerly abducted by the LRA. All except two of them had been given to LRA commanders as 'wives'. Many of the women spoke about abuse and mistreatment in their 'marriages'. The authors also note, however, that 'Women who had been with the LRA for several years had adapted, and they described their role as wives mainly as normal. Some of them told about their husbands and how they provided comfort and protection' (Gustavsson et al., 2017: 698).

Sexual Violence by Government Forces and Cattle Rustlers

Edström and Dolan (2019: 175) underline that male experiences of SGBV 'remain extremely marginalized in research, policy and practice alike'. In Uganda, the work of the Refugee Law Project, which particularly supports male refugees from the African Great Lakes region, has been extremely important in drawing attention to the issue of CRSV against men (Edström et al., 2016). So too has Schulz's (2018a, 2018b, 2021) research, which has also helped to redress the heavy focus within extant scholarship on the LRA's use of sexual violence and the relative lack of discussion about CRSV perpetrated by the Ugandan army.

As discussed in the previous section, the NRA committed serious and systematic human rights abuses with the aim of quelling the north and punishing the Acholi, including for the UNLA's actions in Luwero. According to Schulz (2018a: 1109), during the late 1980s and early 1990s, 'sexual violence against men was geographically widespread enough for the Acholi population to invent a new term to describe this tactic: *tek-gungu*' (see also Esuruku, 2011: 31). Literally meaning to 'bend over' (*gungu*), 'hard' or 'forcefully' (*tek*),

tek-gungu specifically referred to male rape. Indeed, there were particular battalions within the NRA known as '*gungu*-battalions' (Schulz, 2018a: 1109). In addition to anal rape of men, which sometimes occurred in public (Schulz, 2018b: 591), the NRA also committed other acts of sexual violence – including genital beatings, castration and forcing men to carry out or witness sexual abuses against women in their family. Such violence, Schulz argues (2021: 56), was 'widespread and constituted integral components of a wider military campaign centered around interrogation, retaliation, and punishment of the Acholi population at large' (see also Dolan, 2002: 74). He also makes the important point that it is difficult to know whether President Museveni and the top military command ordered the use of sexual violence, or whether orders were issued lower down the chain of command (Schulz, 2021: 65).

It was not only during the early stages of the war that government forces (the UPDF from 1995 onwards) committed acts of sexual violence. Nor were the victims-/survivors only men. Dolan's (2002: 73–74) work, for example, gives an account of several cases of sexual violence by UPDF soldiers against women. Sexual violence against women also occurred in the aforementioned camps or 'protected villages', discussed in the previous section. The camps are an example of how the war increased the risk of sexual exploitation. In Okello and Hovil's (2007: 440) research,

> interviewees reported that rape is linked to women stealing food outside the camps and to 'survival sex,' or 'women having sex for food,' which one informant insisted approximates rape given the woman's lack of choice and the power imbalance between the perpetrator and the victim.

Schools, similarly, often became sites of exploitation. According to Porter (2015: 274), 'Teachers talked in particular about the problems they experienced with sexual exploitation, due to government soldiers stationed nearby and the logistical risks of having such crowded[19] and mixed sleeping arrangements'.

Of the ten Ugandan men who took part in the research underpinning this book (four of them participated in both the quantitative and qualitative phases, discussed in Chapter 3), six were raped by UPDF soldiers between 1996 and 2006. Two of the male Lango participants, moreover, were raped by cattle rustlers from the Karamoja region of north-eastern Uganda. Stites and Howe (2019: 143) point out that nomadic pastoralists from the Karamoja have used sexual violence – against both women and men – 'to terrorise the largely unarmed populations in the neighbouring Acholi and Lango regions' (see also Carlson and Mazurana, 2008: 13). While not directly linked to the war in northern Uganda between the government and the LRA, sexual violence committed in the context of cattle raids can be viewed as part of a deeper conflict within a conflict. Moreover, wider developments in Uganda have shaped the dynamics of cattle raids, which have taken place for decades. As one example, following the ouster of Idi Amin by the Tanzanian army in 1979, weapons such

122 Use of Sexual Violence in Bosnia-Herzegovina, Colombia, Uganda

as AK-47s – left behind by Amin's fleeing soldiers – became readily available. These weapons further fuelled violent cattle raids (Mootz et al., 2017: 371).

★★★

This chapter has given an overview of the conflicts in BiH, Colombia and Uganda. Presenting a broad chronology of events, it has explored particular aspects of the conflicts in more detail – including their changing dynamics and the key actors involved. It has also examined how these actors utilised sexual violence – and for what purposes. The chapter has thus provided an important contextual backdrop for the three empirical chapters that follow. These chapters focus on the experiences of the victims-/survivors of CRSV who participated in this research (and particularly in the interview stage) and on some of the ways that these women and men have demonstrated everyday resilience. In his anthropological research in northern Uganda, Finnström (2008: 14) argues that 'When the surroundings are good, crises and problems of everyday life can be overcome'. The empirical chapters identify particular factors within interviewees' social ecologies (their 'surroundings') that are supportive of resilience and those that are not – as an illustration of what Finnström [2008: 14] calls 'bad surroundings'. More broadly, the chapters apply the framework discussed in Chapter 2 to tell a larger story about resilience through the changing connectivities between individuals and their social ecologies.

Notes

1 According to the 1991 census results, Muslims (Bosniaks) constituted 43.7 per cent of the population, followed by Serbs who made up 31.4 per cent and Croats who accounted for 17.3 per cent. A further 5.5 per cent did not identify with any particular ethnicity and simply declared themselves as Yugoslavs (Meier, 1999: 198).
2 In this small town in eastern BiH in July 1995, the VRS, led by General Ratko Mladić, systematically rounded up and killed more than 7,000 Bosniak men and boys. A contingent of Dutch UN peacekeepers largely stood by as the slaughter unfolded, vastly outnumbered by Bosnian Serb forces and immobilised by a toothless mandate from the UN Security Council (Nettelfield and Wagner, 2014: 15).
3 Talking broadly about Serbs and not just those living in BiH, Allen (1996: 20) comments, for example, that 'the country dwellers, especially those who live in eastern Croatia or western Serbia, are reputed by my informants to be ultranationalistic as a matter of tradition. The country people are the staunchest upholders of the "Great Serbia" notion'.
4 The Četniks were a Serb nationalist movement established in 1941. Today, Serb nationalists, or those perceived to be nationalists or extremists, are commonly referred to as Četniks.
5 According to MacKinnon (1994b: 77), for example, 'pornography saturated Yugoslavia' before the war, with the result that 'a whole population of men' had become 'primed to dehumanize women and to enjoy inflicting assault sexually'.
6 By virtue of resolution 780 of 6 October 1992, the UN Security Council requested the UN Secretary-General to form a Commission of Experts to examine evidence of grave breaches of the Geneva Conventions and other violations of international humanitarian law committed in the territory of the former Yugoslavia.

Use of Sexual Violence in Bosnia-Herzegovina, Colombia, Uganda   123

7 Karadžić was convicted, on 24 March 2016, of genocide, crimes against humanity and violations of the laws or customs of war. He appealed and on 20 March 2019, his original sentence of 40 years was set aside and replaced with life imprisonment. On 22 November 2017, Mladić was also convicted at the ICTY of one count of genocide (in relation to Srebrenica) and multiple counts of crimes against humanity and violations of the laws or customs of war. He was sentenced to life imprisonment, which was upheld on appeal.

8 According to Rodriguez (2020: 215), 'Some of the most conservative studies have estimated that the total death toll of the war may be 220,000'.

9 Some of these organisations, like the Popular Liberation Army (ELP), demobilised in the 1990s.

10 It was also at this time that the FARC added 'People's Army' (*Ejército del Pueblo* in Spanish) to its name, thus becoming the FARC-EP. However, it is most commonly referred to simply as the FARC and this chapter follows that convention.

11 These are crimes that attack an individual's freedom and sexual autonomy. They include rape and other forms of sexual violence.

12 The CNMH (2017: 472–473) has pointed out that the OMC does not include figures from the Victims' Unit that are duplicated, and it also does not include records that are insufficiently lacking in detail to be reliable and/or not directly related to the dynamics of the armed conflict. The OMC, moreover, has explained how it verifies cases (CNMH, 2017: 473). Cases refer to an event and not to individual victims-/survivors. The same individual might have suffered several cases of sexual violence by different armed groups (CNMH, 2017: 474). Thank you to Dr Yoana Fernanda Nieto Valdivieso for translating from Spanish the relevant parts of the CNMH's 2017 report (and its 2018 report).

13 Doom and Vlassenroot (1999: 23), however, argue that 'Kony's aims were political, although it is not clear whether he wanted to topple the regime in Kampala or was limiting his actions to the north'.

14 The LRA did not only recruit children, however (see, e.g., Allen et al., 2020: 666: Victor and Porter, 2017: 593).

15 Mootz et al. (2017: 371) point out that 'There is a dearth of literature about the GBV [gender-based violence] related to these raids'.

16 An important transitional justice development in Uganda was the 2000 Amnesty Act, which granted pardon to any Ugandan engaged – formerly or currently – in acts of rebellion against the government since 1986 (Apuuli, 2006: 183).

17 Carlson and Mazurana (2008: 21) highlight that 'There are also reports that women and girls who failed to conceive were punished, and we collected information that girls or women caught trying to prevent or abort pregnancies were killed'.

18 Donnelly (2018: 470) notes that 'the LRA especially valued educated girls like the "Aboke girls"'.

19 Schools were crowded because they also served as 'night-commuting' centres for children seeking to avoid abduction by the LRA.

References

ABColombia, Sisma Mujer and US Office on Colombia (2013) Colombia: Women, conflict-related sexual violence and the peace process. Available at: https://reliefweb.int/sites/reliefweb.int/files/resources/ABColombia_Conflict_related_sexual_violence_report.pdf (accessed 7 May 2021).

Acosta M, Castañeda A, García D, Hernández F, Muelas D and Santamaria A (2018) The Colombian transitional process: Comparative perspectives on violence against Indigenous women. *International Journal of Transitional Justice* 12(1): 108–125.

Aijazi O and Baines E (2017) Relationality, culpability and consent in wartime: Men's experiences of forced marriage. *International Journal of Transitional Justice* 11(3): 463–483.

Akhavan P (2005) The Lord's Resistance Army case: Uganda's submission of the first state referral to the International Criminal Court. *American Journal of International Law* 99(2): 403–421.

Allen B (1996) *Rape Warfare: The Hidden Genocide in Bosnia and Croatia*. Minneapolis, MN: University of Minnesota Press.

Allen T (1991) Understanding Alice: Uganda's Holy Spirit Movement in context. *Africa* 61(3): 370–399.

Allen T (2008) *Trial Justice: The International Criminal Court and the Lord's Resistance Army*. London: Zed Books.

Allen T, Atingo J, Atim D, Ocitti J, Brown C, Torre C, Fergus CA and Parker M (2020) What happened to children who returned from the Lord's Resistance Army in Uganda? *Journal of Refugee Studies* 33(4): 663–683.

Alsema A (2020) Pandemic leaves Colombia's victims of domestic violence at mercy of their victims. Available at: https://colombiareports.com/pandemic-leaves-colombias-victims-of-domestic-violence-at-mercy-of-their-victimizers/ (accessed 9 October 2021).

Amnesty International (1997) Uganda: 'Breaking God's commands': The destruction of childhood by the Lord's Resistance Army. Available at: www.amnesty.org/en/wp-content/uploads/2021/06/afr590011997en.pdf (accessed 27 October 2021).

Amnesty International (2004) Colombia: 'Scarred bodies, hidden crimes': Sexual violence against women in the armed conflict. Available at: www.amnesty.org/en/wp-content/uploads/2021/06/amr230402004en.pdf (accessed 9 November 2021).

Amnesty International (2009) 'Whose justice?' The women of Bosnia and Herzegovina are still waiting. Available at: www.amnesty.org/en/wp-content/uploads/2021/06/eur630062009eng.pdf (accessed 3 August 2021).

Amnesty International (2020) Why do they want to kill us? Lack of safe space to defend human rights in Colombia. Available at: www.amnesty.org/en/wp-content/uploads/2021/05/AMR2330092020ENGLISH.pdf (accessed 29 September 2021).

Amnesty International (2021) Colombia: Concerning reports of disappearances and sexual violence against protesters. Available at: www.amnesty.org/en/latest/news/2021/05/colombia-preocupan-las-denuncias-de-desapariciones-y-violencia-sexual-contra-manifestantes/ (accessed 3 October 2021).

Amone P'Olak K (2007) Coping with life in rebel captivity and the challenge of reintegrating formerly abducted boys in northern Uganda. *Journal of Refugee Studies* 20(4): 641–661.

Andreas P (2004) The clandestine political economy of war and peace in Bosnia. *International Studies Quarterly* 48(1): 29–51.

Annan J, Blattman C, Mazurana D and Carlson K (2011) Civil war, reintegration and gender in northern Uganda. *Journal of Conflict Resolution* 55(6): 877–908.

Apuuli KP (2006) The ICC arrest warrants for the Lord's Resistance Army leaders and peace prospects for northern Uganda. *Journal of International Criminal Justice* 4(1): 179–187.

Arvelo JE (2006) International law and conflict resolution in Colombia: Balancing peace and justice in the paramilitary demobilization process. *Georgetown Journal of International Law* 37(2): 411–476.

Askin KD (1997) *War Crimes against Women: Prosecution in International War Crimes Tribunals*. The Hague: Kluwer Law International.

Aviles W (2008) US intervention in Colombia: The role of transnational relations. *Bulletin of Latin American Research* 27(3): 410–429.

Baines EK (2007) The haunting of Alice: Local approaches to justice and reconciliation in northern Uganda. *International Journal of Transitional Justice* 1(1): 91–114.

Baines EK (2009) Complex political perpetrators: Reflections on Dominic Ongwen. *Journal of Modern African Studies* 47(2): 163–191.

Baines EK (2014) Forced marriage as a political project: Sexual rules and relations in the Lord's Resistance Army. *Journal of Peace Research* 51(3): 405–417.

Baines EK (2017) *Buried in the Heart: Women, Complex Victimhood and the War in Northern Uganda.* Cambridge: Cambridge University Press.

Banac I (2009) What happened in the Balkans (or rather ex–Yugoslavia)? *East European Politics and Societies* 23(4): 461–478.

Bartell L (2020) Colombia's LGBT community reports increased violence and discrimination. Available at: https://colombiareports.com/colombias-lgbt-community-reports-increased-violence-discrimination/ (accessed 9 November 2021).

Bassiouni MC and McCormick M (1996) *Sexual Violence: An Invisible Weapon of War in the Former Yugoslavia, Occasional Paper No. 1.* Chicago, IL: DePaul University College of Law.

Bates J (2022) The violence of norms: Resisting repertoires of gender violence in post-conflict Colombia. *Journal of Gender Studies* 31(2): 153–164.

BBC (2016) Colombia referendum: Voters reject Farc peace deal. Available at: www.bbc.co.uk/news/world-latin-america-37537252 (accessed 11 October 2021).

BBC (2021) Uganda ordered to end Bobi Wine's house arrest. Available at: www.bbc.co.uk/news/world-africa-55756838 (accessed 3 November 2021).

Bećirević E (2010) The issue of genocidal intent and denial of genocide. *East European Politics and Societies* 24(10): 480–502.

Behrend H (2000) *Alice Lakwena and the Holy Spirits: War in Northern Uganda, 1986–97.* Athens, OH: Ohio University Press.

Berry ME (2018) *Women, War and Power: From Violence to Mobilization in Rwanda and Bosnia-Herzegovina.* Cambridge: Cambridge University Press.

Bieber F (2002) Nationalist mobilization and stories of Serb suffering: The Kosovo myth from 600th anniversary to the present. *Rethinking History* 6(1): 95–110.

Branch A (2009) Humanitarianism, violence and the camp in northern Uganda. *Civil Wars* 11(4): 477–501.

Branch A (2010) Exploring the roots of LRA violence: Political crisis and ethnic politics in Acholiland. In: Allen T and Vlassenroot K (eds.), *The Lord's Resistance Army: Myth and Reality.* London: Zed Press, pp. 25–44.

Burg SL and Shoup PS (2000) *The War in Bosnia-Herzegovina: Ethnic Conflict and International Intervention.* New York, NY: Routledge.

Buss D (2002) Prosecuting mass rape: *Prosecutor v. Dragoljub Kunarac, Radomir Kovac and Zoran Vukovic. Feminist Legal Studies* 10: 91–99.

Calić MJ (2019) *History of Yugoslavia.* West Lafayette, IN: Purdue University Press.

Campbell D (1998) MetaBosnia: Narratives of the Bosnian war. *Review of International Studies* 24(2): 261–281.

Campbell JC (1980) Tito: The achievement and the legacy. *Foreign Affairs* 58(5): 1045–1059.

Carlson K and Mazurana D (2008) Forced marriage within the Lord's Resistance Army, Uganda. Available at: https://fic.tufts.edu/wp-content/uploads/Forced+Marriage+within+the+LRA-2008.pdf (accessed 7 November 2021).

Carmichael C (2015) *A Concise History of Bosnia.* Cambridge: Cambridge University Press.

Chinkin C (1994) Rape and sexual abuse of women in international law. *European Journal of International Law* 5(3): 326–341.

Cigar N (1993) The Serbo-Croatian War, 1991: Political and military dimensions. *Journal of Strategic Studies* 16(3): 297–338.

Clark JN (2017) *Rape, Sexual Violence and Transitional Justice Challenges: Lessons from Bosnia-Herzegovina.* Abingdon: Routledge.

CNMH (2017) *La Guerra inscrita en el cuerpo: Informe nacional de violencia sexual en el conflicto armado.* Bogotá: CNMH.

CNMH (2018) *Memoria histórica con víctimas de violencia sexual: Aproximación conceptual y metodológica.* Bogotá: CNMH.

Cohen LJ and Dragović-Soso J (eds.) (2008) *State Collapse in South-Eastern Europe: New Perspectives on Yugoslavia's Disintegration.* West Lafayette, IN: Purdue University Press.

Copelon R (1994) Surfacing gender: Re-engraving crimes against women in humanitarian law. *Hastings Women's Law Journal* 5(2): 243–266.

Davies SE and True J (2015) Reframing conflict-related sexual and gender-based violence: Bringing gender analysis back in. *Security Dialogue* 46(6): 495–512.

de Waardt M and Weber S (2019) Beyond victims' mere presence: An empirical analysis of victim participation in transitional justice in Colombia. *Journal of Human Rights Practice* 11(1): 209–228.

Demmers J and Gould L (2018) An assemblage approach to liquid warfare: AFRICOM and the 'hunt' for Joseph Kony. *Security Dialogue* 49(5): 364–381.

Diken B and Laustsen CB (2005) Becoming abject: Rape as a weapon of war. *Body & Society* 11(1): 111–128.

Dolan C (2002) Collapsing masculinities and weak states – A case study of northern Uganda. In: Cleaver F (ed.), *Masculinities Matter! Men, Gender and Development.* London: Zed Books, pp. 57–83.

Dolan C (2009) *Social Torture: The Case of Northern Uganda, 1986–2006.* New York, NY: Berghahn Books.

Donnelly P (2018) The interactive relationship between gender and strategy. *Global Society* 32(4): 457–476.

Doom R and Vlassenroot K (1999) Kony's message: A new *Koine*? The Lord's Resistance Army in northern Uganda. *African Affairs* 98(390): 5–36.

Dunn KC (2004) Uganda: The Lord's Resistance Army. *Review of African Political Economy* 31(99): 139–142.

Dunn KC (2010) The Lord's Resistance Army and African international relations. *African Security* 3(1): 46–63.

Edström J and Dolan C (2019) Breaking the spell of silence: Collective healing as activism amongst refugee male survivors of sexual violence in Uganda. *Journal of Refugee Studies* 32(2): 175–196.

Edström J, Dolan C and Shahrokh T, with David O (2016) Therapeutic activism: Men of Hope refugee association Uganda breaking the silence over male rape in conflict-related sexual violence. IDS Evidence Report 182.

Engle K (2005) Feminism and its discontents: Criminalizing wartime rape in Bosnia-Herzegovina. *American Journal of International Law* 99(4): 778–816.

Esuruku RS (2011) Beyond masculinity: Gender, conflict and post-conflict reconstruction in northern Uganda. *Journal of Science and Sustainable Development* 4: 25–40.

Faguet JP, Sánchez F and Villaveces MJ (2020) The perversion of public land distribution by landed elites: Power, inequality and development in Colombia. *World Development* 135: 105036.

Ferizović J and Mlinarević G (2020) Applying international experiences in national prosecutions of conflict-related sexual violence: A case study of application of the ICTY law, findings and practices in prosecutions before the Court of Bosnia and Herzegovina. *Journal of International Criminal Justice* 18(2): 325–348.

Finnström S (2001) In and out of culture: Fieldwork in war-torn Uganda. *Critique of Anthropology* 21(3): 247–258.

Finnström S (2006) Wars of the past and war in the present: The Lord's Resistance Movement/Army in Uganda. *Africa* 76(2): 200–220.

Finnström S (2008) *Living with Bad Surroundings: War, History and Everyday Moments in Northern Uganda.* Durham, NC: Duke University Press.

Fisher DG and Meitus AA (2017) Uprooting or sowing violence? Coca eradication and guerrilla violence in Colombia. *Studies in Conflict & Terrorism* 40(9): 790–807.

Fisher SK (1996) Occupation of the womb: Forced impregnation as genocide. *Duke Law Journal* 46(1): 91–134.

Flisi I (2019) Engendering the understanding of wartime sexual violence in Colombia: Hyper-masculinities and sexual violence against men. In: Danielsson SK (ed.), *War and Sexual Violence: New Perspectives in a New Era.* Leiden: Brill, pp. 243–275.

García-Godos J and Lid KNO (2010) Transitional justice and victims' rights before the end of a conflict: The unusual case of Colombia. *Journal of Latin American Studies* 42(3): 487–516.

Glenny M (1996) *The Fall of Yugoslavia.* 3rd ed. London: Penguin Books.

Goldscheid J (2020) Gender violence against Afro-Colombian women: Making the promise of international human rights law real. *HRLR Online* 4(3): 249–267.

Griffin O (2021) Colombia ELN guerrillas claim responsibility for attacks on oil infrastructure. Available at: www.reuters.com/business/energy/colombias-ecopetrol-reports-attack-oil-pipeline-2021-10-15/ (accessed 17 October 2021).

Guáqueta A (2007) The way back in: Reintegrating illegal armed groups in Colombia then and now. *Conflict, Security & Development* 7(3): 417–456.

Gustavsson M, Oruut J and Rubenson B (2017) Girl soldiers with Lord's Resistance Army in Uganda fighting for survival: Experiences of young women abducted by LRA. *Children's Geographies* 15(6): 690–702.

Gutman R (1994) Foreword. In: Stiglymayer A (ed.), *The War against Women in Bosnia-Herzegovina.* Lincoln, NE: University of Nebraska Press, pp. ix–xiii.

Hammel EA, Mason C and Stevanović M (2010) A fish stinks from the head: Ethnic diversity, segregation and the collapse of Yugoslavia. *Demographic Research* 22: 1097–1142.

Hansen L (2000) Gender, nation, rape: Bosnia and the construction of security. *International Feminist Journal of Politics* 3(1): 55–75.

Hayden RM (1996) Schindler's fate: Genocide, ethnic cleansing and population transfers. *Slavic Review* 55(4): 727–748.

Helms E (2013) *Innocence and Victimhood: Gender, Nation, and Women's Activism in Postwar Bosnia-Herzegovina.* Madison, WI: University of Wisconsin Press.

Helms E (2014) Rejecting Angelina: Bosnian war rape survivors and the ambiguities of sex in war. *Slavic Review* 73(3): 612–634.

Hernández P and Romero A (2003) Adolescent girls in Colombia's guerrilla. *Journal of Prevention and Intervention in the Community* 26(1): 21–38.

Herrera N and Porch D (2008) 'Like going to a fiesta' – The role of female fighters in Colombia's FARC-EP. *Small Wars & Insurgencies* 19(4): 609–634.

Hoare MA (2011) The Bosnian war's forgotten turning point: The Bihać crisis of autumn 1994. *The Journal of Slavic Military Studies* 24(1): 88–114.

Hoare MA (2013) *The Bosnian Muslims in the Second World War: A History*. New York, NY: Oxford University Press.

Holmes JS, Mendizabal AP, De La Fuente DS, Callenes M and Cárdenas Á (2021) Paramilitary violence in Colombia: A multilevel negative binomial analysis. *Defence and Peace Economics* 32(2): 193–219.

HRW (2021a) Left undefended: Killings of rights defenders in Colombia's remote regions. Available at: www.hrw.org/report/2021/02/10/left-undefended/killings-rights-defenders-colombias-remote-communities (accessed 5 October 2021).

HRW (2021b) Colombia: Events of 2020. Available at: www.hrw.org/world-report/2021/country-chapters/colombia (accessed 17 November 2021).

HRW (2022) Colombia – Events of 2021. Available at: www.hrw.org/world-report/2022/country-chapters/colombia (accessed 23 April 2022).

Huneeus A and Rueda Sáiz P (2021) Territory as a victim of armed conflict. *International Journal of Transitional Justice* 15(1): 210–229.

ICMP (2021) ICMP presentation commemorates missing persons in Colombia. Available at: www.icmp.int/news/icmp-exhibition-commemorates-missing-persons-in-colombia/ (accessed 17 December 2021).

ICRC (2019) Bosnia and Herzegovina: 7,000 lives still missing. Available at: www.icrc.org/en/document/bosnia-and-herzegovina-7000-people-still-missing (accessed 14 November 2021).

ICTY (2011) New war demographics feature on the ICTY's webpage. Available at: www.icty.org/en/press/new-war-demographics-feature-icty-website (accessed 5 March 2021).

ICTY (2016) In numbers. Available at: www.icty.org/en/features/crimes-sexual-violence/in-numbers (accessed 31 October 2021).

Inter-American Commission of Human Rights (2009) Annual report of the Inter-American Commission of Human Rights 2009. Available at: www.cidh.org/pdf%20files/ANNUAL2009.pdf (accessed 9 September 2021).

Jackson P (2002) The march of the Lord's Resistance Army: Greed or grievance in northern Uganda. *Small Wars & Insurgencies* 13(3): 29–52.

Jeffrey R (2011) Forgiveness, amnesty and justice: The case of the Lord's Resistance Army in northern Uganda. *Cooperation and Conflict* 46(1): 78–95.

Jolin N (2016) Gender-based violence in Colombia: New legislation targets femicides and acid attacks. *Tulane Law Review* 9(2): 371–404.

Jonsson M, Brennan E and O'Hara C (2016) Financing war or facilitating peace? The impact of rebel drug trafficking on peace negotiations in Colombia and Myanmar. *Studies in Conflict & Terrorism* 39(6): 542–559.

Kan G (2018) The prosecution of a child victim and a brutal warlord: The competing narrative of Dominic Ongwen. *SOAS Law Journal* 5(1): 70–82.

Kaplan O (2017) *Resisting War: How Communities Protect Themselves*. Cambridge: Cambridge University Press.

Kaufman JP and Williams KP (2004) Who belongs? Women, marriage and citizenship. *International Feminist Journal of Politics* 6(3): 416–435.

Kesić V (1994) A response to Catharine MacKinnon's article turning rape into pornography: Postmodern genocide. *Hastings Women's Law Journal* 5(2): 267–280.

Koopman S (2021) Mona, mona, mona! Tropicality and the imaginative geographies of whiteness in Colombia. *Journal of Latin American Geography* 20(1): 49–78.

Kramer S (2012) Forced marriage and the absence of gang rape: Explaining sexual violence by the Lord's Resistance Army in northern Uganda. *Journal of Politics & Society* 23(1): 11–49.

Kravetz D (2017) Promoting domestic accountability for conflict-related sexual violence: The cases of Guatemala, Peru and Colombia. *American University International Law Review* 32(3): 707–762.

Kreft AK (2020) Civil society perspectives on sexual violence in conflict: Patriarchy and war strategy in Colombia. *International Affairs* 96(2): 457–478.

LeoGrande WM and Sharpe KE (2000) Two wars or one? Drugs, guerrillas and Colombia's new 'violencia'. *World Policy Journal* 17(3): 1–11.

Lozano GO and Machado S (2012) The objective qualification of non-international armed conflicts: A Colombian case study. *Amsterdam Law Forum* 4(1): 58–77.

Macdonald A (2019) 'Somehow this whole process became so artificial': Exploring the transitional justice implementation gap in Uganda. *International Journal of Transitional Justice* 13(2): 225–248.

MacKinnon CA (1994a) Rape, genocide and women's human rights. *Harvard Women's Law Journal* 17: 5–16.

MacKinnon CA (1994b) Turning rape into pornography: Postmodern genocide. In: Stiglmayer A (ed.), *Mass Rape: The War against Women in Bosnia-Herzegovina*. Lincoln, NE: University of Nebraska Press, pp. 73–81.

McDonnell FJH and Akallo G (2007) *Girl Soldier: A Story of Hope for Northern Uganda's Children*. Grand Rapids, MI: Chosen Books.

McGee R (2017) Invisible power and visible everyday resistance in the violent Colombian Pacific. *Peacebuilding* 5(2): 170–185.

Meertens D (2001) Facing destruction, rebuilding life: Gender and the internally displaced in Colombia. *Latin American Perspectives* 28(1): 132–148.

Meier V (1999) *Yugoslavia: A History of its Demise*. London: Routledge.

Moloney A (2015) Colombia confronts femicide, the 'most extreme form of violence against women'. Available at: www.reuters.com/article/us-colombia-women-murder-idUSKCN0QP0CM20150820 (accessed 19 December 2021).

Mootz JJ, Stabb JD and Mollen D (2017) Gender-based violence and armed conflict: A community-informed socioecological conceptual model from northeastern Uganda. *Psychology of Women Quarterly* 41(3): 368–388.

Nettelfield LJ and Wagner S (2014) *Srebrenica in the Aftermath of Genocide*. New York, NY: Cambridge University Press.

Niebuhr R (2006) War in Slovenia: Doctrine and defeat. *The Journal of Slavic Military Studies* 19(3): 489–513.

Nkabala HN (2017) The use of violent biblical texts by the Lord's Resistance Army in northern Uganda. *Transformation* 34(2): 91–100.

Norman SV (2018) *Narcotization* as security dilemma: The FARC and drug trade in Colombia. *Studies in Conflict & Terrorism* 41(8): 638–659.

Norwegian Refugee Council (2022) Colombia: 274,000 people affected by violence in two months. Available at: www.nrc.no/news/2022/april/colombia-274000-people-affected-by-violence-in-two-months/ (accessed 24 April 2022).

Nouwen S and Werner (2011) Doing justice to the political: The International Criminal Court in Uganda and Sudan. *European Journal of International Law* 21(4): 941–965.

Nussio E (2011) Learning from shortcomings: The demobilisation of paramilitaries in Colombia. *Journal of Peacebuilding & Development* 6(2): 88–92.

Okello MC and Hovil L (2007) Confronting the reality of gender-based violence in northern Uganda. *International Journal of Transitional Justice* 1(3): 433–443.

Olujić MB (1998) Embodiment of terror: Gendered violence in peacetime and wartime in Bosnia and Croatia. *Medical Anthropology Quarterly* 12(1): 31–50.

OTP-ICC (2012) Situation in Colombia: Interim report – November 2012. Available at: www.icc-cpi.int/sites/default/files/NR/rdonlyres/3D3055BD-16E2-4C83-BA85-35BCFD2A7922/285102/OTPCOLOMBIAPublicInterimReportNovember2012.pdf (accessed 1 October 2021).

Oxfam (2009) Sexual violence in Colombia: Instrument of war. Available at: https://oi-files-d8-prod.s3.eu-west-2.amazonaws.com/s3fs-public/file_attachments/bp-sexual-violence-colombia_4.pdf (accessed 3 September 2021).

Payne WJ (2016) Death-squads contemplating queers as citizens: What Colombian paramilitaries are saying. *Gender, Place & Culture* 23(3): 328–344.

Pham PN, Vinck P and Stover E (2008) The Lord's Resistance Army and forced conscription in northern Uganda. *Human Rights Quarterly* 30(2): 404–411.

Pinzón JC (2016) Colombia back from the brink: From failed state to exporter of security. *Prism* 5(4): 2–9.

Porter HE (2015) 'Say no to bad touches': Schools, sexual identity and sexual violence in northern Uganda. *International Journal of Educational Development* 41: 271–282.

Porter HE (2017) *After Rape: Violence, Justice and Social Harmony in Northern Uganda.* Cambridge: Cambridge University Press.

Porter HE (2019) Moral spaces and sexual transgression: Understanding rape in war and post conflict. *Development and Change* 50(4): 1009–1032.

Prunier G (2004) Rebel movements and proxy warfare: Uganda, Sudan and the Congo (1986–99). *African Affairs* 103(412): 359–383.

Ramet SP (2002) *Balkan Babel: The Disintegration of Yugoslavia from the Death of Tito to the Fall of Milosevic.* 4th ed. New York, NY: Routledge.

Ramsey RW (1973) Critical bibliography on la violencia in Colombia. *Latin American Research Review* 8(1): 3–44.

Rodriguez SP (2020) A second chance on earth: Understanding the selection process of the judges of the Colombian Special Jurisdiction for Peace. *Notre Dame Journal of International & Comparative Law* 10(2): 209–266.

Ruigrok N (2008) Journalism of attachment and objectivity: Dutch journalists and the Bosnian war. *Media, War & Conflict* 1(3): 293–313.

Ruta Pacifica de las Mujeres, Afonso A and Beristain CM (2015) Memory for life: A truth commission proposal from women for Colombia. Available at: https://rutapacifica.org.co/wp/memory-for-life-a-truth-commission-proposal-from-women-for-colombia/ (accessed 3 November 2021).

Saab BY and Taylor AW (2009) Criminality and armed groups: A comparative study of FARC and paramilitary groups in Colombia. *Studies in Conflict & Terrorism* 32(6): 455–475.

Sachseder J (2020) Cleared for investment? The intersections of transnational capital, gender and race in the production of sexual violence and internal displacement in Colombia's armed conflict. *International Feminist Journal of Politics* 22(2): 162–186.

Salzman TA (1998) Rape camps as a means of ethnic cleansing: Religious, cultural, and ethical responses to rape victims in the former Yugoslavia. *Human Rights Quarterly* 20(2): 348–378.

Sanchez AO, Lopez Vivas JN, Rubriche Cardenas D and del Pilar Rengifo Cano M (2011) First survey on the prevalence of sexual violence against women in the context of the Colombian armed conflict, 2001–2009: Executive summary. Available at: https://reliefweb.int/sites/reliefweb.int/files/resources/2011-03-23-Report-English.pdf (accessed 29 August 2021).

Sanford V (2003) Learning to kill by proxy: Colombian paramilitaries and the legacy of Central American death squads, contras and civil patrols. *Social Justice* 30(3): 63–81.

Schulz P (2018a) Displacement from gendered personhood: Sexual violence and masculinities in northern Uganda. *International Affairs* 94(5): 1101–1119.

Schulz P (2018b) The 'ethical loneliness' of male sexual violence survivors in northern Uganda: Gendered reflections on silencing. *International Feminist Journal of Politics* 20(4): 583–601.

Schulz P (2021) *Male Survivors of Wartime Sexual Violence: Perspectives from Northern Uganda.* Oakland, CA: University of California Press.

Shrader CR (2003) *The Muslim-Croat Civil War in Bosnia: A Military History, 1992–1994.* College Station, TX: Texas A & M University Press.

Simić O (2018) *Silenced Victims of Wartime Sexual Violence.* Abingdon: Routledge.

Skjelsbaek I (2012) *The Political Psychology of War Rape: Studies from Bosnia and Herzegovina.* Abingdon: Routledge.

Snyder CS, Gabbard WJ, May D and Zulcic N (2006) On the battleground of women's bodies: Mass rape in Bosnia-Herzegovina. *Affilia* 21(2): 184–195.

Sokolić I (2017) My neighbour, the criminal: How memories of the 1991–1995 conflict in Croatia affect attitudes towards the Serb minority. *Nations and Nationalism* 23(4): 790–814.

Stallone K and Janetsky M (2021) 'I'm not alone': Survivors organise against sexual violence in Colombia. Available at: www.theguardian.com/global-development/2021/jul/22/im-not-alone-survivors-organise-against-sexual-violence-in-colombia (accessed 22 July 2021).

Stiglmayer A (ed.) (1994) *Mass Rape: The War against Women in Bosnia-Herzegovina.* Lincoln, NE: University of Nebraska Press.

Stites E and Howe K (2019) From the border to the bedroom: Changing conflict dynamics in Karamoja, Uganda. *Journal of Modern African Studies* 57(1): 137–159.

Summers N (2012) Colombia's victims' law: Transitional justice in a time of violent conflict? *Harvard Human Rights Journal* 25: 219–236.

Svallfors S (2021) Hidden casualties: The links between armed conflict and intimate partner violence in Colombia. *Politics & Gender*, https://doi.org/10.1017/S1743923X2100043X.

Tanner M (2010) *Croatia: A Nation Forged in War.* 3rd ed. New Haven, CT: Yale University Press.

Tate W (2001) Paramilitaries in Colombia. *The Brown Journal of World Affairs* 8(1): 163–175.

Temmerman E (2009) *Aboke Girls: Children Abducted in Northern Uganda.* Kampala: Fountain Publishers.

Theidon K (2007) Transitional subjects: The disarmament, demobilization and reintegration of former combatants in Colombia. *International Journal of Transitional Justice* 1(1): 66–90.

Theidon K (2016) Peace in Colombia: A time to believe? *Current History* 115(778): 51–59.

Thylin T (2020) Violence, toleration, or inclusion? Exploring variation in the experiences of LGBT combatants in Colombia. *Sexualities* 23(3): 445–464.

Toal G and Dahlman CT (2011) *Bosnia Remade: Ethnic Cleansing and its Reversal.* Oxford: Oxford University Press.

Tournaye C (2003) Genocidal intent before the ICTY. *International and Comparative Law Quarterly* 52(2): 447–462.

Tovar-Restrepo M and Irazábal C (2014) Indigenous women and violence in Colombia: Agency, autonomy and territoriality. *Latin American Perspectives* 41(1): 39–58.

UN (2021) Colombians cling tenaciously to peace gains, Security Council hears. Available at: https://news.un.org/en/story/2021/10/1103132 (accessed 4 October 2021).

UN Commission of Experts (1994) Final report of the Commission of Experts established pursuant to Security Council Resolution 780 (1992), S/1994/674. Available at: www.icty.org/x/file/About/OTP/un_commission_of_experts_report1994_en.pdf (accessed 28 August 2021).

UN Secretary-General (2013) Sexual violence in conflict: Report of the UN Secretary-General. Available at: www.securitycouncilreport.org/atf/cf/%7B65BFCF9B-6D27-4E9C-8CD3-CF6E4FF96FF9%7D/s_2013_149.pdf (accessed 1 August 2021).

UN Secretary-General (2021) Conflict-related sexual violence: Report of the UN Secretary-General. Available at: www.un.org/sexualviolenceinconflict/wp-content/uploads/2021/04/report/conflict-related-sexual-violence-report-of-the-united-nations-secretary-general/SG-Report-2020editedsmall.pdf (accessed 3 August 2021).

UN Secretary-General (2022) Conflict-related sexual violence: Report of the UN Secretary-General. Available at: https://www.un.org/sexualviolenceinconflict/wp-content/uploads/2022/04/auto-draft/SG-Report2021for-web.pdf (accessed 16 July 2022).

UN Security Council (2016) Lord's Resistance Army. Available at: www.un.org/securitycouncil/sanctions/2127/materials/summaries/entity/lord%E2%80%99s-resistance-army (accessed 11 November 2021).

Uribe MV (2004) Dismembering and expelling: Semantics of political terror in Colombia. *Public Culture* 16(1): 79–95.

Valiñas M (2020) The Colombian Special Jurisdiction for Peace: A few issues for consideration when investigating and adjudicating sexual and gender-based crimes. *Journal of International Criminal Justice* 18(2): 449–467.

Van Acker F (2004) Uganda and the Lord's Resistance Army: The new order no one ordered. *African Affairs* 103(412): 335–357.

Victims' Unit (2022) Register of victims. Available at: www.unidadvictimas.gov.co/es/registro-unico-de-victimas-ruv/37394 (accessed 23 April 2022).

Victor L and Porter H (2017) Dirty things: Spiritual pollution and life after the Lord's Resistance Army. *Journal of Eastern African Studies* 11(4): 590–608.

Vinci A (2005) The strategic use of fear by the Lord's Resistance Army. *Small Wars & Insurgencies* 16(3): 360–381.

Vivanco JM (2016) Colombia: Sexual violence by FARC guerrillas exposed. Available at: www.hrw.org/news/2016/08/11/colombia-sexual-violence-farc-guerrillas-exposed# (accessed 8 October 2021).

Viveros-Vigoya M (2016) Masculinities in the continuum of violence in Latin America. *Feminist Theory* 17(2): 229–237.

Vulliamy E (1994) *Seasons in Hell: Understanding Bosnia's War*. New York, NY: St. Martin's Press.

Wienand S and Tremaria S (2017) Paramilitarism in a post-demobilization context? Insights from the department of Antioquia in Colombia. *European Review of Latin American and Caribbean Studies* 103: 25–50.

Wood EJ (2010) Sexual violence during war: Toward an understanding of variation. In: Sjoberg L and Via S (eds.), *Gender, War and Militarism: Feminist Perspectives*. Santa-Barbara, CA: Praeger, pp. 124–137.

Woodward SL (1995) *Balkan Tragedy: Chaos and Dissolution after the Cold War*. Washington, DC: The Brookings Institution.

Yoshida K and Céspedes-Báez LM (2021) The nature of women, peace and security: A Colombian perspective. *International Affairs* 97(1): 17–34.

Zalesne D (2020) Making rights a reality: Access to healthcare for Afro-Colombian survivors of conflict-related sexual violence. *Columbia Human Rights Law Review* 51(2): 668–722.

Žarkov D (2007) *The Body of War: Ethnicity and Gender in the Break-Up of Yugoslavia*. Durham, NC: Duke University Press.

Zimmermann W (1994) A pavane for Bosnia. *The National Interest* 37: 75–79.

Zulver JM (2020) In Colombia, pandemic heightens risks for women social leaders. Available at: https://carnegieendowment.org/2020/05/07/in-colombia-pandemic-heightens-risks-for-women-social-leaders-pub-81736 (accessed 18 September 2021).

Legal Judgements

ICC

Prosecutor v. Ongwen (2021) ICC-02/04–01/15, Trial Chamber Judgement, 4 February 2021.

ICTY

Prosecutor v. Bralo (2005) IT-95–17-S, Sentencing Judgement, 7 December 2005.

Prosecutor v. Češić (2004) IT-95–10/1-S, Sentencing Judgement, 11 March 2004.

Prosecutor v. Furundžija (1998) IT-95–17/1-T, Trial Chamber Judgement, 10 December 1998.

Prosecutor v. Karadžić (2016) IT-95–5/18-T, Trial Chamber Judgement, 24 March 2016.

Prosecutor v. Kunarac et al. (2001) IT-96–93-T, Trial Chamber Judgement, 22 February 2001.

Prosecutor v. Kvočka et al. (2001) IT-98–30/1-T, Trial Chamber Judgement, 2 November 2001.

Prosecutor v. Mladić (2017) IT-09–92-T, Trial Chamber Judgement, 22 November 2017.

Prosecutor v. Mucić et al. (1998) IT-96–21-T, Trial Chamber Judgement, 16 November 1998.

Prosecutor v. Prlić et al. (2013) IT-04–74-T, Trial Chamber Judgement, 29 May 2013.

Chapter 5

Connectivity Stories of Resilience in Bosnia-Herzegovina

A report by Amnesty International (2017: 56) states that two decades after the Bosnian war ended, many women subjected to sexual violence 'are still battling with the pervasive and devastating consequences of these crimes'. It further adds that 'The vast majority of victims suffer in silence' (Amnesty International, 2017: 56). This chapter expressly seeks to develop a different narrative, using the book's connectivity framework presented in Chapter 2. Doing so is not about minimising the fact that victims-/survivors of conflict-related sexual violence (CRSV) in BiH often continue to face challenges, as do many Bosnians who live with the long-term legacies of a war that turned their lives and communities upside down.[1] It is about drawing attention to some of the largely neglected ways that victims-/survivors have demonstrated resilience. By extension, it is about recognising these women and men as actors within their social ecologies, rather than simply locating them at the margins of society – a positioning that contributes to reducing them (and in particular Bosniak women) to 'a caricatured image of silent victimhood' (Helms, 2013: 64; see also Berry, 2018: 189).

In addition to noting interviewees' gender (and age, where relevant), this chapter refers to their ethnicity. Doing so could be interpreted as accentuating differences that nationalist politicians themselves manipulated to help plunge the country into bloodshed. It also potentially puts 'labels' on people that they themselves may not identify with (see Hunt, 2004: 5, 61). The unevenness with which some of the literature has discussed the use of CRSV in BiH, however – as emphasised in the previous chapter – creates a strong rationale for identifying the ethnicity of the interviewees. This is not about creating divides, but about making clear that a person's ethnicity does not make his/her war experiences any less important or less deserving of attention.

Contextualising Experiences of Violence

Highlighted by developments such as the 2014 Global Summit to End Sexual Violence in Conflict, the joint award of the 2018 Nobel Peace Prize to the Congolese gynaecologist Dr Denis Mukwege and the Yazidi activist Nadia

DOI: 10.4324/9781003323532-6

Murad and the creation in 2019 of the Global Survivors Fund, increasing attention is now being given at the international level to CRSV. On one hand, this represents a significant step forward (Askin, 2003: 296). On the other hand, the desirability of this heightened attention to the issue has been questioned. As previously noted in Chapter 2, some scholars have underlined that focusing only or primarily on CRSV overlooks and detracts from other forms of violence – particularly against women (Crawford, 2013: 515; Henry, 2014: 98; Myrttinen and Swaine, 2015: 498). A related argument is that when we treat sexual violence in conflict as something exceptional, we effectively decontextualise it (Boesten, 2017: 511), missing the fact that it often forms part of a broader continuum of violence that cuts across war/peace binaries (Boesten, 2017: 517; Kirby, 2015: 463; Kostovicova et al., 2020: 254).

Certainly, the data from BiH (but also from Colombia and Uganda) strongly support such arguments. More than just continuities of violence, however, what the data highlighted were complex clusters of (often co-occurring) violence that formed important experiential contexts for the analyses. These clusterings are powerfully captured in one of the first themes that emerged from the interview data: *'I am all that I've lived': Connectivities of violence*. Many of the Bosnian interviewees, for example, spoke about physical abuse and mistreatment in detention. Reflecting on the three months that he was held in a camp in eastern BiH, a male Bosniak interviewee recalled: 'A lot, a lot of suffering went on. Beatings, err, cutting of bodies with a knife. They stuck a knife into my father's head. It was in his head, like this, straight up. Big knife, like this [demonstrates the size with his hands]' (interview, BiH, 10 April 2019). A female interviewee from a mixed marriage who identified as Albanian (illustrating how ethnicity in BiH follows a patrilineal logic) described what happened when Serb forces entered her village in 1992:

> We were all taken away from this place. They rounded us up into the buses and drove us away. There is a village close to XXX.[2] We spent two nights and two days there. Then, the buses came and took us to XXX. We spent four days there on the buses. We had no food, nothing. Soldiers used to come in. They were scaring us. Taking out their knives. Threatening us.
>
> (interview, BiH, 20 March 2019)

Many interviewees had also been made to witness violence against others, including, in some cases, loved ones; and some had been forced to flee their homes in what euphemistically became known as 'ethnic cleansing' (Hayden, 1996: 731). Some of the interviewees (although considerably fewer than in Colombia and Uganda) additionally spoke about violence outside the context of war. Two of them, for example, mentioned past domestic violence that they had experienced, and one of them also described the violence that she had suffered as a child at the hands of her mother and brother. Indirectly pointing to broader forms of structural violence, moreover, several female interviewees –

136 Connectivity Stories of Resilience in Bosnia-Herzegovina

from different socio-economic and ethnic backgrounds – articulated the view that women in BiH are not equal to men, either in marriage or in society.[3]

This book is about much more than what the women and men who participated in the research had gone through. It is also about how they were dealing with their experiences, how they were moving on with their lives, how they actively sought out and utilised resources within their social ecologies – all of which are important manifestations of agency that challenge 'infantilizing portrayals of the ever-vulnerable and passive victim' (Touquet and Schulz, 2021: 227). However, it is necessary to locate the book's discussion and analyses of resilience in relation to the breadth of interviewees' experiences of violence and adversity – including but extending beyond CRSV.

An important part of this research is about the effects of multiple stressors (or what Walsh [2020: 899] terms 'a cascade of disruptions') and experiences of violence on individuals' relationships with their social ecologies. In this regard, the idea of fragmentation – which in the context of ecology scholarship refers to the interruption or cessation of connectivity (see Chapter 2) – was recurrent within the interview data. Scholars have observed how stressors can adversely affect social connections, including 'bridging' and 'bonding' social capital (Aiken, 2008: 12; see also Putnam, 2000). In the context of war, conflict and human rights abuses, the significance and implications of fractured and damaged relationships are most often located within broader discussions about transitional justice and/or peacebuilding (Kent, 2011: 442; Neufeldt, 2014: 433). However, these 'harmed' relationships are also highly relevant for thinking about resilience. By extension, broken and ruptured connectivities, which highlight fragmentation and can be understood as lost or diminished resources, have potential implications for how individuals deal with adversity.

It is impossible to discuss all of the broken and ruptured connectivities that interviewees in BiH directly or more indirectly spoke about – and which were linked not only to CRSV but also to the war more generally. The next three sections focus on three broken and ruptured connectivities that were particularly prominent in the Bosnian interview data, the first two of which were coded under the theme *'It isn't there anymore': Connectivities lost.*

Broken and Ruptured Connectivities: Community Relationships

During her anthropological fieldwork undertaken before the Bosnian war, Bringa (1995: 3) experienced a more complex and nuanced reality than depictions of BiH as 'the ideal example of a harmonious and tolerant multicultural society, where people did not classify each other in terms of "Serb", "Muslims", or "Croat"'. What she found was 'both coexistence and conflict, tolerance and prejudice, suspicion and friendship' (Bringa, 1995: 3; see also Hayden, 1996: 741). It is essential, therefore, not to romanticise everyday life in pre-war BiH. Nevertheless, what strongly emerged from the data was that community

Connectivity Stories of Resilience in Bosnia-Herzegovina   137

relations had fundamentally changed as a legacy of the war. While this itself is an unremarkable finding, it does point to the need for greater attention and priority to be given – particularly within the fields of peacebuilding and transitional justice – to aspects of community relations beyond just reconciliation and peaceful co-existence.

First, interviewees' communities had demographically changed as a result of the war – an illustration of how 'communities are never static in their capacities or membership; rather, they are in a constant state of emergence and transformation over time' (Barrios, 2014: 331). A Croat interviewee, for example, maintained that 'Well, my main difficulty is that now just a small number of people live in XXX [her town]. There is a deficit of inhabitants. . . . Those who stayed, well, they are elderly people. At the age of 63, I belong to the younger population'. Lamenting the fact that many of her pre-war friends had left the town, she further underlined: 'Well, the war left its marks. It disrupted our lives, our everyday living and normal life' (interview, BiH, 30 January 2019).

Second, some interviewees talked about how the people in their communities had changed because of the war and their own personal experiences. Reflecting on the fact that the men in his community had been taken to camps where they had suffered multiple human rights violations, a Bosniak interviewee maintained:

> Everyone has a code [meaning post-traumatic stress disorder]. They're not. . . . Well, half of them are not normal. . . . More than half are not normal. Well, and we are here mostly from the camps. We are the majority, we have returned. . . . It is not, like. . . . Not like it was before, prewar. . . . Everything is, like, everyone is on their own, just [out] for their own interests.
>
> (interview, BiH, 10 April 2019)

Third, some interviewees had completely lost their communities. One of them was raped by fellow Croats who were her neighbours. Her 'crime' was that she had married a Serb man. She insisted that she could never go back to her prewar town; 'If we [she and her family] were to return there now, it would all be different. It wouldn't. . . . Simply, there is no more life there to live' (interview, BiH, 19 March 2019). For her part, a Bosniak interviewee talked about living prior to the Bosnian war in an area of what is now *Republika Srpska* (RS). She had never wanted to return there – it held too many bad memories for her – but she also did not feel welcome in the town where she and her family were now living in the BiH Federation. In her words, 'We thought, when we arrived from the Serb territories, that we would be welcomed with full hearts, but you saw immediately the rejection and. . . . Even today, they [referring to her neighbours] say "refugees"'[4] (interview, BiH, 3 February 2019). In other words, she was disconnected from her pre-war community, yet also felt that she had not connected with – or been fully accepted by – her new community.

138 Connectivity Stories of Resilience in Bosnia-Herzegovina

These findings resonate with other studies that have pointed to changed community dynamics (including intra-ethnic dynamics) and neighbourly relations in post-war BiH (see, e.g., Henig, 2012; Lofranco, 2017; Sorabji, 2008). What some of the interviewees in the present research also spoke about, however, was how their own personal experiences – specifically linked to CRSV – had further altered their relationships with the community and created additional breakages and ruptures. Relatively few of them spoke about directly experiencing stigma, which was in striking contrast to the Ugandan interviewees – almost all of whom had faced (and in some cases continued to face) stigma from their families and/or communities (see Chapter 7). More commonly, what some of the Bosnian interviewees expressed was a general feeling that people in the community looked at them or treated them differently because of what they had gone through. When asked what factors had made it difficult for her to rebuild or start to rebuild her life, a Serb interviewee immediately answered: 'Lack of understanding in the community. The community does not, not, not accept this and thinks we did this to ourselves' (interview, BiH, 19 February 2019). A Bosniak interviewee, even though she was now living in a large city that afforded her anonymity, talked about being 'marked' and explained: 'I have the feeling that it can be seen somewhere, as though everyone else, perhaps, even knows about it' (interview, BiH, 3 May 2019).

These various examples of broken and ruptured connectivities are important because community (in the sense of one's neighbours, one's village, etc.) is potentially a resource that supports resilience. The Adult Resilience Measure (ARM; Resilience Research Centre, 2016) – which was discussed in Chapter 3 and measures an individual's protective resources – includes several statements about community (e.g., 'I think it is important to support my community' and 'I feel I belong in my community'). It is interesting to note that in the quantitative phase of this research, Bosnian participants scored lower on the contextual sub-scale of the ARM – the part that includes these community-based questions – than the Colombian and Ugandan participants, as determined by a one-way ANOVA (F(2,445) = 111.923, $p = .026$).[5]

Broken and Ruptured Connectivities: Social Interactions

Bosnian interviewees frequently talked about some of the ways that the emotional and psychological legacies of their experiences had directly affected their interactions with their social ecologies. They spoke most about fear and loss of trust. One of the Bosniak interviewees was living close to Sarajevo when the war broke out and she was raped in May 1992. Thereafter, she returned to her town, which was under the control of the Croatian Defence Council (HVO). Although she did not personally have any bad experiences with the HVO, she felt relieved when her 'own' army – the Army of BiH (ABiH) – entered the town. In her words, 'I thought that maybe this, that this was perhaps an honest army. Serbs raped me.

Croats, well, attacked the village up there. Then I somehow thought, perhaps, that the Bosnian army was a tiny straw of salvation'. She proceeded to explain how soldiers from the ABiH entered and 'looted' Bosniak homes, taking with them whatever they wanted – including food. Reflecting on how this affected her, the interviewee explained: 'Everything was then. . . . All my illusions, all some. . . . Everything went down the drain. You know? Then I became a person who no longer trusted anyone or anything' (interview, BiH, 29 January 2019).

It was significant that the interviewee recounted this story in response to the question 'Are there any parts of your war story which are important to you and which you are never asked about?' More than 20 years after the war ended, BiH remains a fragmented society; 'ethnic divisions have become institutionalized in many sectors' (Simonsen, 2005: 302) and competing ethno-narratives continue to prevail (Mazzucchelli, 2021: 132). In this climate, there is little space for discussion or acknowledgement of crimes and wrongdoings committed by one's 'own' side. At the same time, the interviewee's strong sense of fear and mistrust meant that for years she had never spoken about the sexual violence she suffered; she had first made contact with a non-governmental organisation (NGO) only the previous year. What she repeatedly articulated was a sense of needing to rely on herself. In her words, 'And then you go through life, you fight alone'. While self-reliance might itself be seen as an expression of resilience, the circumstances in which it arises are highly relevant (see Krause and Schmidt, 2020). What stood out in the case of this interviewee, who was 61 years old and lived alone, was the fact that in many respects she had withdrawn from a society that she no longer trusted. It is also noteworthy that of the 126 participants in the total BiH sample, this interviewee had the lowest ARM score (67 out of a possible 140).

Another Bosniak interviewee also accentuated her loss of trust in others. This was not only linked to her war experiences, but also to an incident that had occurred after the war. She had gone to an NGO and had agreed to be interviewed, but not to have her face shown. She claimed, however, that part of the interview subsequently appeared on social media. This interviewee, moreover – who was one of the youngest (aged 42) in the BiH sample – used the word 'fear' 12 times and the word 'afraid' eight times. Such feelings had contributed to a sense of broken and ruptured connections (reflected, for example, in her statement 'No one understands me. Simply no one'); and they were linked to another significant broken connectivity in her life, namely the loss of her father and older sister. The latter had never been found and this was something that the interviewee repeatedly talked about. She suspected who was involved in her sister's disappearance – two Serb soldiers from the town where the interviewee's family had lived up until the war – but said that she had always been too afraid to make a statement. In her words: 'You maybe know what the forests around XXX [her pre-war town] are like. I sometimes go up there, to my mother's grave, to our house. They [the suspected perpetrators] can wait for me' (interview, BiH, 3 February 2019). This interviewee, like the previous interviewee, had a very low ARM score (78) – the fourth lowest within the BiH sample.

It is also important in the context of this discussion to mention the feelings of shame that some interviewees articulated, further affecting their interactions with others. Such feelings reflect, at least in part, broader socio-cultural influences. However, they do not support one-sided claims (see, e.g., Gutman, 1994: x; Healey, 1995: 339) that CRSV had more serious consequences for Bosniak women than for anyone else.[6] Such arguments simplify what it means to be a woman – and in particular a Bosniak woman – in Bosnian society (Majstorović, 2011: 277). The bigger point is that there were interviewees from all three ethnic groups – women and men – who spoke about shame. Moreover, demographic factors played a role in whether they did so, as the following two examples illustrate – both of them involving Croat interviewees.

One of these women lived with her family in a remote mountain village, close to the place where she was born in 1951. She had primary school education and frequently talked about the importance of faith. When asked how the sexual violence that she suffered during the Bosnian war had affected her life and relationships, she said simply 'Badly'. It was a topic that she did not wish to, or was not able to, speak about. Earlier in the interview, and referring to her family, she explained: 'They were always asking, but you cannot say everything. It [the fact that she was raped] is a disgrace, you can't say everything. This will go to the grave with me. It is my obligation to carry it around' (interview, BiH, 21 May 2019).

Another Croat interviewee resided several kilometres away in the nearest town. Born in 1955, she lived by herself (but had family close by) and had studied at university. Rather than carry the 'burden' of the past alone, she had spoken about it publicly and stressed that 'I see it as one notch in my life'. Her experiences during the war had ended a long-term relationship (a broken connectivity in her life) that she described as 'a great love', and she had never had another romantic relationship since then. Overall, however, she did not articulate any feelings of shame and indeed she expressed – perhaps linked to her education and to the job that she had done prior to retiring (which had involved managing and supervising mainly men) – a sense of having ultimately got the upper hand. Not only had she testified against her perpetrators in court, but she also insisted that their attempts to humiliate her had failed. Moreover, rather than simply talk about what they had done to her life, she reversed this and reflected on how the crimes that they committed might have affected their own lives. In her words: 'Sometimes I wish I knew about their lives. Were they able to live normal lives after everything? Are they marked, how do they bear this? Is it worse for them or for me?' (interview, BiH, 30 January 2019).

Broken and Ruptured Connectivities: Health

Bosnian interviewees frequently stressed the importance of health. They also implicitly discussed it as a lost or diminished resource within their lives – an illustration of how 'chronic stress can create allostatic load or "wear and tear" on the body caused by continued activation of multiple stress response systems' (Afifi et al., 2016: 666). As a Bosniak interviewee insisted: 'I had been healthy until I survived that [referring to the 15 months he spent in detention in several different camps in both BiH and Serbia], both mentally and physically'. This 55-year-old man said very little about what he endured in these camps, but he recalled: 'Not for a minute could you feel that you were free, feel alive. You were always watching who was coming, wondering when they will kill you, will they kill you' (interview, BiH, 10 April 2019).

One of the Serb interviewees, similarly, strongly articulated a sense of ruptured health and stressed: 'I was healthy until the war, until . . .'. She too had spent time in a camp, run by the paramilitary Croatian Defence Forces (HOS; see Stiglmayer, 1994: 142); and she linked her experiences to her later diagnosis of breast cancer – for which she underwent surgery in 2007 when she was 51. It was interesting that she partly blamed herself for both the sexual violence ('The worst thing is when you criticise yourself for not doing something that you could have done') and the cancer ('I did not go to the doctor on time'). She had not worked since her surgery, which had affected her family's economic 'health'. In her words, 'health is everything, and when you are healthy you will surely earn money. But when you fall ill, it is hard, really hard' (interview, BiH, 3 July 2019). Furthermore, her connectivity with the city where she lived before the war had been ruptured; she was now internally displaced in a small town where employment opportunities were limited.

A male Serb interviewee effectively described how his own health issues – which he did not attribute directly to the Bosnian war – had ruptured one of the supportive and sustaining connectivities in his life that had helped him to deal with what he went through in a camp. This man, who was about to turn 60, had worked for many years in the building trade and explained that 'while I did some physical work, I felt much better and in a better mood and healthier, and more economically useful and I was smiling then'. He now had several health problems – including a blood coagulation disorder – that meant he had not worked for the last year. This, he said, had affected him emotionally and socially; 'I often avoid company. I often avoid loud noise and everything. It bothers me' (interview, BiH, 2 July 2019).

Some of the many potential health-related consequences of CRSV have been explored within extant scholarship (see, e.g., Akinsulure-Smith, 2014; Dossa et al., 2015; Gilmore and McEvoy, 2021). Health is also a prominent thematic in many discussions about CRSV, particularly at the international policy level (International Committee of the Red Cross [ICRC], 2016; UN Secretary-General, 2019: para. 21; World Health Organization [WHO], 2012: 2). When interviewees talked about health, however, they implicitly illustrated the concept of health ecology, 'a more holistic idea of health' (Collins, 2001: 238). In various ways – and as reflected in the theme *'The problem of ill health is there': Health connectivities and everyday stressors* – the data highlighted that interviewees' wider social ecologies, and more particularly significant stressors within these ecologies, could adversely affect their own individual health (see, e.g., Clark, 2022a; Panter-Brick et al., 2014: 325). This is also consistent with the WHO's (n.d.) definition of health as 'a state of complete physical, mental and social well-being and not merely the absence of disease or infirmity'.

Several interviewees talked about health issues within their families. One of the Bosniak interviewees had an ARM score of 121 when she first completed the study questionnaire, putting her in quartile 3 (the second highest group of ARM scores). When I interviewed her eight months later and re-ran the ARM section of the questionnaire,[7] her score dropped to 94 (quartile 1). Asked whether anything significant (such as a bereavement or relationship breakup) had happened in her life during the interim period, she explained that her elderly mother, who had multiple health issues including epilepsy and diabetes, had suffered a serious seizure two months earlier. The stress of this, the interviewee explained, had taken a toll on her own health; indeed, she looked drained and was noticeably thinner. Her living conditions, another aspect of her social ecology, added to the challenges that she faced in caring for her mother and brother (who had special needs), while also working part-time as a cleaner. She was internally displaced from her home in RS and living in a house that belonged to her mother-in-law (the interviewee was currently separated), but the property was old, in poor condition and did not have a fully functional bathroom (interview, BiH, 2 June 2019).

More broadly, many interviewees pointed to systemic 'health' issues within their environments – from high unemployment[8] and political corruption (Office of the High Representative, 2020) to excessive bureaucratisation (Belloni, 2009: 359) and institutional failings (Bargués and Morillas, 2021: 1328). These examples of 'ill health' further affected interviewees' own health and wellbeing. One of the Serbs, for example, described financial issues as her biggest worry. She did not have a regular job, but she worked when she could as a cleaner.[9] Her husband, a disabled war veteran, could not work and his pension – which they largely relied on – was inadequate.[10] She explained that after they moved to the town where they were currently living in RS, her husband stopped receiving his disability pension. It had taken almost a year to get it reinstated (which had involved navigating multiple layers of bureaucracy), during which time the family had got into debt. The interviewee seemed exhausted mentally and insisted that 'The state is making everything more difficult' (interview, BiH, 6 March 2019).

The broken and ruptured connectivities explored in this section and the previous two do not directly answer the question of how Bosnian interviewees – in interaction with their social ecologies – demonstrated resilience in their everyday lives. What they do provide is an important contextual backdrop, highlighting some of the ways that interviewees' experiences affected which resources they could draw upon. Hobfoll's (2014: 22) Conservation of Resources (COR) theory predicts that 'trauma response will occur when there is major loss of fundamental resources and where this loss occurs rapidly'. Yet, also central to COR is the idea that individuals seek to conserve what resources they have, a process that Hobfoll (2014: 22) refers to as 'building and maintaining "resource caravans"'.

Discussions about CRSV give little attention to individuals' 'resource caravans' – except, implicitly, in the sense of what is missing from them. My intention is not to detract from the importance of victims-/survivors' needs and rights, and nor is it to suggest that all of these women and men have well-resourced 'caravans'. Hobfoll's (2011: 118) work accentuates the relevance of wider social ecologies in 'creating passageways in which resources are supplied, protected, shared, fostered, and pooled'. The dimensions of these 'passageways' necessarily vary hugely in different societies and environments. The key point, however, is that while interviewees in BiH (and in Colombia and Uganda) had suffered many broken and ruptured connectivities, they also frequently spoke about some of the various resources (connectivities) in their lives that were helping them to deal with their experiences of violence and adversity. The next two sections discuss some of these supportive and sustaining connectivities.

Family-Related Supportive and Sustaining Connectivities

Extant scholarship on resilience has extensively explored the 'buffering effects' (Keyes, 2004: 224) of different protective resources (or protective factors/ processes) that potentially limit or offset the impact of shocks and stressors. Relationships – including with family, with teachers, with peers and with community – constitute the core of these protective resources (Darnhofer et al., 2016; Jordan, 2010; Walsh, 2012). Indeed, according to Hartling (2008: 53), 'resilience is all about relationships'.

Scholars writing about CRSV have examined and discussed the significance, inter alia, of survivors' groups and social networks (see, e.g., Edström et al., 2016; Koegler et al., 2019; Schulz and Ngomokwe, 2021). Although not necessarily using terms such as protective resources or social connectedness, such research has demonstrated that relationships and solidarities can constitute valuable sources of support for male and female victims-/survivors. Overall, however, relational resources – beyond survivors' (and survivor-led) groups and networks – remain under-explored in research and policy discussions about CRSV (Clark, 2021).

Both in BiH and in the other two countries, the idea of supportive and sustaining connectivities – encompassed in the theme *'With them I get through it': Relational connectivities* – was very prominent. This research uses the terminology of connectivities, rather than resources, to better reflect some of the deep emotional and sentient dimensions of the relationships that interviewees in all three countries discussed. The supportive and sustaining connectivities that Bosnian interviewees spoke most about centred on spouses/partners, family and children. It is noteworthy that there was a statistically significant difference – as

144 Connectivity Stories of Resilience in Bosnia-Herzegovina

determined by a one-way ANOVA (F(2,446) = 27.709, p = .000) – between the mean scores for each country on the relational sub-scale of the ARM. This includes statements such as 'My family has usually supported me through life' and 'I talk to my family/partner about how I feel' (Resilience Research Centre, 2016). Bosnian participants overall scored highest on this sub-scale.[11]

Spouses/Partners

Scholars have written about some of the ways that the Bosnian war negatively affected family relationships and dynamics (Jurkovic et al., 2005; Klarić et al., 2011; Nelson, 2003). Similarly, scholars have discussed some of the ways that sexual violence committed during the Bosnian war adversely affected the relationships between victims-/survivors and their families, including their spouses. Hansen (2000: 64) has referred to 'the fact that raped Bosnian women have been divorced by their husbands, shunned by their society and in some cases killed'. Writing about wartime rape more broadly and not specifically about BiH, Sackellares (2005: 140) has further generalised that 'Women are either rejected by their husbands, rendered physically unable to bear children or are forced to bear the enemy nation's children'.

Some of the Bosnian interviewees in this research themselves spoke about marital difficulties due to their war experiences. A male Bosniak interviewee blamed the sexual violence that he suffered for the break-up of his marriage ('My life and marriage were destroyed'; interview, BiH, 4 March 2019). One of the Croat interviewees, whose husband spent several months at a time working abroad, explained that she no longer had any sort of relationship with him because he blamed her for being raped. She had testified in court a couple of years earlier and emphasised: 'I went because of this, to prove to you [her husband] that I did not go voluntarily [with the man who raped her]. It was not my own will. I went to court to prove to you, so you cannot mistreat and harass me about this anymore' (interview, BiH, 19 March 2019). This second example accentuates the important point – which was also made in Chapter 2 – that connectivity is not always something positive. In the context of sexual and gender-based violence (SGBV), connectivities can be a significant source of stress or harm; domestic violence and community stigmatisation are just two examples. Furthermore, the dynamic nature of connectivities can result in considerable oscillations and variations in their effects (Afifi et al., 2016: 663).

It was striking, however, that Bosnian interviewees spoke significantly less about marital/relationship issues than the Colombian and Ugandan interviewees. Fourteen of the total 21 Bosnian interviewees were married and one was living with her partner. Of these, nine talked about their spouse/partner as an important source of support in their lives (see also Skjelsbaek, 2006: 386). One of the Serb interviewees explained that her husband had been her friend for 11 years before they married. They had studied together at university (only this interviewee and one other had been to university) and married in 1993.

Connectivity Stories of Resilience in Bosnia-Herzegovina 145

She insisted that 'he brought me back to life', adding that without him, 'God knows how I would have ended up. I mean, I would have probably isolated myself from the rest of the world'. Her husband, she underlined, had never once blamed her for what she went through, and she was therefore able to talk to him without fear of being judged. In her words, 'We focused on surviving and moving on, and it has been ongoing for 26 years of marriage' (interview, BiH, 20 February 2019).

One of the Bosniak interviewees was living with her partner of 15 years and reflected on how he was always there for her ('If I am not in a good mood, he goes out. When I need him, I call him and he is back'). She spoke about the moment she told him what had happened to her, expecting him to reject her, and how he reacted; 'He said: "You are so special to me, and now you are even more special"'. She continued:

> I then started opening up to him, talking. I know it was not easy on him, when I was telling him all this, but I was so ready then. He touched me so deeply. I, well, then I saw in him a very good friend.

This interviewee had experienced domestic violence from her former husband and had also suffered abuse from family members as a child. In contrast to the previous interviewee, whose relationship with her husband was very much a partnership of equals, this 51-year-old woman saw her partner (who was 22 years her senior) as someone who would protect her ('Safety. I would not give him up for anything in the world'). This man had also given her the 'true family' that she had never had; she looked at his two grown-up daughters and young granddaughter as her own (interview, BiH, 22 February 2019).

Wider Families and Children

Beyond simply spouses and partners, Bosnian interviewees frequently referred to supportive and sustaining connectivities with their families (including siblings, children and, in some cases, in-laws) more broadly. A small number spoke about financial support from their families. Primarily what they talked about, however, was non-material support, reflected in statements such as: 'Family, they supported me. With them I get through it'; 'My family were with me when it was the hardest. They looked after me and saved me'; 'My family, firstly, helped me not to fall, to rebound, not to fall into depression' and 'My life is within my family'. The significance of families – illustrating the larger point that 'A crisis can shatter family cohesion if members are unable to turn to one another' (Walsh, 2003: 10–11) – remains little discussed within extant scholarship on the Bosnian war and its aftermath. This is similarly true as regards children.

Chapter 1 provided an overview of how the field of resilience research has grown and developed. Children have always been a strong focus of resilience scholarship (Ungar, 2013: 11). Within research on CRSV, in contrast, children have received far less attention. When they are discussed, the emphasis is most commonly on children born of war (see, e.g., Baines and Oliveira, 2020; Carpenter, 2007; Denov and Piolanti, 2020). Under-explored within both bodies of literature is the idea that children – as a crucial part of individuals' social ecologies – can themselves potentially contribute to fostering resilience (Clark, 2022b; Zraly et al., 2013).

A recurring leitmotif within the Bosnian data was children (regardless of age) as a source of emotional support and strength. Interviewees, only four of whom were not mothers or fathers, gave many examples. Speaking about her two young children, a Serb interviewee maintained that 'they keep me alive. Without them, I think, I would have sunk long ago'. When asked to elaborate further on how they supported her, she answered: 'Well, with their love. They give me, well, something that is the most beautiful thing in the world' (interview, BiH, 19 February 2019). Discussing her three teenage daughters, a Bosniak interviewee explained that whenever they saw her upset, they tried to make it better; 'The children tell me that they are around me to make it easier for me when I need it'. Talking more about the relationship, this woman revealed: 'They hug me, smile at me, say: "Mum, you are the best mum"', and this is enough for me' (interview, BiH, 31 January 2019).

Zraly et al.'s (2013) research comprehensively examines the relationship between motherhood and resilience, drawing on interviews with 63 genocide-rape survivors in Rwanda. In BiH, however, the significance of children as a potential support for resilience extended beyond motherhood. First, all five male interviewees (four Bosniaks and one Serb) spoke about what their children gave them emotionally. One of them had a daughter who was then 2-and-a-half years old and insisted that: 'She is great therapy for me. Her mischief and everything. She sometimes, as they say, takes it too far, but that doesn't matter' (interview, BiH, 11 February 2019). Another Bosniak interviewee was living alone with his 18-year-old son and described him as 'a friend and everything I have'. The two of them worked together (in fruit growing) and the interviewee, speaking directly to the idea of connectivity, stated: 'I see him giving me support. He is connected to me' (interview, BiH, 4 March 2019).

Second, and reflecting the fact that the Bosnian interviewees overall were older than the Colombian and Ugandan interviewees (see Chapter 3, Table 3.1), four of them also spoke about their grandchildren as crucial supports in their lives. One of the Serb interviewees regularly looked after her 6-year-old granddaughter and her face lit up every time that she mentioned her. She was waiting for the little girl to return from school and proudly pointed to some of the latter's drawings displayed on the walls of the lounge where we carried out the interview. Her granddaughter was her priority now, the interviewee explained, and further added that:

The two of us are inseparable. We have not been together today and I can't wait for her to come over. Well, so, this is what fills me up and what I like the most. I relax and forget everything. I go down into her little world.

(interview, BiH, 6 March 2019)

A Croat interviewee, referring to her two grandchildren aged 2 and 6, high-lighted that 'To me, they are. . . . They give me the best happiness, hope. And even when I am saddest, they cheer me up' (interview, BiH, 21 May 2019). As we spoke, the youngest child lay asleep on the sofa next to her grandmother, who rocked her gently throughout the interview.

In their aforementioned research in Rwanda, Zraly et al. (2013: 424) found that 'Being a mother and mothering gave some genocide-rape survivors a life purpose'. Similarly, Bosnian interviewees frequently spoke about their children (or grandchildren) as an important factor that motivated them to get on with their lives and to go forward. Expressing this very literally, a male Bosniak interviewee described his wife and two children as 'the engine that drives me through life' (interview, BiH, 10 April 2019). A female Bosniak interviewee with three children insisted that 'All this has strengthened me. . . . I just think of my children. I have to. I think I have to protect them, so that tomorrow they do not experience what I did' (interview, BiH, 3 February 2019). Several inter-viewees also spoke about 'fighting' for their children (e.g., 'It is for them that I have to be a fighter'; 'I fight, I mean, for my child'; 'I fight, I try to provide for them'; 'I fight for them in a positive sense. I want to always stand behind my children in the future').

It is important to acknowledge that in some cases, children were also a source of stress and worry. Interviewees expressed fears and concerns, inter alia, about their children's futures (would they find jobs, would they have good opportunities in their lives?); and in three cases, the interviewees' children had faced serious health issues. Overall, however, the idea of children (and grandchildren) constituting fun-damental supportive and sustaining connectivities in the interviewees' lives was very salient. While little attention has been given to children in this regard, as previously noted, there is growing research on the concept of family resilience.

According to Walsh (2021: 256), family resilience 'refers to the capacity of the family, as a functional system, to withstand and rebound from adversity' (see also Black and Lobo, 2008). This research is not about family resilience and the interview guide did not include any questions about how interviewees' families had dealt with the shocks and stressors of war or more recent adversities. What Walsh (2003: 10) also argues, however, is that 'Connectedness, or cohesion, is essential for effective family functioning', and this sense of family connected-ness came through very strongly in many of the interviews. Moreover, while interviewees had benefitted from crucial family support, in some ways they had also contributed to their families' resilience, through their determination to get on with life and to fight for their children and their futures.

Other Supportive and Sustaining Connectivities

Besides family-related connectivities, interviewees in BiH also spoke about many other supportive and sustaining connectivities in their lives. While there is not space to discuss all of them, two in particular stood out – relating to the natural environment and health institutions respectively.

148 Connectivity Stories of Resilience in Bosnia-Herzegovina

The Natural Environment

Some interviewees expressed a sense of connectivity to the natural environment and were actively using the wider ecosystems around them to help deal with their experiences and with stressors in their lives. This is significant because 'people-environment relationships' (Stokols et al., 2013) have received little attention in discussions about the Bosnian war and its aftermath – and indeed in research on CRSV more broadly. One of the Bosniak interviewees spoke about her love of mountains and hiking. She explained: 'Well, I find comfort in hiking. I mean, this is where I feel best and I recharge my batteries and I heal, simply. Mountain, mountain, mountain. And then there are no problems, I forget about everything'. The various commitments that she had (her job, caring responsibilities) meant that she had little time for herself and for the things that she enjoyed, but she was a member of a hiking association.

The interviewee's sense of connectivity to place – illustrating Hess et al.'s (2008: 468) argument that 'places are nested collections of human experience, locations with which people and communities have particular affective relationships' – was also something that helped her. Her brother had fought in the ABiH and was in Srebrenica when the town, declared a 'safe area' in April 1993 by the UN Security Council, fell to the Army of RS (VRS) in July 1995. His time in the enclave, and the subsequent genocide that took place, led him to commit suicide. Every year, a peace march takes place in memory of those who perished in the genocide, following the same route taken by those who tried (successfully or unsuccessfully) to reach ABiH-controlled territory. Even though the interviewee's brother was not actually killed in Srebrenica, she talked about why it was important to her to take part in the peace march and how it rejuvenated her. In her own words:

> With the fall of Srebrenica, he [her late brother] passed along that road. And this road draws me to it because I have a feeling, like, that I will see him. You walk day in and day out and this is something that carries you, holds you up and so on. When I come back, I mean, from there, I am a different person. I am functional, I do more work, nothing is hard and nothing is unpleasant. It is easier to do everything. Well, almost. The things I have delayed, I do them all with success after that.
>
> (interview, BiH, 2 June 2019)

A male Bosniak interviewee spoke about the significance in his life of a local lake. When asked how he deals with stress and who or what he turns to, he explained: 'I go alone somewhere. I take the boat, go down along the lake. I also like to drink, and I sit and find solitude and that's it. Until it goes away a bit, and, you know, that's it'. Sometimes friends would come and join him at the lake, but he preferred to be there alone and would often stay until midnight. After his release from the various camps in which he was held for several months in 1992, he briefly lived in another part of BiH (and what had helped him there, he recalled, was walking in woods), but the lake drew him back home ('I am tied to this place'). The lake, he stressed, was a crucial support in his life and something to which he was deeply connected. As he expressed it:

> In fact, the water, water is to me . . . I possibly would not have returned here ever, but it is my birthplace and this lake that I have had since I was a child. . . . I was born in the lake. This is something that keeps me going here.

It was a place where he could 'rest mentally' and not have to think about problems. 'This is it', he said simply. 'My life, here' (interview, BiH, 10 April 2019).

There are important legacies of the Bosnian war that can impede the development of these social-ecological connectivities. Just one example is the fact that there are still a large number of unexploded landmines in the country, particularly in areas close to former front lines. Indeed, 'Bosnia-Herzegovina remains one of the most landmine-contaminated countries in all of Europe, with 1,218.50 km2 or 2.4% of the country's total area still suspected of contamination' (Ryken et al., 2017: 2689). Every year, fatal accidents occur (ICRC, 2017). Furthermore, some interviewees had little opportunity – due to where they lived, health issues or other factors – to form connectivities with the natural environment and actively use them. In those cases where interviewees had done so, however, as in the two previous examples, the data illustrated Hatala et al.'s (2020) framing of resilience as 'a dynamic and contextual process in dialogue with local worlds and environments'.

Health Services and Providers

A final connectivity that must be mentioned relates to health services and providers. This was something that interviewees in all three countries spoke about, but there were some key differences. In Uganda, relatively few of the interviewees had received psychosocial support. In Colombia, interviewees primarily accessed these services through victims' associations and women's (including women-led) organisations. In BiH, similarly, some of the interviewees had received/were receiving therapy and counselling through their contacts with local NGOs, although it was striking that none of the Serb interviewees had done so (reflecting the fact that the majority of NGOs working on the issue of CRSV focus on Bosniak – and to a lesser extent Croat – victims-/survivors).

In contrast to interviewees in the other two countries, some of the Bosnians also had access to a psychologist, psychiatrist or neuro-psychiatrist in a state-run health institution, such as a local hospital or health centre. A female Bosniak interviewee living in a large city explained: 'I have been in treatment for many years. . . . I have my psychiatrist' (interview, BiH, 31 January 2019). A Serb interviewee disclosed that she goes to see a psychiatrist once a month.

This was her outlet because at home, she could not talk to her husband (who did not know that she had been raped) about her feelings. In her words, 'You take the pill [referring to an anti-depressant or a sedative], swallow and keep quiet' (interview, BiH, 7 June 2019). In total, almost half of the interviewees (ten out of 21, including four of the five male interviewees)[12] talked about having support – now or previously – from a mental health professional.

Funk and Berry (2020: 5–6) maintain that 'Despite the intervention of the international community and investments in postwar peacebuilding, there has been no great interest in individual mental health or collective post-traumatic conditions in Bosnia and Herzegovina'. This is arguably only partly true, and two important observations should be highlighted. The first is that there exists in BiH a widespread use of trauma discourse, linked to what Pupavac (2004: 378) has called 'the ascendancy of the international therapeutic paradigm'. Ten of the Bosnian interviewees – in contrast to only four of the Colombian interviewees and none of the Ugandan interviewees – spoke about trauma (e.g., 'It is difficult to live with the trauma'; 'This is what I have the most difficulties with, the traumas'; 'I am aware that I have to live with it, with all my traumas'; 'I guess the trauma affects me'). All of them, moreover, were in contact with or had received support from NGOs which themselves promote a strong trauma narrative (Clark, 2019). The important point – which is not to downplay what interviewees had gone through – is that there has been a strong emphasis on the 'collective post-traumatic conditions in Bosnia and Herzegovina' to which Funk and Berry (2020: 4) refer. People have been 'encouraged' to see themselves as traumatised and to turn to pills as a way of coping with life's challenges (Knežević, 2017).

The second observation is that although several of the interviewees had access to mental health professionals who constituted significant supportive and sustaining connectivities in their lives, many of them said that their appointments were typically short and usually ended with them being given more tablets and pills to take. I was left wondering, thus, consistent with Funk and Berry's aforementioned argument, how much attention was actually being given to their individual mental health. In a heavily trauma-focused culture, moreover, there is little space for these women and men to be something *other than* victims (the term survivors is rarely used in BiH) of sexual violence (Clark, 2019: 255). To cite Berry (2018: 129), '"Rape victim" became their foremost identity in the eyes of the West and its humanitarian aid interlocutors'. This, in turn, can encourage reliance on health professionals and reinforce medicalised ways of dealing with the past (Summerfield, 1999: 1456).

Beyond simply demonstrating that 'Social networks matter' (Putnam and Goss, 2002: 6), this section and the previous one have mapped out some of the supportive and sustaining connectivities that Bosnian interviewees were actively utilising within their social ecologies to help rebuild their lives. To reiterate an earlier point, not only has extant scholarship on CRSV – both in the case of BiH and more broadly – given relatively little attention to these connectivities, but also, relatedly, international political discourse surrounding CRSV has consistently put much more weight on what victims-/survivors want, need and lack, rather than on what they *have* – and on how these connectivities might themselves be supported or strengthened.

New Connectivities: Connecting the Dots

It will be recalled from Chapter 2 that this research links new connectivities to 'the dynamic nature of connectivity' (Reichert et al., 2021: 580) that is accentuated within ecology literature. To be clear, the research is not reducing the complexities of resilience, and the many forms that it can take, to the simple idea of building and forging new connectivities. However, it is significant that interviewees in all three countries spoke, directly and indirectly, about making and developing connectivities (including with themselves and with their wider social ecologies). Moreover, to the extent that these processes of connecting or reconnecting were helping some interviewees to deal with their experiences, they can be viewed as potential expressions of resilience. This section discusses the first of three themes relating to the new connectivities component of the book's conceptual framework.

'Why Did This Have to Be': Making Connections and Finding Meaning

According to Pipher (2002: 61), 'To live is to suffer. To survive is to find meaning in suffering'. Extant research on CRSV has given little attention to the meanings that victims-/survivors attach to their experiences (Gray et al., 2020: 198). This is very relevant because as Dolan et al. (2020: 1153) underline, 'frames of understanding CRSV matter in survivors' attempts to find ways to rebuild their everyday lives and selves in the aftermath of violence through collective and individual meaning-making'. More directly, there is potentially an important relationship between meaning-making and resilience (Park, 2016; Theron and Theron, 2014; Walsh, 2020). Horstman (2019: 1151), for example, argues that resilience 'is a dynamic, changing, and evolving process' which necessitates 'a certain amount of "narrative openness," wherein individuals can re-story their experience, which helps them to come to more fruitful conclusions about the experience' (see also Park, 2016). The very idea of new connectivities that runs through this chapter's final sections can be viewed, to some extent, as a 're-storying' process. For interviewees in all three countries, establishing these new connectivities was partly about trying to create something positive out of negative and deeply painful experiences. Specifically with regards to meaning-making processes, however, the linkage with 're-storying' was often quite limited, and this was certainly the case in BiH.

The interview guide used in this research (see Appendix 1) did not include any questions about meaning-making. Nevertheless, the qualitative data provided many insights, directly and indirectly, into some of the meanings that interviewees ascribed to their experiences. The discussion that follows focuses on several particular aspects of meaning-making that emerged from the Bosnian data. It also reflects on what these meaning-making processes potentially tell us about interviewees' broader social-ecological environments – and some of the 'gaps' and deficits within them.

Just over half of the Bosnian interviewees attributed their war experiences and the suffering that they went through to their ethnicity, insisting that this made others hate them or discriminate against them. Interestingly, however, it was also the case that compared to interviewees in Colombia and Uganda, more Bosnian interviewees engaged in self-blame. As one illustration, the only Albanian interviewee in the sample blamed her good looks. Asked whether the fact of being a woman had affected how she dealt with problems and adversities in life, she confided:

> I don't know whether this is the answer to your question, but I hated myself a bit. I hated the way I look. I hated that I attracted men. And I have always, well, hated my looks. And now, if you'd believe me, when I get up in the morning and I wash my face, there are days when I don't even look at myself in the mirror. I don't like looking at myself in the mirror. And I have often hated my looks.
>
> (interview, BiH, 20 March 2019)

This very striking woman, now in her 60s, was the only interviewee who blamed her physical appearance for what had happened to her. Others blamed themselves, inter alia, for decisions that they had made (why did they stay, why did they not go somewhere else?), and one of the Serb interviewees voiced an inner conflict that she was having with herself. In her own words:

> I am the worst woman for letting this happen to me. But I was powerless. I hated myself. Hated . . . I am disgusting. And then, again, I say: 'Well, what can I do? What happened, happened. Move on. Go on, I mean, we have to live'. But I have said to myself not once but a million times: 'I hate you!' To myself: 'Woman, I hate you!' It's just . . . I have those periods.
>
> (interview, BiH, 7 June 2019)

This quotation powerfully captures the phenomenon of 'competing plotlines storytelling' – which includes 'competing emotional responses or lines of thinking in relation to a specific event or narrative context' (Boritz et al., 2014: 597). Further illustrative of such story-telling was the alternating dynamic in some of the interviews between blaming one's ethnicity and blaming oneself. One of the factors that had contributed to some interviewees blaming themselves was judgement from others. Of the eight interviewees (seven women and one man) who articulated feelings of self-blame, six spoke about hearing comments such as 'Ah, well, she could have evaded that', or 'She herself wanted to go with them [with the rapists], she seduced them'. Interviewees' self-blame and some of the reactions that had helped to fuelled it also reflected broader socio-cultural influences. Female interviewees, for example, maintained, inter alia, that 'Here, in the Balkans, women are not appreciated. They are worth less than men'; 'Here, a woman should just keep quiet'; 'If we say anything, everyone will say that it was our fault. We are blamed. We should have been better, we provoked it'. Kostovicova et al. (2020: 257), similarly, argue that 'A woman [in BiH] is commonly seen as responsible for the very violence committed against her . . . which amnesties men and state institutions from responsibility'.

At the same time, however, it is important not to make sweeping generalisations about the position of women in Bosnian society. As just one example, Majstorović (2011: 282) points out that 'Reality and daily life for women living in the rural and urban areas differ significantly especially when it comes to urban women with higher education'. Indeed, some of the interviewees spoke positively about being a woman, and a Serb interviewee – illustrating Majstorović's argument – particularly stood out in this regard. This 57-year-old woman, who was university educated, had a good job and lived very comfortably, opined: 'I have found fulfilment in all aspects of my life. Through my career. Through earnings. Through family. Through. . . . As a mother' (interview, BiH, 20 February 2019).

Unanswered Questions and the Wider Political Context in BiH

Interviewees' feelings of self-blame were not only the result of socio-cultural factors. I argue that such feelings also partly reflected the 'incompleteness' of individuals' meaning-making processes. Compared to interviewees in the other two countries, Bosnians had the most unanswered questions regarding their experiences, most of which had a 'why me?' focus (e.g., 'Why did I have to be a victim of war?' and 'What did I do to have all this, and this friend of mine, she . . . nothing happened to her?'). Some interviewees also had bigger questions about the war, why it happened and perpetrator motives (e.g., 'What is inside a human being to be able to think of such evil?' 'Why did you [the interviewee was imagining a conversation with the man who violated him] humiliate me like that, why did you do it, why?' 'What are those urges? Can someone talk you into it, pay you, talk you into doing this to a person you have never seen in your life before?').

These questions need to be situated in a context of ruptured meaning-making qua beliefs. A Serb interviewee, for example, revealed: 'I found myself in this, in some. . . . How to say it? A turning point. The things I believed in, suddenly, overnight, all collapsed' (interview, BiH, 3 July 2019). Similarly, a Croat interviewee who was raped by two ABiH soldiers recalled a conversation that she subsequently had with her mother; '"You taught me one thing, some standards of behaviour, and something totally different happened. Someone comes from the street and does things as they please'" (interview, BiH, 30 January 2019). Such examples more broadly illustrate a rupturing of what Park (2016: 1235) calls 'global meaning', encompassing 'people's fundamental beliefs – about themselves, the world, their place in the world, and their sense of meaning and purpose – as well as their unique hierarchies of goals and values'. According to her meaning-making model, the degree of discrepancy between situational meaning (the meaning that an individual assigns to a stressful event) and global meaning shapes how a stressful event is experienced (Park, 2016: 1235). By asking so many questions, Bosnian interviewees were trying to make new connectivities that would give them much-needed answers and advance their meaning-making processes, thereby closing the gap between Park's situational and global meanings.

The wider political context in BiH, however, is arguably not supportive of meaning-making, which is an important part of transitional justice work (Cohen, 2020: 10; Gonzáles-Ayala et al., 2021: 185; Lykes and van der Merwe, 2017: 372). The central meta narrative about the war is an ethnic narrative (Halilovich, 2011: 44), and interviewees' unanswered questions and attempts to somehow 'connect the dots' illuminate the limitations of this narrative in giving them what they needed. Of course, in most cases the questions they asked will remain open precisely because there are no clear-cut answers, but the bigger point is that interviewees were 'reach[ing] for truths that lie beneath official narratives' (Cohen, 2020: 10).

Something else that stood out from the Bosnian interview data in relation to meaning-making was the frequent acknowledgement that 'I was not the only one'. Interestingly, this was one of the few codes where there was a clear correlation with ARM scores. Evidencing the important relationship between connectivity and resilience, none of the passages of text linked to this code came from interviewees in ARM quartile 1 (i.e., those with the lowest ARM scores). Moreover, even though the differences were quite small (reflecting the fact that the total number of interviewees was 21), it was interviewees in ARM quartile 4 (i.e., those with the highest ARM scores) who spoke most about not being the only one.

Some of the Colombian interviewees also talked about this. As will be discussed in detail in the next chapter, this awareness particularly came from their involvement in (or leadership of) women's organisations, NGOs or victims' associations, and from sharing their experiences with other women. In BiH, in contrast, this linkage was far less obvious, and only in one case did there appear to be a direct nexus between the interviewee's interactions with other victims-/survivors (in the context of an NGO that she herself led) and her recognition that 'I was not the only one. There were many of us' (interview, BiH, 7 June 2019). The bigger point is that while interviewees in Colombia frequently articulated a strong sense of solidarity with other victims-/survivors, based on shared experiences, rarely did the interviewees in BiH do so (although this is not to say that such solidarity does not exist at all; see, e.g., O'Reilly, 2017: 146).

Connectivity Stories of Resilience in Bosnia-Herzegovina 155

Part of the explanation lies in the aforementioned fact that BiH remains divided, which has contributed to fostering 'inter-group competitive victimhood' – meaning 'a group's motivation and consequent efforts to establish that it has suffered more than its adversaries' (Noor et al., 2012: 351). During one of the reflections workshops that took place in BiH in June 2021 (see Chapter 3), for example, the workshop convener (the NGO *Snaga Žene*) asked the participants (Bosniaks and one Croat) whether they would be willing to form a network with other women, including Serb women in RS. One of the participants was in favour of this. Another, however, asked: 'Why would we do that among ourselves when, according to the law,[13] the state should provide funding?' A third participant insisted:

> 'She' [a Serb woman] would never accept me and I would not accept her. In Brčko,[14] there are situations where they [Serbs] are making things up and lying. Nothing happened in Brčko, they stayed in Brčko and suddenly they were raped. By whom? Allegedly by Bosniaks. So, I could never accept her. I was present once at the time Ratko Mladić [the former commander of the VRS] was arrested [in May 2011], and Bosnian Serb women were there and they were saying, 'Why was he arrested? He wouldn't hurt a fly'. We can't be together. We can't be together because they have been brainwashed. They have been brainwashed that they are right, that they are just endangered, that we are nobody and nothing, that we do not exist, that we just need to be eliminated.
>
> (reflections workshop, BiH, 7 June 2021)

Bosnian NGOs, both for practical and in some cases political reasons, primarily work within their own entity, which means that victims-/survivors from different ethnic groups do not often have the opportunity to come together and exchange stories. This is another example of how the wider socio-political context in BiH potentially obstructs the building of new connectivities in the sense of cross-ethnic solidarities.[15] So, too, is the fact that victims-/survivors living in the BiH Federation and in RS do not have the same rights and entitlements – thereby illustrating how fundamental disagreements between the two entities have a 'paralysing effect on governance' (Borger, 2015) and on the development of state-level policies.

Victims-/survivors living in the BiH Federation have long been able – although the process is sometimes very protracted – to secure status as a 'civilian victim of war' and to thereby gain entitlement to a monthly social payment, half of which comes from the Federation and half from the cantonal governments (the BiH Federation is divided into ten cantons). The situation has been very different for those living in RS (see Clark, 2017: 177–184). In 2018, however, RS adopted a new law – the Law on Protection of War Torture Victims – which includes within its definition of victims of torture any individual who suffered rape or other forms of sexual violence during the Bosnian war. Even so, this new law does not accord the same level of entitlements as the equivalent law in the BiH Federation.[16]

New Connectivities: With Life

In their research with 32 individuals in Ireland who had experienced mental health issues, Kartalova-O'Doherty et al. (2012: 139) found that 'The participants' main concern was identified as striving to reconnect with life. The core category of recovery, representing the resolution of the main concern, was a gradual progression from disconnection from life to reconnection with life' (see also Jordan, 2010). This 'striving' was similarly a prominent idea within the present study (although this does not mean that all of the interviewees had become 'disconnected' from life – or to the same extent).

'We have to Live': Reconnecting With Life

Interviewees repeatedly underscored the need to accept what had happened, not to dwell on the past and to get on with life. They insisted, inter alia, that: 'I have chosen my direction. I move forward, I don't look back'; 'What happened, it happened, we have to keep on living'; 'Simply, you move on. No stopping'; 'Life goes on'; 'Life is what it is. We have to live'; 'You have to move forward. You have to go somewhere'. In some cases, they spoke about particular factors – including age and education – that had shaped how they dealt with their experiences and, by extension, their resolve to get on with life.

A Bosnian Croat interviewee stood out in this regard. She was 38 years old when she was raped and maintained that her age had helped her to accept what happened to her. She reflected: 'My brother's daughters were 16 and 20, and I, then, I said that it was better that I went through this, if it was meant for it to happen, rather than them'. She also commented on the significance of her education. First, 'if a person is more educated', she opined, 'then they will accept all the problems in life differently'. She had a university degree and her former studies in Sarajevo had given her valuable opportunities to meet and interact with many different people; 'I met with my generation from all over Bosnia-Herzegovina'. Second, the interviewee was involved, with the support of a women's NGO, in growing lavender. Through this work, she had not only forged an important connectivity with the natural environment ('The soil draws out all the negative energy from me'). She had also been able to utilise her education in new ways (e.g., in marketing and selling the lavender oil) that she found helpful for moving forward with her life. She explained: 'Now I am doing what I went to university for, because Economics is about products, promotion, pricing and distribution' (interview, BiH, 30 January 2019).

Interviewees also accentuated the importance of having a focus and pushing away negative thoughts. A Bosniak interviewee recounted that following his release from a camp in 1992, aged 20, 'I was drinking for a while and many other things'. Over time, however, he realised that this 'bad lifestyle' had to stop. He could never forget what happened to him, but he refused to allow the past to be at the forefront of his thoughts; and that meant reconnecting with life in the sense of keeping busy. He had a leadership role in a local association of former camp detainees and his home life also kept him occupied:

> There is always something to do around the house; mow the grass, fix this and that, feed the dog, clean around, get the chickens, this and that. I have bees. So, my days are always full. There is no free time. I always have something to focus on. This is very important, this sort of therapy, to overcome all of this.
>
> (interview, BiH, 11 February 2019)

Indeed, male interviewees were over-represented in the node 'Having a focus/ pushing away negative thoughts'. It is relevant in this regard that they had a very clear idea of what was expected of men in Bosnian society. One of the Bosniak men, who was 54, maintained that 'a man is the pillar of the family, he must earn money, work, think about the family. Simply, he has to stand behind it. He has to protect the family' (interview, BiH, 10 April 2019). A 59-year-old Serb interviewee, for his part, insisted that 'It is expected that he [a man in his community] is his own man, that he has a family. That he has the basics, well, for life' (interview, BiH, 2 July 2019). In other words, notwithstanding their 'masculine vulnerabilities' (Touquet, 2022: 715), getting on with life by keeping busy and having a focus was a way for these interviewees to fulfil their sense of what it meant to be a man – and to support crucial connectivities (above all family) in their lives. In this sense, their relationships with these connectivities were ones of mutual support (Hartling, 2008: 63).

Sources of 'Friction'

Notwithstanding the heavy accent that Bosnian interviewees placed on the need to move forward, they also indirectly identified various sources of 'friction'. Tsing (2005: 3), referring to 'the productive friction of global connections', defines friction as 'the awkward, unequal, unstable, and creative qualities of interconnection across difference' (Tsing, 2005: 4). In the interview data, the idea of friction was not associated with creativity or interconnection but, rather, with a larger push–pull dynamic. The various supportive and sustaining connectivities that this chapter has discussed constituted important 'push' factors that were helping interviewees to move ahead. Yet, there were also significant 'pull' (back) factors that made this process more difficult. These ranged from health issues that were a constant and embodied reminder of a past that interviewees wished to forget (Clark, 2020) to wider systemic issues. Indeed, it is noteworthy that compared to interviewees in Colombia and Uganda, Bosnian interviewees were the most critical of the state – a significant 'frictional layer' (Lettau, 1950) – and pointed to myriad shortcomings on its part. One of the male Bosniak interviewees commented that:

> Daily life is a stress on its own, especially here in Bosnia where many things have not yet been regulated. For example, here in Bosnia and Herzegovina, we still don't have a law on camp prisoners.[17] It is unbelievable that 20-something years after the war ended, there is still no law.
>
> (interview, BiH, 11 February 2019)

Linked to the theme *'It didn't change anything': Justice that connects/makes a difference* (discussed more in the final chapter), some of the interviewees also accused the state of failing to deliver 'justice'. While there has been progress with respect to fighting impunity and bringing perpetrators to account (Ferizović and Mlinarević, 2020: 326), interviewees spoke more frequently about the various ways that they felt let down by the justice system – and how the slow pace of justice (Džidić, 2019) had contributed to taking them back to the past. The Albanian interviewee in the sample, for example, was still waiting to see justice done after more than 20 years and talked about the impact of having to give multiple statements to police and prosecutors. She explained:

> I have not refused to give a statement to anyone. It is hard because these statements shake me. They upset me very much, but I want to give them, so that at least. . . . Let them catch these criminals, so that they never do anything bad to anyone again. I know how I felt that night and everything that went on. You know? I would not want this to happen to anyone again.
>
> (interview, BiH, 20 March 2019)

These obstacles, challenges and 'frictions' may help to explain interviewees' very frequent use of 'fighting' rhetoric – not only in relation to their children, as previously discussed, but also more broadly (e.g., 'We live and we fight and we say, well, we survived'; 'I am a fighter because I know I have to fight, because if I don't fight, well, then I will sink'; 'We never know what awaits us in life, and therefore we need to fight, to survive, to live the best we can'). Part of what motivated some of them to fight, moreover, was having hope. Panter-Brick, discussing her work in Afghanistan, has argued that 'What matters to individuals facing adversity is a sense of "meaning-making" and what matters to resilience is a sense of hope that life does indeed make sense, despite chaos, brutality, stress, worry, or despair' (in Southwick et al., 2014; see also Walsh, 2020: 906). As discussed in the previous section, the interviewees' meaning-making processes were often unfinished and incomplete. Nevertheless, they clung on to a sense of hope that, in the words of one of the male Bosniak interviewees, 'things will be better' (interview, BiH, 10 April 2019). In contrast to many of the Colombian interviewees, however, Bosnian interviewees were much less

Connectivity Stories of Resilience in Bosnia-Herzegovina 159

likely to see themselves as personally having a role to play in building this better future, which leads on to the third theme relating to new connectivities.

New Connectivities: Reaching Out

This final section focuses on the theme *'I want to achieve more': (Re)Building connections and making a difference.* Relatively few passages coded to this theme and its associated sub-themes (including 'fighting as women/for women' and 'experiential connectivity') came from Bosnian interviewees. The overwhelming majority of examples were from Colombia. However, there was a skew in the qualitative data in the sense that many of the Colombian interviewees were community leaders, had their own women's associations or were otherwise engaged in various forms of social and political activism. The profile of the interviewees in this regard is partly linked to the involvement in the study of the feminist organisation *Ruta Pacifica de las Mujeres* and the important role that it played in recruiting some of the research participants (who were members of the organisation; see Chapter 3). However, the composition of the Colombian sample also reflects the long history of women's activism in the country (Lizarazo, 2018; Zulver, 2021).

In BiH, there are also many important examples of women's activism, as scholars such as Berry (2018), Helms (2013) and O'Reilly (2017) have explored in detail, and some victims-/survivors now lead their own organisations. One example is Bakira Hašečić, the head of the NGO *Žena Žrtva Rata* (ŽŽR). She has received an Honorary Doctorate of Laws from Glasgow Caledonian University (2018), 'in recognition of her outstanding contribution to human rights and justice for women in Bosnia'. It is also the case, however, that the majority of ŽŽR's members have not spoken publicly (Helms, 2013: 105); only Hašečić gives frequent statements to the media and has a very public profile. This is an illustration of how activists in BiH often speak on behalf of (other) victims-/survivors of CRSV (see Chapter 3). At least in my own research, moreover, I have seen very few examples of collective activism directly involving victims-/survivors themselves.

Neither the wider systemic context of ongoing ethnic divides in BiH nor the political instrumentalisation of victims-/survivors (Berry, 2018: 188) supports these women and men in becoming politically active (although of course some of them have). As one example, the NVivo code named 'Fighting as women/for women' included only two coding references from BiH (compared to 34 from Colombia) – both from the same Serb interviewee. One of only two interviewees who had her own NGO, this woman underlined that 'I am not the only one. In the end, when you realise a million women[18] have survived this, then we have to move on. There is no other way. We have to fight for our rights, to do something, to have something' (interview, BiH, 7 June 2019). However, she appeared to lack any clear sense of how to do this – or a strong vision of which rights needed to be fought for.

Although there were far fewer examples of social and political activism among the Bosnian interviewees than among the Colombian interviewees, some of the Bosnians were nevertheless 'making a difference' in their own ways. One of the Bosniak interviewees particularly stood out in this respect. In her early 60s, this woman had relatively few supportive and sustaining connectivities in her life. Initially just as a way of earning some extra money, she had started helping elderly people in her community (cooking for them, giving them their medicines, running errands for them). However, this work quickly became something much more meaningful to her. She began to feel more connected, less alone and better about herself. In her own words:

> Then you feel that you are needed by someone, you know. I push myself to be able to help an old guy who can't wait for me to show up at his door. This keeps me going because they made me a better person, these old people.

Above all, she reflected, 'They pulled me up, somehow, from all this sorrow and everything'. Even though this interviewee had the lowest ARM score of all the 126 Bosnian participants who completed a study questionnaire, her efforts to build new connectivities – and thus, to make a difference to others within her social ecology and to herself – were an important expression of everyday resilience. They also illustrate Walsh's (2020: 903) argument that 'Recognition of our essential interdependence is vital for our well-being and resilience. In turning to others for help, we can pay it back and pay it forward' (see also Hartling, 2008: 63).

★★★

The aim of this chapter was to do more than simply give examples of resilience in BiH. Analysing and discussing the Bosnian data within the book's connectivity framework and focusing on the broad ideas of broken and ruptured connectivities, supportive and sustaining connectivities and new connectivities, it has ultimately told a story about these connectivities, about the dynamic relationships between interviewees and their social ecologies and about the role that different parts and layers of these social ecologies have played in fostering or hindering resilience. The next chapter applies the book's conceptual framework to the case study of Colombia.

Notes

1 On this point, I share Summerfield's (1999: 1456) view that:

> Trauma models, where the focus is on a particular event (rape) or particular population group (children) exaggerate the difference between some victims and others, risk disconnecting them from others in their community and from the wider context of their experiences and the meanings they give to them.

2 All place names are redacted to protect the interviewees' identities.

3 Even though gender equality was part of official policy within the Socialist Federal Republic of Yugoslavia (SFRY), Helms (2013: 50) has remarked on the unevenness of this policy in practice, 'especially in areas with large rural and Muslim populations'. Björkdahl (2012: 297), moreover, has emphasised that the multi-party elections that took place in BiH in 1990 'brought to power nationalistic parties that relied upon conservative interpretations of religion with political programs that advocated patriarchal values in which the role of women was marginalized'.

4 People in BiH commonly use the term 'refugees' when they are actually referring to internally displaced persons who have not crossed any international borders.

5 Post-hoc comparisons using the Tukey LSD test indicated that the mean score for the BiH participants (M = 38.58, SD = 5.76) was significantly different statistically from the mean score for the Ugandan participants (M = 40.27, SD = 5.17). I am grateful to Dr Adrian Bromage for these analyses.

6 Based on her extensive research in BiH, Helms (2014: 624) argues that 'In fact, individual and community responses to rape have ranged from support and acceptance to stigma and rejection, but all evidence suggests that such outcomes are not dependent on ethnoreligious belonging'.

7 Ungar et al. (2013: 358) underline that 'Protective and promotive factors that facilitate human development exert a differential impact across contexts and time'. The rationale for asking interviewees to complete the ARM a second time, therefore, was to assess the stability of their resilience scores from the quantitative phase of the research.

8 According to the International Labour Organization (ILO, 2021), 'Employment rates remain low (46% for age 15–64, 2019). Unemployment is high despite a downward trend in recent years (16% in 2020), especially among youth (34% in 2019)'. It adds that BiH 'has one of the lowest female employment rates in the Balkans (around 35%, age 15–64, 2019)' (ILO, 2021).

9 Kostovicova et al. (2020: 261) point out that in BiH, 'The incentives for participation in the informal economy are varied, but by far the strongest is a lack of formal employment'. During the application of the study questionnaire, participants were asked about their employment status. In BiH, 72 per cent of participants said that they were not currently working and a further 8 per cent said that they only sometimes worked.

10 Hronešová (2016: 347) explains that:

> Veteran disability confirmations were first distributed immediately after the war and then during a series of assessments, governmental decisions and revisions. Invalids are required to undergo regular checks to validate their rights to payments. As the mean salary is the measurement benchmark, payments in RS are lower.

11 Post-hoc comparisons using the Tukey LSD test indicated that the mean score for the BiH group (M = 29.09, SD = 4.8) was significantly different from the Colombia group (M = 24.21, SD = 6.65) and the Uganda group (M = 25.26, SD = 5.31). Thank you to Dr Adrian Bromage for these analyses.

12 That these men had sought out help highlights the important point that some male victims-/survivors 'do speak of their experiences and do so in both official and semi-official contexts' (Touquet, 2022: 715).

13 It was not clear which law this interviewee was referring to.

14 Brčko District is a self-governing administrative unit in BiH. It is also ethnically mixed.

15 The Women's Court that took place in Sarajevo in May 2015 (see Clark, 2016) is a good example of how these solidarities might be fostered.

16 One of the Serb interviewees had recently submitted an application under the new law. Although the decision letter acknowledged that she was a victim, it only awarded the right to spa rehabilitation (on the grounds that she had suffered sexual violence

162 Connectivity Stories of Resilience in Bosnia-Herzegovina

[specifically forced nudity] but not rape). This meant little to her, especially as there were no spas close to her town.

17 What the interviewee was referring to here is the continued absence in BiH of a law on torture victims. Several drafts exist of a Law on the Protection of Victims of Torture. However, this has still not been adopted, for political reasons. RS, for example, 'has its own law on wartime torture victims and rejects the idea of a state-level law which would supersede its own legislation' (Bajtarević, 2019).

18 It was not clear which women the interviewee was referring to.

References

Afifi TD, Merrill AF and Davis S (2016) The theory of resilience and relational load. *Personal Relationships* 23(4): 663–683.

Aiken NT (2008) Post-conflict peacebuilding and the politics of identity: Insights for restoration and reconciliation in transitional justice. *Peace Research* 40(2): 9–38.

Akinsulure-Smith AM (2014) Displaced African female survivors of conflict-related sexual violence: Challenges for mental health providers. *Violence Against Women* 20(6): 677–694.

Amnesty International (2017) Bosnia and Herzegovina: 'We need support not pity': Last chance for justice for Bosnia's wartime rape survivors. Available at: www.amnesty.org/en/documents/eur63/6679/2017/en/ (accessed 8 May 2021).

Askin KD (2003) Prosecuting wartime rape and other gender-related crimes under international law: Extraordinary advances, enduring obstacles. *Berkeley Journal of International Law* 41(2): 288–349.

Baines E and Oliveira C (2020) Securing the future: Transformative justice and children 'born of war'. *Social & Legal Studies* 30(3): 341–361.

Bajtarević M (2019) Abandoned by the state: Bosnia's wartime torture victims. Available at: https://balkaninsight.com/2019/05/06/abandoned-by-the-state-bosnias-wartime-torture-victims/ (accessed 29 September 2021).

Bargués P and Morillas P (2021) From democratization to fostering resilience: EU intervention and the challenges of building institutions, social trust, and legitimacy in Bosnia and Herzegovina. *Democratization* 28(7): 1319–1337.

Barrios RE (2014) 'Here, I'm not at ease': Anthropological perspectives on community resilience. *Disasters* 38(2): 392–350.

Belloni R (2009) Bosnia: Dayton is dead! Long live Dayton! *Nationalism and Ethnic Politics* 15(3–4): 355–375.

Berry ME (2018) *Women, War and Power: From Violence to Mobilization in Rwanda and Bosnia-Herzegovina*. Cambridge: Cambridge University Press.

Björkdahl A (2012) A gender-just peace? Exploring the post-Dayton peace process in Bosnia. *Peace & Change* 37(2): 286–317.

Black K and Lobo M (2008) A conceptual review of family resilience factors. *Journal of Family Nursing* 14(1): 33–55.

Boesten J (2017) Of exceptions and continuities: Theory and methodology in research on conflict-related sexual violence. *International Feminist Journal of Politics* 19(4): 506–519.

Borger J (2015) Bosnia's bitter, flawed peace deal, 20 years on. Available at: www.theguardian.com/global/2015/nov/10/bosnia-bitter-flawed-peace-deal-dayton-agreement-20-years-on (accessed 1 October 2021).

Boritz TZ, Bryntwick E, Angus L, Greenberg LS and Constantino MJ (2014) Narrative and emotion process in psychotherapy: An empirical test of the narrative-emotion process coding system (NEPCS). *Psychotherapy Research* 24(5): 594–607.

Bringa T (1995) *Being Muslim the Bosnian Way: Identity and Community in a Central Bosnian Village*. Princeton, NJ: Princeton University Press.

Carpenter RC (ed.) (2007) *Born of War: Protecting Children of Sexual Violence Survivors in Conflict Zones*. Bloomington, CT: Kumarian Press.

Clark JN (2016) Transitional justice as recognition: An analysis of the women's court in Sarajevo. *International Journal of Transitional Justice* 10(1): 67–87.

Clark JN (2017) *Rape, Sexual Violence and Transitional Justice Challenges: Lessons from Bosnia-Herzegovina*. Abingdon: Routledge.

Clark JN (2019) Helping or harming? NGOs and victims-/survivors of conflict-related sexual violence in Bosnia-Herzegovina. *Journal of Human Rights* 18(2): 246–265.

Clark JN (2020) Body memories as a neglected legacy of human rights abuses: Exploring their significance for transitional justice. *Social & Legal Studies* 30(5): 768–789.

Clark JN (2021) Beyond a 'survivor-centred approach' to conflict-related sexual violence? *International Affairs* 97(4): 1067–1084.

Clark JN (2022a) Social ecologies of health and conflict-related sexual violence: Translating 'healthworlds' into transitional justice. *Journal of Human Rights*, https://doi.org/10.1080/14754835.2021.2020627.

Clark JN (2022b) Resilience in the context of conflict-related sexual violence: Children as protective resources and wider implications. *International Journal of Human Rights* 26(4): 634–654.

Cohen CE (2020) Reimaging transitional justice. *International Journal of Transitional Justice* 14(1): 1–13.

Collins AE (2001) Health ecology, land degradation and development. *Land Degradation & Development* 12(3): 237–250.

Crawford FF (2013) From spoils to weapons: Framing wartime sexual violence. *Gender & Development* 21(3): 505–517.

Darnhofer I, Lamine C, Strauss A and Navarrete M (2016) The resilience of family farms: Towards a relational approach. *Journal of Rural Studies* 44: 111–122.

Denov M and Piolanti A (2020) 'Though my father was a killer, I need to know him': Children born of genocidal rape in Rwanda and their perspectives on fatherhood. *Child Abuse & Neglect* 107: 104560.

Dolan C, Baaz ME and Stern M (2020) What is sexual about conflict-related sexual violence? Stories from men and women survivors. *International Affairs* 96(5): 1151–1168.

Dossa NI, Zunzunegui ZE, Hatem M and Fraser WD (2015) Mental health disorders among women victims of conflict-related sexual violence in the Democratic Republic of Congo. *Journal of Interpersonal Violence* 30(13): 2199–2220.

Džidić D (2019) OCSE mission chief: Bosnia 'too slow' in prosecuting war crimes. Available at: https://balkaninsight.com/2019/09/06/osce-mission-chief-bosnia-too-slow-in-prosecuting-war-crimes/ (accessed 4 September 2021).

Edström J, Dolan C and Shahrokh T, with David O (2016) Therapeutic activism: Men of Hope refugee association Uganda breaking the silence over male rape in conflict-related sexual violence. IDS Evidence Report 182.

Ferizović J and Mlinarević G (2020) Applying international experiences in national prosecutions of conflict-related sexual violence. *Journal of International Criminal Justice* 18(2): 325–348.

Funk J and Berry ME (2020) Introduction. In: Funk J, Good N and Berry ME (eds.), *Healing and Peacebuilding after War: Transforming Trauma in Bosnia and Herzegovina*. Abingdon: Routledge, pp. 1–12.

Gilmore S and McEvoy K (2021) Bridging justice and health: Reparations for conflict-related sexual violence. *Obstetrics and Gynaecology* 23(1): 6–8.

Glasgow Caledonian University (2018) Honorary degree for campaigner against war crimes. Available at: www.gcu.ac.uk/theuniversity/universitynews/2018-honorary-degree-for-campaigner-against-war/ (accessed 22 October 2021).

Gonzáles-Ayala SN and Camargo A (2021) Voices of water and violence: Exhibition making and the blue humanities for transitional justice. *Curator* 64(1): 183–204.

Gray H, Stern M and Dolan C (2020) Torture and sexual violence in war and conflict: The unmaking and remaking of subjects of violence. *Review of International Studies* 46(2): 197–216.

Gutman R (1994) Foreword. In: Stiglmayer A (ed.), *Mass Rape: The War against Women in Bosnia-Herzegovina.* Lincoln, NE: University of Nebraska Press, pp. ix–xiii.

Halilovich H (2011) Beyond the sadness: Memories and homecomings among survivors of 'ethnic cleansing' in a Bosnian village. *Memory Studies* 4(1): 42–52.

Hansen L (2000) Gender, nation, rape: Bosnia and the construction of security. *International Feminist Journal of Politics* 3(1): 55–75.

Hartling LM (2008) Strengthening resilience in a risky world: It's all about relationships. *Women & Therapy* 31(2–4): 51–70.

Hatala AR, Njeze C, Morton D, Pearl T and Bird-Naytowhow K (2020) Land and nature as sources of health and resilience among Indigenous youth in an urban Canadian context: A photovoice exploration. *BCM Public Health* 20: 538.

Hayden RM (1996) Schindler's fate: Genocide, ethnic cleansing and population transfers. *Slavic Review* 55(4): 727–748.

Healey SA (1995) Prosecuting rape under the statute of the war crimes tribunal for the former Yugoslavia. *Brooklyn Journal of International Law* 21(2): 327–384.

Helms E (2013) *Innocence and Victimhood: Gender, Nation and Women's Activism in Postwar Bosnia-Herzegovina.* Madison, WI: University of Wisconsin Press.

Helms E (2014) Rejecting Angelina: Bosnian war rape survivors and the ambiguities of sex in war. *Slavic Review* 73(3): 612–634.

Henig D (2012) 'Knocking on my neighbour's door': On metamorphoses of sociality in rural Bosnia. *Critique of Anthropology* 32(1): 3–19.

Henry N (2014) The fixation on wartime rape: Feminist critique and international criminal law. *Social & Legal Studies* 23(1): 93–111.

Hess JJ, Malilay JN and Parkinson JA (2008) Climate change: The importance of place. *American Journal of Preventive Medicine* 35(5): 468–478.

Hobfoll S (2011) Conservation of resource caravans and engaged settings. *Journal of Occupational and Organizational Psychology* 84(1): 116–122.

Hobfoll S (2014) Resource caravans and resource caravan passageways: A new paradigm for trauma responding. *Intervention* 12(4): 21–32.

Horstman HK (2019) Young adult women's narrative resilience in relation to mother-daughter communicated narrative sense-making and well-being. *Journal of Social and Personal Relationships* 36(4): 1146–1167.

Hronešová J (2016) Might makes right: War-related payments in Bosnia and Herzegovina. *Journal of Intervention and Statebuilding* 10(3): 339–360.

Hunt S (2004) *This Was Not Our War: Bosnian Women Reclaiming the Peace.* Durham, NC: Duke University Press.

ICRC (2016) The ICRC and the Preventing Sexual Violence in Conflict Initiative (PSVI). Available at: www.icrc.org/en/document/icrc-and-preventing-sexual-violence-initia-tive-psvi (accessed 7 July 2021).

ICRC (2017) Living with landmines in Bosnia and Herzegovina. Available at: www.icrc. org/en/document/living-landmines-bosnia-and-herzegovina (accessed 5 October 2021).

ILO (2021) About the ILO in Bosnia and Herzegovina. Available at: www.ilo.org/budapest/ countries-covered/bosnia-herzegovina/WCMS_471903/lang – en/index.htm (accessed 6 September 2021).

Jordan J (ed.) (2010) *The Power of Connection: Recent Developments in Relational-Cultural Theory*. Abingdon: Routledge.

Jurkovic GJ, Kuperminc GP, Sarac T and Weisshaar D (2005) Role of filial responsibility in the post-war adjustment of Bosnian young adolescents. *Journal of Emotional Abuse* 5(4): 219–235.

Kartalova-O'Doherty, Stevenson C and Higgins A (2012) Reconnecting with life: A grounded theory study of mental health recovery in Ireland. *Journal of Mental Health* 21(2): 135–143.

Kent L (2011) Local memory practices in East Timor: Disrupting transitional justice narratives. *International Journal of Transitional Justice* 5(3): 434–455.

Keyes CLM (2004) Risk and resilience in human development: An introduction. *Research in Human Development* 1(4): 223–227.

Kirby P (2015) Ending sexual violence in conflict: The Preventing Sexual Violence Initiative and its critics. *International Affairs* 91(3): 457–472.

Klarić M, Frančišković T, Stevanović A, Petrov B, Jonovska S and Nemčić Moro I (2011) Marital quality and relationship satisfaction in war veterans and their wives in Bosnia and Herzegovina. *European Journal of Psychotraumatology* 2(1): 8077.

Knežević G (2017) 'Nothing to be cheerful about': Bosnians, traumatized by war, modern life, turn to antidepressants. Available at: www.rferl.org/a/bosnia-antidepressants-mass-anxiety-postwar-anxiety/28762076.html (accessed 16 September 2021).

Koegler E, Kennedy C, Mrindi J, Bachunguye R, Winch P, Ramazani P, Makambo MT and Glass N (2019) Understanding how solidarity groups – a community-based economic and psychosocial support intervention – can affect mental health for survivors of conflict-related sexual violence in Democratic Republic of the Congo. *Violence Against Women* 25(3): 359–374.

Kostovicova D, Bojicic-Dzelilovic V and Henry M (2020) Drawing on the continuum: A war and post-war political economy of gender-based violence in Bosnia and Herzegovina. *International Feminist Journal of Politics* 22(2): 250–272.

Krause U and Schmidt H (2020) Refugees as actors? Critical reflections on global refugee policies on self-reliance and resilience. *Journal of Refugee Studies* 33(1): 22–41.

Lettau H (1950) A re-examination of the 'Leipzig wind profile' considering some relations between wind and turbulence in the frictional layer. *Tellus* 2(2): 125–129.

Lizarazo T (2018) Alongside violence: Everyday survival in Chocó, Colombia. *Journal of Latin American Cultural Studies* 27(2): 175–196.

Lofranco Z (2017) Negotiating 'neighbourliness' in Sarajevo apartment blocks. In: Donnan H, Hurd M and Leutloff-Grandits C (eds.), *Migrating Borders and Moving Times: Temporality and the Crossing of Borders in Europe*. Manchester: Manchester University Press, pp. 42–57.

Lykes MB and van der Merwe (2017) Exploring/expanding the reach of transitional justice. *International Journal of Transitional Justice* 11(3): 371–377.

Majstorović D (2011) Femininity, patriarchy and resistance in the postwar Bosnia and Herzegovina. *International Review of Sociology* 21(2): 277–299.

Mazzucchelli F (2021) Borders of memory: Competing heritages and fractured memory-scapes in Bosnia and Herzegovina. In: Bădescu G, Baillie B and Mazzucchelli F (eds.),

Transforming Heritage in the Former Yugoslavia: Synchronous Pasts. Cham: Palgrave MacMillan, pp. 131–156.

Myrttinen H and Swaine A (2015) Monster myths, selfies and grand declarations: A conversation on the global summit to end sexual violence in conflict. *International Feminist Journal of Politics* 17(3): 496–502.

Nelson BS (2003) Post-war trauma and reconciliation in Bosnia-Herzegovina: Observations, experiences and implications for marriage and therapy. *The American Journal of Family Therapy* 31(4): 305–316.

Neufeldt RC (2014) Doing good better: Expanding the ethics of peacebuilding. *International Peacekeeping* 21(4): 427–442.

Noor M, Shnabel N, Halabi S and Nadler A (2012) When suffering begets suffering: The psychology of competitive victimhood between adversarial groups in violent conflicts. *Personality and Social Psychology Review* 16(4): 351–374.

Office of the High Representative (2020) Remarks by High Representative Valentin Inzko to the United Nations Security Council. Available at: www.ohr.int/remarks-by-high-representative-valentin-inzko-to-the-united-nations-security-council-18/ (accessed 30 August 2021).

O'Reilly M (2017) *Gendered Agency in War and Peace: Gender Justice and Women's Activism in Post-Conflict Bosnia-Herzegovina*. London: Palgrave Macmillan.

Panter-Brick C, Grimon MP and Eggerman M (2014) Caregiver–child mental health: A prospective study in conflict and refugee settings. *The Journal of Child Psychiatry and Psychology* 55(4): 313–327.

Park CL (2016) Meaning making in the context of disasters. *Journal of Clinical Psychology* 72(12): 1234–1246.

Pipher M (2002) Healing wisdom: The universals of human resilience. *Psychotherapy Networker* 26: 59–61.

Pupavac V (2004) International therapeutic peace and justice in Bosnia. *Social & Legal Studies* 13(3): 377–401.

Putnam RD (2000) *Bowling Alone: The Collapse and Revival of American Community*. New York, NY: Simon & Schuster.

Putnam RD and Goss KA (2002) Introduction. In: Putnam RD (ed.), *Democracies in Flux: The Evolution of Social Capital in Contemporary Society*. Oxford: Oxford University Press, pp. 3–20.

Reichert BE, Fletcher Jr. RJ and Kitchens WM (2021) The demographic contributions of connectivity versus local dynamics to population growth of an endangered bird. *Journal of Animal Ecology* 90(3): 574–584.

Resilience Research Centre (2016) The Resilience Research Centre Adult Resilience Measure (RRC-ARM): User's manual. Available at: https://cyrm.resilienceresearch.org/files/ArchivedMaterials.zip (accessed 9 October 2021).

Ryken KO, Hogue M, Marsh JL and Schweizer M (2017) Long-term consequences of landmine injury: A survey of civilian survivors in Bosnia-Herzegovina 20 years after the war. *Injury* 48(12): 2688–2692.

Sackellares SN (2005) From Bosnia to Sudan: Sexual violence in modern armed conflict. *Wisconsin Women's Law Journal* 20 (1): 137–166.

Schulz P and Ngomokwe F (2021) Resilience, adaptive peacebuilding and transitional justice in post-conflict Uganda: The participatory potential of survivors' groups. In: Clark JN and Ungar M (eds.), *Resilience, Adaptive Peacebuilding and Transitional Justice: How Societies Recover after Collective Violence*. Cambridge: Cambridge University Press, pp. 119–142.

Simonsen SG (2005) Addressing ethnic divisions in post-conflict institution-building: Lessons from recent cases. *Security Dialogue* 36(3): 297–318.

Skjelsbaek I (2006) Victim and survivor: Narrated social identities of women who experienced rape during the war in Bosnia-Herzegovina. *Feminism & Psychology* 16(4): 373–403.

Sorabji C (2008) Bosnian neighbourhoods revisited: Tolerance, commitment and *komšiluk* in Sarajevo. In: Pine F and Pina-Cabral JD (eds.), *On the Margins of Religion*. Oxford: Berghahn, pp. 97–112.

Southwick SM, Bonanno GA, Masten AS, Panter-Brick C and Yehuda R (2014) Resilience definitions, theory and challenges: Interdisciplinary perspectives. *European Journal of Psychotraumatology* 5(1): 25338.

Stiglmayer A (1994) The rapes in Bosnia-Herzegovina. In: Stiglmayer A (ed.), *Mass Rape: The War against Women in Bosnia-Herzegovina*. Lincoln, NE: University of Nebraska Press, pp. 82–169.

Stokols D, Lejano RP and Hipp J (2013) Enhancing the resilience of human-environment systems: A social ecological perspective. *Ecology and Society* 18(1): 7.

Summerfield D (1999) A critique of seven assumptions behind psychological trauma programmes in war-affected areas. *Social Science and Medicine* 48: 1449–1462.

Theron LC and Theron AMC (2014) Meaning-making and resilience: Case studies of a multifaceted process. *Journal of Psychology in Africa* 24(1): 24–32.

Touquet H (2022) Silent or inaudible? Male survivor stories in Bosnia-Herzegovina. *Social Politics* 29(2): 706–728.

Touquet H and Schulz P (2021) Navigating vulnerabilities and masculinities: How gendered contexts shape the agency of male sexual violence survivors. *Security Dialogue* 52(3): 213–230.

Tsing AL (2005) *Friction: An Ethnography of Global Connection*. Princeton, NJ: Princeton University Press.

Ungar M (2013) Resilience after maltreatment: The importance of social services as facilitators of positive adaptation. *Child Abuse & Neglect* 37(2–3): 110–115.

Ungar M, Ghazinour M and Richter J (2013) Annual research review: What is resilience within the social ecology of development? *The Journal of Child Psychology and Psychiatry* 54(4): 348–366.

UN Secretary-General (2019) Conflict-related sexual violence: Report of the United Nations Secretary-General. Available at: www.un.org/sexualviolenceinconflict/wp-content/uploads/2019/04/report/s-2019-280/Annual-report-2018.pdf (accessed 7 May 2020).

Walsh F (2003) Family resilience: A framework for clinical practice. *Family Process* 42(2): 1–18.

Walsh F (2012) Facilitating family resilience: Relational resources for positive youth development in conditions of adversity. In: Ungar M (ed.), *The Social Ecology of Resilience*. New York, NY: Springer, pp. 173–185.

Walsh F (2020) Loss and resilience in the time of COVID-19: Meaning making, hope and transcendence. *Family Process* 59(3): 898–911.

Walsh F (2021) Family resilience: A dynamic systemic framework. In: Ungar M (ed.), *Multisystemic Resilience: Adaptation and Transformation in Contexts of Change*. New York, NY: Oxford University Press, pp. 255–270.

WHO (2012) Mental health and psychosocial support for conflict-related sexual violence: Principles and interventions. Available at: http://apps.who.int/iris/bitstream/handle/10665/75179/WHO_RHR_HRP_12.18_eng.pdf;jsessionid=7A2FBDCF55026CAAD3DD4595A48956D1?sequence=1 (accessed 2 August 2021).

WHO (n.d.) Constitution. Available at: www.who.int/about/governance/constitution (accessed 6 March 2020).

Zraly M, Rubin SE and Mukamana D (2013) Resilience and motherhood among Rwandan genocide-rape survivors. *Ethos* 41(4): 411–439.

Zulver JM (2021) The endurance of women's mobilization during 'patriarchal backlash': A case from Colombia's reconfiguring armed conflict. *International Feminist Journal of Politics* 23(3): 440–462.

Chapter 6

Connectivity Stories of Resilience in Colombia

Jineth Bedoya Lima is a Colombian journalist who was kidnapped, tortured and gang raped while on her way to interview an imprisoned right-wing paramilitary leader in May 2000. In October 2021, the Inter-American Court of Human Rights ruled that Colombia was 'internationally responsible for the violation of the rights to [Bedoya Lima's] personal integrity, personal freedom, honor, dignity and freedom of expression' (Parkin Daniels, 2021). The Court found that Bedoya Lima's attackers would not have been able to do what they did 'without the acquiescence and collaboration of the state' (Parkin Daniels, 2021). This award-winning journalist's very public fight for justice over more than 20 years – despite facing death threats and myriad obstacles – offers a powerful example of resilience.

The Colombians who participated in this research did not have Bedoya Lima's high profile, and they often had considerably fewer resources to draw upon. Yet, many of them also exhibited resilience in their efforts to get on with their lives and to fight for those around them, including their children and other victims-/survivors. This chapter focuses on the complex, changing and multi-layered connectivities between interviewees and their social ecologies that define the book's approach to and analysis of resilience as a quintessentially relational concept. For comparative purposes, the chapter adopts the same structure as the Bosnian chapter (and the Ugandan chapter that follows), through application of the book's connectivity framework.

For reasons explained in Chapter 3, this chapter, like the previous one, will note interviewees' gender and ethnicity (and in some cases age). What it does not do is capture the diversity that exists within broad ethnic categories in Colombia – and this was never a specific research aim – because the total number of interviewees (as in the other two countries) was 21. Of these, four were Afro-Colombian. It is impossible, therefore, to do more than acknowledge that 'Black communities in Colombia are marked by differences of region, local histories, class, occupation, and political ideology, among other factors' (Asher, 2007: 14). Similarly, the chapter does not address different Indigenous cultures and traditions (the three Indigenous interviewees were from the Embera Chami, Nasa and Pastos peoples respectively).

DOI: 10.4324/9781003323532-7

170 Connectivity Stories of Resilience in Colombia

Seven of the 21 interviewees did not identify with any of the ethnicity options listed in the study questionnaire,[1] and two of them did not understand the question about ethnicity.[2] A crucial point in this regard – although it is not specific to Colombia – is that ethnicity fundamentally intersects with other identities (Melo, 2015: 1031). Consequently, some participants refrained from putting themselves into neat categories that could 'never quite encapsulate the complexity of their reality' (Ng'weno, 2007: 418). Some of them just saw themselves as Colombian. Others placed a strong accent on their rural identities. In hindsight, *campesino/campesina* (peasant/small farmer) should have been included as one of the options in the questionnaire, to better reflect some of the different ways that people in Colombia identify themselves. The demographic profile of many of the interviewees, however, means that this chapter does encapsulate some of the experiences of rural populations who have borne the brunt of the armed conflict (Merriman, 2020: 25).

Contextualising Experiences of Violence

The theme *'I am all that I've lived': Connectivities of violence*, which all three empirical chapters explore, highlights interviewees' multiple experiences of ' "living-in" violence' (Al-Masri, 2017: 37) – and more specifically of 'living-in', and with or through, different forms of intersecting violence that reach across war/armed conflict and 'peace'. Relatedly, it demonstrates that interviewees' 'experiential histories' (Sturge-Apple et al., 2012: 238) of violence, direct and indirect, are an integral part of thinking about and analysing resilience. However, there were important differences – linked to the respective dynamics of the conflicts in Bosnia-Herzegovina (BiH), Colombia and Uganda, and to wider contextual and structural factors – regarding the specific types of violence that interviewees in each country emphasised. Colombian interviewees particularly spoke about forced displacement, which is discussed in the next section. They also frequently talked about witnessing violence against others and about everyday forms of violence (especially from family members), illustrating 'naked infinities of the layering of violence upon violence' (Barad, 2019: 541).

Witnessing Violence Against Others

It is significant that interviewees in Colombia, compared to those in BiH and Uganda, had seen much more direct combat between armed groups fighting for 'territorial dominance' (Meertens and Segura-Escobar, 1996: 168). An interviewee who identified as mixed-race (Mestizo) talked about being caught in a crossfire between the army and the Revolutionary Armed Forces of Colombia (FARC). She recalled:

The army made us stick close to the banks of the river, where they were, and then the guerrillas opened fire on them. I mean, I'd never seen anything like it, but that day I saw what it looks like when a M60 [machine gun] gets fired.

(interview, Colombia, 10 February 2019)

Another interviewee, who did not understand the question about her ethnicity, recalled that 'there was a lot of killing in the *vereda* [a type of administrative unit]. There were three factions fighting each other: there was the army, the FARC and the paramilitaries' (interview, Colombia, 13 March 2019).

The presence in an area of different armed groups exposed civilians to considerable risk. Becoming 'the "pat-ball" of all' (Meertens and Segura-Escobar, 1996: 167), they could be forced to collaborate with one or more of these groups (Rojas, 2009: 239). Emphasising that 'We were in-between a rock and a hard place', one of the male interviewees who did not identify with any particular ethnic group explained that it was necessary to 'work with' both the guerrillas (he specifically named the FARC)[3] and the army. This resulted in the FARC accusing him and his family of giving information about them to the army. He explained that 'when they [the guerrillas] took over the ranch [run by the interviewee's uncle], they locked us all up. Then they did whatever they pleased, as they say, with the men, women'. The interviewee's mother was raped in front of him – and he was raped in front of her (interview, Colombia, 30 January 2019).

Uribe (2004: 91) has pointed out that simply being seen doing business with, talking to or showing hospitality to another group was 'reason enough to be considered an enemy collaborator (auxiliador)'. Indeed, several interviewees talked about violence that they had witnessed against individuals accused of collaborating. An Afro-Colombian interviewee had previously lived with her family in a town controlled by guerrillas and stressed that it was necessary to do what the latter wanted. As one example, 'if a guerrilla comes along or if some other armed group come along and they say they want you to cook them some plantain, then you have to cook'.[4] When paramilitaries arrived in the town, they looked for several people whom they accused of aiding the guerrillas, including the interviewee's cousin. She recalled: 'So, let's see, that was when my cousin fell – they killed him. They burned his face with acid and killed him' (interview, Colombia, 30 March 2019).

Everyday Violence

Zulver (2017: 1502) underlines that 'women in Colombia do not experience violence solely as a result of having been displaced by armed groups, but also because of a patriarchal society in which women are subject to broader forms of violence on a daily basis'. Colombian women who participated in this

172 Connectivity Stories of Resilience in Colombia

research spoke about ongoing violence and threats of violence, linked, inter alia, to the presence of armed groups and criminal gangs (known as BACRIM) in their neighbourhoods, and to the work that some of them (interviewees) were engaged in as human rights defenders and social leaders. They also frequently talked about violence – including sexual violence – that they had experienced from family members. Wood (2014: 460) has pointed out that:

> According to a survey in fifteen conflicted municipalities in Colombia, 3.4% of women reported having been raped between 2000 and 2009. The reported rate of rape by family members was triple the reported rate by combatants and 50% more than the reported rate by strangers.

A mixed-race interviewee narrated how, as a child, her parents would leave her alone on the family ranch with her brothers. 'My elder brother abused me', she explained, 'and, for me, it made my life really hard from that point. Well, I mean, my life changed completely because I told my Mum but she didn't believe me'. The interviewee was now living with her second husband, with whom she had a son. She also had two children with her previous husband. Referring to the latter, she disclosed that 'I didn't want another child and he raped me and that left me pregnant. So, that's how I got my second child' (interview, Colombia, 3 February 2019).

An interviewee who did not identify with any ethnic group recounted how, growing up, she was abused by her grandfather. Later, FARC guerrillas raped her and she was subsequently violated by her stepfather. Reflecting on this second rape, the interviewee recalled:

> I felt so ill and I went to the bathroom and splashed water onto myself and I . . . not again, not again! It was the same thing that had happened with the guerrillas and I said: 'Oh God, what's happening to me?'

When the interviewee married, her husband also abused and demeaned her. In her words, 'I was treated like a dog by that man' (interview, Colombia, 14 March 2019).

Such examples support the argument that conflict-related sexual violence (CRSV) constitutes part of 'a spectrum of women's (violent) oppression grounded in patriarchal structures' (Kreft, 2019: 221). At the same time, however, the data arguably suggested something more than just a 'continuum of gender-based violence that springs out of gender inequality and permeates both war and peace' (Houge and Lohne, 2017: 760). Some interviewees (including those in BiH and Uganda) expressed the sense that their lives were caught up in perpetual cycles or 'diachronic loops' (McKittrick, 2016: 13) of violence. My point is not to problematise the concept of a continuum of violence, but simply to accentuate that it does not necessarily capture how individuals themselves experience or make sense of violence in their lives.

Broken and Ruptured Connectivities: Uprooting and Family Relationships

As Chapter 2 discussed, an important element of the book's connectivity framework – linked to the concept of fragmentation in ecology scholarship – is broken and ruptured connectivities, reflected particularly in the theme '*It isn't there anymore': Connectivities lost.* This section and the next explore three broken and ruptured connectivities that were especially prominent in the Colombian data, relating to forced displacement, family and health, respectively.

Forced Displacement

More than five decades of armed conflict in Colombia have resulted in large-scale internal displacement (predominantly from rural to urban areas). Indeed, in 2016 – the year that the government and the FARC signed a historic peace agreement – the country 'had the largest internal displacement crisis in the world' (Sachseder, 2020: 168). Notwithstanding the peace agreement and the demobilisation of more than 13,000 FARC guerrillas (Meernik et al., 2021: 537), forced displacement is still happening in Colombia as multiple armed groups continue to fight for control of resource-rich territory, supported by international interests (see, e.g., Escobar, 2004: 19).[5] According to the Internal Displacement Monitoring Centre (IDMC, 2020), the activities of these armed groups 'triggered about 106,000 new displacements in 2020' (see also United Nations Refugee Agency [UNHCR], 2021).

Forced displacement, an issue that both reflects and illustrates 'the complementarities of war and agrarian extractivism' (Berman-Arévalo and Ojeda, 2020: 1583), was one of the many broken and ruptured connectivities prevalent in the stories of Colombian interviewees. Taking different forms in different areas (Meertens and Segura-Escobar, 1996: 170), displacement had variously disconnected interviewees, temporarily or permanently, from their land, communities and entire ways of life (Schultz et al., 2014). One interviewee, who emphasised her *campesina* identity – as a Colombian woman from the countryside – had been forcibly displaced by the FARC in 2006. Aged 52 and now living in a tiny flat on the outskirts of a large city, in a neighbourhood that she described as unsafe (due to the presence of criminal gangs and drug dealers), she reflected:

> The only thing I long for, in order to be able to live well, in peace, is to get some farmland and be able to keep cows, pigs, chickens. To have what I long for. That would be the only thing that would enable me to rebuild; for everything to be as it was before in XXX [the place where she had lived prior to being displaced].[6] It would be having a farm again, being able to keep animals and all the things I had there. You see, here you can't really have anything. Living here is like being imprisoned.
>
> (interview, Colombia, 3 April 2019)

174 Connectivity Stories of Resilience in Colombia

Highlighting the reciprocal and nurturing relationships between *campesinos/campesinas* and their land, Lederach (2017: 592) posits that 'The violent severing of these relationships results in an extended sense of being lost (*perdido*) and uprooted (*desarraigado*)'. If the above interviewee implicitly conveyed a sense of being lost in her new environment of graffiti-covered apartment blocks, a research participant[7] in one of the reflections workshops organised in 2021 (see Chapter 3) openly objected to being called 'displaced'. In her words, 'We are not displaced. We are uprooted because they [armed groups] detached us like a yucca plant'[8] (reflections workshop, Colombia, 30 June 2021).

Forced displacement has particularly affected Afro-Colombian and Indigenous populations (IDMC, 2020; Schultz et al., 2014). For one of the Afro-Colombian interviewees, being displaced in a sprawling city on Colombia's Caribbean coast meant no longer having neighbours who would always look out for her and offer help when she needed it. It additionally meant – further conveying the idea of uprooting – no longer having easy access to natural food sources that she and her children had been able to rely on when they were hungry. The interviewee specifically mentioned the *papoche* plant, explaining that 'it's a tiny plantain that grows on riverbanks and you can cut it and eat it'. Life in the city, this 61-year-old underscored, was much harder; 'It has been a big change' (interview, Colombia, 30 March 2019). This example and the previous one, thus, also illuminate a rupturing of what Lemaitre (2016: 552) calls 'the stewardship of life' – an integral part of women's traditional roles in rural areas. This stewardship 'begins with taking care of themselves . . . as much as being able to take care of their home . . . and being able to take care of their family' (Lemaitre, 2016: 552–553).

An interviewee from the Indigenous Pastos people also spoke about displacement and loss of land ('They [guerrillas] took 32 hectares of my land and until now they've not returned them' [interview, Colombia, 4 February 2019]). Although she did not elaborate further or discuss what it meant to her to be disconnected from her land, Tovar-Restrepo and Irazábal (2014: 42) argue that 'Indigenous women's cosmogonies, beliefs, and traditions often put them in virtually seamless relation to their environment, with land and natural resources, particularly the ones that directly nurture their livelihood, being conceived of and treated as extensions of the self' (see also Sweet and Ortiz Escalante, 2017: 595). This is an important example of how cultural context and belief systems can potentially enhance or further contribute to experiential ruptures linked to displacement.

Loss of Loved Ones/Broken Families

According to Oslender (2008: 78), 'violence runs like a red thread' not only through Colombia's official history, 'but also through the personal, intimate life histories of most Colombians'. Everyone, he points out, 'seems to have a story to tell about a relative blackmailed, a friend kidnapped, a neighbor shot, a colleague

Connectivity Stories of Resilience in Colombia   175

disappeared, or family friends driven off their lands' (Oslender, 2008: 78). In this research, Colombian interviewees' stories often focused on and involved their families. As Chapter 5 explored, families can act as crucial protective resources (Afifi and MacMillan, 2011: 268; Ahern et al., 2006: 105; Black and Lobo, 2008: 35). It is significant in this regard that salient within the Colombian data were some of the many ways that the armed conflict had broken and ruptured interviewees' relationships and connectivities with their families.

Patterson (2002: 354) points out that 'All families at some time or another are faced with challenges to their usual way of relating and accomplishing life tasks'. For many of the interviewees, however, their families had not just faced challenges. The loss and/or disappearance of loved ones had fundamentally altered family structures and dynamics (see also Goldscheid, 2020: 257; Suárez-Baquero et al., 2022: 1309), in turn affecting how interviewees accomplished 'life tasks' – and the resources and connectivities that they relied on to do so.

The Colombian interviewees, of course, were not alone in having lost family members. During the application of the study questionnaire in 2018, affirmative responses to family-related questions in the Traumatic Events Checklist (TEC) were high across all three countries (see Chapter 3, Figure 3.1). As one illustration, 63.49 per cent of Bosnian participants, 66.08 per cent of Colombian participants and 88.16 per cent of Ugandan participants answered yes to TEC question 11 ('Had members of your family killed'). However, it is also significant that analysis of responses to the Adult Resilience Measure (ARM; Resilience Research Centre, 2016) revealed that participants in Colombia had the lowest scores on the relational sub-scale of the ARM,[9] which includes questions about family support. Indeed, these questions triggered strong emotional responses from some of the Colombian participants, either because they did not have such support (e.g., due to unresolved issues and tensions within their families) or because the armed conflict had taken from them crucial family members. The qualitative part of the research further accentuated these cross-country differences. Overall, Colombian interviewees spoke far less than the Bosnian interviewees about their families as supportive and sustaining connectivities in their lives, and they talked much more than the Bosnian interviewees (but less than the Ugandan interviewees) about the impact of armed conflict on their families.

An interviewee who referred to herself as a *costeña* – meaning a woman from the coast – narrated how she was raped in front of her grandmother (who had raised her) when she was 14 years old (she was now 32). She also talked about the two-year disappearance of her stepfather. In both cases, she blamed guerrillas,[10] arguing that they had sought reprisals against her family because of her stepfather's refusal to smuggle an explosive device into the local army base. Later, her beloved grandmother died, after having her leg amputated. The interviewee stressed that:

> My family was totally destroyed, we couldn't . . . I couldn't make any bonds of friendship or harmony with my siblings, nor with my mum or

with my stepfather because . . . I wanted to have a family but what they [the guerrillas] did was total destruction.

Her family members were now widely scattered; her sister and uncle had moved abroad, and her mother and brother were living in different parts of Colombia. Underlining that 'we'll never be back together as a family', the interviewee explained: 'I've always been alone, I've gone through it all alone' (interview, Colombia, 2 May 2019).

An interviewee from the Indigenous Pastos people recounted how armed groups had killed her husband. She had additionally lost a brother and had conceived two children – after being raped on two separate occasions by members of the guerrillas and the paramilitaries. She disclosed that 'Of the two children, one was taken by them [she did not specify which armed group] and killed when it was two months old and the other died in the womb'. She had three other children but two months before she was interviewed for this research, one of her sons was killed. She maintained that the police had 'done a false positive on him', meaning that they had deliberately misrepresented him as a guerrilla fighter who was lawfully killed in combat.[11] This interviewee had helped to organise an association of displaced people and explained 'I bury myself in all this community work to forget that I exist, that I'm going through what I'm going through' (interview, Colombia, 4 February 2019). For some of the other interviewees, similarly, their social activism and work in the community were partly a way of dealing with broken and ruptured family connectivities – and of building new connectivities (discussed in the final sections).

It is also important, however, to recognise another dimension of broken and ruptured connectivities within the data. There were 'bad connectivities' in some interviewees' lives that they wanted to break and rupture but could not. In some cases, moreover, these bad connectivities were linked to broken and ruptured family connectivities. The story of one of the Afro-Colombian interviewees was particularly illustrative in this regard. She described how paramilitaries disappeared her brother and subsequently killed her husband. Five years later, they disappeared her son. She borrowed money through a loan scheme called *gota a gota* (drop by drop) to try and find him ('I had such high hopes of finding my son'). Moneylenders, who are often involved in criminal networks, offer these loans – also known as payday loans – 'at predatory interest rates which maintain a vicious cycle of indebtedness' (Martinez and Rivera-Acevedo, 2018: 120).

The interviewee was desperate to complete the payments and to have no further dealings with the moneylenders, whom she described as 'cruel'. However, her precarious economic situation, fuelled by wider structural factors,[12] maintained these potentially dangerous financial connectivities. According to Forero (2016: 247), those who fall behind with their payments 'face the enforcers (*chulqueros*), who are not reluctant to use paramilitary methods including murder'. This story illuminates some of the complex dialectics and dynamics between different types or strands of connectivity, and specifically between broken and ruptured connectivities and bad connectivities.

Broken and Ruptured Connectivities: Health

When interviewees spoke about families, sometimes they also talked specifically about relationships with spouses and problems with intimacy. Issues of intimacy, highlighting embodied ruptures, were often linked, in turn, to broader health-related issues. As reflected in the theme *'The problem of ill health is there': Health connectivities and everyday stressors*, health was another significant broken and ruptured connectivity prominent in the qualitative data from Colombia (and indeed from all three countries).

Embodied Ruptures

Elbers et al. (2021), reflecting on embodied resilience as 'a quality of the dynamic relationships between the affected body and what happens in our surroundings', write about bodies *'opening or closing* from the world around them' (emphasis in the original). This, they argue, constitutes 'an important part of getting in touch with what is alive in the surroundings' (Elbers et al., 2021). What some of the Colombian interviews evidenced was a more complex 'opening and closing' dialectic. An Indigenous interviewee from the Nasa people, for example, had very viscerally opened herself up to other victims-/survivors, sharing with them her pain and tears. She had established her own association in 2016 and in the context of discussing her work, she articulated a desire to reconnect with her body – and to enable other victims-/survivors to do the same. As she described it, 'We're trying to get back in touch with our own bodies, to be able to feel again. To remember how to touch our heads, our breasts, which are sometimes overlooked'. Yet, at the same time, she expressed rupture, in the sense of being disconnected from the sensual side of herself that had once experienced desire and arousal. Revealing that she had not had a relationship with anyone since she was raped, she emphasised 'That all died for me, it died, it's dead'. She further added that 'I could watch a sexy film, but it would be like when I was two or three. It does nothing for me, it doesn't interest me. So, you see, all that died for me' (interview, Colombia, 6 March 2019). Another interviewee, also Indigenous and from the Pastos people, similarly used the words 'it died in me', insisting that 'there isn't the same pleasure in your body from being touched' (interview, Colombia, 4 February 2019). These women were in their 50s and 60s.

If, as Sviland et al. (2018: 372) argue, 'difficult life experiences may cause ruptured narratives in embodied and sensuous ways', what the previous examples show is that difficult life experiences can cause or contribute to embodied ruptures that affect how bodies relate and 'connect' with other bodies. In some cases, moreover, interviewees' bodies had been ruptured in the sense that they were no longer 'whole'. De Welde (2003: 267) refers to 'the body that has been degraded, ruptured, and dislocated through violence'. Some interviewees had lost integral parts of their bodies (including wombs) due to the extreme violence inflicted on them.

Before she had even been asked the first question in the interview guide, an interviewee who did not identify with any particular ethnic group explained: 'I lost my internal organs because of the beatings they [referring to FARC guerrillas] gave me. My insides are a mess'. The violence carried out on her body had resulted in damage to her ovaries and womb, which had consequently been removed. Reflecting on everything that had happened and on her ongoing health issues, this woman underlined that 'So, as I say, it's still going on and I am still suffering from the armed conflict. All the memories are still with me'. In other words, while her experiences had resulted very literally in broken and ruptured embodied connectivity, her body also 'stored' the memory of everything that she had gone through (Minge, 2007: 266), illustrating Scarry's (1985: 109) argument that 'what is "remembered" in the body is well remembered'. The interviewee further spoke about the impact of her experiences on her intimate relations with her husband. In her words, 'It took years for me to be with my partner again and it was even worse when I lost my organs. I felt worse at that point than right at the beginning' (interview, Colombia, 29 March 2019). At the very start of the interview, she underlined that she did not wish her husband to see the scars – 'a bodily marker of rupture' (Riessman 2015: 1063) – all over her body.

An Afro-Colombian interviewee – raped by four paramilitaries – talked about being 'horribly scarred' by this experience.[13] In her words, 'That hour, it will never leave me. Like when you screw up a sheet of paper, no matter how hard you try to smooth it out again, it stays [creased]. . . . The wound is like that'. Her scars were also physical; part of her womb had been removed (to reduce the risk of cervical cancer) after her rapists infected her with the human papilloma virus. She further spoke about how this embodied rupture had affected her relationship with her late husband (killed by paramilitaries). She recalled that 'It was two years before I could have sexual relations with him again. Out of fear. You see, I thought it would hurt, that it would harm me'. There were thus multiple broken and ruptured connectivities in her life; and she herself reinforced this imagery when, explaining how she understood the concept of victim, she opined that 'it's as if they've cut your wings off and you try to fly, but you can't' (interview, Colombia, 30 March 2019).

If, as these examples illustrate, intimacy issues reflect embodied ruptures linked, in some cases, to broader health issues, health was a prominent and recurring thematic within the data – and a resource which, for some interviewees, had been substantially impaired. In the study questionnaire, for example, 69 per cent of Colombian participants evaluated their health as either poor or fair. Only 5.26 per cent considered it to be excellent. Relatedly, interviewees frequently underlined some of the various ways that their experiences continued to affect them emotionally and psychologically. A male interviewee who did not identify with any ethnic group explained that 'when I start thinking about those things that happened, I feel [he hits the table] that I'm locked up again, tied up' (interview, Colombia, 30 January 2019). His words 'tied up' evoke connectivity, and interviewees particularly accentuated feelings of emotional pain which kept them connected – a further illustration of bad connectivities – to a past that they desperately wanted to forget or erase.

Another interviewee, who also did not identify with any specific ethnic group, spoke about some of the nightmares she had. As she explained:

> It can happen that if anything unsettles me, I can't control it, it's something... it mostly happens when I'm deep asleep. Then I wake up scared and I don't know where I am, disorientated as if I'm . . . as if I'm in a wasteland . . . like I'm hurt all over again.
>
> (interview, Colombia, 11 February 2019)

Her use of the term 'wasteland' was particularly evocative, further conveying ideas of scarring and rupture. Writing about a post-industrial wasteland in Kyrgyzstan, Pelkmans (2013: 17) argues that 'The entire territory of Ak-Tiuz is covered with scars, reminders of a different and better past, of the pain of recent rupture, but also of the process of healing'. This reference to healing is interesting because it accentuates the importance of social ecologies – and what Burton (2011: 26) refers to as 'the ecology of the pain experience' – in the sense of how they can contribute to or alleviate emotional pain. The larger point is that health is intrinsically connected to wider social ecologies (Taylor et al., 1997).

Social-Ecological Health

In Colombia, as in the other two countries, interviewees gave various examples of ill health within their social ecologies that added to the stressors in their lives. The Indigenous Embera Chami interviewee commented that her father's illness had created new financial worries for the family. She also referred to the ill health of her environment in the sense that 'Trying to bring up children in the society we live in at the moment with so many drugs, so many . . . such immense things for children to cope with, we don't know where to begin. It's a fight' (interview, Colombia, 11 February 2019). An interviewee who identified as mixed-race similarly accented the unhealthy nature of her environs in as far as they posed a risk to personal safety (Taylor et al., 1997: 439). 'It's best to stay quiet', she stressed, 'because there have been threats – I was threatened when I had to go out and about. So, that's been hard; being without money, going without things, it makes it hard to integrate with the community again' (interview, Colombia, 3 February 2019). In this example, a crime-ridden environment was helping to maintain some of the broken and ruptured connectivities in the interviewee's life.

The COVID-19 pandemic has contributed to further strengthening armed groups in Colombia. According to Human Rights Watch (HRW, 2020), groups in different parts of the country have imposed curfews and other measures to curb the spread of the virus, and have 'threatened, killed, and attacked people they perceive as failing to comply' with their rules. Moreover, in one of the reflections workshops that took place in Colombia in 2021, participants emphasised that restrictions on their movement – the very opposite of connectivity (Bishop et al., 2017: 9) – and the threats posed by armed actors had affected their mental health (reflections workshop, Colombia, 24 June 2021).

From the perspective of thinking about and exploring resilience, the broken and ruptured connectivities that this section and the previous section have discussed are significant because – building on this chapter's first section – they provide further insights into interviewees' experiences and the many stressors that they had faced (and often continued to face). They are also important because they bring to the forefront the issue of resources – and some of the resources that interviewees had either lost or could no longer use and access in the same way that they could previously. Broken and ruptured connectivities, however, were only one part of the interviewees' stories. All of them spoke about supportive and sustaining connectivities across different layers of their social ecologies, captured in the theme *'With them I get through it': Relational connectivities*, and it is to these connectivities that the chapter now turns.

Supportive and Sustaining Connectivities: Faith and Spirituality

Theron (2019: 328) refers to 'differentially-impactful resilience enablers'. This terminology is linked to Ungar's (2018: 6) discussion of differential impact theory, which seeks to elucidate 'which interventions with children are likely to have the most impact'. The key point is that supportive and sustaining connectivities, or protective resources, will have varying levels of 'protective value' (Theron, 2019: 329), depending on wider contextual factors and the particular stressors that individuals are facing. Gillum et al.'s (2006: 247) research with women in the United States (US) who had suffered domestic violence, for example, found that 'race moderated the relationship between religious involvement and social support', in the sense that 'Higher religious involvement was a predictor of greater social support for women of color but not for Caucasian women'. Barnes-Lee and Campbell's research on the juvenile justice system and predictive validity of the Protective Factors for Reducing Juvenile Reoffending (PFRJR) measure further illustrates the relevance of differential impact. The authors found that 'PFRJR scores significantly predicted desistance for White youth, but not racial minority juveniles' (Barnes-Lee and Campbell, 2020: 1402).

The fact that this book's three empirical chapters discuss the supportive and sustaining connectivities that interviewees in each country collectively spoke most about itself highlights how particular connectivities have different saliences and significance in different settings. This section focuses on faith and spirituality – one of the two supportive and sustaining connectivities that were especially pronounced in the Colombian interview data.

Scholars have explored the relationship between spirituality and resilience in various contexts (see, e.g., Alawiyah et al., 2011; Fernando and Ferrari, 2011; Glenn, 2014; Jones et al., 2016; Roberto et al., 2020). In general, however, relatively little attention has been given to the (potential) significance of faith and spirituality in the lives of individuals who have experienced CRSV. Moreover, research that has addressed the topic has primarily focused on African victims-/survivors (see, e.g., Akinsulure-Smith, 2014; Kelly et al., 2017; Yohani and Okeke-Ihejirika's, 2018).

In this research, it was Colombian interviewees who spoke the most about faith and spirituality. It is important to note that 'Colombia is a highly religious country (94% of Colombians are religiously affiliated). Specifically, 79% of Colombians are Roman Catholic Christian, 13% are Protestant Christian, 2% have another religious affiliation, and only 6% are religiously unaffiliated' (Chen et al., 2021: 84). This section, however, refers to faith and spirituality rather than religion. Although these terms are frequently used interchangeably, they are not the same. For example, 'spirituality can exist without religion and religion can exist without spirituality' (Farley, 2007: 4). What is important to underline is that religion, to cite Delgado (2005: 158), 'is the term used for formal or ritualized belief practices that are shared with a group of others' – and this is primarily not what the Colombian interviewees spoke about. Although some did talk about religion in an organised sense, faith and spirituality arguably better capture the very personal relationships with God that many interviewees articulated outside of formal religious frameworks and institutionalised belief systems. Lunn (2009: 937) defines spirituality as 'the personal beliefs by which an individual relates to and experiences the supernatural realm; and faith as the human trust or belief in a transcendent reality'.

Interviewees in all three countries identified faith and God as sources of support and strength in their lives. It was nevertheless striking that substantially more of the Colombian interviewees (19) did so compared to the Bosnian (9) and Ugandan (8) interviewees. When Colombians spoke about faith and spirituality, there were no obvious demographic patterns linked to factors such as age or ethnicity. It was interviewees' experiences that were often most relevant for contextualising the role that faith and spirituality played in their lives.

One of the interviewees (she did not identify with any particular group) had been raped by a group of paramilitaries while her children were screaming in the room next door, her husband had been killed by paramilitaries and the family had been forcibly displaced twice. Within these multiple and entangled experiences of violence, the interviewee's relationship with God had become one of the pivotal supportive and sustaining connectivities in her life. As she described: 'For me, it has been very hard, having five children [one of whom was disabled] with me. I sometimes think about it and then I pray to the Lord: "Give me strength. Give me the strength to carry on"'.

She had also relied on her faith when she had no one else to turn to or talk to – and in those periods when she was forced to remain silent. She explained, for example, that after paramilitaries raped her, 'They said to me: "If you talk to the police or make a statement, we'll come back here and finish off your family. You have to leave, you have to go or we'll kill you"'. Having already lost the family home and ranch, the interviewee subsequently moved with her children to a city where she 'didn't know a soul'. Faith and spirituality had thus been an enduring connectivity in her life and a way of dealing with so many broken and ruptured connectivities. 'I pray to God all the time', she revealed (interview, Colombia, 12 March 2019).

Paramilitaries had also killed the husband of one of the Afro-Colombian interviewees and disappeared her son. Using the word 'God' nine times and the word 'Christ' 13 times, this interviewee insisted that 'My only comfort has been Jesus Christ, who has been my support through this. The rest has been very cruel'. She further maintained that had Christ not been there for her, 'I believe that I wouldn't be here either'. Like the previous interviewee, this woman spoke about silence imperatives that her environment – and armed actors within that environment – had created, in the sense that 'in this country we never know who's who. It's more that they want to keep us in fear, so that people don't know if they should make a complaint or not'. This was the reason, she disclosed, that she had never made an official complaint about the CRSV that she had suffered; she worried that the individuals who took her statement could turn out to be informers. In this context, her faith and spirituality provided not only support, but also a sense of safety and security. Interestingly, while this interviewee initially called her life story 'No End in Sight', she ultimately changed it to 'Hope in Christ'. By way of explanation, she reflected: 'I feel that Christ is the one who is going to help us all, so we can all get through this and leave it all behind. He will give each of us what we most need' (interview, Colombia, 30 March 2019).

Other interviewees, similarly, expressed the strong conviction that God took care of them. An interviewee from the Indigenous Nasa people, for example, was 62 years old and claimed that no one would give her a job because of her age. She had the additional financial worry of looking after her elderly parents. Although money was tight, she was able to 'scrape together' enough to get by and maintained that this was thanks to God. In her own words, 'The thing is to believe in yourself, believe in things – that Our Lord will provide'. She further explained that 'I'm a very spiritual person. I'm a strong believer in God and I don't think that God will let me fall, because although I have setbacks

I always get back on track. Spirituality, that's the most important thing' (interview, Colombia, 6 March 2019).

The Indigenous Embera Chami interviewee also stressed that 'having faith and trust is everything'. She talked about the financial difficulties she faced in looking after her children and her dream was to become a dressmaker. She prayed to God about this, regarding Him as her main source of support, and trusted that He would look out for her. She earned money by making dress alterations for local people and disclosed that 'What I do is every day, I get up and ask God: "What can I do? Where shall I start?" And I ask him to send me clients who want me to do alterations'. It is important to underline that this interviewee, who was 40 years old, was not passively relying on God for help (and indeed none of the interviewees were). She was very actively trying to improve her financial situation ('I'm fighting for a little [street] booth to sell coffees and pastries'), but the point is that her faith and spirituality were aiding her in this regard. As she underscored, 'We carry on fighting with God's help. That's the most important thing' (interview, Colombia, 11 February 2019).

One of the two male Colombian interviewees also spoke about the importance of faith in his life. This 38-year-old man, who identified as mixed-race, called his life story 'Mary', explaining that 'I believe deeply in God, in Our Lady of Carmen and the Virgin Mary and the Holy Remedy'. Compared to many of the other interviewees, he spoke more about organised religion (going to church, attending an annual religious festival), but he too also articulated the idea of God as protector;

> I want God to be close to me in my life, right? God will protect me wherever I go, wherever I am – with my friends. God will look after me. Sometimes I pray to God a lot – asking Him to protect me wherever I go and wherever I am.
>
> (interview, Colombia, 29 January 2019)

Religious coping has been defined as 'the use of religious beliefs or behaviors to facilitate problem-solving to prevent or alleviate the negative emotional consequences of stressful life circumstances' (Koenig et al., 1998: 513). Although there is a significant and growing body of literature on religious coping (e.g., Harrison et al., 2001; Mesidor and Sly, 2019; Pargament et al., 2000), this sub-section does not use such terminology. First, 'coping' potentially detracts from the many challenges that interviewees – in Colombia but also in BiH and Uganda – continued to face. Second, 'religious coping' elevates religion over the many other ways that individuals – drawing on their social ecologies and the relationships that they have within these ecologies – deal with their experiences and rebuild their lives. What the earlier examples from the interview data primarily demonstrate is that faith and spirituality, as important supportive and sustaining relational connectivities, can be 'an integral part [albeit only one part] of how individuals . . . rise to the challenges of adversity' (Popham et al., 2021: 370).

Supportive and Sustaining Connectivities: Women's and Non-governmental Organisations

The Comparative Picture

In one of the reflections workshops that took place in Colombia in 2021, a participant articulated her understanding of resilience. In her words:

> For me, resilience is related to the environment. You have to analyse a little that broad environment that is helping you to be resistant. In resilience, there are a series of people, of situations around us that can help us to get that resilience.
>
> (reflections workshop, Colombia, 30 June 2021)

She thus expressed a social-ecological understanding of resilience, consistent with this book's own theorisation of the concept.

An environmental connectivity that was extremely important both to this participant and indeed to many of the Colombian interviewees was their relationships with, involvement in and/or leadership of women's organisations and non-governmental organisations (NGOs). In the quantitative part of the study, a higher percentage of Colombian respondents (73 per cent), compared to Bosnian (47.93 per cent) and Ugandan respondents (33.5 per cent), answered that they were in contact with women's organisations, although a higher percentage of Bosnian respondents (90 per cent) than Colombian (70.76 per cent) and Ugandan respondents (38.8 per cent) said they were in contact with NGOs. The distinction between women's organisations and NGOs is necessarily fluid and there were some country differences in this regard. In particular, the terminology of NGOs is much more common in BiH and Uganda (even in relation to organisations that work with women), while women's organisations/associations is a widely used term in Colombia.

It is also necessary to point out that the in-country organisations which supported the fieldwork played a crucial role in facilitating access to research participants, as discussed in Chapter 3. Moreover, many (although by no means all) of the participants were already known to these organisations or were in contact with other organisations. These factors may have contributed to slanting the data, in terms of the emphasis that interviewees – and particularly those in Colombia – put on women's organisations and NGOs. However, it may also simply reflect the important work that these organisations do on the ground. Especially in Colombia, moreover, women's organisations and NGOs have long been a significant part of the country's socio-political landscape (which is also linked to the duration of the armed conflict). Kreft (2019: 231), for example, notes that high levels of mobilisation around the issue of CRSV in Colombia gave 'the impetus for the establishment of women's and victims' organizations from the 1970s onwards'.

Connectivity Stories of Resilience in Colombia 185

Ugandan interviewees mainly spoke about the financial and livelihood support that they had received from organisations, including Village Savings and Loan Associations (VSLA) known locally as *Bol icup* (see Chapter 7). Many of them had also received basic existential support (clothes, blankets, cooking utensils) from international organisations such as World Vision. Colombian interviewees (and those in BiH) talked far less about such forms of support and focused much more on psychosocial support. The Indigenous Embera Chami interviewee, for example, spoke about the support and holistic care that she had received from a local women's organisation. She reflected: 'Each little thing has been very useful. Because when you go there, they look after you, they see that you eat well, that you sleep well and all that'. She had been 'trapped', she maintained, and the organisation – which had also given her access to a psychologist – 'helped me get out of the hole I was in' (interview, Colombia, 11 February 2019).

An Afro-Colombian interview also underlined the importance of the psychological support that she had received from various women's organisations. She was now able to speak about her experiences (she had previously dealt with the past by putting everything that she had gone through in her 'trunk of things to forget'), and this had made a huge difference to her wellbeing. She stressed that 'I'm not the same sad woman I was before, in those days when what happened to me happened [she was kidnapped by a guerrilla from the Popular Liberation Army (ELP)[14] and held as a sexual slave]. I feel different now' (interview, Colombia, 30 March 2019).

From a psychological perspective, what had also enormously helped many of the Colombian interviewees was having the opportunity to meet, interact with and share their stories with fellow women in the safe environment of organisations such as *Ruta Pacífica de las Mujeres*, *El Meta con Mirada de Mujer* and the *Red de Mujeres Víctimas y Profesionales*. These interactions helped to foster what I refer to as experiential solidarity, the existence of which illustrates that supportive and sustaining connectivities can be reciprocal as well as one-directional.

Experiential Solidarity

An interviewee who identified as mixed-race referred to two women's organisations that had given her 'huge support' and explained:

> That's why I'm such a great believer in the power of community. I tell you, for women who've been through so many different ways of being victimised, it helps so, so, so much in life to be surrounded by other women who support you and give you a hand.
>
> (interview, Colombia, 10 February 2019)

Another interviewee, who did not identify with any ethnic group, spoke about one of the same two organisations, which she had first established contact with some six years earlier. She recalled that hearing the stories of other women, which were sometimes worse than her own, had an immensely positive impact on her; 'It was amazing because I could tell myself that it could have been worse, but I got on with life. If they can do it, so can I. That has helped me so much'. She also stressed that talking to other women had enabled her to overcome the sense of guilt that she had felt for a long time ('I always felt that everything that happened was my fault'), and she had gone on to officially report the sexual violence that she experienced – something that she had previously not felt able to do (interview, Colombia, 11 February 2019).

Indeed, there are many examples of experiential solidarity in Colombia. The organisation *Narrar para Vivir*, established in 2001 in the Montes de María region of northern Colombia to bring together *campesina* women and give them the opportunity to speak about their experiences, is just one illustration. According to Lemaitre and Sandvik (2015: 29), the women's activities 'focus on building trust and creating networks of affection among women, within which they feel safe talking about themselves, their grief, and their fears'. From a resilience perspective, these 'networks of affection' constitute highly significant resources which, as the final chapter will argue, need to be invested in and supported as part of both transitional justice and policy work on CRSV.

Lemaitre and Sandvik (2015: 29) further argue that *Narrar para Vivir* gives women an opportunity to express identities – for example, as mothers, teachers or shop owners – 'that go beyond their identities as "victims of war crimes"'. It is important to note in this regard that the interviewees who participated in this research did not view women's organisations simply as spaces for sharing their pain and affirming their victimhood. They also frequently spoke about new skills that they had learned or developed through training courses and workshops, and some of them were now leading their own organisations, fighting for the rights of other women and thus giving back to their social ecologies. In short, the organisations played a crucial role in nourishing what Lemaitre (2016: 556) refers to as 'gendered strength', which manifests through caretaking. In her words, 'the stronger the woman, the wider she casts the net of her caretaking . . . beginning with herself and extending to her family, neighbors, and community' (Lemaitre, 2016: 557).

One of the two male interviewees, who did not identify with any ethnic group, also spoke about receiving help from an organisation, and in particular about going to workshops and learning new skills, 'so we know where we are and how to keep going forwards; how to keep doing things and survive day to day' (interview, Colombia, 30 January 2019). However, he could not remember the name of the organisation, and it transpired that he was actually referring to the state-run Victims' Unit rather than to an NGO. The second male interviewee, who identified as mixed-race, did not speak about organisations at all. Nevertheless, both of these men did have important sources of support in their lives. They spoke about friends, for example, and the first interviewee also stressed the significance of his mother, to whom he referred ten times. He explained that: 'Until now, my mother has taught me everything. Seeing how my mother has got through so much has given me the strength to do the same' (interview, Colombia, 30 January 2019).

Neither man said anything about sharing his experiences with fellow male victims-/survivors of CRSV. In his work on northern Uganda, Schulz (2019) has explored and underlined the importance of survivors' groups for men. He argues that:

> in contexts where the formal justice system is inaccessible or unavailable for survivors, and where institutionalized TJ [transitional justice] processes are irresponsive to male sexual and gendered harms, groups can offer an avenue for survivors to engage with their experiences, remedy their harms and thereby attain a sense of justice.
>
> (Schulz, 2019: 186)

Such groups, however, are relatively rare, and so too are resources specifically aimed at male victims-/survivors – or which are genuinely (as opposed to just nominally) inclusive of them.

One organisation in Colombia that does offer some support to male victims-/survivors – and specifically to men (and women) who are part of the LGBT (lesbian, gay, bisexual, transgender) community – is *Colombia Diversa*. Its work in defending LGBT rights is hugely important. This particular focus, however, together with the organisation's modest resources, means that *Colombia Diversa* can necessarily only reach a limited number of male victims-/survivors. Even if more support did exist for these men, they may not readily use it for a host of reasons, including inhibiting feelings of shame, fear and cultural factors (Traunmüller et al., 2019: 2036; see also Manivannan, 2014: 650–651).

As a final point with which to conclude this section, it was striking that experiential solidarity and the benefits of sharing one's experiences with other victims-/survivors were far less prominent in the Bosnian and Ugandan datasets compared to the Colombian dataset. It is also important to reiterate that Bosnian and Ugandan interviewees primarily spoke about organisations in the sense of what they had received from them (materially and/or psychologically). Indeed, these organisations were set up precisely to provide such support. In Colombia, however, and reflecting a long tradition of women's activism (see, e.g., Asher, 2004; Hernandez Reyes, 2019; Zulver, 2022), many of the organisations have much broader agendas. For example, *Casa de la Mujer*, a feminist organisation established in 1982, 'has prioritized strengthening women's autonomy, sexual health, and reproductive rights'; and the feminist movement *Ruta Pacífica de las Mujeres* 'has been committed to strengthening the role of women in a negotiated solution to the armed conflict' (Kreft, 2019: 225). The ambitious goals of these organisations require women to work together and fight together – and the sharing of stories, pain and emotions is the first step in building deeper activist solidarities.[15]

New Connectivities: Building Connections Through Meaning-Making

In its efforts to do more than simply give examples of resilience from the Colombian interview data, this chapter has thus far focused on two particular dimensions of its connectivity framing of resilience (and on the themes linked to them) – broken and ruptured connectivities and supportive and sustaining connectivities. The final two sections concentrate on the third dimension – new connectivities. Before continuing, it is important to reiterate that this book is not reducing the many layers and complexities of resilience to new connectivities. What it seeks to demonstrate is that exploring the broad idea of new connectivities is one possible way – and '*a* story, necessarily selected from fluid possibilities' (Riessman, 2015: 1067; emphasis in the original) – of thinking about what everyday resilience 'looks' like and how it manifests. It is also essential to stress that the book's emphasis on and analysis of new connectivities must be situated in the context of its overall aim of telling a story about resilience through the fluid and dynamic relationships between individuals and their social ecologies – and how the two 'co-facilitate' resilience (Theron, 2019: 327).

As noted in the previous chapter, I developed three particular themes (relevant to BiH, Colombia and Uganda) linked to new connectivities. However, to avoid unnecessarily repeating some of the same points made in the Bosnian chapter, and to reflect the fact that one of the themes (*'I want to achieve more': (Re)Building connections and making a difference*) was especially significant in the Colombian data, this section and the next focus on just two of the three themes relating to new connectivities. This section is about new connectivities in the sense of meaning-making.

'Why Did This Have to Be': Making Connections and Finding Meaning

According to Brockmeier (2009: 230), 'Reaching for meaning . . . might be the ultimate form of human agency'. In general, scholarship on CRSV has given relatively little attention to how victims-/survivors interpret their experiences and endeavour to make sense of them (Dolan et al., 2020: 1153). There are, however, some exceptions. Coulter's (2009) work in Sierra Leone, for example, has explored how contextual factors shaped women's stories and interpretations of CRSV; and also how 'local moral imperatives' (Coulter, 2009: 126) influenced the way that these women dealt with their experiences in order to survive. In her research in Peru, similarly, Theidon has discussed the wider social and narrative context in which women situated – and made sense of – their experiences of rape. The women, she explains,

> detailed the preconditions that structured vulnerability and emphasized their efforts to minimize harm to themselves and to the people they cared

for. With their insistence on context, women situated their experience of sexual violence – those episodes of brutal victimization – within womanly narratives of heroism.

(Theidon, 2013: 118)

More recently, and based on interviews with representatives of Colombian civil society, some of whom had themselves experienced CRSV, Kreft (2020: 459) found that 'The women interviewed overwhelmingly see CRSV as grounded in patriarchal structures that are deeply embedded in Colombian society'. The present research also supports this finding. Specifically, some interviewees linked their experiences of violence to entrenched structural factors. An interviewee who did not identify with any ethnic group and who, as previously discussed, was raped by FARC guerrillas and by her own stepfather, insisted, for example, that 'What has happened to me has only happened to me because I'm a woman' (interview, Colombia, 14 March 2019).

Structural factors, moreover, are often entangled with cultural factors. An Afro-Colombian interviewee underlined both her gender and the significance of cultural stereotypes about Black (hyper)sexuality.[16] According to her:

lots of men seem to have the idea that Afro women have wonderful bodies, that they have a vagina. I don't know if you understand me? That their vaginas are big. So, they [men] want to try it out with us because they have the idea that we're hot.

(interview, Colombia, 30 March 2019)[17]

An interviewee who viewed herself as a *costeña* referred to the existence of similar cultural stereotypes about women from the coast, which had partly informed her own meaning-making process and understanding of why she was targeted. She argued that 'There are things that they [people in general] always say about you, to stereotype you. That the coastal women are hot, that they're up for it' (interview, Colombia, 2 May 2019).

Very few of the Colombian interviewees engaged in self-blaming, and they frequently stated explicitly that they were not at fault. In making this point, some interviewees drew attention to the circumstances in which they were subjected to CRSV, which often involved the use of threats. An Afro-Colombian interviewee stressed that when paramilitaries arrived in her *vereda* and liked the look of a particular woman, she had to go with them and had no choice in the matter. This interviewee further recounted her own experiences with a particular paramilitary;

He came and he said to me: 'Come on'. . . . And he was touching me and he often said to me: 'If you don't come with me, I'll kill your mother, I'll kill your children'. So, what could I do about it?

(interview, Colombia, 4 March 2019)

Another interviewee, who did not identify with a specific ethnic group, described how a unit of the FARC had threatened to harm her young nephew if she did not go along with their wishes. In her words: 'I had to do as they said because they threatened the child. They had a grenade. So, what did I have to do? I had to let them do whatever they liked' (interview, Colombia, 14 March 2019).

I discuss these examples as illustrating new connectivities, linked to resilience, in the sense that interviewees were making connections between their experiences and the wider structural, cultural and contextual circumstances surrounding those experiences – and doing so in ways that were helping them to deal with what they had gone through and to rebuild their lives. Significant in this regard is Antonovsky's (1993: 725) concept of Sense of Coherence (SOC), referring to 'a way of seeing the world which facilitated successful coping with the innumerable, complex stressors confronting us in the course of living'. More specifically, Antonovsky's conceptualisation of salutogenesis, meaning the origins of health (Antonovsky, 1996: 13), posits that SOC, which is shaped by life experiences, 'helps one mobilise resources to cope with stressors and manage tension successfully' (Mittelmark and Bauer, 2017: 7). Applying this to the qualitative data, interviewees' experiences and their interpretation of those experiences had contributed to a SOC which was one factor motivating them to fight for resources – not only for themselves but also, in many cases, for the benefit of others within their social ecologies – as will be discussed in the next section.

Post-traumatic Growth

Compared to the Bosnian and Ugandan interviewees, more of the Colombian interviewees had found positive meaning in their experiences. This, by extension, illuminates the relevance of post-traumatic growth (PTG), a concept first introduced by Tedeschi and Calhoun (1996) and which has since been explored in a variety of different contexts (see, e.g., Hefferon et al., 2009; Shamia et al., 2015; Vazquez et al., 2021; Woodward and Joseph, 2003). The core idea is that PTG, as both a process and an outcome, develops 'out of a cognitive process that is initiated to cope with traumatic events that extract an extreme cognitive and emotional toll' (Tedeschi et al., 1998: 1).

Notwithstanding a wealth of literature on the concept, Jayawickreme and Blackie (2014: 32) point out that many researchers are in broad agreement that the positive transformations in beliefs and behaviour which characterise PTG 'can be manifested in at least five forms: improved relations with others, identification of new possibilities for one's life, increased perception of personal strength, spiritual growth and enhanced appreciation of life'. These are also the five factors (onto which 21 different items load) that constitute Tedeschi and Calhoun's (1996) PTG Inventory.

Scholars have explored the relationship between resilience and PTG, and it is frequently argued that the two are distinct concepts (see, e.g., Ewert and

Tessneer, 2019: 284; 285; Schaefer et al., 2018: 18). Tedeschi and Calhoun (2004: 4), for example, comment that PTG 'refers to a change in people that goes beyond an ability to resist and not be damaged by highly stressful circumstances'. It thus has 'a quality of transformation, or a qualitative change in functioning', unlike the 'apparently similar' concept of resilience (Tedeschi and Calhoun, 2004: 4). Levine et al.'s (2009: 285) research, moreover, has found an inverse relationship between resilience (narrowly conceptualised and measured by the absence of post-traumatic stress disorder) and PTG. Nevertheless, there are significant overlaps between PTG and resilience (Infurna and Jayawickreme, 2019: 155); and although resilience can exist without PTG, the latter can be an example or expression of resilience. This was particularly evident in Colombia.

This research (and specifically the study questionnaire) did not use the aforementioned PTG Inventory, and the interview guide did not include any questions about 'growth'. Some of the interviewees, however, spoke about personal strength (factor III in the PTG Inventory), and specifically about renewed strength as a result of their experiences. An Afro-Colombian interviewee explained that 'I see myself as a woman who's a fighter, a warrior; a woman who's become stronger, so that today she doesn't fear anything' (interview, Colombia, 30 March 2019). Reflecting on her life today, an interviewee who did not identify with any ethnic group opined that 'I feel it has changed a great deal – in the sense that I am much stronger than before'. Elaborating on this, she added that:

> I want to fight for the things I want; I want to change my life; I want to study. I want to help my children get ahead – that's the most important thing. I don't want to be humiliated by anyone anymore.
> (interview, Colombia, 2 May 2019)

Although to a much lesser extent, some of the Bosnian and Ugandan interviewees also maintained that their experiences had made them stronger. Moreover, interviewees in all three countries frequently evidenced an appreciation of life (factor V in Calhoun and Tedeschi's PTG Inventory). The biggest difference between the Colombian interviews compared to the Bosnian and Ugandan interviews, however, was in relation to factor II of the Inventory, namely new possibilities. Fundamentally, some of the Colombian interviewees were effectively creating new possibilities (and new meanings), as discussed in the final section.

New Connectivities: Fighting for Change

This book, as part of its connectivity framework for thinking about resilience, places a strong accent on broken and ruptured connectivities – an idea explored in all three empirical chapters. A fundamental reason why the book utilises connectivity as its framework, as discussed in Chapter 2, is to make a novel conceptual and empirical contribution to existing scholarship on resilience and on social-ecological systems (SES), by examining the changing relational dynamics within these systems in contexts of war and armed conflict. Precisely because SES are in constant movement and flux, any rupture in the relationship between different components of these systems is not necessarily something negative and need not be destabilising.

Highlighting this, the back loop (release and reorganisation phases) of the adaptive cycle (Gunderson and Holling, 2002), outlined in Chapter 1, is quintessentially about rupture; it is when things break up and come apart. It entails 'the collapse of accumulated connections and the release of bound-up knowledge and capital' (Holling, 2004). This rupture and breaking apart mean that the back loop can therefore offer opportunities for things to be significantly different (Miller et al., 2021). According to Wakefield (2017: 86), for example, 'What the back loop suggests to us is that the Anthropocene is now a time to explore, to let go – of foundations for thinking and acting – and open ourselves to the possibilities offered to us here and now'. It should be emphasised that changes resulting from the back loop do not necessarily make things better or worse, but they can be positive or negative (Holling, 2004).

When rupture occurs in the context of individuals' experiences of armed conflict and large-scale violence, the resultant changes can be deeply disruptive to lives that will never be the same again. Nevertheless, the Colombian data, in particular, also offered some important examples of 'the opportunities that are opened up by . . . rupture' (King et al., 2021: 2786). In short, notwithstanding the many broken and ruptured connectivities that interviewees had experienced, many of them were now engaged in what Zulver (2021: 443) has termed 'transformational repertoires of action', through the building of new connectivities aimed at bringing about positive change within their social ecologies.

'*I Want to Achieve More*': (Re)Building Connections and Making a Difference

The aforementioned concept of experiential solidarity is itself partly about new connectivities. Some of the interviewees, moreover, had built on this solidarity – and on the crucial support that they had received from women's organisations and NGOs – to forge further connectivities. As one illustration, an interviewee who identified as mixed-race reflected that 'sharing with other people has let me see that it wasn't just me who suffered these things [referring to CRSV]'. This had helped her to reconnect with life; she maintained that 'I've started afresh, right? I've started again with my life in the community. Before, I'd abandoned everything, for a while I abandoned it all. I've come back into society because I want to help other women in my community'. She had resolved to make something good out of what happened to her ('I use my experience to help other women'), and she talked about some of the work that she was now doing in her community. This included fostering income-generating opportunities for women (e.g., sourcing laying-hens for those who had land; finding the necessary materials for those who wanted to engage in craftwork). In her words, 'I try to organise projects for the women. You see, many of them are mothers and the main breadwinner – they are mostly widows – so I try to, at the very least, I try to support them, right?' (interview, Colombia, 4 February 2019).

The interviewee from the Indigenous Nasa people insisted that 'I'm very resilient and I've resisted. I've resisted against the pain, of keeping quiet about it [CRSV], keeping it to myself. Do you understand?' She also spoke about 'letting all the pain go and allowing something good to flourish'. There were two aspects to this. First, she maintained that she had undergone a psychological transformation – 'like a butterfly coming out of its chrysalis and spreading its wings'. As part of this process, she had reconnected with life and with herself. In her words:

> It's a good life when you start living again, start thinking again and wanting to feel again. When you no longer fear yourself and can recognise yourself as a woman again. I can touch myself again. I'm not afraid to touch myself again.

Second, when specifically asked how the sexual violence that she suffered during the armed conflict had impacted on her life, she opined that: 'For me, it's become something good – not because of what was done to me, but, rather, because of what I'm doing with it now'.[18] This interviewee had established her own association (which had 130 members) to help other women, and the experiential solidarity that was implicit in her interview was based on shared experiences not only of CRSV but also, more broadly, of continued struggle. As she reflected, 'We've lived with the conflict since our parent's time, and they've survived alongside us. Think about it, it's like a chain; that's what survival is, that we're surviving still and now with the conflict'.

At the outset, this Indigenous interviewee explained that 'My life is very busy at the moment', and this was fundamentally linked to her work as a women's leader. It was work that required her to build new connectivities, and to creatively use them, in order to support other women. She gave the following example:

> If I don't have what I need, I have to look for someone who does have the resources. To help someone else, I have to go looking – at least knocking on doors. 'Look here, let's do this. Let's do a jumble sale'. 'But how? I don't have any clothes!' 'But I want to have a jumble sale to generate some cash'. 'Who's it for?' 'To help the girls'. 'What sort of clothes?' 'Whatever you have, that you don't need, that you're going to throw out or don't want anymore and then we'll sell them for 1,000 Pesos or more'. So, with all this knocking on doors, opportunities open up and all that.

She also made clear, however, that the work she did was very much a collective effort ('We work together'), based on the deep connectivities that she had forged with the women in her association whom she described as her main source of support. They were, she insisted, 'friends who are always around and always ready to see what we need to do, where we're going next, what we're doing and aiming for' (interview, Colombia, 6 March 2019).

The Wider Context

Had it been possible to make contact with Colombian victims-/survivors of CRSV without enlisting the support of organisations such as *Ruta Pacifica de las Mujeres*, some of the recurrent ideas within the data – such as experiential solidarity and helping other women – might have been less prominent.[19] The utility of the book's connectivity approach to resilience, however, is precisely that it tells a broad narrative based on its three core elements, while also leaving sufficient space for exploring what those elements look like in very different contexts. In Colombia, interviewees' leadership positions and relationships with women's organisations and/or NGOs were a fundamental part of the context in which they were dealing with their experiences, seeking to move forward with their lives and engaging in the process of building new connectivities with their social ecologies.[20]

To pick up on an earlier point made by the Indigenous Nasa interviewee, it is also highly significant that 'For Colombian women the armed conflict is an everyday reality. It is not an isolated event or incident, it has been part of their life for more than six decades' (Sanchez et al., 2011: 9). Hence, simply living with – and finding ways to live with – this reality itself represents a form and expression of everyday resilience. More than this, however, some of the interviewees were actively resisting the status quo by standing up against violence, continuing with their social activism and/or fighting for institutional and structural change. In this regard, as Rodriguez Castro (2021: 356) argues, 'The voices of Colombian women need to be heard, not as victims, but as agents and political subjects creating and enacting other worlds to resist and re-exist' (see also Sachseder, 2020: 174; Zulver, 2017: 1512).

An interviewee who did not identify with any particular ethnic group described herself as a victims' leader. Part of her work, which focused not only on victims-/survivors of CRSV, was about supporting women to speak about their experiences of violence and to officially report them. Making the decision to talk, she stressed, was not easy, particularly when the person taking the statement did not demonstrate sensitivity or understanding. 'I went into so many offices', she recalled, 'where they [officials] asked me questions that made me feel even more dirty than I already did, and there are still women who have that experience when I take them to make their statements'. Seeking to change this, the interviewee regularly followed up on women's cases and had actively built new institutional connectivities as a way of ensuring that the members of her organisation were treated with the dignity and respect that they deserved. Of particular importance was the relationship that she had established with the *Defensoría del Pueblo* (Ombudsman), which, she maintained, 'is like our second home'.

Interestingly, what the interviewee also implicitly expressed was a resistance to connectivity. Underlining the challenges that she faced as a victims' leader in securing the necessary resources to help other women, she explained, for example, that:

> You hear about a project and you get involved, but the project doesn't get off the ground because you're not from the same political party as them. That's sad and it's humiliating to have them rub your face in the dirt all the time.

Rather than submitting to clientelism, however, which is fundamentally about connections in the sense of patron–client networks (Veenendaal and Corbett, 2020),[21] this woman insisted that 'If one door shuts, we look for another door' (interview, Colombia, 29 March 2019).

Another interviewee, who identified as mixed-race, spoke about the mistreatment of women within her municipality and what she was doing about this. She began the interview by stating that 'I'm working on the land. That's what I know how to do. I've always been on the land'. Through her involvement with a local women's organisation, however, she had gained important skills and legal knowledge that she was now using to establish new connectivities within her social ecology in the sense of confronting officials with the truth that they were often unwilling to acknowledge. 'It's always the same', she stressed, 'the way they are like "noooo!" They try to mask the way things are, but I have the law on my side. I use the law and go knocking on doors – the direct approach' (interview, Colombia, 10 February 2019).

There is an obvious lack of any reference to male victims-/survivors of CRSV in this particular discussion. Neither of the two male interviewees held social leadership roles nor were they involved in advocacy work, which is partly a reflection of wider contextual factors. These include the absence of a history of men's activism in Colombia, linked, in turn, to the fact that 'men's and women's experiences and actions during conflict are determined by gender roles and identities assigned by society' (Moser and Clark, 2001: 30). With respect to new connectivities, the larger point is that men and women do not necessarily have the same opportunities to build new connectivities in some contexts. Potentially, this could be construed as a flaw in the book's connectivity framework. It is, however, a problem that almost certainly would not have arisen had it been possible to generate a more gender-balanced interview sample (which is also a reflection of context) and had the profile of the female interviewees themselves been a little more diverse.

★★★

196 Connectivity Stories of Resilience in Colombia

This chapter has sought to capture and convey some of the depth and richness of the interviews on which it has drawn. While it has not been able to cover everything, and while it has fully acknowledged some of the limitations of the research, it has told a novel story about resilience, centred on the connectivities between interviewees and their social ecologies and on the different types and dynamics of connectivity in the interviewees' lives. What it has also aimed to show is the significance of connectivity for providing a broader context in which to understand and situate interviewees' expressions of resilience. It has followed the same structure as the previous chapter on BiH (and the next chapter on Uganda), a decision that carried the very real risk of the chapters becoming repetitive. The elasticity of the book's conceptual framework, however, means that it allows for comparison across the three case studies, while also leaving wide scope for analysis of its three connectivity dimensions and what they look like in each country. The next and final case study chapter further demonstrates this.

Notes

1 These were Afro-Colombian, Indigenous, Mestizo, Raizal and Roma or Gitano/a.
2 Of the 171 Colombian participants who completed a study questionnaire, 47 did not identify with any of the ethnic groups listed and 12 did not understand the question about ethnicity.
3 Interviewees often identified which armed group(s) had committed violence. However, in some cases they were unsure. Alluding to the fact that all of the armed actors wore the same uniform, Uribe (2004: 92) has referred to them simply as 'the people in camouflage'.
4 As in BiH, interviewees sometimes spoke in the present tense when referring to past events. This is an illustration of how 'life stories continuously jump back and forth' (Brockmeier, 2000: 56; see also Riessman, 2015: 1057). One explanation is that 'every narrative about my past is always also a story told in, and about, the present as well as [a] story about the future' (Brockmeier, 2000: 56).
5 Transnational corporations have been heavily implicated in the armed conflict in Colombia (see, e.g., Holmes and Gutiérrez De Piñeres, 2011: 574; Sachseder, 2020: 165).
6 All place names are redacted to protect the interviewees' identities.
7 It should be noted that demographic information is not available for the Colombian workshop participants as the workshop convenors anonymised the transcripts.
8 The interviewee's reference to a plant – and one that has deep and strong roots – is particularly interesting in this context. According to Calhoun (2020: 19):

> the science of botany, both historically and structurally, is predicated on an initial process of uprooting (*déracinement*). This foundational act of violence severs the flower from its natural habitat – tears it from its ground (*sol*) – and carries it away from any point of origin in order to mount or fix it somewhere else.

9 As noted in the previous chapter, there was a statistically significant difference between the group means of each country's total score on the relational sub-scale of the ARM, as determined by a one-way ANOVA ($F(2,446) = 27.709$, $p = .000$). Post-hoc comparisons using the Tukey LSD test indicated that the mean score for Colombia (M = 24.21, SD = 6.65) was significantly different from the mean score for BiH (M = 29.09,

SD = 4.8) – but not from the mean score for Uganda (M = 25.26, SD = 5.31). Thank you to Dr Adrian Bromage for these analyses.

10 Interviewees often simply referred to the 'guerrillas' without specifically naming a particular group.

11 According to Gordon (2017: 133), false positive crimes 'were primarily committed between 2002 and 2008 and involved the execution of over 3,000 civilians'. She further adds that 'The scandal constitutes one of the most shocking global examples in recent years of crimes of the powerful: crimes committed by state actors against the most dispossessed and marginalized members of society' (Gordon, 2017: 133).

12 Sanchez-Barrios et al. (2015: 889) point out that research evidence 'indicates that racial minorities [in Colombia] continually face higher rejection rates and receive less favorable terms than other types of financial service consumers of equal credit risks'.

13 Indeed, several interviewees talked about being scarred – e.g., 'You're scarred forever'; 'The scars that it left are on my body and in my mind'; 'And that's something that leaves a mark on you – scars you for your whole life'.

14 Established in 1965, the EPL was the military wing of Colombia's Marxist-Leninist Party. It demobilised in 1991 and formed a political party called Hope, Peace and Freedom.

15 During the negotiations that eventually resulted in the 2016 peace agreement between the government and the FARC, for example, a gender sub-committee was set up in 2014. Boutron (2018: 116) points out that 'The gender subcommittee was established thanks to the combined endeavours of women's organisations and those of the actors from the international community engaged in promoting the gender lens in Colombian peacebuilding'.

16 Discussing representations of Black sexuality in Latin America more broadly, Wade (2013: 215) argues that 'Black women have commonly been portrayed as sexually loose and available, hypersexual and desirable'.

17 Sachseder (2020: 178), similarly, notes that 'Some of my interviewees told me how specifically Black women with their "curly hair," "big breasts," and "broad hips" were targeted'.

18 Interestingly, and in contrast to the other two Indigenous interviewees, this interviewee also regarded her ethnicity as relevant to how she had dealt with her experiences. In her words:

> I think that I take certain risks sometimes because my parents and my grandparents were Indigenous and they were very powerful people. So yes, coming from those roots makes you feel like a warrior, strong. You are not easily intimidated. . . . If you start to fall back, you say to yourself: 'No, I can do this!' and I pick up what I need and well, go for the top.
>
> (interview, Colombia, 6 March 2019)

19 Nine of the 21 interviewees, for example, answered in the study questionnaire that they held leadership positions within women's organisations. Five of the Bosnian interviewees and ten of the Ugandan interviewees also answered in the affirmative to the question about leadership. However, while leadership was a very prominent theme in the Colombian interviews, this was not the case at all in the Bosnian and Ugandan interviews.

20 The results of a Mann-Whitney non-parametric test on the questionnaire data indicated that participants (in all three countries) who said that they held leadership roles had higher overall ARM scores (M = 112) than those who did not (M = 108), U = 19490, p = .011. Thank you to Dr Adrian Bromage for these analyses.

21 Eaton and Chambers-Ju (2014: 88) argue that 'Even for Latin America, a region widely marked by patron-client relations, Colombia stands out for the pervasiveness and extensiveness of its clientelistic networks'.

References

Afifi TO and MacMillan HL (2011) Resilience following child mistreatment: A review of protective factors. *Canadian Journal of Psychiatry* 56(5): 266–272.

Ahern NR, Kiehl EM, Sole ML and Byers J (2006) A review of instruments measuring resilience. *Issues in Comprehensive Pediatric Nursing* 29(2): 103–125.

Akinsulure-Smith AM (2014) Displaced African female survivors of conflict-related sexual violence: Challenges for mental health providers. *Violence Against Women* 20(6): 677–694.

Alawiyah T, Beli H, Pyles L and Runnels RC (2011) Spirituality and faith-based interventions: Pathways to disaster resilience for African American Hurricane Katrina survivors. *Journal of Religion & Spirituality in Social Work* 30(3): 294–319.

Al-Masri M (2017) Sensory reverberations: Rethinking the temporal and experiential boundaries of war ethnography. *Contemporary Levant* 2(1): 37–47.

Antonovsky A (1993) The structure and properties of the sense of coherence scale. *Social Science & Medicine* 36(3): 725–733.

Antonovsky A (1996) The salutogenic model as a theory to guide health promotion. *Health Promotion International* 11(1): 11–18.

Asher K (2004) Texts in context: Afro-Colombian women's activism in the Pacific lowlands of Colombia. *Feminist Review* 78(1): 38–55.

Asher K (2007) *Ser y Tener*: Black women's activism, development and ethnicity in the Pacific lowlands of Colombia. *Feminist Studies* 33(1): 11–37.

Barad K (2019) After the end of the world: Entangled nuclear colonialisms, matters of force and the material force of justice. *Theory & Event* 22(3): 524–550.

Barnes-Lee AR and Campbell CA (2020) Protective factors for reducing juvenile reoffending. *Criminal Justice and Behavior* 47(11): 1390–1408.

Berman-Arévalo E and Ojeda G (2020) Ordinary geographies: Care, violence and agrarian extractivism in 'post-conflict' Colombia. *Antipode* 52(6): 1583–1602.

Bishop MJ, Meyer-Pinto M, Airoldi L, Firth LB, Morris RL, Loke LHL, Hawkins SJ, Naylor LA, Coleman RA, Chee SY and Dafforn KA (2017) Effects of ocean sprawl on ecological connectivity: Impacts and solutions. *Journal of Experimental Marine Biology and Ecology* 492: 7–30.

Black K and Lobo M (2008) A conceptual review of family resilience factors. *Journal of Family Nursing* 14(1): 33–55.

Boutron C (2018) Engendering peacebuilding: The international gender nomenclature of peace politics and women's participation in the Colombian peace process. *Journal of Peacebuilding & Development* 13(2): 116–121.

Brockmeier J (2000) Autobiographical time. *Narrative Inquiry* 10(1): 51–73.

Brockmeier J (2009) Reaching for meaning: Human agency and the narrative imagination. *Theory & Psychology* 19(2): 213–233.

Burton T (2011) Painful memories: Chronic pain as a form of re-membering. *Memory Studies* 4(1): 23–32.

Calhoun D (2020) Flowers for Baudelaire: Urban botany and allegorical writing. *Nineteenth-Century French Studies* 14(1–2): 17–34.

Chen ZJ, Ortega Bechara A, Worthington EL, Davis EB and Csikszentmihalyi M (2021) Trauma and well-being in Colombian disaster contexts: Effects of religious coping, forgiveness and hope. *The Journal of Positive Psychology* 16(1): 82–93.

Coulter C (2009) *Bush Wives and Girl Soldiers: Women's Lives through War and Peace in Sierra Leone*. Ithaca, NY: Cornell University Press.

Delgado C (2005) A discussion of the concept of spirituality. *Nursing Science Quarterly* 18(2): 157–162.

De Welde K (2003) Getting physical: Subverting gender through self-defense. *Journal of Contemporary Ethnography* 32(3): 247–78.

Dolan C, Baaz ME and Stern M (2020) What is sexual about conflict-related sexual violence? Stories from men and women survivors. *International Affairs* 96(5): 1151–1168.

Eaton K and Chambers-Ju C (2014) Teachers, mayors and the transformation of clientelism in Colombia. In: Brun DA and Diamond L (eds.), *Clientelism, Social Policy and the Transformation of Democracy*. Baltimore, MD: John Hopkins University Press, pp. 88–113.

Elbers E, Baur V, te Winkel B and Duyndam J (2021) Embodied resilience: A phenomenological perspective. *Indo-Pacific Journal of Phenomenology* 21(1): e1965857.

Escobar A (2004) Development, violence and the new imperial order. *Development* 47: 15–21.

Ewert A and Tessneer S (2019) Psychological resilience and posttraumatic growth: An exploratory analysis. *Journal of Experiential Education* 42(3): 280–296.

Farley YR (2007) Making the connection. *Journal of Religion & Spirituality in Social Work* 26(1): 1–15.

Fernando C and Ferrari M (2011) Spirituality and resilience in children of war in Sri Lanka. *Journal of Spirituality in Mental Health* 13(1): 52–77.

Forero JE (2016) State, illegality and territorial control: Colombian armed groups in Ecuador under the Correa government. *Latin American Perspectives* 43(1): 238–251.

Gillum TL, Sullivan CM and Bybee DI (2006) The importance of spirituality in the lives of domestic violence survivors. *Violence Against Women* 12(3): 240–250.

Glenn CBT (2014) A bridge over troubled waters: Spirituality and resilience with emerging adult childhood trauma survivors. *Journal of Spirituality in Mental Health* 16(1): 37–50.

Goldscheid J (2020) Gender violence against Afro-Colombian women: Making the promise of international human rights law real. *Human Rights Law Review Online* 4(3): 249–267.

Gordon E (2017) Crimes of the powerful in conflict-affected environments: False positives, transitional justice and the prospects for peace in Colombia. *State Crime Journal* 6(1): 132–155.

Gunderson LH and Holling CS (eds.) (2002) *Panarchy: Understanding Transformations in Human and Natural Systems*. Washington, DC: Island Press.

Harrison MO, Koenig HG, Hays JC, Eme-Akwari AG and Pargament KI (2001) The epidemiology of religious coping: A review of recent literature. *International Review of Psychiatry* 13(2): 86–93.

Hefferon K, Grealy M and Mutrie N (2009) Post-traumatic growth and life threatening physical illness: A systematic review of the qualitative literature. *British Journal of Health Psychology* 14(2): 343–378.

Hernandez Reyes CE (2019) Black women's struggles against extractivism, land dispossession, and marginalization in Colombia. *Latin American Perspectives* 46(2): 217–234.

Holling CS (2004) From complex regions to complex worlds. *Ecology and Society* 9(1): 11.

Holmes JS and Gutiérrez De Piñeres SA (2011) Conflict-induced displacement and violence in Colombia. *Studies in Conflict & Terrorism* 34(7): 572–586.

Houge AB and Lohne K (2017) End impunity! Reducing conflict-related sexual violence to a problem of law. *Law & Society Review* 51(4): 755–789.

HRW (2020) Colombia: Armed groups' brutal COVID measures. Available at: www.hrw.org/news/2020/07/15/colombia-armed-groups-brutal-covid-19-measures (accessed 17 December 2021).

IDMC (2020) Colombia. Available at: www.internal-displacement.org/countries/colombia (accessed 16 November 2021).

Infurna FJ and Jayawickreme E (2019) Fixing the growth illusion: New directions for research in resilience and posttraumatic growth. *Current Directions in Psychological Science* 28(2): 152–158.

Jayawickreme E and Blackie LER (2014) Post-traumatic growth as positive personality change: Evidence, controversies and future directions. *European Journal of Personality* 28(4): 312–331.

Jones K, Simpson GK, Briggs L and Dorsett P (2016) Does spirituality facilitate adjustment and resilience among individuals and families after SCI? *Disability and Rehabilitation* 38(10): 921–935.

Kelly J, Albutt J, Kabanga A, Anderson K and VanRooyen M (2017) Rejection, acceptance and the spectrum between: Understanding male attitudes and experiences towards conflict-related sexual violence in eastern Democratic Republic of Congo. *BCM Women's Health* 17: 127.

King C, Iba W and Clifton J (2021) Reimagining resilience: COVID-19 and marine tourism in Indonesia. *Current Issues in Tourism* 24(19): 2784–2800.

Koenig HG, Pargament KI and Nielsen J (1998) Religious coping and health status in medically ill hospitalized older adults. *The Journal of Nervous and Mental Disease* 186(9): 513–521.

Kreft AK (2019) Responding to sexual violence: Women's mobilization in war. *Journal of Peace Research* 56(2): 220–233.

Kreft AK (2020) Civil society perspectives on sexual violence in conflict: Patriarchy and war strategy in Colombia. *International Affairs* 96(2): 457–478.

Lederach AJ (2017) 'The *campesino* was born for the *campo*': A multispecies approach to territorial peace in Colombia. *American Anthropologist* 119(4): 589–602.

Lemaitre J (2016) After the war: Displaced women, ordinary ethics and grassroots reconstruction in Colombia. *Social & Legal Studies* 25(5): 545–565.

Lemaitre J and Sandvik KB (2015) Shifting frames, vanishing resources and dangerous political opportunities: Legal mobilization among displaced women in Colombia. *Law & Society Review* 49(1): 5–38.

Levine SZ, Laufer A, Stein E, Hamama-Raz Y and Solomon Z (2009) Examining the relationship between resilience and posttraumatic growth. *Journal of Traumatic Stress* 22(4): 282–286.

Lunn J (2009) The role of religion, spirituality and faith in development: A critical theory approach. *Third World Quarterly* 30(5): 937–951.

Manivannan A (2014) Seeking justice for male victims of sexual violence in armed conflict. *New York University Journal of International Law and Politics* 46(2): 635–680.

Martinez L and Rivera-Acevedo JD (2018) Debt portfolios of the poor: The case of street vendors in Cali, Colombia. *Sustainable Cities and Society* 41: 120–125.

McKittrick K (2016) Diachronic loops/deadweight tonnage/bad made measure. *Cultural Geographies* 23(1): 3–18.

Meernik J, Henao JG and Baron-Mendoza L (2021) Insecurity and the reintegration of former armed non-state actors in Colombia. *European Political Science Review* 13(4): 528–546.

Meertens D and Segura-Escobar N (1996) Uprooted lives: Gender, violence and displacement in Colombia. *Singapore Journal of Tropical Geography* 17(2): 165–178.

Melo JB (2015) The intersection of race, class, and ethnicity in agrarian inequalities, identities, and the social resistance of peasants in Colombia. *Current Sociology* 63(7): 1017–1036.

Merriman DR (2020) Contentious bodies: The place, race, and gender of victimhood in Colombia. *Transforming Anthropology* 23(1): 24–40.

Mesidor JK and Sly JF (2019) Religious coping, general coping strategies, perceived social support, PTSD symptoms, resilience, and posttraumatic growth among survivors of the 2010 earthquake in Haiti. *Mental Health, Religion and Culture* 22(2): 130–143.

Miller MA, Alfajri, Astuti R, Grundy-Warr C, Middleton C, Tan ZD and Taylor DM (2021) Hydrosocial rupture: Causes and consequences for transboundary governance. *Ecology and Society* 26(3): 21.

Minge JM (2007) The stained body: A fusion of embodied art on rape and love. *Journal of Contemporary Ethnography* 36(3): 252–280.

Mittelmark MB and Bauer GF (2017) The meanings of salutogenesis. In: Mittelmark MB, Sagy S, Eriksson M, Bauer GF, Pelikan JM, Lindström B and Espnes GA (eds.), *The Handbook of Salutogenesis*. Cham: Springer, pp. 7–13.

Moser C and Clark F (2001) Gender, conflict, and building sustainable peace: Recent lessons from Latin America. *Gender & Development* 9(3): 29–39.

Ng'weno B (2007) Can ethnicity replace race? Afro-Colombians, indigeneity and the Colombian multicultural state. *Journal of Latin American and Caribbean Anthropology* 12(2): 414–440.

Oslender U (2008) Another history of violence: The production of 'geographies of terror' in Colombia's Pacific coast region. *Latin American Perspectives* 35(5): 77–102.

Pargament KI, Koenig HG and Perez LM (2000) The many methods of religious coping: Development and initial validation of the RCOPE. *Journal of Clinical Psychology* 56(4): 519–543.

Parkin Daniels J (2021) Colombia found responsible for 2000 kidnap and torture of journalist. Available at: www.theguardian.com/global-development/2021/oct/19/jineth-bedoya-colombian-state-responsible-kidnap-torture-journalist (accessed 20 October 2021).

Patterson JM (2002) Integrating family resilience and family stress theory. *Journal of Marriage and Family* 64(2): 349–360.

Pelkmans M (2013) Ruins of hope in a Kyrgyz post-industrial wasteland. *Anthropology Today* 29(5): 17–21.

Popham CM, McEwen FS and Pluess M (2021) Psychological resilience in response to adverse circumstances: An integrative developmental perspective in the context of war and displacement. In: Ungar M (ed.), *Multisystemic Resilience: Adaptation and Transformation in Contexts of Change*. New York, NY: Oxford University Press, pp. 395–416.

Resilience Research Centre (2016) The Resilience Research Centre Adult Resilience Measure (RRC-ARM): User's manual. Available at: https://cyrm.resilienceresearch.org/files/ArchivedMaterials.zip (accessed 9 October 2021).

Riessman CK (2015) Ruptures and sutures: Time, audience and identity in an illness narrative. *Sociology of Health & Illness* 37(7): 1055–1071.

Roberto A, Sellon A, Cherry ST, Hunter-Jones J and Winslow H (2020) Impact of spirituality on resilience and coping during the COVID-19 crisis: A mixed-method approach investigating the impact on women. *Health Care for Women International* 41(11–12): 1313–1334.

Rodriguez Castro L (2021) 'We are not poor things': *Territorio cuerpo-tierra* and Colombian women's organised struggles. *Feminist Theory* 22(3): 339–359.

Rojas C (2009) Securing the state and developing social insecurities: The securitisation of citizenship in contemporary Colombia. *Third World Quarterly* 30(1): 227–245.

Sachseder J (2020) Cleared for investment? The intersections of transnational capital, gender and race in the production of sexual violence and internal displacement in Colombia's armed conflict. *International Feminist Journal of Politics* 22(2): 162–186.

Sanchez AO, Lopez Vivas JN, Cardenas DR and del Pilar Rengifo Cano M (2011) First survey on the prevalence of sexual violence against women in the context of the Colombian armed conflict, 2001–2009: Executive summary. Available at: https://reliefweb.int/sites/reliefweb.int/files/resources/2011-03-23-Report-English.pdf (accessed 29 August 2021).

Sanchez-Barrios LJ, Giraldo M, Khalik M and Manjarres R (2015) Services for the underserved: Unintended well-being. *The Service Industries Journal* 35(15–16): 883–897.

Scarry E (1985) *The Body in Pain: The Making and Unmaking of the World.* New York, NY: Oxford University Press.

Schaefer LM, Howell KH, Schwartz LE, Bottomley JS and Crossnine CB (2018) A concurrent examination of protective factors associated with resilience and posttraumatic growth following childhood victimization. *Child Abuse & Neglect* 85: 17–27.

Schulz P (2019) 'To me, justice means to be in a group': Survivors' groups as a pathway to justice in northern Uganda. *Journal of Human Rights Practice* 11(1): 171–189.

Schultz JM, Garfin DA, Espinel Z, Araya R, Oquendo MA, Wainberg ML, Chaskel R, Gaviria SL, Ordóñez AE, Espinola M, Wilson FE, Muñoz García M, Gómez Ceballos ÁM, Garcia-Barcena Y, Verdeli H and Neria Y (2014) Internally displaced 'victims of armed conflict' in Colombia: The trajectory and trauma signature of forced migration. *Current Psychiatry Reports* 16(10): 475.

Shamia NA, Thabet AAM and Vostanis P (2015) Exposure to war traumatic experiences, post-traumatic stress disorder and post-traumatic growth among nurses in Gaza. *Journal of Psychiatric and Mental Health Nursing* 22(10): 749–755.

Sturge-Apple ML, Davies PT and Cicchetti D (2012) Interparental violence, maternal emotional unavailability and children's cortisol functioning in family contexts. *Developmental Psychology* 48(1): 237–249.

Suárez-Baquero DFM, Bejarano-Beltrán MP and Dimmitt Champion J (2022) Rural women in Colombia, facing the postconflict: A qualitative synthesis. *Trauma, Violence & Abuse* 23(4): 1302–1316.

Sviland R, Martinsen K and Råheim M (2018) Towards living with my body and accepting the past: A case study of embodied narrative identity. *Medicine, Healthcare and Philosophy* 21: 363–374.

Sweet EL and Ortiz Escalante S (2017) Engaging *territorio cuerpo-tierra* through body and community mapping: A methodology for making communities safer. *Gender, Place & Culture* 24(4): 594–606.

Taylor SE, Repetti RL and Seeman T (1997) Health psychology: What is an unhealthy environment and how does it get under the skin? *Annual Review of Psychology* 48(1): 411–447.

Tedeschi RG and Calhoun LG (1996) The posttraumatic growth inventory: Measuring the positive legacy of trauma. *Journal of Traumatic Stress* 9: 455–471.

Tedeschi RG and Calhoun LG (2004) Posttraumatic growth: Conceptual foundations and empirical evidence. *Psychological Inquiry* 15(1): 1–18.

Tedeschi RG, Park CL and Calhoun LG (1998) Posttraumatic growth: Conceptual issues. In: Tedeschi RG, Park CL and Calhoun LG (eds.), *Posttraumatic Growth: Positive Changes in the Aftermath or Crisis.* Mahwah, NJ: Lawrence Erlbaum Associates, pp. 1–22.

Theidon K (2013) *Intimate Enemies: Violence and Reconciliation in Peru.* Philadelphia, PA: University of Pennsylvania Press.

Theron L (2019) Championing the resilience of sub-Saharan adolescents: Pointers for psychologists. *South African Journal of Psychology* 49(3): 325–336.

Tovar-Restrepo M and Irazábal C (2014) Indigenous women and violence in Colombia: Agency, autonomy and territoriality. *Latin American Perspectives* 41(1): 39–58.

Traunmüller R, Kijewski S and Freitag M (2019) The silent victims of sexual violence during war: Evidence from a list experiment in Sri Lanka. *Journal of Conflict Resolution* 63(9): 2015–2042.

Ungar M (2018) The differential impact of social services on young people's resilience. *Child Abuse & Neglect* 78: 4–12.

UNHCR (2021) Colombia – August 2021. Available at: https://reporting.unhcr.org/sites/default/files/Colombia%20Operational%20Update%20August%202021.pdf (accessed 16 November 2021).

Uribe MV (2004) Dismembering and expelling: Semantics of political terror in Colombia. *Public Culture* 16(1): 79–95.

Vazquez C, Valiente C, García FE, Contreras A, Peinado A, Trucharte A and Bentall RP (2021) Post-traumatic growth and stress-related responses during the COVID-19 pandemic in a national representative sample: The role of positive core beliefs about the world and others. *Journal of Happiness Studies* 44: 2915–2935.

Veenendaal W and Corbett J (2020) Clientelism in small states: How smallness influences patron-client networks in Caribbean and the Pacific. *Democratization* 27(1): 61–80.

Wade P (2013) Blackness, indigeneity, multiculturalism and genomics in Brazil, Colombia and Mexico. *Journal of Latin American Studies* 45(2): 205–233.

Wakefield S (2017) Inhabiting the Anthropocene back loop. *Resilience* 6(2): 77–94.

Wood EJ (2014) Conflict-related sexual violence and the policy implications of recent research. *International Review of the Red Cross* 96(894): 457–478.

Woodward C and Joseph S (2003) Positive change processes and post-traumatic growth in people who have experienced childhood abuse: Understanding vehicles of change. *Psychology & Psychotherapy* 76(3): 267–283.

Yohani S and Okeke-Ihejirika P (2018) Pathways to help-seeking and mental health service provision for African female survivors of conflict-related sexualized gender-based violence. *Women & Therapy* 41(3–4): 380–405.

Zulver JM (2017) Building the City of Women: Creating a site of feminist resistance in a northern Colombian conflict zone. *Gender, Place & Culture* 24(10): 1498–1516.

Zulver JM (2021) The endurance of women's mobilization during 'patriarchal backlash': A case from Colombia's reconfiguring armed conflict. *International Feminist Journal of Politics* 23(3): 440–462.

Zulver JM (2022) *High-Risk Feminism in Colombia: Women's Mobilization in Violent Contexts.* New Brunswick, NJ: Rutgers University Press.

Chapter 7

Connectivity Stories of Resilience in Uganda

During the reflections workshops that took place in Bosnia-Herzegovina (BiH), Colombia and Uganda in 2021, research participants were individually asked to draw a spider's web, with the multiple threads of the web denoting the different connectivities in their lives. This idea generated particularly rich discussions in Uganda. Explaining his drawing, a male Acholi participant emphasised that the war in northern Uganda had tangled the threads of his web, limiting his access to support. He further maintained that this web functioned like a net which stopped good things passing through it and into his life (reflections workshop, Uganda, 8 September 2021). Describing her own web, a Lango participant provided a detailed explanation of her drawing. As she outlined:

> My web speaks about how I can connect with other people. It shows how good things can come out of such connections. Some lines are closer together and straighter than others, to show that sometimes my life is harder and other times it is a little easier, and that's when I feel people are closer to me. Life can never be the same at all times. Where the lines run straight, life is easier. Where the lines are broken means that life is sometimes hard. The circular threads also show hardship, especially where the thread is broken or crooked.
> (reflections workshop, Uganda, 13 September 2021)

In other words, some participants referred not only to the threads constituting their webs, but also to the condition, shape and positioning of those threads. This is significant as it reinforces the book's argument that connectivities – which are deeply contextual – tell a story, just as the act of story-telling 'articulates webs of connections' (Rose, 2017: 501–502). This chapter explores the connectivities and their storied dimensions that were prominent in the Ugandan qualitative data, as part of a larger connectivity story about resilience.

Extant scholarship on the war in northern Uganda has overwhelmingly focused on the Acholi people. According to Apio (2016: 24), 'This "Acholisation" of the LRA conflict is problematic and probably due to the understanding that the war was an "Acholi issue"'. Little attention has been given to the

DOI: 10.4324/9781003323532-8

stories of Lango women and men. In this research, ten of the interviewees (selected from a quantitative dataset of 152 Ugandan participants) were Lango and 11 were Acholi. Of the four male interviewees, two were Lango and two were Acholi. Consistent with the two previous chapters, this chapter will note interviewees' ethnicity and gender (and age, where relevant), to draw attention to particular experiences that have been largely overlooked.

Contextualising Experiences of Violence

While this book uses the terminology of victims-/survivors of conflict-related sexual violence (CRSV), it has also stressed that research participants in all three countries had faced multiple (and in some cases ongoing) forms of violence. Like the silk capture threads in a spider's web, these different experiences were sticky and entangled – as this section briefly explores through its focus on the theme *'I am all that I've lived': Connectivities of violence*. Ugandan interviewees spoke particularly about direct violence and mistreatment linked to their experiences of abduction and captivity, as well as about indirect violence against loved ones.

Abduction and Captivity

The majority of the Ugandan interviewees had been abducted by the Lord's Resistance Army (LRA) during the latter's two-decade-long war with President Museveni's National Resistance Army (NRA), which in 1995 became the Uganda People's Defence Forces (UPDF). Some interviewees had been abducted on more than one occasion, including by government forces or by cattle rustlers from the Karamoja region in north-east Uganda. Abduction – which was typically 'extremely brutal' (Vinci, 2005: 370) – and mistreatment in captivity, including beatings, were therefore central parts of many interviewees' stories (see also Porter, 2015a: 84).

A Lango woman recounted how she was abducted when she was 18 years old and pregnant with her first child. She spent three months with the LRA and spoke about the suffering that was part of everyday life in the bush. 'We walked to the extent that even if your feet were extremely swollen, they [the LRA] would not care about you', she recalled. She also spoke about an occasion when she tried to escape and was caught by a group of LRA soldiers. In her own words:

> I was in luck because their leader appeared, raised his hand and said I should be left to live, not killed. . . . But they tied up my hands and led me to where people had gathered and caned me so that. . . . Then they placed a machete on my neck and said that whoever thinks of escaping will have their necks cut.

She did eventually succeed in escaping from the LRA with several other girls, and all of them were subsequently captured and detained for a week by government soldiers. 'They disturbed us very much', the interviewee disclosed, meaning that the soldiers had raped them (interview, Uganda, 11 June 2019). On this point, it was striking that both Acholi and Lango interviewees frequently made only indirect references or used euphemistic language when speaking about CRSV – a reflection of some of the cultural taboos surrounding sex in northern Uganda (Amone P'Olak et al., 2015).[1] This is discussed further in the chapter's penultimate section.

An Acholi man also talked about the violence that he had experienced from both the LRA and government soldiers. Recalling the cruelty of life in the bush following his abduction in 1998 (and on two further occasions in 1999), he maintained that 'The worst problem is hunger and walking on swollen legs. Life becomes somewhat easy only after your leg is pierced, pus removed and the legs harden'. He further added that 'If you refuse to walk, you immediately get killed for planning to escape'.[2] Prior to being abducted by the LRA, this man had been captured by NRA soldiers – on the grounds that his brother was reportedly in the bush with the LRA (which was in fact a case of mistaken identity). Upon being captured, he was put into a pit with nine other men, and his mother, wife and sister were taken to a dwelling a few metres away. He spent a week in the pit and three commanders would regularly call out individual men; 'At night, they would pick someone, they get out and they say: "bend over"'. He added that 'Once you have bent, they will start sleeping with you' (interview, Uganda, 26 March 2019). In addition to experiencing *tek-gungu* (male rape, sodomy), this man revealed that the same commanders who violated him also raped his wife and sister.

Violence Against Loved Ones

Interviewees frequently spoke about violence (which in some cases they had personally witnessed) against members of their immediate family, including their spouses. Such violence was perpetrated not only by the LRA and/or government forces but also, in a small number of cases, by cattle rustlers from the Karamoja region. These cattle raids, which have a long history (Nannyonjo, 2005: 473), were not specifically part of the war between the LRA and government forces. There are claims, however, that President Museveni tolerated cattle raids as a way of disrupting the LRA's war efforts (see, e.g., Knighton, 2003: 427).

A Lango woman explained that she was captured by cattle rustlers in 1987 (when she was 25 years old) and sexually abused by three of them ('I then became a wife to them'). Additionally, she spoke about the violence that cattle rustlers inflicted on her husband, who was badly beaten and left for dead. Hospital scans revealed the severity of his injuries. He had suffered a bleed on the brain and according to the interviewee, 'He then started living like someone whose head had got spoiled' (interview, Uganda, 2 April 2019). He survived like this for ten years. When he died, he left the interviewee alone with seven children.

An Acholi woman similarly spoke, inter alia, about violence against her husband, but what her story also accentuated is that connectivities of violence can have significant cross-temporal dimensions. She explained that one year during farming season (she said it was sometime in the 1980s),[3]

> They [cattle rustlers from the Karamoja] were the ones that came and found my husband and me in the garden. They came and took the oxen, they murdered my husband. Then they abused [raped] me right there in the garden. They stole the bulls and went away with them.

The interviewee had been in her late teens at the time. Years later, she continued, 'it' (meaning sexual violence) happened again. This time she could remember the year. It was 2006 and she was living in one of the many camps – discussed in Chapter 4 – set up by the government on the pretext of 'protecting' civilians from the LRA (see Lundgren et al., 2019: 388). The interviewee had briefly left the camp and returned to her homestead to collect food. On the way, she was abducted by LRA rebels and subsequently spent two years in the bush. Following her escape, she returned home 'with a stomach [pregnant]' and infected with human immunodeficiency virus (HIV; interview, Uganda, 12 June 2019). Her child, she revealed, also had HIV. This young boy was thus living with the intergenerational legacy of violence done to his mother's body.

This section does not in any way do justice to the totality of the interviewees' multiple interconnected experiences of violence, but it does provide insights into some of the many adversities that they had faced. Reverting back to the analogy of the spider's web with which this chapter began, O'Rourke (2015: 122) has referred to 'the web of harms against women'. What the data revealed, in various ways, was a 'web of harms' against women and men – and against parts of their social ecologies. These multiple harms, in turn, had either contributed to or themselves developed into important broken and ruptured connectivities in the interviewees' lives.

In the Ugandan data, it was particularly difficult to separate these breakages and ruptures – reflected in the theme *'It isn't there anymore': Connectivities lost* – as they were often deeply intertwined. The following three sections explore a particular cluster of co-tangled broken and ruptured connectivities – namely, lost (ruptured) opportunities, stigma and health, respectively. In so doing, they demonstrate how breakages and ruptures, like adversities and disadvantages, can accumulate (Mazer, 2018: 115; Wolff and De-Shalit, 2007: 120).

Broken and Ruptured Connectivities: Lost Opportunities

The meta theme of broken and ruptured connectivities is fundamentally about lost resources, and in this research these lost resources often had an important futurity dimension. Interviewees in all three countries articulated the idea that their experiences of CRSV, and of war or armed conflict more broadly, had greatly affected their lives and futures in the sense of what *might* have been. In the Ugandan data, the idea of lost opportunities and, relatedly, of ruptured futures was especially pronounced, and interviewees particularly spoke about lost opportunities linked to education and marriage.

Education and Job Prospects

Education and access to education constitute protective resources in diverse contexts (Aly et al., 2014: 369–370; Betancourt and Khan, 2008: 322; Theron, 2020: 80). As Benzies and Mychasiuk (2009: 105) argue, 'Increased skills and training can provide people with flexibility and more available options to effectively deal with problems'. What some of the Ugandan interviewees accentuated is that the war had essentially ruptured their opportunities to get an education (or to complete their education), and thus to build a better future for themselves and their families. One of the Acholi women told the story of how she was abducted by the LRA in 2004 (when she was 16 years old) and held in captivity for eight months. Reflecting on everything that happened, she insisted that 'it spoiled my future because I was still a student at the time I was abducted. So that's the way my studies ended'. She herself powerfully conveyed the idea of rupture when she revealed that 'I was expecting something for myself in the future, to be somebody in life. But the way my life turned out, it got cut off'.

In Uganda, many children do not have the possibility to complete their schooling (United Nations International Children's Emergency Fund [UNICEF], n.d.). Moreover, 'Only 1 in 4 children who starts primary school makes it to secondary school' (UNICEF, n.d.; see also UNICEF, 2019: 9). This is despite Uganda becoming the first country in sub-Saharan Africa (in 2007) to introduce universal secondary education (Kavuma, 2011). It is necessary, therefore, to see the interviewee's ruptured education in this broader context and to acknowledge the fact that despite the war, she had received more education than some Ugandan children will. What also stood out from her interview, however, was that there were deeper structural factors adding to her sense of being disconnected from opportunities that would enable her to build a better life and future. She had applied for a job spraying mosquitoes, but 'they [the employer] said women cannot manage that work'. She had also applied for a job immunising children and lamented that 'no woman was given the job'. Moreover, she felt doubly disadvantaged as a woman with HIV, a corporeal legacy of her time in the bush, arguing that this made it even more difficult for her to access opportunities (interview, Uganda, 20 March 2019).

Another Acholi interviewee, similarly, maintained that her abduction by the LRA at a young age and the nine years that she spent in the bush 'destroyed my future', in the sense of rupturing opportunities that she might otherwise have had to develop herself and to get a job (she did not speak about systemic and structural impediments in this regard). She frequently compared herself to her uncle's daughter and explained that 'We both started Primary 2 [second year of primary school] at the same time. But she is now a health worker at Lacor [a hospital in Gulu]. But for me, I do not have anything that I can do'. If circumstances had been different and she had not been abducted, she mused, 'maybe I would have trained to be some kind of teacher. Even if it meant teaching at nursery school only, I would be there. But now, I see that my future is not good'.

It was particularly interesting that this interviewee's sense of lost opportunities and a destroyed future existed alongside, or in the broader context of her understanding that the circumstances in which she was raped effectively constituted a rupture with Acholi norms and traditions. Porter (2015a: 87) argues that 'In Acholi, there are strong beliefs that sex "in the bush" is inappropriate and carries negative cosmological consequences. It violates norms that define the purposes of sex around the creation of and cementation of "a home"' (see also Porter, 2015b: 316). Articulating such beliefs herself, the interviewee stressed that 'In Acholi culture, it is said that "it is not right that you are slept with under a tree in some bush". That deed is not in harmony with Acholi culture'. She also expressed fears that her experiences in the bush had left bad luck or a curse (kiir)[4] on her body, which had further implications for her future. Using the second person, she explained that: 'Now it has affected how to get a good man who would wish to marry you' (interview, Uganda, 1 February 2019). Her concerns about finding a husband illustrate a second important example of lost opportunities (often entangled with the issue of stigma) that Ugandan interviewees frequently spoke about.

Marriage Prospects

A Lango woman narrated how she was abducted by the LRA in 2003 and taken to the bush. In contrast to some of the other interviewees who talked about being raped by different men within the LRA,[5] this interviewee had been 'given' to one particular commander;

> We were taken and then distributed, each of us, to a man. The person you were sent to would stay with you as your husband. He was responsible for providing for you, including what to eat. I was 12 years old.[6]

She spent three months in the bush and insisted that her experiences had 'spoiled' her relationships. Underscoring three times that 'my future is no longer there', she maintained that she had no prospects of finding a husband 'because it's now common knowledge that I am LRA. It doesn't matter where I go, people will still abuse me with the same tongue'.

In the eyes of some members of her community, the interviewee remained experientially connected to the LRA (and to her past) in a way that impeded her from having the married life – and the resources that it could offer her – that she desired. The cultural significance of this ruptured opportunity, and of future connectivities related to it (e.g., land),[7] can be better appreciated in the context of Kiconco and Nthakomwa's (2018: 68) argument that 'Marriage status is still such an important aspect of an individual's socialization, a rite of passage (in terms of recognition, respect, pride) and a source of well-being'.

The interviewee, who was 32 years old, had in fact been married twice and had three children born to three different fathers. 'Different men', she explained, 'because each time I try to settle down, it fails'. She was now raising her children alone and had little help from her family in this regard; 'They accuse me of gathering home children of the wild [i.e., having children outside marriage]' (interview, Uganda, 10 June 2019). Two of her children were not actually born outside wedlock. However, in accordance with Lango marriage and kinship norms, they remained jurally affiliated to their respective fathers' patriclans (Apio, 2016: 23), even though the interviewee was no longer married to these men. The children's connectivity to these patriclans meant that the interviewee could not rely on her natal family to help raise them. Only her third child, born after the interviewee had divorced her second husband, was affiliated with the natal patriline and thus welcome within the natal home.[8]

In the context of this discussion about broken and ruptured connectivities and marriage, the case of an elderly Lango interviewee was particularly interesting. She could not remember when LRA rebels captured her, but she said it was during the same year that the Aboke girls were abducted (discussed in Chapter 4), which was in 1996. The interviewee was 50 years old at the time.[9] According to her story, she spent only a day in the bush before she was released. In addition to being beaten, she revealed that 'My life was made dirty through sleep' (a euphemism for rape) and referred to two LRA soldiers doing 'bad deeds on my body'. The interviewee initially claimed that her husband had died 'long ago' (she also stated in the study questionnaire that she was a widow) and stressed that 'Life was somehow better when his body was there'. Without his support in digging and cultivating crops, getting enough food to eat was a daily challenge.

Later in the interview, this woman revealed that after the LRA released her, 'My husband said that he could never again be intimate with one whom the LRA had sat [had sex] with'. She had been one of her husband's two wives and he left her to live with his other wife. The loss of her husband was a major rupture in the interviewee's life, and it seems that she had psychologically dealt with it by creating a story that he had died. What she strongly expressed was a deep sense of being alone. In her words, 'I stayed alone, on my own. I did not enter into any love relationship with anybody. I remained by myself. I have grown old in my house alone' (interview, Uganda, 16 May 2019).

Broken and Ruptured Connectivities: Stigma

Stigma[10] and rejection were especially recurring ideas within the Ugandan interviews (although it is important to acknowledge that stigma is not always about rejection; see, e.g., Macdonald and Kerali, 2020: 785). Interviewees frequently

Connectivity Stories of Resilience in Uganda 211

spoke about 'bad tongues' and about *cimo tok* (literally, 'pointing at the back of one's head'). That their experiences of CRSV often went against acceptable social norms, including payment of *luk*,[11] was a powerful driver of stigma. In the case of male interviewees, stigma was also related to the fact that 'Within a heteronormative and patriarchal context, penetrative male anal rape is considered as rendering male survivors feminine and thus inferior in the gender hierarchy, depriving them of their manhood, power and status' (Schulz, 2020: 24).

None of the male interviewees explicitly spoke about feeling less of a man.[12] One of the two Acholi men, however, was very clear that 'Men and men do not sleep with each other' (interview, Uganda, 26 March 2019; see also Dolan et al., 2020: 1163). The other Acholi man, similarly, underlined that 'Men must not be sat with'. This interviewee suffered *tek-gungu* from government soldiers (they had accused him and other villagers of supporting the LRA) and recounted how people in his community had verbally abused him, telling him '"you stupid person, you allowed your fellow man to sleep with you"' (interview, Uganda, 13 June 2019).

Stigma was additionally linked, inter alia, to the reality that some of the interviewees had 'complex identities as "victim-perpetrators"' (Macdonald and Kerali, 2020: 771). Their return from the bush caused fear within their communities that they might be bringing with them the polluting spirits (*cen*)[13] of the dead. An Acholi woman who returned with two children, for example, explained that whenever the latter got into trouble, 'people will say, "look at these children, Kony's *cen* is afflicting their heads"' (interview, Uganda, 1 February 2019). Another Acholi interviewee described neighbours telling her that she has *lacen* – an evil spirit (Bedigen, 2021: 472) – in her head (interview, Uganda, 20 March 2019).

It is beyond the scope of this chapter to discuss and explore in depth the many layers and complexities of stigma (Akello, 2019; Gray et al., 2020; Kiconco and Nthakomwa, 2022; Macdonald and Kerali, 2020). A key point to underline, however, is that when research participants talked about stigma, they provided important insights into some of the connectivities in their lives – and their thoughts and feelings about those connectivities. One of the Acholi men who took part in the all-male reflections workshop, for example, underlined that although his spider's web consisted of many different connectivities, some of them were of no use to him and actually caused problems in his life. He further explained that 'when you hear somebody say something bad about you, all those threads or ropes [of the web] that connect to you cannot work' (reflections workshop, Uganda, 8 September 2021). He had actively sought to rupture some of these connectivities – at least temporarily – by moving away from his natal homestead and from the people who verbally abused him.

While emphasising the importance of family, some workshop participants also stressed that stigma and *cimo tok* primarily came from family members (including spouses and brothers). 'Stigma lives in the home', a female Lango participant maintained (reflections workshop, Uganda, 6 September 2021).

212 Connectivity Stories of Resilience in Uganda

What thus became clear from the workshops, where participants directly engaged with the concept of connectivity through discussion of the research findings, was that it is impossible to speak about connectivities without also speaking about stigma.

Broken and Ruptured Connectivities: Health

Health was a salient broken and ruptured connectivity across all three datasets. However, passages of interview text relating to the issue of health were ultimately coded not to the aforementioned theme *'It isn't there anymore': Connectivities lost*, but to the related theme *'The problem of ill health is there': Health connectivities and everyday stressors*. Making health a theme in its own right was important for conveying its significance within the data and the frequency with which interviewees spoke about it – a reflection of how war is 'multiply written upon the body' (McSorley, 2014: 121). Health was also an issue that powerfully highlighted connectivity in the sense of 'the interdependence of minds, bodies, and environment' (Marchand, 2010: 2).

Individual Health Legacies and the Physical Performativity of the Body

It was the Ugandan interviewees who spoke most about the toll that war and their experiences had taken on their bodies. They strongly underscored physical pain, which was often the result of beatings. According to one of the Acholi women, 'I find that the spot on my back that was severely beaten keeps giving me pain and it spreads to the rest of my chest. The beatings were both by canes and machetes' (interview, Uganda, 19 March 2019). In addition to physical pain, the interviewees spoke more generally about bodily weakness and loss of physical strength, which they often attributed to the fact of being forced to carry heavy loads in the LRA (see, e.g., Akhavan, 2005: 407–408). Describing his time in the bush, an Acholi man recalled: 'You walk for long with no food to eat. Loads. They give you heavy loads, so that now my chest cannot allow me to do anything' (interview, Uganda, 26 March 2019). That some interviewees were infected with HIV was a further factor contributing to diminished physical strength.

Krieger (2005: 350) argues that 'Just as the proverbial "dead man's bones" do in fact tell tales, via forensic pathology and historical anthropometry, so too do our living bodies tell stories about our lives, whether or not these are ever consciously expressed'. The interviewees' bodies told stories about the multiple sufferings that they had experienced, but also about the transformation of those bodies in the sense of their performative capacities. Fundamentally, some of the interviewees accentuated that they were no longer able to rely on their bodies in the same way that they had before the war. This emerged strongly from the data in two ways.

First, two of the male interviewees explained that their health issues related to the war had affected them in a sexual sense. One of them, an Acholi, disclosed that due to the 'sleep abuse' that he suffered from government soldiers during the mid-1990s, 'my strength in bed, which I had in the past has gone down' (interview, Uganda, 26 March 2019). Although he did not elaborate, he made it clear that this remained a problem in his life. The other interviewee, a Lango man, talked about living through a cattle raid by groups from the Karamoja region and revealed how 'that job' (sexual violence) continues to affect him today. He described deep pain in his abdomen area and stressed that 'there is no power to be with a woman' (interview, Uganda, 22 February 2019). These examples support the argument that CRSV against men entails 'an attack on the sexual subjectivity of the male body' (Drumond, 2019: 1279), while also illustrating how such violence potentially affects or ruptures the sexual 'performance of masculinity' (Dalley-Trim, 2007: 199).

Second, interviewees' cumulative experiences of violence and related health issues had in some cases affected and altered their bodies as income-generating and livelihood-sustaining resources. It is important to highlight in this regard that many of the Ugandan research participants were subsistence farmers. An Acholi interviewee who was HIV positive underlined that 'The problem of sickness spoiled the renewal of my life because I do not have the capacity to work the way I used to. I have no strength, even to do things like digging'. This woman, who was 31 years old at the time of the interview, relied on farming to support herself and her two children. The previous year, however, due to sickness, she had only been able to plant beans and nothing else. That was when she had started antiretroviral (ARV) therapy,[14] she explained, and 'I lost all of my physical energy' (interview, Uganda, 20 March 2019).

The aforementioned Acholi man who revealed that he has reduced strength in the sense of sexual performativity also talked more broadly about the effects on his body of the beatings that he suffered from government soldiers – and of the subsequent physical demands put on him following his abduction by the LRA. He was not doing well in life, he maintained, because 'I now have to hire a person to perform some of the work my heart wants'. He was 44 years old and further added that he was no longer able to make charcoal – an important income-generating activity in rural Uganda (Okello et al., 2013: 59; Sankhayan and Hofstad, 2000: 117). 'Charcoal-burning is not possible if your chest is weak', he lamented (interview, Uganda, 26 March 2019).

Health, in sum, is a significant resource that many of the Ugandan interviewees no longer had – at least not to the same extent that they had pre-war. This in and of itself constituted an important broken and ruptured connectivity in their lives. At the same time, their health issues contributed to further broken and ruptured connectivities in the sense of disconnecting them, to different degrees, from resources that they had previously freely utilised.

When Ugandan interviewees talked about how their experiences had affected them psychologically and emotionally, they spoke relatively little about issues such as loss of trust, difficulties sleeping or feelings of fear and anxiety (in contrast to the Bosnian and Colombian interviewees). Instead, there were many references to the head. Reflecting on her time in the bush, for example, an Acholi woman explained: 'I found that one [referring to CRSV] very painful in my life. It was painful in my head and that thing will never disappear' (interview, Uganda, 19 March 2019).

For her part, a Lango interviewee described how, a year before the interview, she had 'run mad'. She had lived in the bush, she claimed, barely eating or drinking, and it was prayers that made her better; 'People started helping me with prayer. And then changes started to happen' (interview, Uganda, 4 March 2019). A study by Okello and Ekblad, albeit focused on the Baganda people,[15] makes it clear that the term 'madness' can have several meanings, reflecting different degrees of severity. One meaning is 'mild madness', which means that a person's head has 'become mixed up' (Okello and Ekblad, 2006: 295). It is important to underline in this regard that few of the Ugandans had received or had access to professional psychosocial support, in particular contrast to the some of the Bosnian interviewees (see Chapter 5).

Like interviewees in BiH and especially Colombia, what the Ugandan interviewees did express was a deep sense of emotional hurt and pain (e.g., 'it is my heart that bleeds'; 'the pain is in our hearts'; 'it touched my life painfully, because a person shouldn't be captured and forcefully sat with without the person's consent'). These feelings of hurt and pain were a reflection of the many breakages and ruptures that interviewees had experienced (including loss of loved ones, loss of physical health, loss of opportunities, loss of virginity). Stigma and insults from family members and/or members of the community had, in some cases, further contributed to such feelings. One of the two Acholi men detailed how people in his home area had verbally abused him on account of the CRSV that he suffered from government soldiers. 'It bled my heart', he stressed; 'It took my mind back to those things of the past' (interview, Uganda, 13 June 2019).

Social-Ecological Health

The bigger point is that interviewees' health – and especially their psychological and emotional health – was entangled with their social ecologies, and with the 'healthiness' of those ecologies. Highlighting the vulnerability of sub-Saharan Africa to climate change (see Simtowe et al., 2019), some interviewees, for example, spoke about drought and how this had added to their economic worries. 'There is drought', one of the Acholi women stressed, 'and so there is nothing to feed the children. So, I find my life is too hard'. Recent drought also meant that she was unable to generate sufficient income to pay for her three children's school fees. In the interviewee's words, 'Even the strength to send the children to school is no longer there' (interview, Uganda, 15 April 2019).

A male Acholi interviewee, similarly, spoke about the impact of drought on his family's resources – and on his capacity to fulfil the demands of his culturally expected 'provider role' (Madhani and Baines, 2020). Severe drought the previous year meant that he had no beans to sell, and he had turned to repairing bicycles as a way of generating income for food (interview, Uganda, 26 March 2019). According to Branch (2018: 311), the issue of drought in northern Uganda 'can be understood as embedded within the legacies of war, as a form of violence that has continued into the post-conflict period'.

Some of the Ugandan interviewees, like those in BiH and Colombia, also expressed deep concerns about the health of loved ones within their social ecologies – worries that had further affected their own health and wellbeing. An Acholi woman infected with HIV had returned from the bush carrying a child and spoke about her early fears that he too might be infected ('That was the problem that entered my heart painfully') – and about the challenges that she had faced in getting her son (aged 9 at the time of the interview) tested. He had been diagnosed with HIV only in 2018 and the interviewee recalled how she felt at the time; 'I just wanted to vanish, to lose my life. Why has this thing [HIV] been found on my child and not only on me? Does it mean that all the trials and tribulations in this world are only targeting me?' (interview, Uganda, 12 June 2019).

A Lango woman was divorced and living with her mother and four children. Her mother, she explained, took care of her and her children, but this elderly woman was 'fractured' (in the sense that she had a broken leg but also in the broader sense that she was infirm and weak). The situation was a great source of concern to the interviewee, who was 30 years old. She revealed: 'My worry is how to help myself and my children. When I am left alone, I worry every day and night. Sometimes it brings tears to my eyes' (interview, Uganda, 4 March 2019). What these examples illustrate is that the frequent intersection of interviewees' own health issues with broader health-related issues within their social ecologies (Clark, 2022) further stripped them, in some cases, of important resources.

This section and the two previous sections have focused on some of the various broken and ruptured connectivities that were prominent in the Ugandan interviews. As in the other two countries, however, these breakages and ruptures – while very significant in the context of thinking about resilience – were only one part of the interviewees' stories. These women and men also had access to important supportive and sustaining connectivities which they were actively using to move on with their lives. The following three sections focus on three supportive and sustaining connectivities that Ugandan interviewees frequently talked about – namely family, community and land.

Supportive and Sustaining Connectivities: Family

Interviewees in all three countries had various supportive and sustaining connectivities in their lives (although some had more than others), reflected in the theme *'With them I get through it': Relational connectivities*. From a comparative perspective, the main differences between the countries were less in the types of connectivities that interviewees spoke about and more in the degrees of emphasis that they placed on particular connectivities. There were also differences in how common connectivities functioned, linked to wider contextual factors. For example, while family was one of the main supportive and sustaining connectivities that both Bosnian and Ugandan interviewees spoke about, in Uganda family support – which consisted of three main types – was often closely linked to the previously discussed issue of stigma.

Family Support and the Repair of Broken and Ruptured Connectivities

Some interviewees effectively spoke about their families helping them to mend broken and ruptured (or at least damaged) connectivities in their lives, including their marital relations. Following her abduction by LRA rebels and subsequent detention by government soldiers, for example, a Lango woman returned home to her husband and described the latter's reaction. 'He did not want to welcome me back into his house', she recalled, 'since many people raped me in the bush'. Intervention by the interviewee's parents, however, ultimately changed her husband's view of the situation ('My parents said "first allow her to stay, don't chase her. It was never her wish nor in her thoughts to go to that place [the bush]"').

Interestingly, while some interviewees experienced abuse from their husbands' families, this particular woman had additionally benefitted from further support in this regard. Her in-laws, she explained, had 'cooled her husband's heart' (calmed his feelings of anger). Furthermore, her spouse's grandmother had impressed upon him that he should allow his wife to stay, reminding him that he had paid bride price – an important cultural practice that the war severely disrupted as people lost livestock and had fewer opportunities to earn money (Whyte et al., 2013: 291).[16] The interviewee further noted that her husband's grandmother had welcomed her back by making her step on an egg; 'You are made to step on a chicken egg,[17] so that never again will you return to that place [the bush]' (interview, Uganda, 12 June 2019). The act of stepping on the egg involved a symbolic rupturing of the experiential connectivity between the interviewee and her past in the LRA.

An Acholi woman gave a detailed account of the verbal abuse that she and her mother had received from people in the community whom she referred to as 'relatives', primarily on the side of her late father. Some of these relatives, who were not immediate family,[18] had themselves lost children in the bush and were angry with the interviewee's mother that her own daughter had returned home (see also Baines and Rosenoff Gauvin, 2014: 291). Some of them, moreover, had accused the interviewee, who spent eight years in the bush and admitted 'I was a soldier and a serious fighter', of killing their children. This example highlights the importance of social harmony within Acholi society (Porter, 2017: 3), which, from the perspective of people in the interviewee's community, she had destabilised and transgressed by 'engaging in acts of *kiir*, "taboo/abomination"' (Kiconco and Nthakomwa, 2022: 660).

The interviewee spoke about her mother's attempts to defend her, but relationships remained ruptured and the abuse continued. For her own safety, and with her mother's help, she moved to another area. Her mother then became the main target of people's abuse and the situation only started to improve after the interviewee's uncle, who had been a government soldier, intervened (interview, Uganda, 1 February 2019). What especially stood out from this story were the many ways that the interviewee's mother had supported her – and the personal risks that the latter had taken to try and appease some of the anger that her daughter's return to the community had provoked.

Emotional Support

In some cases, interviewees' families also constituted important supportive and sustaining connectivities by providing them with vital emotional support, comfort and solace. One of the Acholi men explained that what had made it hard for him to rebuild his life was that his heart 'was bleeding' for his four brothers who were killed in a massacre by UPDF forces. However, he also stressed fundamental connectivities with his 'brothers' (agnates), who were part of his extended family. They had 'counselled' him by telling him not to keep thinking about the past and to live his life freely. This advice, he maintained, 'propped my back' (supported him) and 'strengthened my heart' (interview, Uganda, 13 June 2019).

Another Acholi interviewee spoke about crucial support that she had received from her spouse (her story was relatively unusual in this regard). She had returned from the LRA in 2002 to find that her parents were dead. Not wanting to be alone, she started a relationship with a man but when her pregnancies kept miscarrying, he left her (claiming that she had aborted the pregnancies). She had also faced stigma from the Lango community in which she was living; 'I'm abused that I am a "go-spread"/"go-tell"[19] and that I should be chased back there [to the bush]'. Her new husband, she stressed, was always there for her, from taking her to hospital to find out why she kept miscarrying (she was ultimately diagnosed with syphilis) to lifting her spirits whenever she faced hurtful comments. In her words, 'he consoles me and gives me strength to persevere as he will be with me when people are distressing me' (interview, Uganda, 12 February 2019).

Financial Support

Another important way that some interviewees' families were supporting them, which sometimes overlapped with the two previous types of support discussed, was in a financial sense. A Lango woman described how abuse from her in-laws had ruptured her relationship with her husband, resulting in her decision to leave. She had married a second time, but she experienced similar relationship difficulties and had thus returned to her natal home. Although her children (two with her first husband and two with her second husband)[20] technically belonged to their fathers' clans, her parents had welcomed them – illustrating the argument that 'Home is a form of social and emotional relatedness' (Whyte, 2005: 156) – and given the interviewee a livelihood working on the land. Perhaps because the war had put an end to her own education ('if they [the LRA] had left me to remain at school and continue with my education, I would not be like this'), and also because her father was a retired teacher, the interviewee stressed the importance of schooling. What was greatly helping her in this regard was the fact that her father was paying her eldest child's school fees (interview, Uganda, 21 February 2019).

An Acholi woman similarly spoke about important material support from her father. Just the previous week, he had paid her 14-year-old daughter's school fees (as a loan until she could repay him). He had also given the interviewee some land, which she had cultivated for two years. This had enabled her and her husband to buy some land of their own – a new supportive and sustaining connectivity. Despite her father's valuable support (and thanks to his interventions, stigma from people in the community had greatly lessened), the interviewee stressed that she did not have much to sustain herself (interview, Uganda, 21 May 2019). The interviewer therefore purchased some eggplants from this 35-year-old woman at the end of their discussion and her post-interview notes stated the following:

> When we had concluded the brief sale by the car, she introduced a man [her husband], who later asked for a lift to the trading centre. We agreed. I saw the interviewee quickly put into his hand one of the notes that I had given her as payment for her eggplants. We later left him [her husband] at the trading centre, where he hurried across the road towards a group of men perched on little wooden chairs enjoying the local potent gin.
>
> (post-interview notes, 21 May 2019)

This is an interesting detail. It raises the question of whether these two important connectivities in the interviewee's life – her father and her husband – were effectively working against each other, in the sense that her husband's drinking was diluting the benefits of her father's financial support (and indeed of her own hard work).

What this discussion about family has shown is that notwithstanding the prevalence of stigma as a recurrent thematic within the interviewees' stories, their experiences of facing verbal abuse were entangled with – and often accentuated the importance of – the crucial support that they had received from immediate and, in some cases, extended family. These dynamics, which themselves emphasise storied dimensions of connectivity, remain little explored within existing discussions about stigma in northern Uganda.

Supportive and Sustaining Connectivities: Community

Khadiagala (2001: 58) underscores that 'Interrogating the notion of community is important in Africa where the tendency to idealize local spaces is an enduring one'. Discussions about the meaning of community in the context of northern Uganda are difficult to find, but helpful in this regard is Khadiagala's (2001: 58) argument that community is not an entity but a process. According to her,

> It is a series of social practices that constitute closures, boundaries, and divisions that create insiders and outsiders, delineate who has the right to set the rules, and determine the morality which guides social conduct and the legitimacy of claims.
>
> (Khadiagala, 2001: 59)

It was precisely these social practices that were supporting interviewees in different ways, in turn illuminating the concept of community resilience (Berkes and Ross, 2013; Cutter et al., 2008; Koliou et al., 2020).

Resilient Communities and Connections

Discussing community resilience, Chaskin (2008: 65) distinguishes between community as context and community as an agent of change. 'Community as context', he argues, 'focuses on communities as local environments providing a set of risk and protective factors that have an influence on the well-being of community members' (Chaskin, 2008: 65). Community as an agent of change means thinking about how 'communities exhibit resilience themselves . . . as *actors* that respond to adversity' (Chaskin, 2008: 66; emphasis in the original). Both conceptualisations, which may overlap in practice, are useful for thinking about community in relation to the Ugandan interview data. Interviewees' stories clearly illustrated the idea of 'community as context'; risk factors within the community existed alongside, and were often entangled with, protective factors. This lends support to the argument that communities stigmatise not only to exclude, but also 'as part of social processes designed to reintegrate returnees back into the fold of village life' (Macdonald and Kerali, 2020: 783).

Regarding 'community as an agent of change', and how communities respond to adversity, the interview material exposed an interesting dialectic. On one hand, it illustrated the disruptive effects of CRSV on social harmony and 'cosmological equilibrium within Acholi communities' (Porter, 2017: 3). From a resilience perspective, this is significant because it has implications for the wider stability of social-ecological systems (SES), of which communities are an important part (and example). On the other hand, some interviewees' descriptions of the various ways that their communities were supporting them indicate that there were emic resources within these communities that helped them to absorb shocks and respond to adversity. Particularly pertinent is Ellis and Abdi's (2017: 290) argument that 'social connection is at the heart of resilient communities and suggests that any strategy to increase community resilience must both harness and enhance existing social connections while endeavoring to not damage or diminish them'. The war in Uganda did damage some of these connections, yet the data also pointed to the existence of enduring – and hence resilient – connections.

As one example, interviewees often talked about members of the community 'advising', 'counselling' or 'consoling' them. It was one of the Acholi women who gave a particularly detailed narrative in this regard. When asked what had helped her in the process of rebuilding or starting to rebuild her life, she answered: 'The advice that people kept giving me strengthened my heart'. These were people from her community with whom she had lived before the war and she talked about some of the ways that they had supported her when she returned;

> When they heard that I had returned from the bush, they came. When I would be about to think of ending my life because I had gone through many problems, they also kept giving me advice: 'Stay. You are not the only one' [in the sense of what she had gone through].

Community support had been especially important to this interviewee in 2018 when she found out that the child with whom she returned (pregnant) from the bush was HIV positive. At this time, she felt angry with the world, she explained, but people in the community were there for her and 'made my heart stronger'. Describing her life as 'prayerful', she also talked about the support and advice that she had received from members of the local Protestant church, underlining that going to church every Sunday 'has pressed [soothed] my heart very much' (interview, Uganda, 12 June 2019).

Another Acholi interviewee, similarly, described how some of her neighbours had stepped in to help her when she needed it. In her words, 'I have suffered great sadness, because I was abused, but people kept consoling me; "You should not be thinking about what people are saying [referring to stigma]. You didn't do anything bad"'. Such support, she maintained, had been crucial and helped her to 'persevere' (interview, Uganda, 12 February 2019).

Indeed, several interviewees talked about persevering/perseverance (*akanyo*), which can be viewed as a cultural and contextual expression of resilience. In support of this, Abonga and Brown's (2022) research found that Acholi youth understand resilience as 'a generalised ability to "persevere"'. The authors also make clear, however, that individual and community resilience are not independent of each other (Abonga and Brown, 2022). In the context of this book, the important point is that interviewees' enduring relational connectivities with their

Connectivity Stories of Resilience in Uganda   221

communities – or more accurately with particular parts of their communities – were one of the factors helping them to 'persevere'.

The Local Council System

Another community resource, and one unique to the Ugandan participants, was the Local Council system, which starts at the village level (LC1) and goes up to the district level (Devas and Grant, 2003: 311). According to Oosterom (2011: 404),

> Women will first discuss domestic problems with their father-in-law, and then with the clan leaders of their husbands. If a problem is not resolved, a woman can still go to the chair person of the Local Council at village level, but many will not do this.

Several of the female interviewees, however, had turned to their Local Councils for support. One of them reflected that 'Being an Acholi has helped me. When I go to a leader who is an Acholi and I explain my problems, they will help me, saying: "This is my fellow Acholi, I have to help her"'. By way of illustration, she spoke about occasions when her children had got into trouble (e.g., fights with other children) and how this had further fuelled her experiences of stigmatisation through the extension of stigma to her children. In such cases, the Local Council chairperson would regularly step in to calm the situation. As the interviewee explained:

> Whenever the matter gets to the Local Council, we would be brought together with the mother of the other child and then he [chairperson] would start speaking. He would speak to us well, saying, 'I do not want any confusion. Every human being is equal. There is no bush that shows on a person's body. People are equal'.
>
> (interview, Uganda, 1 February 2019)

Although the LC1 system is often male dominated (Oosterom, 2011: 404), and hence it can reinforce patriarchal structures and gender inequalities (Khadiagala, 2001),[21] the interviewee commented that the LC1 chairperson was currently a woman. A Lango interviewee had also benefitted from the intervention of her Local Council chairperson. She talked about ongoing verbal abuse from certain members of the community, most recently from a man who had ordered some beer from her and then refused to pay for it. When the interviewee insisted that he pay for what he had ordered, 'he let out his tongue on my body [verbally abused her]'. Asked how she deals with such situations, she explained that 'I take the people who are abusing me to the Local Council chairman and now the insults have gone down somewhat' (interview, Uganda, 11 June 2019).

These examples do not diminish the fact that many of the interviewees continued to face stigma. The key point is that stories about stigma, in some cases, were interwoven with stories about community support, and hence it is crucial that the former do not eclipse or occlude the latter. Indeed, the prevalence of stigma had arguably enhanced the significance – and thus contributed to the resilience – of social practices that interviewees were able to draw on as supportive and sustaining connectivities in their lives.

Supportive and Sustaining Connectivities: Land

The importance of land in northern Uganda cannot be overstated. Existing scholarship has tended to focus particularly on the issue of land conflicts (see, e.g., Joireman, 2018; Meinert et al., 2017; Mugizi and Matsumoto, 2021). Hopwood (2022: 52), however, maintains that 'hegemonic mistranslations and misuse of tropes such as "land conflict" and "customary land" have warped debate on a complex situation of very real problems around how families cope with evolving social change and resource deficiencies'. If the interview data captured some of this complexity, it also told a bigger story about the diverse ways that land mattered in the interviewees' lives.

Most of the Ugandan interviewees had some land, or at least access to land, and as previously noted many of them relied on subsistence farming. Their relationships with land, therefore, were primarily expressed through 'knowing' and the 'competent performance of one's knowledge' (Anderson, 2000; 117); and this knowledge was an important resource that interviewees were actively using to deal with certain challenges in their lives. An Acholi woman, for example, stressed that 'I am doing my best to pay fees for my children in school. I farm a lot, so that the children may get an education and find ways to live well'. However, she also made the point that farming is not a reliable source of income; 'You know us peasant farmers. If we don't dig and get good harvests, it is impossible to pay school fees' (interview, Uganda, 12 June 2019). In resilience research, stability is often discussed as a property of systems. In the context of both ecological systems and SES (see Chapter 1), for example, 'resilience is related to stability' (Adger, 2000: 349). The interviewee thus drew attention to the fact that everyday resources themselves can be highly unstable – and deeply affected by other systems (e.g., climate).

In some cases, however, larger systemic factors had enhanced interviewees' resources. Another Acholi woman spoke about planting beans, maize and sesame. Discussing the previous year's harvest, she commented that 'The beans got spoiled and we could only get a bag [100kg] from the harvest. But we harvested two bags of sesame' (interview, Uganda, 29 May 2019). Uganda is the world's fifth largest producer of sesame, 'a high value crop with ready domestic, regional and international markets' (Munyua et al., 2013: 1). When the interviewee found that sesame was selling at a better price than it had been previously, she focused on that and made enough money to pay her children's school fees.

Land also supported interviewees in the sense of enabling them to expand their resources. As one example, a Lango woman did not have her own land; she recounted how her paternal uncle had 'violently refused' to allow her to cultivate her late father's land. Her first husband had rejected her and the child with whom she returned from the bush. She subsequently had a relationship and children with another man (who already had a wife), but his family did not accept her, calling her a 'wife of the LRA'. She was now single and had moved away from her natal land due to the issues with her uncle. 'I survive by hiring land to dig', she explained, and talked about growing rice and using the money she earned from it to buy livestock to rear.

Her animals had been a crucial resource during a recent and very difficult situation when her son had accidentally hit a neighbour with his motorbike. The interviewee had used her cattle to pay part of the *kwor* (blood compensation) to the deceased's family and stressed that 'If I wasn't a farmer, I would have no means to address my problems'. The payment of *kwor* meant that this 44-year-old woman no longer had any oxen for ploughing, further illustrating the instability of resources. It was nevertheless important to her that she had been able to make the payment, thereby challenging entrenched gender norms and expectations (although she paid the blood compensation as a member of her clan and not simply as her son's mother). People in the community had not expected her to be in a position to do so; 'But afterwards, they found out that I indeed paid it. They then said that I am stronger than a man' (interview, Uganda, 28 February 2019).

New Connectivities: Building Meaning

The final two sections of this chapter focus on the new connectivities part of the book's overall framework. This section is specifically about meaning-making, a theme that was also discussed in the two previous chapters. To reiterate, there are important connections between resilience and meaning-making (Park and Blake, 2020; Yang, 2020); the meaning that an individual attaches to a particular experience or set of experiences can shape how s/he deals with adversity (Theron and Theron, 2014: 25). Meaning-making is itself strongly influenced by wider contextual and socio-cultural factors (see, e.g., Theron and Theron, 2014: 23; Wexler et al., 2009: 565).[22] Some of the discussions that took place during the reflections workshops in Uganda were particularly illustrative in this regard.

Workshop participants were asked to imagine themselves as spiders in a web, and to think about the different connectivities (good and bad) that constituted the threads of their web. The Ugandan participants engaged much more directly (and in some cases very literally) with the idea than the Bosnian and Colombian participants. Furthermore, some of them did not like the spider (*obworopyen*) analogy because for them it had negative connotations. One of the male Acholi participants associated spiders with greed and stressed that:

> If a person is compared to *obworopyen*, it means that person is bad. It means that person associates with everything and anything, gathering all sorts of

things in his/her life. A bad person indeed because a spider traps everything in its net.

(reflections workshop, Uganda, 8 September 2021)

An elderly Acholi interviewee, for her part, associated *obworopyen* with being a poor widow with no prospect of being inherited. She explained that 'When a widow has no brother-in-law to inherit her and the problems she suffers, that is poverty. It's terrible poverty because it deprives you of inheriting your husband's property' (reflections workshop, Uganda, 6 September 2021). To contextualise this, it should be noted that according to Acholi customary law, 'If her husband dies, traditionally a widow will be "inherited" by one of her brothers-in-law in a levirate marriage' (Hopwood, 2015: 401). The interviewee and the other women in this particular workshop were from a very rural part of eastern Acholi and continued to strongly associate with patriarchal customary law (although not all of the interviewees did so, as will be discussed). They accordingly agreed among themselves that while they liked the idea of the web, they would leave out the spider.

Dolan et al. (2020: 1152) have explored the significance of meaning-making in Uganda, focusing on 'some of the ways in which survivors [of CRSV] comprehend – and indeed theorize – the sexual in SV'. In contrast to Dolan et al.'s research, the study underpinning this book did not set out to explore how the participants understood the violence committed against them; and as Chapter 5 previously noted, the interview guide did not include any questions related to meaning-making. Interviewees, however, frequently provided insights – through their answers to other questions – into their meaning-making processes. This section will discuss three particular points that stood out from the Ugandan interview data linked to the theme *'Why did this have to be'*: *Making connections and finding meaning.*

The Importance of God

There was a common tendency among Ugandan interviewees to invoke God as part of their meaning-making. They particularly underlined that they were still alive because God had 'saved' them. As one illustration, a Lango woman detailed how, in 2002, LRA rebels locked her and her family in a hut and set it alight. 'As they started the fire', she recalled, 'I shouted out to them. I said: "You are burning us, yet I have 700,000 Shillings [approximately £147] that I have kept with me. Please help us"'. Upon hearing this, the rebels opened the door of the hut and the interviewee (together with her family) escaped, but not before some burning debris fell on her. Reflecting on this experience, she insisted that 'I was supposed to die, but God is great'.

She further maintained that it was thanks to God that she had earlier returned from ten months in the bush (following her abduction by the LRA in 1991). 'Had the Creator not wanted me to survive', she argued, 'I could have remained in the bush and not come back home'. This woman expressed a strong sense of needing to get on with life and spoke about her resolve to 'persevere' whenever she faced problems. Giving her life story the title *chan* – which means poverty, but in more than just an economic sense – she further articulated the belief that when God saves people, He intends for them to learn from *chan* (interview, Uganda, 28 February 2019).

If religious meaning-making partly reflects the influence of religion in Ugandan cultural life,[23] some interviewees also spoke more specifically about the help and support that they had received from religious institutions. According to Porter (2017: 179), in a context where levels of impunity remain high, 'it is no wonder that the church's primary role after rape is spiritual consolation, supporting an internal process which women have power to pursue regardless of the social constraints of relatives or impotence of formal justice mechanisms'. An Acholi interviewee, for example, had spent eight years in the bush following her abduction by the LRA, and during this time she sustained a bullet wound to the leg. Due to the pain from this wound, which had never fully healed, the interviewee had previously reached a point where she wanted to end her own life. Her friend, however, had stepped in and called on the local pastor. Recalling the latter's words, and how he reminded her that God brought her back from the bush because He loves her, the interviewee explained: 'That was when I started accepting the pastor's words. Then I started to . . . then I started being saved, then I started welcoming the Lord as my Lord and Saviour'. The interviewee, who was 44 years old and described herself as a born-again Christian,[24] further stressed that notwithstanding the many challenges and difficulties that she continues to face, God must have His reasons 'for letting these things pass through my life' (interview, Uganda, 1 February 2019).

Chapter 1 discussed some common neoliberal critiques of resilience. One of Reid's (2013: 355) trenchant criticisms, for example, is that 'The resilient subject is a subject . . . that accepts the disastrousness of the world it lives in as a condition of partaking in that world'. Regarding the two women discussed in this sub-section, it could be argued that their meaning-making processes had led them to simply 'accept' the terrible things that they had gone through. Moreover, they were not alone in this regard; there were interviewees in all three countries who expressed such acceptance. Yet, the very fact that they did so is important because it reveals how neoliberal critiques of resilience can lack contextual nuance. The crucial point is that the two women, like many of the interviewees in all three countries – in different ways and to different degrees – were actively forging new connectivities in the sense of meaning-making frameworks that were helping them to get on with their lives. Interviewees' meaning-making processes – which may be viewed, in part, as expressions of resilience – were not a reflection of implicit neoliberal agendas, but of deeper contextual and cultural factors within their social ecologies.

'*It Was Not My Will*'

The meaning of rape in international criminal law, and the relationship between consent and force/coercion, are important issues that have generated considerable discussion and jurisprudence (see, e.g., Adams, 2018; Obote-Odora, 2005; Schomburg and Paterson, 2007). In the Kunarac case at the International Criminal Tribunal for the former Yugoslavia (ICTY), the Appeals Chamber stated that 'the circumstances . . . that prevail in most cases charged as either war crimes or crimes against humanity will be almost universally coercive. That is to say, true consent will not be possible' (Prosecutor v. Kunarac et al., 2002: para. 130). The International Criminal Court's (ICC) definition of rape, contained in its Element of Crimes, does not explicitly include consent. However, as Dowds (2018: 629) underlines, 'the issue has re-emerged in cases and there remains a lack of clarity around the role of consent: do the existing elements in the definition constitute evidence of lack of consent or do they operate independently from consent?'

What was striking about many of the Ugandan interviewees was that they frequently highlighted both coercion/force *and* lack of consent. They repeatedly used the words 'force' and 'forcefully' (e.g., 'He was staying with me forcefully'; 'He slept with me by force'; 'The people of Kony slept with us forcefully'; 'They kept doing things by force'). Additionally, they consistently underlined, inter alia, that 'It was not my will'; 'It was never my wish'; 'It did not happen of my own will'; 'It touched my life because it is something that was against one's will'. One factor that had arguably contributed to the interviewees' strong sense that they were not blameworthy was the everyday brutality of life in the bush that many of them had suffered. Another factor was the aforementioned support that some interviewees had received from family and members of the community, including reassurances that they themselves were not at fault for what they had gone through. Chapter 1 noted the existence of crucial feedback loops within complex SES (see, e.g., Huber et al., 2013; Walker and Meyers, 2004). Similarly, there were important feedback loops within interviewees' social ecologies, in the sense of connectivities that positively shaped meaning-making processes.

The young age of some of the interviewees when they suffered CRSV was almost certainly another relevant factor. It should be noted in this regard that when Ugandan interviewees stated that they were abducted and/or suffered CRSV at a particular age, there were often discrepancies. An Acholi interviewee, as one illustration, maintained that she was 10 years old when the LRA captured her in 2000 and 'maybe 11 or 12' the first time that she was made to have sex. She stressed that 'my time had not yet come to do that thing. I was forced and I did it by force' (interview, Uganda, 19 March 2019). Yet, according to the demographic data that she provided in the study questionnaire, she was born in 1983. If this date was correct, and if she was in fact abducted by the LRA in 2000, she would have been 17 years old at the time. Such discrepancies may simply evidence 'fragmented and/or disorganized trauma memories' (Gray and Lombardo, 2001: 171). However, they may also reflect a heightened sense of lost childhood, making some interviewees think that they were several years younger than they actually were when they were abused.

Use of Euphemisms

The previous interviewee who stated that she was abducted at the age of 10 revealed that she had never been able to tell her mother (her father had died) or her natal family about the issue of 'forced sleeping'. She worried that they would not believe that it happened by force, and she stressed 'That thing [CRSV], I find, brought a lot of shame on my head' (interview, Uganda, 19 March 2019). In particular contrast to the Bosnian interviewees, however, very few of the Ugandan interviewees explicitly spoke about shame. They expressed it more implicitly through their very frequent use of euphemisms when referring to the CRSV that they had suffered. It is interesting to note that while Ugandan male interviewees were proportionally under-represented in the nodes relating to meaning-making, perhaps suggesting that they had spent less time thinking about and trying to make sense of their experiences, they used euphemisms just as frequently as the female interviewees, including 'sleep-abuse', 'that one' (e.g., 'that one is difficult to speak about'), 'that thing' and 'sitting with'.

The common use of euphemisms highlighted an interesting dialectic within the data. On one hand, interviewees' euphemistic and indirect references to the CRSV that they had experienced were interwoven with and reflected deeper socio-cultural ideas about sex and sexual morality. Ebila (2020: 247) argues that euphemisms constitute 'a culturally milder and more acceptable sexual reference – to mediate (even mute) the traumatic experience of forced sexual intercourse'. On the other hand, through their repeated insistence that they themselves were not to blame, interviewees were implicitly challenging and resisting these ideas by asserting their own side of the story. If this dialectic illustrates 'the on-going nature of meaning-making and that meanings assigned can change over time' (Theron and Theron, 2014: 30; see also Walsh, 2020: 906), resistance can itself be an important cultural expression of resilience (Raider-Roth et al., 2012; Ryan, 2015). This will be explored further in the final section.

New Connectivities: Getting on With Life and (Re)Building Connections

Two further themes (relevant to all three countries) were developed from the qualitative data that broadly spoke to the idea of new connectivities, namely *'We have to live': Reconnecting with life* and *'I want to achieve more': (Re)Building connections and making a difference*. For the purposes of this chapter, it was appropriate to merge these two themes and to examine especially significant elements from both.

In their research on social repair and motherhood in northern Uganda, Oliveira and Baines (2022: 750) explore 'the ways women repair webs of kin relations to secure a future no longer dictated by the circumstances of their children's birth'. Specifically, the authors interpret mothers' efforts to unite their children with paternal relatives as important acts of social repair, in the sense of 'reifying systems of relatedness that had been torn apart by war violence' (Oliveira and Baines, 2022: 766). There were no directly comparable examples within the interview data, but some of the ways that female interviewees spoke about women particularly stood out.

The Socio-Cultural Importance of Women

An Acholi interviewee underlined that:

> A woman will not let her children sleep hungry if she has children. She will do her best, to what? To find food for the children to eat. And a woman will find it painful if her children miss going to school while other people's children are in school.

Emphasising, further, that 'it is a woman who cares for a home', the interviewee argued that 'all women stand with their families, taking care of the family' (interview, Uganda, 19 March 2019). A Lango interviewee, for her part, stressed that 'A woman starts caring for children right from when she rises from bed. Then, whenever she goes to dig the fields, she will have her baby with her'. Men come and go, she claimed, returning home when it suits them, while 'all this time, the woman will be taking care of the child. That is how I see it' (interview, Uganda, 10 June 2019).

These examples reveal interviewees' strong sense of their socio-cultural importance as women and mothers, which they actively manifested through acts of care towards their social ecologies. According to Tronto (1993: 103), care is 'everything that we do to maintain, continue and repair "our world" so that we can live in it as well as possible' – a world, she maintains, 'that includes our bodies, our selves, and our environment, all of which we seek to interweave in a complex, life sustaining web'. Some of the participants in the 2021 reflections workshops, as previously noted, did not like the spider analogy that was used. The important point, however, is that just as 'most spiders produce various kinds of silk fibers' (Moon and Kim, 2005: 133), Tronto's reference to a 'life sustaining web' usefully illustrates how, in engaging in acts of care, interviewees were themselves effectively spinning multiple fibres. In so doing, they evidenced their central role within the home and, relatedly, their efforts to hold everything together (and hence they themselves constituted important connectivities). Indeed, this was one of the factors driving them to get on with

Connectivity Stories of Resilience in Uganda 229

life and, as much as possible, to put the past behind them. As one of the Acholi women explained, 'I feel that if I continue thinking about things past, raising my children might defeat me since it is said that too much thinking can bring illness to the body' (interview, Uganda, 29 May 2019).

'Renewal'

Something else that was prominent within the Ugandan data was the frequency with which interviewees spoke (and certainly much more so than the Bosnian and Colombian interviewees) about their lives positively changing. In particular, they talked about their lives 'renewing' (roc), and many different factors had contributed to this sense of renewal. For one of the Lango women, 'the most important factor in renewing my life was starting to get back to my body', by which she meant reconnecting with herself and with other people. She recalled that at one stage, 'I would not have managed to respond to what you [referring to the interviewer] are saying to me now' (interview, Uganda, 16 May 2019). For his part, one of the Acholi men described himself as 'someone whose life is renewed'. He explained that when his male relatives gave him a goat, which he had used to prepare burial ceremonies for his brothers who were killed by the UPDF, this was something that had helped him to renew his life in the sense of starting to let go of the past (interview, Uganda, 13 June 2019).

For many interviewees, addressing and resolving economic worries was a crucial part of renewing their lives, and some of them spoke about coming together with others as a way of doing this. When asked what had helped her in the process of rebuilding or starting to rebuild her life, an Acholi interviewee answered: 'Interacting with other people. I would interact with other women. Women actually started a village saving's scheme, and that helped us in interacting'. Through these interactions in the context of the local Village Savings and Loan Association (VSLA, known locally as *Bol icup*),[25] the interviewee had been able to start selling silver fish at the market. While this had not resolved her economic worries in the long term, she reflected that the opportunity to sell fish 'gradually helped me to start an easy life among the women' (interview, Uganda, 15 April 2019).

Another Acholi interviewee similarly spoke about coming together with other women in a VSLA. With the loan that she had received, she explained, 'I go and buy tomatoes in the villages to sell in the market. Once people buy my tomatoes, I repay the loan and then I borrow again to strengthen myself [economically] and that is what keeps me going' (interview, Uganda, 17 April 2019). In other words, these women had actively helped to establish important new supportive and sustaining connectivities in their lives, not just in an economic sense but also in a social sense (Baines and Rosenoff Gauvin, 2014: 297; Musinguzi, 2016: 506). While the male interviewees themselves did not speak about the importance of such interactions, research has explored the value that some men in Uganda do attach to being in a group with fellow victims-/survivors (see, e.g., Schulz, 2019; Schulz and Ngomokwe, 2021).

Resisting New Connectivities

According to Oliveira and Baines (2022: 756), 'One becomes a respected woman or man through marriage' in northern Uganda. Some of the female interviewees, however, were actively resisting socio-cultural norms and expectations by choosing not to form new connectivities – and specifically new connectivities with men. Two interviewees' stories were particularly illustrative. One interviewee was a 54-year-old Acholi woman whose husband was killed by cattle rustlers during the late 1980s. She was subsequently 'inherited' by her late husband's brother,[26] but he went away with his other wife and left her. The interviewee spoke about the 'big tongue' (verbal abuse) that she had experienced, including from potential suitors who mocked and ridiculed her when she refused them. She had made the decision, however, to remain alone (with her five children), and felt that this had benefitted her. She spoke about feeling untied/unbound, thus conveying the sense that her active choice not to form new relationships with men had left her much freer. She further maintained that being a single woman had given her more strength because it meant that 'I am free from the hard life or the abuses that men direct at their wives' (interview, Uganda, 12 June 2019).

A Lango interviewee, also a widow, explained that after her husband died, she refused to be inherited. Regarding the practice of 'widow inheritance' (levirate), known in Luo as *laku*, Oleke et al. (2005: 2632) comment that 'Langi and other Luo ethnography reveals that the widow herself had a decisive say in whether or not she were to be "inherited"'. They add that 'Other sources, however, note that although in principle a woman can decide her own destiny upon her husband's death, her options are severely constrained by the strongly patrilineal principles of Luo culture' (Oleke et al., 2005: 2632). The interviewee herself, who was 57 years old, talked about some of these constraints, recalling that when she made it clear that she did not wish for anyone to inherit her, there was discussion about reporting her to the clan. Yet, this did not change how she felt. In her words: 'I don't owe anybody anything. I am struggling to ensure that these children of yours [referring to the fact that her children belonged to the clan] grow, but I am not struggling so that someone comes and messes up my family's future'.

Her concern was that a man might take advantage of her, expecting her to prepare three meals a day while doing nothing to help her, and hence she had resolved to remain alone. People in the community had questioned how she would raise her children without a man, but she paid no attention and talked about 'silently scolding them in my heart' (interview, Uganda, 2 April 2019).

These examples offer important cultural expressions of resilience qua everyday resistance. The interviewees were actively challenging what the norms and traditions within their social ecologies expected from them as widows; and in so doing, they were seeking to carve out new roles for themselves within these ecologies. They were also thus making very active choices about the sorts of connectivities that they did and did not wish to build and cultivate in their lives.

★★★

Connectivity Stories of Resilience in Uganda 231

This chapter has sought to convey some of the richness and complexity of the Ugandan data, while also telling an overall story about the data and the interviewees' lives. Like the Bosnian and Colombian chapters previously, it has used the concept of connectivity – and specifically the three broad narrative frames of broken and ruptured connectivities, supportive and sustaining connectivities and new connectivities – to construct and shape this story. The final chapter explores the significance of these connectivities in relation to transitional justice. If these connectivities, as an analytical framework for thinking about resilience, are fundamentally about the relationships between individuals and their social ecologies, the final chapter uses them to examine how the field of transitional justice might itself be developed in new social-ecological directions – and what this would mean in practice.

Notes

1 In their research on the gendered nature of naked protests, Ebila and Tripp (2017: 38) cite a male Acholi participant who explained that:

> Acholi culture is not like other cultures where people bare themselves often in public [*kima-sulo*]. Even speaking about sex openly is taboo. In fact, while growing up you do not know some of the names of your body parts, they are not even spoken out loud.

2 The interviewee's use of the present tense when narrating past events was striking. Indeed, this was a pattern that was common in many of the interviews – and not only in Uganda. One explanation is that past events were still very present in interviewees' minds and lives, eliding neat temporal compartmentalisation. Research has also found that 'narrative temporal structure reflects the intensity of the narrator's current affective state' (Pølya, 2021: 288), meaning that experiences that evoke particularly intense emotions may be narrated in the present tense (see also Pillemer, 1998: 138).
3 Cattle raids were particularly prevalent during the second half of the 1980s (Apio, 2016: 25).
4 Discussing the meaning of *kiir*, a female Acholi interviewee explained that 'In Acholi tongue, they would say that you have done an abomination [*gwok*] that can kill a person' (interview, Uganda, 26 March 2019; see also Leman, 2009: 116).
5 Several interviewees spoke about experiencing CRSV outside the context of forced marriage and often involving more than one perpetrator.
6 In the study questionnaire, however, the interviewee stated that she was born in 1987. Based on this, she would have been 16 and not 12 if she was abducted in 2003 (she was very specific about the date).
7 In patrilineal societies like Uganda, 'women derive rights to land from marriage' (Khadiagala, 2001: 60).
8 Thank you to Dr Eunice Otuko Apio for this explanation.
9 Existing scholarship overwhelmingly focuses on the LRA's abduction of children and young adults, due to the sheer numbers (see, e.g., Pham et al., 2008). However, the LRA did also abduct a small number of considerably older (and elderly) women and men (see, e.g., Human Rights Watch [HRW], 2003; Prosecutor v. Ongwen, 2021: paras. 1828, 1971 n3140).
10 Pescosolido and Martin (2015: 91) define stigma as 'the mark, the condition, or status that is subject to devaluation' and stigmatisation as 'the social process by which the mark affects the lives of all those touched by it'. Because there was significant overlap between stigma and stigmatisation in the interviewees' stories, this chapter primarily uses the term stigma to encompass both.

232 Connectivity Stories of Resilience in Uganda

11 In Acholi society, 'the payment of *luk* (customary payments which recognize and formalize sexual access), or the intention of payment, is a key distinction between socially acceptable sex that contributes to social harmony and that which damages it' (Porter, 2015c: 280; for a discussion of *luk* in Lango society, see Apio, 2016: Chapter 3). It can be reasonably assumed that because the interviewees suffered sexual violence in a conflict context, *luk* would not have been paid.

12 Interestingly, one of the male Lango interviewees insisted that he still is, and still sees himself as a man. He also emphasised that 'There is no problem in my being a man [referring to his ability to perform sexually]. There is no issue with it' (interview, Uganda, 20 February 2019). This might be read as a form of resistance to the 'displacement from gendered personhood' that Schulz (2018) discusses.

13 *Cen*, as Baines (2010: 420) notes, 'is the vengeful spirit of persons who either died badly (murder, neglect) or were treated badly in death (failure to give a proper burial or treating a corpse without respect)'.

14 According to the interviewee, she did not start ARV treatment until 2018 – four years after she was diagnosed with HIV – because the local health centre did not have the resources to check her CD4 count. CD4 count and viral load are 'the two most important laboratory tests to determine whether [ARV] treatment should begin' (Piacenti, 2006: 1112).

15 The Baganda are a Bantu ethnic group in southern Uganda.

16 Some connections, thus, could not be 'properly established according to what many considered Acholi [or Lango] tradition' (Whyte et al., 2013: 290–291).

17 Baines (2007: 94) notes that 'stepping on an egg' (*nyono tong gweno*) ceremonies were 'practised across the region to promote forgiveness in communities and to encourage others to take advantage of the amnesty [an amnesty law came into force in 2000] and return home'.

18 Kiconco and Nthakomwa (2018: 65) explain that 'The patriarchal setting in rural Acholiland is based on extended families. A typical *dog gang* (family) consists of a husband, wife(s), and unmarried children, grandparents (parents to the husband), unmarried siblings, offspring of deceased siblings, among other relatives'.

19 The LRA frequently targeted civilians whom it accused of collaborating with government soldiers. It would, for example, cut off people's lips and order them to 'spread the word' that the LRA was responsible, as a way of instilling fear.

20 At the time of the interview, this woman had six children. However, she subsequently lost three of them, two of whom died from hepatitis B almost three years after the interview took place.

21 Devas and Grant (2003: 312) note, however, that 'Gender and minority interests are protected (in principle at least) through reserved seats for women, youth and disabled at each level'.

22 Ungar (2013: 260), moreover, has underlined that 'embedded in culture are expectations regarding appropriate ways to cope with adversity that influence Environment x Individual interactions'.

23 Uganda's 2014 census results revealed that 'Catholics are the largest religious denomination constituting close to 40 percent of the population followed by Anglicans with 32 percent and Moslems with about 14 percent' (Ugandan Bureau of Statistics, 2016: 19).

24 Williams (2021: 561) argues that Pentecostal-Charismatic churches 'have flourished in northern Uganda since the war, as in so many other parts of the world, and it seemed that people were turning here for solace, recovery, and community'. According to Uganda's 2014 census, Pentecostals constitute 11.1 per cent of the country's population, compared to 4.7 per cent in 2002 (Ugandan Bureau of Statistics, 2016: 19).

25 Musinguzi (2016: 501) argues that:

> the benefits – and unintended consequences – of participation in VSLAs are found in the networks of friendships and social relations that predate the VSLA. These social

networks influence women's decisions to join VSLAs and to challenge structural barriers, and they enable women to expand and maintain friendship networks.

26 Mkutu (2008: 248) points out that:

> Part of the cultural provision for widows in many societies in Africa is wife inheritance: the transfer of women and their children to the husband's brother or lineage. Marriage is seen in terms of clans rather than individuals, so children and wife belong to the clan.

References

Abonga F and Brown C (2022) Restoration and renewal through sport: Gendered experiences of resilience for war-affected youth in northern Uganda. *Civil Wars*, https://doi.org/10.1080/13698249.2022.2015216.

Adams A (2018) The legacy of the International Criminal Tribunals for the former Yugoslavia and Rwanda and their contribution to the crime of rape. *European Journal of International Law* 29(3): 749–769.

Adger WN (2000) Social and ecological resilience: Are they related? *Progress in Human Geography* 24(3): 347–364.

Akello G (2019) Reintegration of amnestied LRA ex-combatants and survivors' resistance acts in Acholiland, northern Uganda. *International Journal of Transitional Justice* 13(2): 249–267.

Akhavan P (2005) The *Lord's Resistance Army* case: Uganda's submission of the first state referral to the International Criminal Court. *American Journal of International Law* 99(2): 403–421.

Aly A, Taylor E and Karnovsky S (2014) Moral disengagement and building resilience to violent extremism: An education intervention. *Studies in Conflict & Terrorism* 37(4): 369–385.

Amone-P'Olak K, Ovuga E and Jones PB (2015) The effects of sexual violence on psychosocial outcomes in formerly abducted girls in northern Uganda: The WAYS study. *BMC Psychology* 15: 46.

Anderson DG (2000) *Identity and Ecology in Arctic Siberia: The Number One Reindeer Brigade.* Oxford: Oxford University Press.

Apio EO (2016) Children born of war in northern Uganda: Kinship, marriage and the politics of post-conflict reintegration in Lango society. PhD thesis, University of Birmingham. Available at: https://etheses.bham.ac.uk/id/eprint/6926/ (accessed 4 January 2022).

Baines E (2007) The haunting of Alice: Local approaches to justice and reconciliation in northern Uganda. *International Journal of Transitional Justice* 1(1): 91–114.

Baines E (2010) Spirits and social reconstruction after mass violence: Rethinking transitional justice. *African Affairs* 109(436): 409–430.

Baines E and Rosenoff Gauvin L (2014) Motherhood and social repair after war and displacement in northern Uganda. *Journal of Refugee Studies* 27(2): 282–300.

Bedigen W (2021) Honyomiji: The local women's peacebuilding institution in South Sudan. *Peacebuilding* 9(4): 457–476.

Benzies K and Mychasiuk R (2009) Fostering family resiliency: A review of the key protective factors. *Child & Family Social Work* 14(1): 103–114.

Berkes F and Ross H (2013) Community resilience: Toward an integrated approach. *Society & Natural Resources* 26(1): 5–20.

Betancourt TS and Khan KT (2008) The mental health of children affected by armed conflict: Protective processes and pathways to resilience. *International Review of Psychiatry* 20(3): 317–328.

Branch A (2018) From disaster to devastation: Drought as war in northern Uganda. *Disasters* 42(2): 306–327.

Chaskin RC (2008) Resilience, community and resilient communities: Conditioning contexts and collective action. *Child Care in Practice* 14(1): 65–74.

Clark JN (2022) Social ecologies of health and conflict-related sexual violence: Translating 'healthworlds' into transitional justice. *Journal of Human Rights*, https://doi.org/10.1080/14754835.2021.2020627.

Cutter SL, Barnes L, Berry M, Burton C, Evans E, Tate E and Webb J (2008) A place-based model for understanding community resilience to natural disasters. *Global Environmental Change* 18(4): 598–606.

Dalley-Trim L (2007) 'The boys' present . . . Hegemonic masculinity: A performance of multiple acts. *Gender and Education* 19(2): 199–217.

Devas N and Grant U (2003) Local government decision-making – Citizen participation and accountability: Some evidence from Kenya and Uganda. *Public Administration and Development* 23(4): 307–316.

Dolan C, Baaz ME and Stern M (2020) What is sexual about conflict-related sexual violence? Stories from men and women survivors. *International Affairs* 96(5): 1151–1168.

Dowds E (2018) Conceptualizing the role of consent in the definition of rape at the International Criminal Court: A norm transfer perspective. *International Feminist Journal of Politics* 20(4): 624–643.

Drumond P (2019) What about men? Towards a critical interrogation of sexual violence against men in global politics. *International Affairs* 95(6): 1271–1287.

Ebila F (2020) Loss and trauma in Ugandan girls' ex-child-soldier autobiographical narratives: The case of Grace Akallo and China Keitetsi. *Auto/Biography Studies* 35(3): 533–555.

Ebila F and Tripp AM (2017) Naked transgressions: Gendered symbolism in Ugandan land protests. *Politics, Groups and Identities* 5(1): 25–45.

Ellis BH and Abdi S (2017) Building community resilience to violent extremism through genuine partnerships. *American Psychologist* 72(3): 289–300.

Gray H, Stern M and Dolan C (2020) Torture and sexual violence in war and conflict: The unmaking and remaking of subjects of violence. *Review of International Studies* 46(2): 197–126.

Gray MJ and Lombardo TW (2001) Complexity of trauma narratives as an index of fragmented memory in PTSD: A critical analysis. *Applied Cognitive Psychology* 15(7): 171–186.

Hopwood J (2015) Women's land claims in the Acholi region of northern Uganda: What can be learned from what is contested. *International Journal on Minority and Group Rights* 22(3): 387–409.

Hopwood J (2022) An inherited animus to communal land: The mechanisms of coloniality in land reform agendas in Acholiland, northern Uganda. *Critical African Studies* 14(1): 38–54.

HRW (2003) Human rights abuses by the Lord's Resistance Army. Available at: www.hrw.org/reports/2003/uganda0703/uganda0703a-04.htm#P376_64817 (accessed 23 January 2022).

Huber R, Briner S, Peringer A, Lauber S, Seidl R, Widmer A, Gillet F, Buttler A, Le QB and Hirschi C (2013) Modeling social-ecological feedback effects in the implementation of payments for environmental services in pasture-woodlands. *Ecology and Society* 18(2): 41.

Joireman JF (2018) Intergenerational land conflict in northern Uganda: Children, customary law and return migration. *Africa* 88(1): 81–98.

Kavuma RM (2011) Free universal secondary education in Uganda has yielded mixed results. Available at: www.theguardian.com/global-development/poverty-matters/2011/oct/25/free-secondary-education-uganda-mixed-results (accessed 3 February 2022).

Khadiagala L (2001) The failure of popular justice in Uganda: Local councils and women's property rights. *Development and Change* 32(1): 55–76.

Kiconco A and Nthakomwa M (2018) Marriage for the 'new woman' from the Lord's Resistance Army: Experiences of female ex-abductees in Acholi region of Uganda. *Women's Studies International Forum* 68: 65–74.

Kiconco A and Nthakomwa M (2022) Wartime captivity and homecoming: Culture, stigma and coping strategies of formerly abducted women in post-conflict northern Uganda. *Disasters* 46(3): 654–676.

Knighton B (2003) The state as raider among the Karamojong: 'Where there are no guns, they use the threat of guns'. *Africa* 73(3): 427–455.

Koliou M, van de Lindt JW, McAllister TP, Ellingwood BR, Dillard M and Cutler H (2020) State of the research in community resilience: Progress and challenges. *Sustainable and Resilient Infrastructure* 5(3): 131–151.

Krieger N (2005) Embodiment: A conceptual glossary for epidemiology. *Journal of Epidemiology & Community Health* 59(5): 350–355.

Leman P (2009) Singing the law: Okot p'Bitek's legal imagination and the poetics of traditional justice. *Research in African Literatures* 40(3): 109–128.

Lundgren R, Burgess S, Chantelois H, Oregede S, Kerner B and Kågesten AE (2019) Processing gender: Lived experiences of reproducing and transforming gender norms over the life course of young people in northern Uganda. *Culture, Health & Sexuality* 21(4): 387–403.

Macdonald A and Kerali R (2020) Being normal: Stigmatization of Lord's Resistance Army returnees as 'moral experience' in post-war northern Uganda. *Journal of Refugee Studies* 33(4): 766–790.

Madhani DP and Baines E (2020) Fatherhood in the time of war and peace: The experiences of demobilized male soldiers in northern Uganda. *Women's Studies International Forum* 83: 102415.

Marchand THJ (2010) Making knowledge: Explorations of the indissoluble relation between minds, bodies and environment. *Journal of the Royal Anthropological Institute* 16(1): 1–21.

Mazer S (2018) New hazardscapes for old. *Performance Research* 23(4–5): 111–115.

McSorley K (2014) Towards an embodied sociology of war. *The Sociological Review* 62(2): 107–128.

Meinert L, Willerslev R and Seebach SH (2017) Cement, graves and pillars in land disputes in northern Uganda. *African Studies Review* 60(3): 37–57.

Mkutu KA (2008) Uganda: Pastoral conflict and gender relations. *Review of African Political Economy* 35(116): 237–254.

Moon MJ and Kim TH (2005) Microstructural analysis of the capture thread spinning apparatus in orb web spiders. *Entomological Research* 35(2): 133–140.

Mugizi FMP and Matsumoto T (2021) From conflict to conflicts: War-induced displacement, land conflicts and agricultural productivity in post-war northern Uganda. *Land Use Policy* 101: 105149.

Munyua B, Orr A and Okwadi J (2013) Open sesame: A value chain analysis of sesame marketing in northern Uganda. *International Crops Research Institute for the Semi-Arid Tropics,* available at: https://citeseerx.ist.psu.edu/viewdoc/download?doi=10.1.1.658.3455&rep=rep1&type=pdf (accessed 6 January 2022).

Musinguzi LK (2016) The role of social networks in savings groups: Insights from village savings and loan associations in Luwero, Uganda. *Community Development Journal* 51(4): 499–516.

Nannyonjo J (2005) Conflicts, poverty and human development in northern Uganda. *The Round Table* 94(381): 473–488.

Obote-Odora A (2005) Rape and sexual violence in international law: ICTR contribution. *New England Journal of International and Comparative Law* 12(1): 135–160.

Okello C, Pindozzi S, Faugno S and Boccia L (2013) Development of bioenergy technologies in Uganda: A review of progress. *Renewable and Sustainable Energy Reviews* 18: 53–63.

Okello ES and Ekblad S (2006) Lay concepts of depression among the Baganda of Uganda: A pilot study. *Transcultural Psychiatry* 42(2): 287–313.

Oleke C, Blystad A and Rekdal AB (2005) 'When the obvious brother is not there': Political and cultural contexts of the orphan challenge in northern Uganda. *Social Science and Medicine* 61(12): 2628–2638.

Oliveira C and Baines E (2022) 'It's like giving birth to this girl again': Social repair and motherhood after conflict-related sexual violence. *Social Politics* 29(2): 750–770.

Oosterom M (2011) Gender and fragile citizenship in Uganda: The case of Acholi women. *Gender & Development* 19(3): 395–408.

O'Rourke C (2015) Feminist scholarship in transitional justice: A de-politicising impulse? *Women's Studies International Forum* 51: 118–227.

Park CL and Blake EC (2020) Resilience and recovery following disasters: The meaning making model. In: Schulenberg S (ed.), *Positive Psychological Approaches to Disaster*. Cham: Springer, pp. 9–25.

Pescosolido BA and Martin LK (2015) The stigma complex. *Annual Review of Sociology* 41(1): 87–116.

Pham PN, Vinck P and Stover E (2008) The Lord's Resistance Army and forced conscription in northern Uganda. *Human Rights Quarterly* 30(2): 404–411.

Piacenti FJ (2006) An update and review of antiretroviral therapy. *Pharmacotherapy* 26(8): 1111–1133.

Pillemer DB (1998) *Momentous Events, Vivid Memories*. Cambridge, MA: Harvard University Press.

Pølya T (2021) Temporal structure of narratives reveals the intensity of the narrator's current affective state. *Current Psychology* 40: 281–291.

Porter HE (2015a) After rape: Comparing civilian and combatant perpetrated crime in northern Uganda. *Women's Studies International Forum* 51: 81–90.

Porter HE (2015b) Mango trees, offices and altars: The role of relatives, non-governmental organizations and churches after rape in northern Uganda. *International Journal on Minority and Group Rights* 22(3): 309–334.

Porter HE (2015c) 'Say no to bad touches': Schools, sexual identity and sexual violence in northern Uganda. *International Journal of Educational Development* 41: 271–282.

Porter HE (2017) *After Rape: Violence, Justice and Social Harmony in Uganda*. Cambridge: Cambridge University Press.

Raider-Roth M, Stieha V and Hensley B (2012) Rupture and repair: Episodes of resistance and resilience in teachers' learning. *Teacher and Teacher Education* 28(4): 493–502.

Reid J (2013) Interrogating the neoliberal biopolitics of the sustainable development-resilience nexus. *International Political Sociology* 7(4): 353–367.

Rose DB (2017) Connectivity thinking, animism and the pursuit of liveliness. *Educational Theory* 67(4): 491–508.

Ryan C (2015) Everyday resilience as resistance: Palestinian women practising *sumud*. *International Political Sociology* 9(4): 299–315.

Sankhayan PL and Hofstad O (2000) Production and spatial price differences for charcoal in Uganda. *Journal of Forest Research* 5: 117–121.

Schomburg W and Paterson I (2007) Genuine consent to sexual violence under international criminal law. *American Journal of International Law* 101(1): 121–140.

Schulz P (2018) Displacement from gendered personhood: Sexual violence and masculinities in northern Uganda. *International Affairs* 94(5): 1101–1119.

Schulz P (2019) 'To me, justice means to be in a group': Survivors' groups as a pathway to justice in northern Uganda. *Journal of Human Rights Practice* 11(1): 171–189.

Schulz P (2020) Examining male wartime rape survivors' perspectives on justice in northern Uganda. *Social & Legal Studies* 29(1): 19–40.

Schulz P and Ngomokwe F (2021) Resilience, adaptive peacebuilding and transitional justice in post-conflict Uganda: The participatory potential of survivors' groups. In: Clark JN and Ungar M (eds.), *Resilience, Adaptive Peacebuilding and Transitional Justice: How Societies Recover after Collective Violence*. Cambridge: Cambridge University Press, pp. 119–142.

Simtowe F, Marenya P, Amondo E, Worku M, Rahut DB and Erenstein O (2019) Heterogeneous seed access and information exposure: Implications for the adoption of drought-tolerant maize varieties in Uganda. *Agricultural and Food Economics* 7: 15.

Theron LC (2020) Adolescent versus adult explanations of resilience enablers: A South African study. *Youth & Society* 52(1): 78–98.

Theron LC and Theron AMC (2014) Meaning-making and resilience: Case studies of a multifaceted process. *Journal of Psychology in Africa* 24(1): 24–32.

Tronto JC (1993) *Moral Boundaries: A Political Argument for an Ethic of Care*. New York, NY: Routledge.

Ugandan Bureau of Statistics (2016) The national population and housing census 2014 – Main report. Available at: www.ubos.org/wp-content/uploads/publications/03_20182014_National_Census_Main_Report.pdf (accessed 9 February 2022).

Ungar M (2013) Resilience, trauma, context and culture. *Trauma, Violence & Abuse* 14(3): 255–266.

UNICEF (2019) UNICEF Uganda: Annual report 2019. Available at: www.unicef.org/uganda/media/6806/file/UNICEF_UgandaAR2019-WEBhighres.pdf (accessed 21 January 2022).

UNICEF (n.d.) Education. Available at: www.unicef.org/uganda/what-we-do/education (accessed 21 January 2022).

Vinci A (2005) The strategic use of fear by the Lord's Resistance Army. *Small Wars & Insurgencies* 16(3): 360–381.

Walker B and Meyers JA (2004) Thresholds in ecological and social-ecological systems: A developing database. *Ecology and Society* 9(2): 3.

Walsh F (2020) Loss and resilience in the time of COVID-19: Meaning making, hope, and transcendence. *Family Process* 59(3): 898–911.

Wexler LM, DiFluvio G and Burke TK (2009) Resilience and marginalized youth: Making a case for personal and collective meaning-making as part of resilience research in public health. *Social Science & Medicine* 69(4): 565–570.

Whyte SR (2005) Going home? Belonging and burial in the era of AIDS. *Africa* 75(2): 154–172.

Whyte SR, Babiiha SM and Mukyala R (2013) Remaining internally displaced: Missing links to security in northern Uganda. *Journal of Refugee Studies* 26(2): 283–301.

Williams LH (2021) 'An automatic Bible in the brain': Trauma and prayer among Acholi Pentecostals in northern Uganda. *Transcultural Psychiatry* 58(4): 561–572.

Wolff J and De-Shalit A (2007) *Disadvantage*. Oxford: Oxford University Press.

Yang M (2020) Resilience and meaning making amid the COVID-19 epidemic in China. *Journal of Humanistic Psychology* 60(5): 662–671.

Legal Judgements

ICC

Prosecutor v. Ongwen (2021) ICC-02/04–01/15, Trial Chamber Judgement, 4 February 2021.

ICTY

Prosecutor v. Kunarac et al. (2002) IT-96–23/1-A, Appeals Chamber Judgement, 12 June 2002.

Chapter 8

Resilience and Why Social Ecologies Matter for Transitional Justice

Through its focus on resilience, this book has sought to address a pronounced gap within extant literature on conflict-related sexual violence (CRSV). Adopting a social-ecological approach to resilience, it has used the idea of connectivity – borrowed from ecology scholarship – to develop its own conceptual framework within which to analyse the interview data from Bosnia-Herzegovina (BiH), Colombia and Uganda. In doing so, it has constructed an overall narrative about resilience focused on the multiple connectivities, and the stories of those connectivities, between individuals and their social ecologies, in the sense of everything that they have around them. This final chapter – which has wider relevance beyond just CRSV – pulls the different threads of the research together, specifically by discussing and reflecting on their significance for transitional justice theory and practice.

A small number of exceptions notwithstanding (see, e.g., Clark, 2022a; Clark and Ungar, 2021; Gilmore and Moffett, 2021; Kastner, 2020; Wiebelhaus-Brahm, 2017), 'transitional justice discourses and scholarship have, so far, remained relatively indifferent to the concept of resilience' (Kastner, 2020: 369). However, there are some important synergies between resilience and core transitional justice goals. In his research on hybrid courts[1] and resilience, Wiebelhaus-Brahm (2020: 1027) notes that:

> If one accepts the premise that hybrid courts have the potential to help repair relationships and promote the rule of law, the development literature suggests that these societies should more easily rebound from natural disasters and economic and political crises.

Flipping this around, the larger point is that relational repair and reconciliation, the (re)establishment of the rule of law and, relatedly, building peace are all long-term processes that arguably necessitate resilience in the sense of systems that can withstand shocks and stressors, thereby providing crucial stability. Even if it is not explicitly associated with resilience, capacity-building – which has been an important part of the work and legacies of international judicial

DOI: 10.4324/9781003323532-9

institutions (see, e.g., Barria and Roper, 2008; Dieng, 2011) – can be viewed as a way of helping to create or develop such systems (Clark, 2021a: 532).

The concept of connectivity is also implicit within transitional justice processes in several ways. Staub (2006: 876), for example, emphasises that 'Trauma creates insecurity, mistrust, and disconnection from people'. Reconciliation, thus, is quintessentially about re-establishing or rebuilding connectivities. Moreover, transitional justice mechanisms such as criminal trials and truth commissions require individuals to remember (Humphrey, 2003: 177; Manning, 2012: 165), and memory is itself about connectivity. As Schacter and Welker (2016: 242) point out, 'an important recent trend in cognitive and neuroscientific approaches to memory in individuals explores the realization that memory serves to connect individuals not only to their pasts but also to their futures'. What has been significantly missing from transitional justice theory and practice to date, however, is recognition of and attention to the complex and multi-dimensional connectivities between individuals and their social ecologies and, more importantly, the relevance of these connectivities for processes of dealing with the past.

The focus of this chapter is precisely on demonstrating why and how the social ecologies – and connectivities – that are central to this book's understanding of resilience also matter for transitional justice. Herremans and Destrooper (2021: 577) explain that their use of the term 'the justice imagination' refers to 'what we believe can be achieved through various kinds of justice processes and initiatives, and how we stretch the boundaries of what is conceivable in terms of justice and accountability'. This chapter itself is an expression of 'the justice imagination'. It uses the book's analysis of resilience to 'stretch the boundaries', in the sense of putting forward a new – and broadly sketched – social-ecological framework that both effects and constitutes an important epistemic shift in how we think about transitional justice. This framework means, inter alia, locating individuals and the harms that they experience within broader relational assemblages and 'infinite webs of interconnectedness' (Tschakert, 2022: 291), and thus foregrounding the crucial dialectics and feedbacks between individuals and their social ecologies.

To be clear, this is primarily a conceptual chapter aimed at exploring and demonstrating what it might mean to think in new social-ecological ways about transitional justice. Its objective is not to prescriptively lay out a series of steps needed to translate an idea into practice. However, a question that Roelvink (2018: 137) poses in the context of his work on climate justice is also highly pertinent to this research, namely: 'how do we get from an abstract ontological revisioning to a glimmer or a whiff of what to do on the ground?' This chapter makes several suggestions aimed at answering this question, and more specifically the question of what a social-ecological framing of transitional justice might look like – and require – in practice.

It is important to highlight several recent developments in Colombia that reflect social-ecological thinking. In 2011, Decree-Law 4633 recognised that

Why Social Ecologies Matter for Transitional Justice 241

the armed conflict had produced territorial and cultural harms that threatened Indigenous peoples and their very existence (McClanahan, 2019: 76). In so doing, the legislation acknowledged that Indigenous peoples 'have "special and collective ties" with "Mother Earth" (Article 3) and have the right to "harmonious coexistence in the territories" (Article 29)' (Izquierdo and Viaene, 2018). More recently, in 2020, Colombia's Special Jurisdiction for Peace (JEP) – established as part of the 2016 peace agreement between the government and the Revolutionary Armed Forces of Colombia (FARC) – declared that the territories of three Indigenous communities and two Black communities have been victims of the armed conflict (Huneeus and Rueda Sáiz, 2021).

The importance of these developments and the potential precedent that they set for expanding transitional justice in new directions cannot be over-emphasised. Fundamentally, the posthumanist concept of territory-as-victim gives legal expression to the idea that armed conflict does not only affect and harm human lives and relationships, 'but also relations with non-humans, including animals, plants, ecosystems and natural entities or "earth beings" such as rivers and mountains, and the spiritual world' (Huneeus and Rueda Sáiz, 2021: 211).[2] In short, the JEP has made a major contribution to redefining 'the interplay between the environment and armed conflict' (Yoshida and Céspedes-Báez, 2021: 34). The framing that this chapter puts forward, however, is about more than just recognising the impact of war, armed conflict and large-scale violence on the natural environment. It both entails and requires a 'profound rethinking of [transitional justice] problems and possible solutions' (Hoddy and Gready, 2020: 563) in the context of the multiple relationships and connectivities between individuals and their social ecologies. While these social-ecological environments necessarily include land, water systems, trees and other aspects of the natural environment, they are also much broader in scope.

This chapter begins by exploring how the interviewees in BiH, Colombia and Uganda spoke about justice. It particularly draws attention to examples from the data of implicit social-ecological thinking about transitional justice. The second, third and fourth sections demonstrate how the three core elements of the book's conceptual framework – broken and ruptured connectivities, supportive and sustaining connectivities and new connectivities – are relevant to transitional justice and its future development in ways that capture the significance of individuals' social ecologies and the 'co-evolving elements of social-ecological systems' (Stagl, 2007: 52). These sections respectively discuss the ideas of harm and relationality, adaptive capacity and mutuality.

Interviewees' Reflections on Transitional Justice

It would be premature to move straight into a deeper discussion of why social ecologies matter for transitional justice without first examining some of the ways that the interviewees in BiH, Colombia and Uganda themselves broadly spoke about transitional justice processes, including their personal experiences,

242 Why Social Ecologies Matter for Transitional Justice

expectations and/or grievances. The three preceding chapters analysed the interview data with reference to seven core themes, all of them linked to the book's connectivity framework. The eighth and final theme, which primarily speaks to the new connectivities part of the framework, is '*It didn't change anything': Justice that connects/makes a difference.*

The two parts of this theme illuminate the issue of top-down/bottom-up disconnects within transitional justice processes, which extant scholarship has extensively discussed (see, e.g., Lundy and McGovern, 2008; McAuliffe, 2017; McEvoy and McGregor, 2008; Ranasinghe, 2019). Reflected in the first part of the theme, what interviewees frequently articulated was a strong sense of disillusionment and disappointment with transitional justice. This was largely based on a common sentiment that whatever transitional justice work had taken place in their respective countries, it was effectively 'space-capsule justice' (Gow et al., 2013) that had not positively changed anything in – and was removed from – the interviewees' everyday lives.

Transitional justice work in BiH has taken a predominantly judicial form, through the work of the International Criminal Tribunal for the former Yugoslavia (ICTY; see, e.g., Orentlicher, 2018) and, subsequently, the State Court of BiH and other local courts (see, e.g., Meernik and Barron, 2018). Unsurprisingly, therefore, Bosnian interviewees spoke most about criminal prosecutions. More particularly, they talked about their frustrations with the outcomes of proceedings, the length of sentences handed down and the slow pace of the justice process.[3] Discussing her own experiences, a Bosnian Serb interviewee angrily insisted that: 'It does not mean anything to me that he [the man who raped her] was arrested 21 years later and then released after three years. What is that? Nothing. It's as if it [the rape she suffered] never happened. I got nothing out of the trial process' (interview, BiH, 20 February 2019). She further underlined that her perpetrator should have stood trial much sooner and not simply been allowed to get on with his life for so many years while she could not.

Colombian interviewees tended to speak most about reparations, which some of them had received from the country's Victims' Unit, and they identified important flaws in the process. An interviewee from the Indigenous Pastos people, for example, pointed out that 'Nobody ever asks you: "How do you feel?", or "What did you lose?" or "How are you doing, as a woman, as a mother?" And this is like a huge hole'. She continued: 'That's what I was saying about how they [the Victims' Unit] just hand over the award letter [granting reparations] and that's it, finished' (interview, Colombia, 4 February 2019).

Consistent with the fact that BiH, Colombia and Uganda are at very different stages in addressing the legacies of past human rights violations, Ugandan interviewees had the least experience of transitional justice. Some of them, however, had received amnesty under the country's 2000 Amnesty Act (see, e.g., Raymond, 2013: 428–429).[4] Reflecting on her experiences in this regard, an Acholi woman maintained that she was glad to have an amnesty card from the Amnesty Commission as it gave her opportunities. For example, she needed to show the card to be able to join a tailoring group, she explained. She had also received some money from the Amnesty Commission, which had enabled her to buy three goats. Yet, she had mixed feelings about the amnesty process, stressing that she had not done anything that needed to be pardoned. In her words:

> I was abducted, taken by force and that's why I went [to the bush]. And so, when I was given amnesty to say that I had been forgiven, I kept thinking 'but what wrong have I done?' I did not commit any wrongs.
>
> (interview, Uganda, 19 March 2019)

In other words, although the amnesty process had made some small differences to this interviewee's life, in her view it was disconnected from and failed to recognise the reality of what she herself had gone through in the bush.

If the aforementioned examples support Hinton's (2018: 9) argument for 'a phenomenological approach to transitional justice that refocuses attention on lived experience', some interviewees were also deeply sceptical about the very idea of 'justice' – and whether it could be achieved in a way that would be meaningful to them. It was overwhelmingly the Bosnian interviewees – from all ethnic groups – who expressed such sentiments, almost certainly linked to the fact that more than 25 years after the Bosnian war ended, 'justice' has remained an elusive concept for many (Korjenić, 2020). Relatedly, some interviewees stressed that the ideal of 'justice for all' was completely at odds with reality. One of the Croat interviewees underlined that 'the poor and little people[5] always get the thin end. Anyone can do whatever they want with them' (interview, BiH, 21 May 2019).

Several of the Colombian interviewees articulated similar views, thereby situating the operationalisation of justice within 'intersecting matrices of privilege and oppression' (Buchanan and Wiklund, 2020: 318). One woman, for example, who did not identify with any particular ethnic group, asserted that:

> Here in Colombia, justice is, in many ways, like politics – [it's] about connections. For instance, in everything that has happened to us, to the poor people, nobody has helped us. The police will just tell us. . . . Like, if we go to them and tell them that we've been raped, they won't lift a finger. Because we're nobodies. If we were someone higher up, they'd be on the case immediately, looking for who was responsible, whatever.
>
> (interview, Colombia, 29 January 2019)

While interviewees articulated various issues with transitional justice, the second part of the aforementioned eighth theme – *Justice that connects/makes a difference* – demonstrates that these women and men also had very clear ideas about what they wanted and needed. It is significant in this regard that some of them were implicitly thinking, at least to some extent, in social-ecological ways about transitional justice. That it was particularly (although by no means exclusively) the Colombian interviewees who did so is consistent with some of the social-ecological developments that have unfolded in the context of Colombia's transitional justice work, noted in the introduction to this chapter.

As an illustration of some of the social-ecological ideas woven into the qualitative data, a Colombian interviewee who did not identify with any ethnic group told the story of how she was raped by a paramilitary commander and several members of his entourage.[6] Accentuating that she had lost faith in justice, she explained that this man was very powerful. 'So, when I come along and make accusations against him', she stated, 'well, I'm just a nobody, trying to . . . accusing someone who has it all'. Even if she had little hope of ever seeing justice done in her case, she nevertheless expected more from transitional justice. She had travelled to various places to give individual statements, but she felt that this had decontextualised her story because what happened to her was not an isolated event. What she desperately wanted was for investigators from the JEP to visit her area and essentially to understand some of the social-ecological dynamics that protected the 'heroic' image of the commander (who had ultimately been killed), sustained his legacy and kept people living in fear. In her words:

> It [the JEP] has to come here, to this region. It has to investigate and recognise that there are victims here of a person who seems to be untouchable.[7] I mean, he has cost the lives of so many people. And like me, there are lots of women in this region who've suffered these things [referring to CRSV].
>
> (interview, Colombia, 11 February 2019)

It is necessary to stress that the interviewee was not proposing anything new in expressing what she wanted; comprehensive judicial investigations necessarily entail extensive on-the-ground enquiries and research. What is significant is that this woman was thinking about justice in more than an individual sense. She wanted justice not only for herself, but also for other people whose stories were entangled with her own – and whose lives continued to be deeply affected by wider political machinations within their social ecologies. In the context of the interviewee's comments, it should also be noted that the JEP has so far opened seven 'macro cases'[8] that aggregate multiple perpetrators (Braithwaite, 2021: 272–273). Some of these cases, like case 03 on extrajudicial assassinations and forced disappearances by the state, are primarily thematic. Others have a regional/territorial focus, like case 04 on the Urabá region and case 05 on the north of Cauca and the Valle del Cauca.[9] Certainly, the JEP's macro approach has the potential to tell a bigger story about events and one that encompasses individuals' wider social ecologies.

Turning to a second example of social-ecological thinking within the data, all interviewees were asked about reparations and specifically about whether their preference was for individual or collective reparations. Interviewees in all three countries primarily favoured the former. Some of them, however, spoke about the importance of collective reparations – which Szoke-Burke (2015: 486) defines as 'forms of distribution of public goods or services that are designed for the benefit of all members of a region, group, or community, rather than for specific individual victims' – in the shape of community projects. A female Bosnian interviewee who identified as ethnic Albanian stressed that:

> What I would like the most is for something to be opened, so that people have jobs. They have nothing. There is very little work. I would like something to be opened, a factory or something[10] – anything – to stop people from migrating.[11]
>
> (interview, BiH, 20 March 2019)

For her part, a Lango woman in Uganda believed that reparations should benefit more than just individuals. Preferring a collective form of reparations, such as the building of a new school, she reflected that 'This is more important than paying me alone because if a school is built, it will not only help me but will also help my children and other people's children' (interview, Uganda, 21 February 2019).

While Gready (2022: 185) sees collective reparations as potentially transformative, in the sense of addressing the elemental causes of conflict, the crucial point is that they are also – even if they are not actually framed as such within extant scholarship – a social-ecological concept (see, e.g., Balasco, 2017). Fundamentally, implicit in some interviewees' expressions of support for collective reparations were concerns about their social ecologies and recognition that their own wellbeing was closely intertwined with these ecologies.

The data from BiH, Colombia and Uganda also revealed that interviewees did not only, or even primarily, associate reparations with repair of the multiple harms that they had suffered (and indeed some of them insisted that these harms could never be repaired or compensated). They frequently saw reparations as enabling and linked to new opportunities. Some of the Colombian interviewees, for example, outlined how the award of reparations would enable them to help (or to help more) fellow victims-/survivors within their social ecologies. An Afro-Colombian woman stressed that she would like reparations in the form of opportunities to study. 'I want to study', she explained, 'because I'm here with the fact that I was a victim of sexual violence and my dream is to become a lawyer to protect victims of sexual violence'. Interestingly, she added that 'Nobody has ever asked me: "what are your dreams?" I would say: "I want to study, that's what I want," but I don't have the means and nobody has talked to me about working out how I could study' (interview, Colombia, 30 March 2019).

Another Colombian interviewee who did not identify with any specific ethnic group maintained that:

> They've never asked me – not even the state organisations – what it is that I want. It happened only once. A magistrate, I don't remember the name, asked me: 'what do you want the state to give you to try to repair, in some part, the hurt that was done to you?'

What the interviewee wanted, she underlined, was a home that she could call her own. Not only would this benefit her and her family, but it would also give her more possibilities to help the women in her association. At present, she was living in a small apartment in a converted house, and she spoke about her dreams of owning the property and being able to use the space downstairs. Outlining her aspirations and the plans that she had mapped out in her head, she enthused:

> I'd make one room into a living space where the women could be at ease and the other two would be workspaces for them. There would be a bakery. We'd set up a bakery and café, and in the other we'd set up a dressmaking studio. That's what I dream of.
>
> (interview, Colombia, 29 March 2019)

In the previous two examples, it is significant that both interviewees highlighted what for them were important questions that they had not been asked. This lends some support to the argument put forward by the Global Survivors Fund (2021: 12) – launched in 2019 by the joint Nobel Peace Prize laureates Dr Denis Mukwege and Nadia Murad – that reparations programmes should be 'co-created with survivors'. Such 'co-creation', however, necessarily raises enormous practical challenges, particularly when there are large numbers of victims-/survivors.[12] Co-creation, therefore, can arguably only ever be a partial process, and it is difficult to envisage how broad reparations programmes can fully address needs, wants and priorities that are deeply interconnected with and shaped by victims-/survivors' context-specific social ecologies. The larger point is that resilience, as this book has underlined, is itself a co-creation or co-construction (Haysom, 2017: 1; Theron et al., 2021: 361). By explaining how they would use reparations to support and contribute to their social ecologies, interviewees thus implicitly made linkages, largely unexplored to date, between transitional justice and resilience.

The examples discussed in this section are important because they illustrate some of the ways that the interview data have directly informed the social-ecological framing of transitional justice that this chapter advocates and develops. The remainder of the chapter examines the significance of the book's connectivity framework, and of the interview data more indirectly, for thinking in social-ecological ways about transitional justice. Specifically, it explores how the three meta themes of broken and ruptured connectivities, supportive and sustaining connectivities and new connectivities – which were used to analyse the qualitative data and to structure the empirical chapters – themselves translate into social-ecological ideas relevant for transitional justice theory and practice. The following three sections link the meta themes, respectively, to the concepts of harm and relationality, adaptive capacity and mutuality.

Harm and Relationality (Broken and Ruptured Connectivities)

Harm is a fundamental concept within transitional justice theory and practice. In addressing the legacies of past human rights abuses, transitional justice processes essentially seek to repair and remedy – to the extent possible – multiple and complex harms. Yet, there is also a sizeable body of scholarship that is critical of how transitional justice has traditionally approached and understood harm.

Some Harm-Based Critiques of Transitional Justice

Some feminist scholars, in particular, have argued that transitional justice prioritises specific gendered harms in a decontextualised way, by neglecting the reality that these harms are 'inextricably linked to broader gender power dynamics that both precede and follow periods of political violence' (O'Rourke, 2015: 120). The example of CRSV illustrates this point. If laws prohibiting sexual violence in wartime 'languished ignored for centuries' (Askin, 2003: 288), there have been major developments over the last three decades (see, e.g., Amann, 1999; Brammertz and Jarvis, 2016; Sellers, 2011). As Chapter 2 discussed, however, these developments, and, relatedly, the dominant international policy framing of CRSV as a 'weapon of war',[13] have generated concerns. These relate, inter alia, to the 'hypervisibility' (Laverty and de Vos, 2021) of such violence[14] – and what it potentially obscures (Žarkov, 2016: 122). Some scholars, for example, argue that CRSV is too often portrayed as 'an exceptionalized event' (Crosby et al., 2016: 267). It is thus conceptually divorced from experiences of everyday or 'routine' sexual and gender-based violence (SGBV), in turn 'facilitating the easy dislocation of one kind of harm from the other' (Aoláin, 2014: 626; see also Rubio-Marín, 2012: 73; Swaine, 2015: 759).[15]

Accordingly, there have been calls for transitional justice processes to adopt more gender-sensitive understandings that acknowledge the reality of multiple and intersecting harms (Aoláin, 2012; Lemaitre and Sandvik, 2014). Discussing the Peruvian Truth and Reconciliation Commission, for example, Theidon (2007: 458–459) has underlined that the women who testified gave 'thick' descriptions of their experiences, narrating 'a much broader set of truths about systemic injustice, the gross violations of their socioeconomic rights, the lacerating sting of ethnic discrimination, and the futility of seeking justice from the legal systems that operated nationally and locally'. In other words, thinking comprehensively about gender-based harms means giving greater attention to some of the deeper structures that underpin and foster such harms (and not only against women) and their permeation across war/peace binaries.

A related critique of transitional justice, but one that has a broader application beyond just the issue of SGBV, is precisely that it fails to take seriously and address structural violence (see, e.g., Evans, 2016; McGill, 2017; Nagy, 2008). An important example is the structural violence of colonialism and its legacies (Maddison and Shepherd, 2014; Park, 2020; Rolston and Aoláin, 2018; Yusuf, 2019).[16] Balint et al. (2014: 216) maintain that 'In settler colonial states, where questions of historical and structural injustice risk being downplayed and discredited, the imperative to explore new ways of conceptualizing and responding to the harms inflicted on indigenous peoples . . . remains strong'. Some scholars have therefore called for a more 'transformative' justice that brings about systemic change, by addressing everyday violence and challenging 'unequal and intersecting power relationships and structures of exclusion at both the local and the global level' (Gready and Robins, 2014: 314; see also Atallah and Masud, 2021; Gready and Robins, 2019; Lambourne, 2014). The underlying structures within a society can be generative of violence and human rights violations, and hence they cannot be treated simply as '"inert" background' (Hoddy and Gready, 2020: 572).

The narrowness with which transitional justice has traditionally approached the concept of harm is intrinsically linked to its ideological foundations. The field developed in what Teitel (2000: 5) has referred to as 'the distinctive context of transition' – and specifically transition from authoritarianism to liberal democracy. From the outset, therefore, transitional justice has been conceptually associated with liberalism (Arthur, 2009: 337; Hinton, 2018: 6; Mutua, 2015: 3). Indeed, according to Sharp (2015: 150), 'the idea of transitional justice as handmaiden to liberal political transitions . . . remains a deeply embedded narrative that has helped to shape dominant practices and conceptual boundaries'.

Liberalism, of course, is not a single school of thought, politically or economically, and it encompasses many different theories (Walt, 1998: 32). What they broadly share, however, is 'an emphasis on the individual' (Mahon, 2008: 343) and on the importance of personal autonomy (Colburn, 2010; Dworkin, 2015; Taylor, 2005) – even if there is disagreement about how to conceptualise this autonomy.[17] The central point is that because transitional justice has its roots in liberal theory, it has 'continued mostly to operate in accordance with an individualistic legal framework without facilitating a deep engagement with structural injustices and the types of interventions needed to address them' (Balint et al., 2014: 198).

More fundamentally, this individualistic focus is discordant with the crucial fact that many of the harms that individuals experience in societies undergoing conflict and large-scale violence are deeply relational, as the book's empirical chapters have demonstrated through their analyses of broken and ruptured

Why Social Ecologies Matter for Transitional Justice   249

connectivities. Hence, an important aspect of developing the field of transitional justice in new social-ecological directions is precisely to explore – and ultimately to operationalise – more relational ways of thinking about harm and its legacies. There are two particular relational 'routes' that merit further attention: the posthumanist and the systemic.

Harm, Relationality and Posthumanism

Relationality has been extensively discussed in many different contexts. Leopold (1949: 120), an ecologist and conservationist, famously used the phrase 'thinking like a mountain'. He thus expressed his non-anthropocentric view of the world and his conceptualisation of civilisation as 'mutual and interdependent cooperation between human animals, other animals, plants, and soils' (Leopold, 1991: 183). These ideas deeply resonate with Indigenous cosmologies (see, e.g., Hatala et al., 2020; Izquierdo and Viaene, 2018; Murdock, 2018). As one illustration, Tynan (2021: 600) points out that Aboriginal people in Australia frequently greet each other by asking '"Who are you? Where are you from?"' These are fundamentally questions about relational ties and connections. Asking someone where they are from, for example, 'decentres the human and looks for relational ties based on Country (ancestral or lived) and more-than-human' (Tynan, 2021: 600). In a very different context, Cruikshank's beautifully written book *Do Glaciers Listen?* explores human and more-than-human relationalities through its focus on glaciers and their significance for Indigenous Tlingit and Athapaskan peoples in North America. Glaciers are actors in her book, sentient beings who directly communicate with Indigenous communities by expressing their moods and feelings. As Cruikshank (2005: 8) notes, 'I was informed . . . of firm taboos against "cooking with grease" near glaciers, which are offended by such smells'.

There are important synergies, in turn, between Indigenous onto-epistemologies and posthumanism (Braidotti, 2013; Haraway, 2003; Wolfe, 2010).[18] While it is essential to underline the enormous diversity and richness that these concepts reflect,[19] they broadly emphasise relationality and problematise or reject human/nature binaries that privilege and elevate humans over other life forms. To cite Crellin and Harris (2021: 473), 'human beings are one of many components that make up our world, and . . . cannot be understood apart from the wider relational assemblages . . . of which they are part'. For posthumanists, therefore, a common aim is not to remove humans from the analysis, which would detract from the consequences of human actions and from human responsibility for those actions (Barad, 2006: 136; Díaz de Liaño and Fernández-Götz, 2021: 547). The goal, rather, is to de-centre or 'unseat' *Homo sapiens* as the main focus of social enquiry (Margulies and Bersaglio, 2018: 104) – and, from a related new materialist perspective, to 'understand the materializing effects of particular ways of drawing boundaries between "humans" and "non-humans"' (Barad, 2011: 123–124).

To date, transitional justice literature has engaged very little with posthumanist ideas,[20] although some scholars have discussed environmental harms (see, e.g., Bradley, 2017; Killean and Dempster, 2022; Klinsky and Brankovic, 2018). As Celermajer and O'Brien (2020: 502) argue, the broad field of transitional justice has overwhelmingly focused on 'intra-human' relationships. This, in turn, only further accentuates the significance of recent developments in Colombia, and in particular the JEP's aforementioned recognition of territory as a victim of the armed conflict – an illustration of what Lyons (2018: 421) refers to as 'evidentiary ecologies'.[21] These developments might cautiously be viewed as nascent examples of posthumanist transitional justice and what it could look like. However, it is also necessary to take note of Huneeus and Rueda Sáiz's (2021: 228) argument that 'For us to propose that a concept forged by Colombia's indigenous people should carry over into non-indigenous law risks recreating exploitative relations through cultural appropriation'.

It is beyond the scope of this chapter to engage in an extensive discussion of posthumanism or to reflect on how posthumanist ideas – of which there were some implicit examples within the interview data (Clark, 2022b) – could be incorporated into transitional justice theory and practice. The crucial point is that posthumanism offers a largely unexplored framework – as part of a wider social-ecological approach to transitional justice – for thinking about harm that reflects 'a deeply connected way of being-in-the-world' (Hébert, 2014: 32; see also Theidon, 2022: 7). It thus has the potential to greatly expand the field of transitional justice beyond its liberal origins and exclusive focus on violations of *human* rights.[22] As Haraway (2016: 55) argues, living inside the world is about living inside 'ongoing multispecies stories'.

Harm, Relationality and Social-Ecological Systems

The book's connectivity approach to resilience – itself deeply relational – has told a story, inter alia, of multiple broken and ruptured connectivities between interviewees (in all three countries) and different parts of their social ecologies, including family, community and land. It is of course a truism to argue that CRSV (and the many other forms of violence with which it frequently co-occurs) affects and implicates multiple relationships. In their research with Indigenous Mayan survivors[23] in Guatemala, for example, Crosby and Lykes (2011: 472) remark that these women 'live within families and communities', and that 'their identities as women come into being within the lived experience of these social relations, including the experience of sexual violence, which is deeply structural and relational rather than only an individuated experience of bodily harm'. Discussing the issue of CRSV in the eastern Democratic Republic of Congo (DRC), Mertens and Pardy (2017: 964) note that it has 'destroyed basic tissues of social life, it has damaged spousal bonds and child-parent relationships and it has seriously fractured the sense of community'.

Why Social Ecologies Matter for Transitional Justice   251

Rather than simply identifying relational harms, this chapter argues for a systemic way of recognising and exploring these harms that also constitutes, like posthumanism, an epistemological shift away from liberalism and its decontextualised focus on individual harms (on this point, see also Theidon, 2022). To this end, it advocates conceptualising societies that have suffered large-scale violence and rights violations as social-ecological systems (SES). It will be recalled from Chapter 1 that the basic SES concept accentuates the deep interconnections and enmeshments between social and ecological systems. As Walker and Salt (2006: 31) articulate, 'We all live and operate in social systems that are inextricably linked with the ecological systems in which they are embedded; we exist *within* social-ecological systems' (emphasis in the original). Chapter 1 also emphasised, however, that some of the discussions about SES within extant scholarship are very abstract, making it difficult to nail down precisely what these systems are and how they function. To be clear, therefore, this chapter invokes the concept of SES specifically to put forward a way of thinking about societies such as BiH, Colombia and Uganda as multi-layered and multi-systemic connectivities between individuals and their social ecologies. In so doing, it gives prominence to the dynamic movement of harms, and their reverberations, through these systems in the sense of myriad broken and ruptured connectivities.

Existing research has primarily focused on the resilience of SES (Berkes et al., 2003; Folke, 2006; Walker et al., 2004). It has examined these systems' capacity to deal with shocks and disturbances – such as floods or hurricanes – and to absorb them in order 'to retain essential structures, processes and feedbacks' (Adger et al., 2005: 1036). SES have not been discussed or explored in a transitional justice context. Some scholars, however, have utilised similar concepts. Fletcher and Weinstein (2002: 581), for example, previously called for 'an ecological model of social reconstruction that considers a spectrum of interventions that includes, but is broader than, criminal trials'. However, while they invoked ecological language, their focus was squarely on social systems and 'the complexities involved in social repair' (Fletcher and Weinstein, 2002: 637). It was not on SES or on harms needing 'repair' across these systems.

In his own work, Hinton (2018: 24) has used the analogy of an ecosystem to contrast 'flat' models of transitional justice – which frame ' "the local" as a static, stagnant space that is acted upon' – with 'dynamic' models that render local–global binaries obsolete (Hinton, 2018: 24). In his words, 'this suggestion of ecosystem is holistic and takes account of fluidity and a multitude of generative interactions masked by a surface-level, experience-distant, facadist perspective of "global justice" ' (Hinton, 2018: 24). More recently, in their research on Guatemala, Evrard et al. (2021: 440) discuss transitional justice as 'an ecosystem of dynamic spaces' and challenge the construction of spatial binaries within transitional justice, especially distinctions between formal and informal spaces. They underline that 'victims move through multiple spaces that are connected in an ecosystemic rather than a binary fashion' (Evrard et al., 2021: 440). This, in turn, has important implications for what happens within these spaces, including how their dynamics and boundaries are shaped – and by whom (Evrard et al., 2021: 440).

Such examples demonstrate the rationale for, and utility of, incorporating ecological ideas into transitional justice. While this chapter further builds on them, the implications of its arguments – an extension of the book's connectivity framework – and emphasis on societies as SES are more far-reaching. The first crucial point is that fundamental feedbacks operate within SES; changes within an ecological system can bring about changes within a social system – and vice versa.[24] In short, SES are systems 'composed of networks of relations and interactions between humans and nonhuman entities' (Schlüter et al., 2019). Within such a framework, it is therefore impossible to think in only anthropocentric ways about harm. Contextualising transitional justice harms within broader SES would therefore create important scope for posthumanist developments within the field and for new discussions about and theorisations of the relationship between transitional justice and environmental justice (SES can be thought of as an important bridging concept between the two). As Ong (2017: 219) argues, 'achieving "environmental" justice' can be considered as 'an additional means of achieving comprehensive justice within a transitional society' (see also Hulme, 2017: 135; Killean, 2021: 339).

The second point to underline is that SES are dynamic and fluid, continually changing and evolving in response to external shocks and stressors and internal developments (Biggs et al., 2015). These systems, thus, do not have a centre. This is very relevant for discussions about 'victim-centred justice' (see, e.g., Kent, 2019; Robins, 2011) and the concept of a 'survivor-centred approach' to CRSV (see, e.g., United Nations [UN] Security Council, 2019). Thinking about and situating these 'centring' concepts in the context of deeply decentred systems is not about rejecting or dismissing them. It is about reflecting critically on what they might miss or leave out (see Clark, 2021b). Discussing the implications of the JEP's recognition of territory as a victim of Colombia's armed conflict, Huneeus and Rueda Sáiz (2021: 229) argue that 'to create a viable transitional justice intervention, the surrounding ecosystem must be understood and incorporated'. More broadly, locating victims-/survivors of CRSV, or indeed any form of violence, within SES is ultimately about recognising the impossibility of fully supporting individuals without also supporting the social ecologies that shape their needs, wants, priorities and concerns – and which themselves suffer harm. As Mertens and Pardy (2017: 970) underline in the context of their research in the eastern DRC, 'For many, addressing individual needs can only ever be a partial response because the community and eco-systems they are part of are crucial in addressing the collective trauma of sexual violence'.

Adaptive Capacity (Supportive and Sustaining Connectivities)

SES as Complex Adaptive Systems

For the purposes of a social-ecological framing of transitional justice, what is also significant about SES is that they are complex adaptive systems (CAS; Holland, 1992; Levin et al., 2013; Preiser et al., 2018). They are 'characterized by many interactions, feedbacks and processes within and among social and ecological components and over multiple scales' (Arlinghaus et al., 2017: 5; see also Anderies and Janssen, 2013: 515). Indeed, such is the importance of relationality for how CAS function and behave that they can be seen as 'a network of relationships and interactions, in which the whole is very much more than the sum of the parts' (Glouberman et al., 2006: 328). Examples of CAS range from developing embryos and the immune system to ant colonies, cities and ecosystems.

Due to the inherent complexity of CAS, there is some disagreement regarding their essential elements (see, e.g., Holland, 1995; Levin, 1998). In the context of this chapter, however, two characteristics of CAS are especially relevant. The first of these characteristics is non-linearity (Kok et al., 2021). As Spannring and Hawke (2021) discuss, there is no unidirectional causation within CAS as these systems 'are characterized by autopoietic processes through iteration over time and feedback mechanisms'. Anticipating that they will behave in a certain way can therefore result in errors (Levin et al., 2013: 125). The non-linearity and inherent dynamism of CAS can be contrasted with traditional conceptualisations of transitional justice that 'assume a teleological movement (the "transition")' from authoritarianism to liberal democracy (Hinton, 2018: 15; see also Bueno-Hansen, 2018: 141; Leebaw, 2008: 117). The significance of non-linear thinking when applied to transitional justice is precisely that it challenges simplistic cause-effect expectations that doing a, b and c will result in x, y and z.

The second characteristic of CAS that makes them very pertinent to this research, even if they do operate at high levels of abstraction (Lansing, 2003: 184), relates directly to the supportive and sustaining connectivities component of the book's connectivity framework. The 'pivotal characteristic' (Holland, 1992: 19) of CAS is their inherent and eponymous ability to adapt (Hartvigsen et al., 1998: 428). As Preiser et al. (2018) emphasise, there are adaptive components and capacities within CAS that enable these systems 'to change and evolve over time in response to feedbacks and changes in the system context'. This chapter argues that the various supportive and sustaining connectivities that interviewees in BiH, Colombia and Uganda talked about, and which were helping them in different ways to deal with their experiences and rebuild their lives, can be viewed as evidencing this deep adaptive capacity.

Investing in Adaptive Capacity

The idea that societies have adaptive capacities, and in-built resources that help them to deal with shocks and stressors, has important implications for transitional justice. In research focused on the Karamoja region of north-east Uganda, Bimeny et al. (2021) argue – albeit not specifically in relation to transitional justice – that interventions aimed at promoting resilience can in fact have the opposite effect. As one illustration, they note that while the Ugandan government has repeatedly sought to restrict the mobility of pastoralists within the Karamoja region, viewing this mobility as a security threat, such efforts have undermined the 'survival mechanisms' that pastoralist communities have developed and adapted to deal with the harshness and unpredictability of their environment (Bimeny et al., 2021). What this example more broadly illustrates is that while the outcomes of transitional justice processes and interventions can never be predicted with any certainty, it is essential that they do not disrupt or weaken adaptive capacities that exist within a society, for example by fostering new divisions (see, e.g., Winter, 2013: 241).

This, in turn, means that transitional justice work should not focus only on deficits – in the sense of what societies, and individual victims-/survivors of violence living in these societies, lack. Attention should also be given to the resources that they have. In particular, transitional justice work should actively invest in and strengthen these resources wherever possible (Clark, 2021b). In their research on the resilience of refugee children, for example, Kuru and Ungar (2021: 4219) accentuate that:

> child development in refugee camps requires attention be focussed not only on individual children, but also on the wellbeing of their caregivers, as well as the potential supports provided by many other co-occurring systems with which both mothers and children interact.

In other words, the resources and systems that these children have around them also need care and attention. In the framework of this research, similarly, the fact that Bosnian, Colombian and Ugandan interviewees – to differing degrees – all had crucial connectivities in their lives that were helping them and sustaining them powerfully reinforces the argument that supporting individual victims-/survivors necessarily also means supporting their social ecologies.

An important example in this regard is Nadia's Initiative. Established in 2018 by the Yazidi activist and Nobel Peace Prize laureate Nadia Murad, Nadia's Initiative – focused on the Yazidi homeland of Sinjar in northern Iraq – adopts a 'comprehensive peace-building approach' (Nadia's Initiative, 2021a). This also includes some transitional justice elements.[25] What is particularly noteworthy is that Nadia's Initiative programmes are a hybrid, in the sense that they are framed as both survivor-centred and community-focused. The accent on centring survivors is fundamentally about listening to them and 'helping women rebuild their lives, provide for their families, and serve as leaders in their communities'

(Nadia's Initiative, 2020: 18). The Murad Code[26] – which was formally launched in April 2022 – is an example of centring; the Foreword states that the Code 'reflects universal, non-negotiable core standards which should be applied by all actors in all contexts to uphold a survivor-centred approach' (Nadia's Initiative et al., 2022). Implicitly, however, what Nadia's Initiative also recognises is that the wellbeing of survivors is deeply connected to and inseparable from their wider social ecologies,[27] making it impossible to focus on one without the other. The organisation accordingly works with its partners on the ground in Sinjar to, inter alia, 'design and support projects that promote the restoration of education, healthcare, livelihoods, WASH (water, sanitation, and hygiene), women's empowerment, and culture in the region' (Nadia's Initiative, 2020: 8).

The work of rebuilding and restoring resources destroyed by violence is hugely important. Yet, so too, as this section has underscored, is supporting and enhancing the resources that victims-/survivors already have. Interviewees in all three countries, for example, spoke in different ways about their children (and, in some cases, grandchildren) as supportive and sustaining connectivities in their lives. At the same time, however, some of them also expressed various worries, particularly of a socio-economic nature, about their children. One way that transitional justice processes could help to alleviate these worries, and thereby strengthen crucial supportive and sustaining connectivities within individuals' social ecologies, is by investing more directly in future generations. Orjuela (2020: 361) points out that 'the role of youth in transitional justice has received increased emphasis'. Much of this emphasis, however, has been on ways of engaging young people in transitional justice work, as well as on the linkages between transitional justice and education (see, e.g., Bellino et al., 2017; Cole, 2007; Scarlett, 2009).

It will be recalled from Chapter 7 that Ugandan interviewees frequently spoke about the financial challenges that they faced in sending their children to school. This highlights, more broadly, the importance of transitional justice initiatives aimed at ensuring that children get an education. Such initiatives would be a way of supporting individuals' protective resources, but also of fostering more long-term and sustainable approaches to dealing with the past that invest in families – and relatedly communities – as important parts of CAS (and SES). This is an example of the many potential linkages between transitional justice and resilience which, to date, remain largely unexplored. The key point is that within CAS, 'Interconnections make learning and co-evolution possible' (Chaffee and McNeill, 2007: 233). Hence, these interconnections – the supportive and sustaining connectivities that were a significant component of the three empirical chapters – must be nurtured and cared for.

Mutuality (New Connectivities)

In her discussion of Relational-Cultural Theory (RCT), referred to in Chapter 2, Jordan (2013: 73) notes that RCT 'suggests that resilience resides not in the individual but in the capacity for connection'. What strongly emerged from the qualitative data on which this book is based is that interviewees in BiH, Colombia and Uganda, in different ways, were actively building new connectivities, as the empirical chapters explored. In other words, they had a strong 'capacity for connection', but there are broader questions about how transitional justice processes themselves can foster and enhance this capacity. Mutuality is important in this regard. Jordan and Walker (2004: 3) argue that mutuality, a key concept within RCT, 'involves profound mutual respect and mutual openness to change and responsiveness'. Mutuality is also a core aspect of SES (Edwards, 2021: 3087–3088; Renaud et al., 2011: 7), and this section focuses specifically on mutuality in the sense of the connectivities between individuals and their social ecologies – and the relevance of this mutuality for the chapter's social-ecological framing of transitional justice.

Mutuality Through Solidarity and Story-Sharing

Scholarship has discussed some of the ways that victims-/survivors of CRSV can draw support from interactions with others who have gone through similar experiences (see, e.g., Koegler et al., 2019; Nieder et al., 2019; Schulz and Ngomokwe, 2021). Reflecting on her time spent with other women, and on the dolls that they made together as a way of expressing their thoughts and feelings, Reilly (2021: 85) underlines that:

> We connected and were connected. We conversed kindly with one another as we worked on our dolls, and we helped each other. We tenderly spoke of and to our dolls. We carried them gently. We reached out and touched each other softly.

In this research, as Chapter 6 explored, it was the Colombian interviewees who particularly expressed a sense of connectedness to, and experiential solidarity with, other victims-/survivors of violence. This was linked to the fact that many of them were actively involved in, and in some cases were leaders of, women's and victims' organisations.

More broadly, however, interviewees in all three countries frequently underlined (and drew some comfort from the knowledge) that 'I was not the only one', 'there are lots of us, people who've been through more or less the same as me', 'we are indeed very many'. Similarly, in their interviews and focus groups with Mayan women survivors who took part in Guatemala's Tribunal of Conscience in 2010, Crosby and Lykes (2011: 469) found that:

> respondents emphasized the importance of hearing the testimonies of their fellow survivors from other regions of the country: 'It wasn't just me. Before, I thought that this had only happened to me, but now I see that it happened in all of Guatemala'.

Notwithstanding the strong accent that transitional justice places on story-telling, which enables various forms of story-sharing to occur (Mussi, 2021: 4), there are often limited opportunities for victims-/survivors – of CRSV or any other form of violence – to directly share their stories with each other. This is significant because stories and story-sharing can be 'powerful agents or aids in the service of change, as shapers of a new imagination of alternatives' (Sandercock, 2005: 308). A good example of this is SEMA – The Global Network of Victims and Survivors to End Sexual Violence in Conflict.[28] Established in 2017, with the support of the Dr Denis Mukwege Foundation, and bringing together (female) victims-/survivors from 21 different countries across six continents, SEMA creates opportunities for these women to 'share and learn from each other, to fight for their rights, to raise awareness and conduct international advocacy together, and to influence policies and programmes which impact them' (Dr Denis Mukwege Foundation, n.d.).[29]

The bigger point is that just as CAS learn through interactions (Holland, 2006: 1), so too do people – as part of these complex systems. The reflections workshops that took place in 2021 illustrated this. First and foremost, these workshops were about sharing some of the core research findings, but they were also, indirectly, a form of story-sharing that allowed participants in each of the countries to learn something about the experiences of victims-/survivors in the other two countries. Some of the participants, moreover, found the workshops useful for precisely this reason. After learning, for example, that some of the Ugandans involved in this research were dealing with the challenges of drought (an issue discussed in Chapter 7), a female Bosniak participant revealed: 'I've never even thought about this issue until now, and now I'm really thinking about it. And I think everyone should put themselves in a position of imagining what real hunger feels like' (reflections workshop, BiH, 14 June 2021). A Croat woman in the same workshop reflected critically on the situation in her own town after learning about some of the ways that the Colombian interviewees were supporting and caring for each other. In her words:

> I have always said that there are no problems in XXX [her town], but there are. We now have two associations [for women, but not exclusively victims-/survivors of CRSV]. There was previously only one but then divisions developed, and so now there are two associations and the leaders ended up not talking to each other. So, there is no solidarity.
> (reflections workshop, BiH, 14 June 2021)

On this latter point, there was a sense, at the end of the workshop, that the participants wanted women to work together, even if deep disconnects – in the form of ethnic divisions and nationalist politics – remained within their socio-political environment.

In Uganda, an Acholi man spoke about gaining new insights from the workshop in which he participated. He commented, for example, that 'I find that some of the things in the other two countries are similar to what I experience here' (reflections workshop, Uganda, 8 September 2021). A Lango participant, similarly, opined that she had found it helpful to learn that there were other people in the world dealing with some of the same problems that she was struggling with (reflections workshop, Uganda, 13 September 2021). A Lango woman in a different workshop talked about learning that 'it is a good thing to join hands as a strategy for dealing with *chan* [poverty – in the broad sense of general hardship and life's difficulties]' (reflections workshop, Uganda, 10 September 2021).

Participants in the three Colombian reflections workshops primarily spoke about learning in the sense of learning from each other, through their involvement in and leadership of women's and victims' organisations. One of them[30] made the interesting point that the sexual violence that women had suffered during the armed conflict had also 'opened the possibility for good things, such as meeting new people, learning new things, empowering ourselves and defying the domination of our husbands'. Moreover, she referred to the reflections workshop as one of these 'good things' and as forming part of her own learning experience (reflections workshop, Colombia, 13 September 2021).

These examples of learning – and indeed of potentially 'galvanised' learning[31] – illustrate the late Martin Luther King Jr.'s (1963) words that 'All life is interrelated. . . . We're caught in an inescapable network of mutuality'. What this chapter underscores is that transitional justice has an important role to play in both recognising and giving effect to this mutuality. Particular attention should be given to creating opportunities for victims-/survivors to forge new connectivities in their lives through story-telling and story-sharing with each other.[32] This, in turn, makes it clear that there is much creative scope for exploring not only local and national dimensions of transitional justice, but also transnational dimensions. A Bosniak who took part in one of the reflections workshops in BiH led her own organisation and described how, prior to the COVID-19 pandemic, the women regularly came together to weave and sew. In her words, 'We were in the world of colours, in the world of our threads, and that's our network' (reflections workshop, BiH, 14 June 2021). Part of the process of developing transitional justice in new social-ecological directions means expanding this world of threads and connectivities. In short, it means facilitating, fostering and supporting explorations of mutuality and interconnectedness, experiential solidarity and learning not only within but also across diverse social ecologies and SES.

Mutuality Through Giving Back and Story-Making

There is a second important and related aspect of mutuality that matters for this discussion. This book, as part of its connectivity framework, has placed a

Why Social Ecologies Matter for Transitional Justice   259

heavy accent on the multi-systemic supportive and sustaining connectivities that interviewees in all three countries had available to them (structural connectivity) – and which they were actively utilising (functional connectivity).[33] These connectivities are strongly accentuated within extant resilience scholarship, where they are commonly referred to as resources or protective factors (see Chapter 1). In a recent article, for example, Theron et al. (2022) argue that 'prioritising African youth resilience is intertwined with advancing an understanding of the multisystemic promotive and protective factors and processes . . . that support their school engagement'. What the data from BiH, Colombia and Uganda also brought to the forefront, however, was the mutuality of interviewees' connectivities. In various ways, these women and men were actively contributing to and giving back to their social ecologies, including through leadership roles, everyday caring practices and work on the land.

This reinforces the argument that victims-/survivors of CRSV should not be viewed only or primarily as individuals in need; and it is important here to repeat the words of an Afro-Colombian interviewee cited in the first section of this chapter: 'nobody has ever asked me: "what are your dreams?"' (interview, Colombia, 30 March 2019). Asking victims-/survivors not only about what they need and lack, but also about what they want to *do* is hugely important.[34] It is not just a recognition of their agency, but also a way of operationalising the idea of reparations as enabling (and, thus, reflective of mutuality). Creating opportunities for victims-/survivors of CRSV (and/or other forms of violence) to make a difference within their social ecologies, where it is their wish to do so,[35] is therefore another important way in which transitional justice praxis could further support adaptive capacity and directly engage with social-ecological discourse and ideas.

A final point to underline is that if story-telling and story-sharing are integral aspects of transitional justice, so too is story-building. Fundamentally, 'we do not merely tell stories but are active in creating them with our lives' (Sandercock, 2005: 305). A Colombian interviewee who identified as mixed-race had actively participated in creating the *Fragmentos* 'counter-monument' to war. The idea of Colombian artist Doris Salcedo, *Fragmentos* – which counters and challenges 'the static, figurative and mostly heroic dimension of official monuments such as men on horseback, obelisks or victory columns' (Huyssen, 2021: 2) – is made from the decommissioned and melted down weapons of former FARC guerrillas. The interviewee was one of the women who took part in reshaping the metal, to form the tiles of *Fragmentos*. She explained that 'we took part in making it, we were there. We cast the moulds and every blow we struck there was like we were releasing ourselves from that hatred, that resentment . . . the silence that we'd been keeping for so long' (interview, Colombia, 10 February 2019).

The sound of the hammers smashing against the metal had broken that silence; and the reshaping of the weapons, and of the trauma that they symbolised, marked the start of a new story that the women themselves were actively involved in building. In this process, they had contributed to their social ecologies in the sense of transforming a small part of the physical landscape in a way that could help other victims-/survivors of the armed conflict. In the interviewee's words, 'we've got a place where women can stop and say: "look, once weapons like this were pointed at me and now, here I am, standing on them"' (interview, Colombia, 10 February 2019).

The mutuality between individuals and their social ecologies is an elemental part of story-building. The latter is an expression of this mutuality and it has an important part to play within transitional justice. The 'motherwork' (Lawson and Flomo, 2020) undertaken by women in Liberia illustrates this. The women's activism – which is 'rooted in politicised motherhood' (Lawson and Flomo, 2020: 1866), spans multiple social-ecological levels and includes efforts to maintain social harmony – 'holds the potential to address local needs related to transitional justice in more comprehensive and holistic ways' (Lawson and Flomo, 2020: 1876). Story-building thus illuminates broader issues – and avenues for further investigation – not only about the various ways that individuals participate, formally and informally, in transitional justice processes (Evrard et al., 2021: 437), but also about how they shape and contribute to these processes. Moreover, as 'a shifting relational encounter which offers potential for reimagining . . . our relationship with each other and the world in troubled times' (Stephenson et al., 2022: 73), story-building further accentuates significant, if largely unexplored, linkages and connectivities between resilience and core transitional justice goals.

★★★

When I designed the research project that constitutes the foundations of this book, I had planned to develop a new 'social-ecological model' of transitional justice. 'Model' was not the right way of thinking about what I wanted to do. It was too prescriptive and too 'neat'. What this chapter has done is to outline a much looser and more flexible social-ecological framing of transitional justice that draws on key elements of the book – resilience, SES (and relatedly CAS) and connectivity – and on some of the empirical data. More specifically, it has analysed how the three core elements of the book's connectivity framework – broken and ruptured connectivities, supportive and sustaining connectivities and new connectivities – form a basis for thinking in social-ecological ways about transitional justice. To do so, it has linked the three parts of the framework to the concepts of harm and relationality, adaptive capacity and mutuality.

The chapter should primarily be read as a conceptual reflection – or more accurately a set of reflections – about transitional justice and resilience. While it has also made several practical suggestions, it has inevitably raised many new questions – without claiming to have all the answers. Ultimately, however, it has demonstrated that adding a resilience 'lens' to transitional justice creates expansive scope for advancing the field 'into new terrain' (Huneeus and Rueda Sáiz, 2021: 210) – and, above all, into new terrain that captures and reflects the many layered and storied connectivities between individuals and their social ecologies.

Notes

1 Such courts, which are a hybrid (a mixture of international and national) as regards both their jurisdiction and composition, have included the Special Court for Sierra Leone and the (ongoing) Special Tribunal for Lebanon.

2 In their research on Indigenous Wiwa spiritual advocacy and the role of female spiritual leaders (Sagas) in Colombia's Sierra Nevada de Santa Marta, for example, Pastor and Santamaria (2021: 90) argue that:

> The effect of army activities and criminals on sacred sites is indicative of the fragility of the Sagas' spiritual consultation and communication with 'Mother Earth.' The armed conflict has affected the spiritual power of Sagas and their capacities to balance the world of divinities and human beings.

3 Human Rights Watch (HRW, 2020) notes, for example, that 'According to information provided by the OSCE [Organization for Security and Co-operation in Europe], in August 2019 there were 250 war crimes cases against 512 defendants in the post-indictment phase pending before all courts in BiH'.

4 Bradfield (2017: 831) notes that 'Between the years 2000 and 2011, over 13,000 LRA fighters received amnesty and returned home to their communities'.

5 In using the term 'little people', the interviewee meant ordinary people with no political importance or influence.

6 To preserve the interviewee's anonymity, it has been necessary to omit crucial details that made her story so powerful.

7 It was interesting that the interviewee repeatedly spoke about the commander as if he were still alive.

8 See www.jep.gov.co/especiales1/macrocasos/index.html.

9 There have been calls, including from women's organisations, for the JEP to open a macro case on sexual and gender-based violence (SGBV). According to Valiñas (2020: 465), however,

> Such a thematic case may risk de-contextualizing the acts of sexual violence. The case may also focus too much on drawing patterns of sexual violence, instead of presenting broader patterns of criminality of which sexual violence acts were an integral part.

10 As Kurtović (2021: 879) notes, 'socialist-era firms and factories were broken up, sold off, and eventually shut down or buried in long bankruptcy proceedings, generating a vast and deserted post-industrial landscape'.

11 According to a survey conducted by the United Nations Population Fund (UNFPA, 2021) in early 2021, based on a representative sample of 5,001 Bosnians aged between 18 and 29 years old, 47 per cent of young people in BiH are considering leaving the country, whether temporarily or permanently, in search of a better quality of life and more opportunities.

12 It is different when the numbers are small. In 2016, for example, a court in Guatemala issued a historic verdict in the Sepur Zarco trial, convicting two former members of the country's military of sexual violence committed in Guatemala's civil war (see Martin and SáCouto, 2020). Fifteen Maya Q'eqchi' women participated in the trial and in the reparations hearing. According to Evrard et al. (2021: 443):

> As a result, the reparations not only included economic compensation but also development measures related to health and education, in addition to tackling historical and structural causes of the conflict, such as land dispossession, by ordering the legalization of land titles.

13 Buss (2009: 150) observes that 'The conception of "rape as a weapon of war"... laid the groundwork for the legal recognition of rape as a crime by the Rwanda and Yugoslav Tribunals'. Discussing it in the context of the 1994 Rwandan genocide, however, she argues that 'This focus on the generalised pattern of rape ... can lead to a problematic homogenisation in which wartime rape is treated as seemingly inevitable' (Buss, 2009: 161).

14 Crosby et al. (2016: 268), moreover, accentuate that 'the story women are repeatedly asked to tell is one of sexual harm and degradation, in contrast to the perpetrators, who are not asked to tell the horrific details of their crimes'. While the rigours of the legal process require the precise facts of what happened and how, this is 'probably not the story that victims would want, or feel comfortable, to tell' (Henry, 2020: 1106).

15 Henry (2014: 99), however, maintains that:

> while it is correct that a vast array of gender-based harms have either been routinely ignored in post-conflict justice mechanisms or not specifically framed as gendered harms, it is possible that the very attention given to sex crimes against women within international jurisdictions has at least opened up possibilities for pursuing other forms of gendered violence.

16 It is also highly pertinent in this regard that the field of transitional justice remains 'largely white' (McEvoy, 2018: 189).

17 Dworkin (1988: 9) refers to 'one concept and many conceptions of autonomy'.

18 Henriksen et al. (2022: 465) maintain that 'Indigeneity can be positioned as ontologically prior to posthumanism'.

19 Braidotti (2018: 206), for example, has commented on 'the enormous spectrum of positions posthumanism spans'.

20 A forthcoming 2023 special issue of the *International Journal of Transitional Justice* will address the theme of nature and transitional justice. This is likely to generate considerable interest, not least because 'the victim status of non-human entities' is already 'an emerging and important area of concern within green criminology' (White, 2018: 240) – and indeed within fields such as the blue humanities (see, e.g., González-Ayala and Camargo, 2021).

21 Elucidating the term, Lyons (2018: 421) explains that ' "evidentiary ecologies" ... cannot help but retain the traces of violence enacted against them'.

22 Bradley (2017: 405), for example, has stressed the need for 'broader engagement among transitional justice scholars and practitioners with harms that have anthropogenic and environmental dimensions'.

23 Here I refer just to survivors (and to not to victims-/survivors), consistent with the terminology that Crosby and Lykes use.

24 Discussing the island of Tikopia in the Solomon Islands, for example, Walker and Meyers (2004) note that the first 1,000 years of settlement (which began around 900 BC) had a significant impact on soil, as well as on native flora and fauna. They also point out that 'Instead of a collapse of both the human population and the environment ... the feedback on social behavior led the society to change' (Walker and Meyers, 2004), including with regards to its agricultural practices.

25 The website states, for example, that 'We seek justice through fighting to hold perpetrators accountable for their crimes and to enable survivors to heal and rebuild their lives' (Nadia's Initiative, 2021b).

26 The official name of the Murad Code is the Global Code of Conduct for Gathering and Using Information about Systematic and Conflict-Related Sexual Violence.

27 While emphasising the individuality of survivors, for example, the Murad Code states that 'We will tailor our approach to their specific identities, characteristics, groups and contexts, such as their age, gender, evolving capacities, resilience, relationships with and

Why Social Ecologies Matter for Transitional Justice 263

connections to others, socio-economic and political situation, and the discrimination they face' (Nadia's Initiative et al., 2022: Principle 1.1).

28 See www.semanetwork.org

29 Such initiatives, however, cannot reach everyone. Moreover,

> life threatening poverty, emotional trauma and the disintegration of social support networks caused by violence and displacement greatly diminish the most disadvantaged women's capacity to participate in mutual support and political empowerment programmes thereby exacerbating the social and political status of women.
>
> (Fiske and Shackel, 2015: 113)

30 No information was collected regarding the ethnicity of the participants in the Colombian workshops. Although all of them had taken part in the questionnaire stage of the study (and in some cases also the interview stage), and although all of them signed consent forms, the workshop transcripts were fully anonymised. In Uganda, two of the workshops consisted of Acholi participants and the other two brought together some of the Lango participants. In BiH, I knew from the informed consent forms who took part in the workshops, and in some cases I was able to identify participants (and their ethnicity) from what they said.

31 According to Sandercock (2005: 308):

> When people are immersed in local battles, they are often so locally focused that they have no idea what's happening elsewhere. To discover that some other neighbourhood or social movement in your city or country has won some similar battle can be inspiring and galvanizing.

32 Cultural factors are important in this regard. Mbazumutima (2021: 79), for example, points out that 'Story sharing and listening are not new to the African context, nor to the Burundian one for that matter. Burundians educate one another and create new understanding through stories'. It is also essential to underline, however, that some victims-/survivors – regardless of where they are – may never want or feel able to engage in storytelling and story-sharing. This must be respected.

33 The concepts of structural and functional connectivity were discussed in detail in Chapter 2.

34 In their work in Liberia, for example, Lawson and Flomo (2020: 1864) assert that:

> Liberian women are not merely interested in keeping peace but are also actively invested in what an emerging peace economy allows them to do: participate in the political process, make rights-based claims, exercise a degree of agency over their lives, ensure the viability of their families and contribute to rebuilding their communities.

35 This is an example of what Robbins (2013: 458) calls the 'anthropology of the good', highlighting 'the ways people come to believe that they can successfully create a good beyond what is presently given in their lives'.

References

Adger WN, Hughes TP, Folke C, Carpenter SR and Rockström J (2005) Social-ecological resilience to coastal disasters. *Science* 309(5737): 1036–1039.

Amann DM (1999) Prosecutor v. Akayesu. Case ICTR-96-4-T. *The American Journal of International Law* 92(1): 195–199.

Anderies JM and Janssen MA (2013) Robustness of social-ecological systems: Implications for public policy. *Policy Studies Journal* 41(3): 513–536.

Aoláin FN (2012) Advancing feminist positioning in the field of transitional justice. *International Journal of Transitional Justice* 6(2): 205–228.

Aoláin FN (2014) Gendered harms and their interface with international criminal law. *International Feminist Journal of Politics* 16(4): 622–646.

Arlinghaus R, Alós J, Beardmore B, Daedlow K, Dorow M, Fujitani M, Hühn D, Haider W, Hunt LM, Johnson BM, Johnston F, Klefoth T, Matsumura S, Monk C, Pagel T, Post JR, Rapp T, Riepe C, Ward H and Wolter C (2017) Understanding and managing freshwater recreational fisheries as complex adaptive social-ecological systems. *Reviews in Fisheries Science & Aquaculture* 25(1): 1–41.

Arthur P (2009) How transitions reshaped human rights: A conceptual history of transitional justice. *Human Rights Quarterly* 31(2): 321–367.

Askin KD (2003) Prosecuting wartime rape and other gender-related crimes under international law: Extraordinary advances, enduring obstacles. *Berkeley Journal of International Law* 21(2): 288–349.

Atallah DG and Masud HR (2021) Transitional or transformative justice? Decolonial enactments of adaptation and resilience within Palestinian communities. In: Clark JN and Ungar M (eds.), *Resilience, Adaptive Peacebuilding and Transitional Justice: How Societies Recover after Collective Violence*. Cambridge: Cambridge University Press, pp. 234–256.

Balasco LM (2017) Reparative development: Re-conceptualising reparations in transitional justice processes. *Conflict, Security & Development* 17(1): 1–20.

Balint J, Evans J and McMillan M (2014) Rethinking transitional justice, redressing indigenous harm: A new conceptual approach. *International Journal of Transitional Justice* 8(2): 194–216.

Barad K (2006) *Meeting the Universe Halfway: Quantum Physics and the Entanglement of Matter and Meaning*. Durham, NC: Duke University Press.

Barad K (2011) Nature's queer performativity. *Qui Parle* 19(2): 121–158.

Barria LA and Roper SD (2008) Judicial capacity building in Bosnia and Herzegovina: Understanding legal reform beyond the completion strategy of the ICTY. *Human Rights Review* 7: 317–330.

Bellino MJ, Paulson J and Anderson Worden E (2017) Working through difficult pasts: Toward thick democracy and transitional justice in education. *Comparative Education* 53(3): 313–332.

Berkes F, Colding J and Folke C (eds.) (2003) *Navigating Social-Ecological Systems: Building Resilience for Complexity and Change*. Cambridge: Cambridge University Press.

Biggs RO, Rhode C, Archibald S, Kunene LM, Mutanga SS, N Nkuna, Ocholla PO and Phadima LJ (2015) Strategies for managing complex social-ecological systems in the face of uncertainty: Examples from South Africa and beyond. *Ecology and Society* 20(1): 52.

Bimeny P, Angolere BP, Nangiro S, Sagal IA and Emai J (2021) From warriors to mere chicken men, and other troubles: An ordinary language survey of notions of resilience in Ngakarimjong. *Civil Wars*. https://doi.org/10.1080/13698249.2022.2015215.

Bradfield P (2017) Reshaping amnesty in Uganda. *Journal of International Criminal Justice* 15(4): 827–855.

Bradley M (2017) More than misfortune: Recognizing natural disasters as a concern for transitional justice. *International Journal of Transitional Justice* 11(3): 400–420.

Braidotti R (2013) *The Posthuman*. Cambridge: Polity Press.

Braidotti R (2018) Affirmative ethics, posthuman subjectivity and intimate scholarship: A conversation with Rosi Braidotti, interviewed by Kathryn Strom. In: Strom K, Mills T and Ovens A (eds.), *De-Centering the Researcher in Intimate Scholarship: Critical Posthuman Methodological Perspectives in Education*. Bingley: Emerald Publishing, pp. 205–220.

Braithwaite J (2021) Scaling up crime prevention and justice. *Crime and Justice* 50(1): 247–299.

Brammertz S and Jarvis M (eds.) (2016) *Prosecuting Conflict-Related Sexual Violence at the ICTY*. Oxford: Oxford University Press.

Buchanan NT and Wiklund LO (2020) Why clinical science must change or die: Integrating intersectionality and social justice. *Women & Therapy* 43(3–4): 309–329.

Bueno-Hansen P (2018) The emerging LGBTI rights challenge to transitional justice in Latin America. *International Journal of Transitional Justice* 12(1): 126–145.

Buss DE (2009) Rethinking 'rape as a weapon of war'. *Feminist Legal Studies* 17: 145–163.

Celermajer D and O'Brien A (2020) Transitional justice in multispecies worlds. In: Celermajer D, Chatterjee S, Cochrane A, Fishel S, Neimanis A, O'Brien A, Reid S, Srinivasan K, Schlosberg D and Waldow A, Justice through a multispecies lens. *Contemporary Political Theory* 19(3): 475–512.

Chaffee MW and McNeill MM (2007) A model of nursing as a complex adaptive system. *Nursing Outlook* 55(5): 232–241.

Clark JN (2021a) Thinking systemically about transitional justice, legal systems and resilience. In: Ungar M (ed.), *Multisystemic Resilience: Adaptation and Transformation in Contexts of Change*. New York, NY: Oxford University Press, pp. 530–550.

Clark JN (2021b) Beyond a 'survivor-centred approach' to conflict-related sexual violence? *International Affairs* 97(4): 1067–1084.

Clark JN (2022a) Storytelling, resilience and transitional justice: Reversing narrative social bulimia. *Theoretical Criminology* 26(3): 456–474.

Clark JN (2022b) Resilience in the context of conflict-related sexual violence and beyond: A "sentient ecology" framework. *British Journal of Sociology* 73(2): 352–369.

Clark JN and Ungar M (eds.) (2021) *Resilience, Adaptive Peacebuilding and Transitional Justice: How Societies Recover after Collective Violence*. Cambridge: Cambridge University Press.

Colburn B (2010) *Autonomy and Liberalism*. New York, NY: Routledge.

Cole EA (2007) Transitional justice and the reform of history education. *International Journal of Transitional Justice* 1(1): 115–137.

Crellin RJ and Harris OJT (2021) What difference does posthumanism make? *Cambridge Archaeological Journal* 31(3): 469–475.

Crosby A and Lykes MB (2011) Mayan women survivors speak: The gendered relations of truth-telling in postwar Guatemala. *International Journal of Transitional Justice* 5(3): 456–476.

Crosby A, Lykes MB and Caxaj B (2016) Carrying a heavy load: Mayan women's understandings of reparation in the aftermath of genocide. *Journal of Genocide Research* 18(2–3): 265–283.

Cruikshank J (2005) *Do Glaciers Listen? Local Knowledge, Colonial Encounters and Social Imagination*. Vancouver, BC: University of British Columbia Press.

Díaz de Liaño GD and Fernández-Götz M (2021) Posthumanism, new humanism and beyond. *Cambridge Archaeological Journal* 31(3): 543–549.

Dieng A (2011) Capacity-building efforts of the ICTR: A different kind of legacy. *Northwestern University Journal of International Human Rights* 9(3): 403–422.

Dr Denis Mukwege Foundation (n.d.) SEMA – The Global Network of Victims and Survivors to End Wartime Sexual Violence. Available at: www.mukwegefoundation.org/sema/ (accessed 7 February 2022).

Dworkin G (1988) *The Theory and Practice of Autonomy*. Cambridge: Cambridge University Press.

Dworkin G (2015) The nature of autonomy. *Nordic Journal of Studies in Educational Policy* 2015(2): 28479.

Edwards MG (2021) The growth paradox, sustainable development and business strategy. *Business Strategy and the Environment* 30(7): 3079–3094.

Evans M (2016) Structural violence, socioeconomic rights and transformative justice. *Journal of Human Rights* 15(1): 1–20.

Evrard E, Bonifazi GM and Destrooper T (2021) The meaning of participation in transitional justice: A conceptual proposal for empirical analysis. *International Journal of Transitional Justice* 15(2): 428–447.

Fiske L and Shackel R (2015) Gender, poverty and violence: Transitional justice responses to converging processes of domination of women in eastern DRC, northern Uganda and Kenya. *Women's Studies International Forum* 51: 110–117.

Fletcher LE and Weinstein HM (2002) Violence and social repair: Rethinking the contribution of justice to reconciliation. *Human Rights Quarterly* 24(3): 573–639.

Folke C (2006) Resilience: The emergence of a perspective for social-ecological systems analyses. *Global Environmental Change* 16(3): 253–267.

Gilmore S and Moffett L (2021) Finding a way to live with the past: 'Self-repair', 'informal repair' and reparations in transitional justice. *Journal of Law and Society* 48(3): 455–480.

Global Survivors Fund (2021) Global reparations study executive summary report of preliminary findings. Available at: https://static1.squarespace.com/static/5ff7d9f4dd4cdc650b24f9a4/t/61558febcd56d515c8012904/1632997364374/2021 + 09 + 27+GSF+Report_UNGA_Preliminary_Findings.pdf (accessed 27 February 2022).

Glouberman S, Gemar M, Campsie P, Miller G, Armstrong J, Newman C, Siotis A and Groff P (2006) A framework for improving health in cities: A discussion paper. *Journal of Urban Health* 83: 325–338.

González-Ayala SN and Camargo A (2021) Voices of water and violence: Exhibition making and the blue humanities for transitional justice. *Curator* 64(1): 183–204.

Gow J, Michalski M and Kerr R (2013) Space capsule justice: The ICTY and Bosnia – Image, distance and disconnection. *The Slavonic and East European Review* 91(4): 818–846.

Gready P and Robins S (2014) From transitional to transformative justice: A new agenda for practice. *International Journal of Transitional Justice* 8(3): 339–361.

Gready P and Robins S (eds.) (2019) *From Transitional to Transformative Justice*. Cambridge: Cambridge University Press.

Gready S (2022) The case for transformative reparations: In pursuit of structural socioeconomic reform in post-conflict societies. *Journal of Intervention and Statebuilding* 16(2): 182–201.

Haraway DJ (2003) *The Companion Species Manifesto: Dogs, People and Significant Otherness*. Chicago, IL: Prickly Paradigm Press.

Haraway DJ (2016) *Staying with the Trouble: Making Kin in the Chthulucene*. Durham, NC: Duke University Press.

Hartvigsen G, Kinzig A and Peterson G (1998) Use and analysis of complex adaptive systems in ecosystem science: Overview of special section. *Ecosystems* 1(5): 427–430.

Hatala AR, Njeze C, Morton D, Pearl T and Bird-Naytowhow K (2020) Land and nature as sources of health and resilience among Indigenous youth in an urban Canadian context: A photovoice exploration. *BCM Public Health* 20: 538.

Haysom L (2017) Moving the social ecology to the centre: Resilience in the context of gender violence. *Agenda* 31(2): 1–2.

Hébert IM (2014) Mountain reflections: Reverence for the consciousness of nature. In: Vakoch DA and Castrillón F (eds.), *Ecopsychology, Phenomenology and the Environment: The Experience of Nature*. New York, NY: Springer, pp. 27–46.

Henriksen D, Creely E and Mehta R (2022) Rethinking the politics of creativity: Posthumanism, indigeneity and creativity beyond the Western Anthropocene. *Qualitative Inquiry* 25(5): 465–475.

Henry N (2014) The fixation on wartime rape: Feminist critique and international criminal law. *Social & Legal Studies* 23(1): 93–111.

Henry N (2020) The impossibility of bearing witness: Wartime rape and the promise of justice. *Violence Against Women* 16(10): 1098–1119.

Herremans B and Destrooper T (2021) Stirring the justice imagination: Countering the invisibilization and erasure of Syrian victims' justice narratives. *International Journal of Transitional Justice* 15(3): 576–595.

Hinton AL (2018) *The Justice Facade: Trials of Transition in Cambodia*. New York, NY: Oxford University Press.

Hoddy ET and Gready P (2020) From agency to root causes: Addressing structural barriers to transformative justice in transitional and post-conflict settings. *Contemporary Social Science* 15(5): 561–576.

Holland JH (1992) Complex adaptive systems. *Daedalus* 121(1): 17–30.

Holland JH (1995) *Hidden Order: How Adaptation Builds Complexity*. Reading, MA: Addison-Wesley.

Holland JH (2006) Studying complex adaptive systems. *Journal of Systems Science and Complexity* 19: 1–8.

HRW (2020) Bosnia and Herzegovina – Events of 2019. Available at: www.hrw.org/world-report/2020/country-chapters/bosnia-and-herzegovina# (accessed 2 March 2022).

Hulme K (2017) Using a framework of human rights and transitional justice for post-conflict environmental protection and remediation. In: Stahn C, Iverson J and Easterday JS (eds.), *Environmental Protection and Transitions from Conflict to Peace: Clarifying Norms, Principles and Practices*. Oxford: Oxford University Press, pp. 119–142.

Humphrey M (2003) From victim to victimhood: Truth commissions and trials as rituals of political transition and individual healing. *The Australian Journal of Anthropology* 14(2): 171–187.

Huneeus A and Rueda Sáiz P (2021) Territory as a victim of armed conflict. *International Journal of Transitional Justice* 15(1): 210–229.

Huyssen A (2021) Doris Salcedo's compelling counter monument. *ReVista* 20(3): 1–9.

Izquierdo B and Viaene L (2018) Decolonizing transitional justice from Indigenous territories. *Peace in Progress* 34. Available at: www.researchgate.net/profile/Lieselotte-Viaene/publication/325961679_Decolonizing_transitional_justice_from_indigenous_territories/links/5b2fedf34585150d23cf16e3/Decolonizing-transitional-justice-from-indigenous-territories.pdf (accessed 11 February 2022).

Jordan JV (2013) Relational resilience in girls. In: Goldstein S and Brooks RB (eds.), *Handbook of Resilience in Children*. New York, NY: Springer, pp. 73–86.

Jordan JV and Walker M (2004) Introduction. In: Jordan JV, Walker M and Hartling LM (eds.), *The Complexity of Connection: Writings from the Stone Center's Jean Baker Miller Training Institute*. New York, NY: The Guildford Press, pp. 1–8.

Kastner P (2020) A resilience approach to transitional justice? *Journal of Intervention and State-building* 14(3): 368–388.

Kent L (2019) Rethinking 'civil society' and 'victim-centred' transitional justice in Timor-Leste. In: Kent K, Wallis J and Cronin C (eds.), *Civil Society and Transitional Justice in Asia and the Pacific*. Acton, ACT: Australian National Press, pp. 23–38.

Killean R (2021) From ecocide to eco-sensitivity: 'Greening' reparations at the International Criminal Court. *The International Journal of Human Rights* 25(2): 323–347.

Killean R and Dempster L (2022) 'Greening' transitional justice? In: Evans M (ed.), *Beyond Transitional Justice: Transformative Justice and the State of the Field (or Non-Field)*. Abingdon: Routledge, pp. 54–64.

King ML, Jr. (1963) Letter from Birmingham jail. Available at: www.africa.upenn.edu/Articles_Gen/Letter_Birmingham.html (accessed 2 March 2022).

Klinsky S and Brankovic J (2018) *The Global Climate Regime and Transitional Justice*. Abingdon: Routledge.

Koegler E, Kennedy C, Mrindi J, Bachunguye R, Winch P, Ramazani P, Makambo NT and Glass N (2019) Understanding how solidarity groups – a community-based economic and psychosocial support intervention – can affect mental health for survivors of conflict-related sexual violence in Democratic Republic of the Congo. *Violence Against Women* 25(3): 359–374.

Kok KPW, Loeber AMC and Grin J (2021) Politics of complexity: Conceptualizing agency, power and powering in the transitional dynamics of complex adaptive systems. *Research Policy* 50(3): 104183.

Korjenić S (2020) How many victims are still waiting for justice to be done? Available at: https://trialinternational.org/latest-post/how-many-victims-are-still-waiting-for-justice-to-be-done/ (accessed 9 March 2022).

Kurtović L (2021) When the 'people' leave: On the limits of nationalist (bio)politics in post-war Bosnia-Herzegovina. *Nationalities Papers* 49(5): 873–892.

Kuru N and Ungar M (2021) Refugee children's resilience: A qualitative social ecological study of life in a camp. *Journal of Refugee Studies* 34(4): 4207–4224.

Lambourne W (2014) Transformative justice, reconciliation and peacebuilding. In: Buckley-Zistel S, Beck TK, Braun C and Mieth F (eds.), *Transitional Justice Theories*. Abingdon: Routledge, pp. 19–39.

Lansing JS (2003) Complex adaptive systems. *Annual Review of Anthropology* 32: 183–204.

Laverty C and de Vos D (2021) Reproductive violence as a category of analysis: Disentangling the relationship between 'the sexual' and 'the reproductive' in transitional justice. *International Journal of Transitional Justice* 15(3): 616–635.

Lawson ES and Flomo VK (2020) Motherwork and gender justice in peace huts: A feminist view from Liberia. *Third World Quarterly* 41(11): 1863–1880.

Leebaw BA (2008) The irreconcilable goals of transitional justice. *Human Rights Quarterly* 30(1): 95–118.

Lemaitre J and Sandvik KB (2014) Beyond sexual violence in transitional justice: Political insecurity as a gendered harm. *Feminist Legal Studies* 22 (2014): 243–261.

Leopold A (1949) *A Sand County Almanac: And Sketches Here and There*. Oxford: Oxford University Press.

Leopold A (1991) The conservation ethic. In: Flader SL and Callicott JB (eds.), *The River of the Mother of God and Other Essays by Aldo Leopold*. Madison, WI: University of Wisconsin Press, pp. 181–92.

Levin SA (1998) Ecosystems and the biosphere as complex adaptive systems. *Ecosystems* 1: 431–436.

Levin SA, Xepapadeas T, Crépin AS, Norberg J, de Zeeuw A, Folke C, Hughes T, Arrow K, Barrett S, Daily G, Ehrlich P, Kautsky N, Mäler KG, Polasky S, Troell M, Vincent JR and Walker B (2013) Social-ecological systems as complex adaptive systems: Modeling and policy implications. *Environment and Development Economics* 18(2): 111–132.

Lundy P and McGovern M (2008) Whose justice? Rethinking transitional justice from the bottom up. *Journal of Law and Society* 35(2): 265–292.

Lyons K (2018) Chemical warfare in Colombia, evidentiary ecologies and *senti-actuando* practices of justice. *Social Studies of Science* 48(3): 414–437.

Maddison S and Shepherd LJ (2014) Peacebuilding and the postcolonial politics of transitional justice. *Peacebuilding* 2(3): 253–269.

Mahon R (2008) Varieties of liberalism: Canadian social policy from the 'golden age' to the present. *Social Policy & Administration* 42(4): 342–361.

Manning P (2012) Governing memory: Justice, reconciliation and outreach at the Extraordinary Chambers in the Courts of Cambodia. *Memory Studies* 5(2): 165–181.

Margulies JD and Bersaglio B (2018) Furthering post-human political ecologies. *Geoforum* 94: 103–106.

Martin C and SáCouto S (2020) Access to justice for victims of conflict-related sexual violence: Lessons learned from the *Sepur Zarco* case. *Journal of International Criminal Justice* 18(2): 243–270.

Mbazumutima T (2021) Land restitution in postconflict Burundi. *International Journal of Transitional Justice* 15(1): 66–85.

McAuliffe P (2017) Localised justice and structural transformation: How new approaches to transitional justice pull in different directions. *Human Rights & International Legal Discourse* 11(1): 96–107.

McClanahan B, Sanchez Parra T and Brisman A (2019) Conflict, environment and transition: Colombia, ecology and tourism after demobilisation. *International Journal for Crime, Justice and Social Democracy* 8(3): 74–88.

McEvoy K (2018) Travel, dilemmas and nonrecurrence: Observations on the 'respectabilisation' of transitional justice. *International Journal of Transitional Justice* 12(2): 185–193.

McEvoy K and McGregor L (eds.) (2008) *Transitional Justice from Below: Grassroots Activism and the Struggle for Change*. Portland, OR: Hart Publishing.

McGill D (2017) Different violence, different justice? Taking structural violence seriously in post-conflict and transitional justice processes. *State Crime Journal* 6(1): 79–101.

Meernik J and Barron J (2018) Fairness in national courts prosecuting international crimes: The case of the War Crimes Chamber of Bosnia-Herzegovina. *International Criminal Law Review* 18(4): 712–734.

Mertens C and Pardy M (2017) 'Sexurity' and its effects in eastern Democratic Republic of Congo. *Third World Quarterly* 38(4): 956–979.

Murdock EG (2018) Storied with land: 'Transitional justice' on Indigenous lands. *Journal of Global Ethics* 14(2): 232–239.

Mussi F (2021) Land and storytelling: Indigenous pathways towards healing, spiritual regeneration and resurgence. *The Journal of Commonwealth Literature*, https://doi.org/10.1177/00219894211031716.

Mutua M (2015) What is the future of transitional justice? *International Journal of Transitional Justice* 9(1): 1–9.

Nadia's Initiative (2020) Annual report. Available at: https://static1.squarespace.com/static/5e4ed852d5526563e04b189a/t/616fc3aa46d98f0eac8b37d1/1634714717021/NI_2020_AnnualReport_Final.pdf (accessed 18 February 2022).

Nadia's Initiative (2021a) Our approach. Available at: www.nadiasinitiative.org/our-approach (accessed 17 February 2022).

Nadia's Initiative (2021b) About Nadia's Initiative. Available at: www.nadiasinitiative.org/nadias-initiative (accessed 17 February 2022).

Nadia's Initiative, Institute for International Criminal Investigations and the Preventing Sexual Violence in Conflict Initiative (2022) Global code of conduct for gathering and using information about systematic and conflict-related sexual violence (Murad Code). Available at: www.muradcode.com/murad-code (accessed 24 April 2022).

Nagy R (2008) Transitional justice as global project: Critical reflections. *Third World Quarterly* 29(2): 275–289.

Nieder C, Muck C and Kärtner J (2019) Sexual violence against women in India: Daily life and coping strategies of young women in Delhi. *Violence Against Women* 25(14): 1717–1738.

Ong DM (2017) Prospects for transitional environmental justice in the socio-economic reconstruction of Kosovo. *Tulane Environmental Law Journal* 30(2): 217–272.

O'Rourke C (2015) Feminist scholarship in transitional justice: A de-politicising impulse? *Women's Studies International Forum* 51: 118–227.

Orentlicher D (2018) *Some Kind of Justice: The ICTY's Impact in Bosnia and Serbia*. New York, NY: Oxford University Press.

Orjuela C (2020) Passing on the torch of memory: Transitional justice and the transfer of diaspora identity across generations. *International Journal of Transitional Justice* 14(2): 360–380.

Park ASJ (2020) Settler colonialism, decolonization and radicalizing transitional justice. *International Journal of Transitional Justice* 14(2): 260–279.

Pastor L and Santamaria A (2021) Experiences of spiritual advocacy for land and territorial itineraries for the defense of Wiwa women's rights in postconflict Colombia. *International Journal of Transitional Justice* 15(1): 86–107.

Preiser R, Biggs R, De Vos A and Folke C (2018) Social-ecological systems as complex adaptive systems: Organizing principles for advancing research methods and approaches. *Ecology and Society* 23(4): 46.

Ranasinghe C (2019) Good intentions and flawed outcomes: The impact of international actors on Sri Lanka's transitional justice process. *Sri Lanka Journal of International Law* 27 (2019): 77–112.

Raymond RE (2013) When two elephants fight, it is the grass that suffers: Proposed amnesty legislation for peace and justice. *Syracuse Journal of International Law and Commerce* 40(2): 407–438.

Reilly RC (2021) Reclaiming my sister, Medusa: A critical autoethnography about healing from sexual violence through solidarity, doll-making and mending myth. *Cultural Studies ↔ Critical Methodologies* 21(1): 80–87.

Renaud FG, Dun O, Warner K and Bogardi J (2011) A decision framework for environmentally induced migration. *International Migration* 49(1): 5–29.

Robbins J (2013) Beyond the suffering subject: Toward an anthropology of the good. *Journal of the Royal Anthropological Institute* 19(3): 447–462.

Robins S (2011) Towards victim-centred transitional justice: Understanding the needs of families of the disappeared in postconflict Nepal. *International Journal of Transitional Justice* 5(1): 75–98.

Roelvink G (2018) Community economies and climate justice. In: Jacobsen SG (ed.), *Climate Justice and the Economy: Social Mobilization, Knowledge and the Political*. London: Routledge, pp. 147–165.

Rolston B and Aoláin FN (2018) Colonialism, redress and transitional justice: Ireland and beyond. *State Crime Journal* 7(2): 329–348.

Rubio-Marín R (2012) Reparations for conflict-related sexual and reproductive violence: A decalogue. *William & Mary Journal of Women and the Law* 19(1): 69–104.

Sandercock L (2005) Out of the closet: The importance of stories and storytelling in planning practice. In: Stiftel B and Watson B (eds.), *Dialogues in Urban and Regional Planning 1*. London: Routledge, pp. 299–321.

Scarlett MH (2009) Imagining a world beyond genocide: Teaching about transitional justice. *The Social Sciences* 100(4): 169–176.

Schacter DL and Welker M (2016) Memory and connection: Remembering the past and imagining the future in individuals, groups and cultures. *Memory Studies* 9(3): 241–244.

Schlüter M, Haider LJ, Lade SJ, Lindkvist E, Martin R, Orach K, Wijermans N and Folke C (2019) Capturing emergent phenomena in social-ecological systems: An analytical framework. *Ecology and Society* 24(3): 11.

Schulz P and Ngomokwe F (2021) Resilience, adaptive peacebuilding and transitional justice in post-conflict Uganda: The participatory potential of survivors' groups. In: Clark JN and Ungar M (eds.), *Resilience, Adaptive Peacebuilding and Transitional Justice: How Societies Recover after Collective Violence*. Cambridge: Cambridge University Press, pp. 119–142.

Sellers PV (2011) Wartime female slavery: Enslavement? *Cornell International Law Journal* 44(1): 115–144.

Sharp DN (2015) Emancipating transitional justice from the bonds of the paradigmatic transition. *International Journal of Transitional Justice* 9(1): 150–169.

Spannring R and Hawke S (2021) Anthropocene challenges for youth research: Understanding agency and change through complex, adaptive systems. *Journal of Youth Studies*, https://doi.org/10.1080/13676261.2021.1929886.

Stagl S (2007) Theoretical foundations of learning processes for sustainable development. *International Journal of Sustainable Development & World Ecology* 14(1): 52–62.

Staub E (2006) Reconciliation after genocide, mass killing or intractable conflict: Understanding the roots of violence, psychological recovery and steps toward a general theory. *Political Psychology* 27(6): 867–894.

Stephenson L, Daniel A and Storey V (2022) Weaving critical hope: Story making with artists and children through troubled times. *Literacy* 56(1): 73–85.

Swaine A (2015) Beyond strategic rape and between the public and private: Violence against women in armed conflict. *Human Rights Quarterly* 37(3): 755–786.

Szoke-Burke S (2015) Not only 'context': Why transitional justice programs can no longer ignore violations of economic and social rights. *Texas International Law Journal* 50(3): 465–494.

Taylor RS (2005) Kantian personal autonomy. *Political Theory* 33(5): 602–628.

Teitel RG (2000) *Transitional Justice*. New York, NY: Oxford University Press.

Theidon K (2007) Gender in transition: Common sense, women and war. *Journal of Human Rights* 6(4): 453–478.

Theidon K (2022) *Legacies of War: Violence, Ecologies and Kin*. Durham, NC: Duke University Press.

Theron LC, Levine D and Ungar M (2021) African emerging adult resilience: Insights from a sample of township youth. *Emerging Adulthood* 9(4): 360–371.

Theron LC, Ungar M and Höltge J (2022) Pathways of resilience: Predicting school engagement trajectories for South African adolescents living in a stressed environment. *Contemporary Educational Psychology* 69: 102062.

Tschakert P (2022) More-than-human solidarity and multispecies justice in the climate crisis. *Environmental Politics* 31(2): 277–296.

Tynan L (2021) What is relationality? Indigenous knowledges, practices and responsibilities with kin. *Cultural Geographies* 28(4): 597–610.

UNFPA (2021) Citing poor life quality, almost half of young people in Bosnia and Herzegovina ponder emigration, UNFPA survey finds. Available at: https://eeca.unfpa.org/en/news/citing-poor-life-quality-almost-half-young-people-bosnia-and-herzegovina-ponder-emigration (accessed 7 March 2022).

UN Security Council (2019) Resolution 2467.

Valiñas M (2020) The Colombian Special Jurisdiction for Peace: A few issues for consideration when investigating and adjudicating sexual and gender-based crimes. *Journal of International Criminal Justice* 18(2): 449–467.

Walker B and Meyers JA (2004) Thresholds in ecological and social-ecological systems: A developing database. *Ecology and Society* 9(2): 3.

Walker B and Salt D (2006) *Resilience Thinking: Sustaining Ecosystems and People in a Changing World*. Washington, DC: Island Press.

Walker B, Holling CS, Carpenter SR and Kinzig A (2004) Resilience, adaptability and transformability in social-ecological systems. *Ecology and Society* 9(2): 5.

Walt SM (1998) International relations: One world, many theories. *Foreign Policy* 110: 29–44.

White R (2018) Green victimology and non-human victims. *International Review of Victimology* 24(2): 239–255.

Wiebelhaus-Brahm E (2017) After shocks: Exploring the relationships between transitional justice and resilience in post-conflict societies. In: Duthie R and Seils P (eds.), *Justice Mosaics: How Context Shapes Transitional Justice in Fractured Societies*. New York, NY: International Center for Transitional Justice, pp. 140–165.

Wiebelhaus-Brahm E (2020) The concept of resilience and the evaluation of hybrid courts. *Leiden Journal of International Law* 33(4): 1015–1028.

Winter S (2013) Towards a unified theory of transitional justice. *International Journal of Transitional Justice* 7(2): 224–244.

Wolfe C (2010) *What is Posthumanism?* Minneapolis, MN: University of Minnesota Press.

Yoshida K and Céspedes-Báez LM (2021) The nature of women, peace and security: A Colombian perspective. *International Affairs* 97(1): 17–34.

Yusuf HO (2019) Colonialism and the dilemmas of transitional justice in Nigeria. *International Journal of Transitional Justice* 12(2): 257–276.

Žarkov D (2016) Co-option, complicity, co-production: Feminist politics on war rapes. *European Journal of Women's Studies* 23(2): 119–123.

Conclusion

Final Reflections and Connecting the Threads

Brown (2014: 107) maintains that 'In the wake of a sudden event or disaster we witness calls for increased resilience, or narratives about how resilient people and communities are, or perhaps how resilient ecosystems are or nature itself is in the wake of disturbance'. During the five years of research on which this book is based, two particularly momentous events of global significance occurred that illustrate Brown's argument. The first of these was the ongoing COVID-19 pandemic, which has generated a great deal of new research on resilience. Scholars have explored, inter alia, the impact of lockdowns, social isolation and loss of loved ones on individuals' emotional health and wellbeing (Marchini et al., 2021), the buffering role of protective factors (Nitschke et al., 2021) and the importance of social context (Fernández-Prados et al., 2021). The second event was the unlawful invasion of Ukraine by Russian forces on 24 February 2022. In the context of the continuing war, bloodshed and suffering in the country, there have been many references to resilience. According to a statement by the North Atlantic Treaty Organization (NATO, 2022) on 24 March, for example, 'We have trained Ukraine's armed forces, strengthening their capabilities and capacities and enhancing their resilience'. A day earlier – and reflecting Ukraine's significance as a major exporter of wheat and other grains – the European Commission (EC) adopted the communication on 'Safeguarding food security and reinforcing the resilience of food systems'. This underlines the need 'to ensure that our food system is resilient to external shocks, like the one we are now experiencing' (EC, 2022).

These examples illustrate some of the many uses and the widespread application of the term resilience, which Anderson (2015: 62) describes as 'empirically multiple'. Some commentators therefore insist that the terminology of resilience 'is everywhere these days' (Keyes, 2004: 223; see also Brassett et al., 2013: 223). It is striking, however, that this omnipresence does not extend to scholarship on conflict-related sexual violence (CRSV), in which there are very few direct references to or discussions about resilience. Far from being 'everywhere', resilience is largely absent from this literature. This interdisciplinary book, as the first major (and comparative) study of resilience with a particular focus on victims-/survivors of CRSV – and based on empirical data

DOI: 10.4324/9781003323532-10

274 Conclusion

from Bosnia-Herzegovina (BiH), Colombia and Uganda – has made a significant contribution to addressing that gap. In so doing, it has demonstrated, both conceptually and empirically, that there are important reasons for taking resilience seriously within research and discussions about CRSV. Above all, it has sought to make clear that talking about and exploring resilience in this context does not mean promoting self-help ideologies that place the burden of responsibility on victims-/survivors themselves to positively adapt to adversity and uncertainty. Quite the opposite. Indeed, this research has explicitly rejected, and challenged, framings of resilience as 'a neoliberal notion of decontextualized individual choice and responsibility' (Zembylas, 2021: 1967).

Looking Beyond Individual-Centred Framings of Resilience

Resilience is mentioned, albeit briefly, in some policy documents about CRSV. The International Committee of the Red Cross (ICRC), for example, adopted a 2018–2022 Strategy on Conflict-Related Sexual Violence. This discusses ways of reducing the risk of sexual violence in conflict (as well as in detention and in other situations of violence) by, inter alia, 'Increasing resilience and supporting coping mechanisms of communities at risk' (ICRC, 2018: 13). The meaning of resilience is left undefined, as if its meaning were self-evident. What is apparent from other policy documents, however, is that resilience is often narrowly construed. A report by the UN Secretary-General (2021: para. 14), António Guterres, for example, states that 'Survivors continued to demonstrate their agency and resilience, playing a key role in their own recovery'. In December 2021, the Special Representative of the Secretary-General on Sexual Violence in Conflict, Pramila Patten, delivered a speech in Guatemala in which she extended a 'very warm greeting to the survivors of Sepur Zarco who are here with us today' (Office of the Special Representative of the Secretary-General on Sexual Violence in Conflict [OSRSG-SVC], 2021). Speaking directly to the Indigenous Maya Q'eqchi' women who suffered sexual and other forms of violence in Sepur Zarco (where the Guatemalan army set up a military rest outpost in 1982) and subsequently fought for justice, Patten told them: 'Your courage and resilience are an inspiration to us all' (OSRSG-SVC, 2021).

The second edition of the International Protocol on the Documentation and Investigation of Sexual Violence in Conflict makes several references to resilience.[1] Elaborating on the meaning of the term, it emphasises that 'Resilience is multifaceted, and includes the ability to withstand injury and maintain functioning, the speed and ease of recovery, and the ability to positively adapt in the face of trauma' (Foreign and Commonwealth Office [FCO], 2017: 232). It also lists a number of protective (and risk) factors for resilience. However, it consistently refers to 'individual resilience' – and additionally mentions 'psychological resilience' (FCO, 2017: 232); and it explains that its use of the term 'victim' (rather than 'survivor') 'is in no way meant to diminish the agency, autonomy and resilience of individual victims' (FCO, 2017: 19).

What stands out prominently from all the above examples is that when resilience is alluded to or discussed in the context of policy work on CRSV, there is a strong individualist emphasis. Individual factors are of course relevant; Massad et al. (2018: 288), for example, refer to resilience as 'a process supported by various traits, capacities, and emotional orientations toward hardship'. To over-accentuate them, however, is problematic for several reasons. First, individualism is closely associated with neoliberalism, as is the use of terms such as autonomy. To cite Joseph (2013: 46), 'Neoliberalism is about constructing the conditions for autonomy'. It is very important, therefore, that policy references to and framings of resilience do not unintentionally feed neoliberal critiques or, relatedly, foster reductive ways of thinking about the concept that simplify its many layers.

Second, the conceptual location of resilience in individuals raises consequential issues about the possible (albeit unintentional) creation of hierarchies. Various scholars writing about CRSV have critically discussed the problem of hierarchies, including gender and victim hierarchies (Dolan, 2016; du Toit and le Roux, 2021; Simić, 2018). Aroussi (2018: 283), for example, maintains that 'In practice, the prioritization of militarized sexual violence establishes a hierarchy of victims, crimes and areas for interventions that inevitably translates into differential access to justice and services targeted for survivors of rape'. References to resilience that focus on the attributes of individual victims-/survivors of CRSV potentially risk fostering further hierarchies that distinguish those who 'are resilient' from those who are not. This book has expressly not discussed resilience in this way. Indeed, it has adopted an approach that 'purposely decenters individuals' (Ungar, 2013: 256) – in the sense of personal traits and characteristics – by emphasising their relationships with their social ecologies.

Third, narrow person-centred framings not only miss important developments and shifts within resilience scholarship (discussed in Chapter 1), but they also fail to do justice to the significance and relevance of resilience in the context of CRSV. Resilience is a process that develops through the relationships and interactions between individuals and everything that they have around them – emotionally, spiritually, culturally, physically – from people and places to organisations and institutions. What this book has demonstrated, therefore, is that exploring resilience can provide fresh insights into the everyday lives of victims-/survivors of CRSV, their social ecologies and the myriad ways that these social ecologies (including what they provide as well as lack) shape and influence the legacies of sexual violence in conflict – positively and negatively. Thinking about resilience, in other words, potentially enriches and diversifies common narratives about such violence which can foster the idea that all victims-/survivors have similar experiences (e.g., of stigmatisation).[2]

In multiple contexts, use of the term resilience is sometimes prefixed by 'extraordinary' or similar adjectives (see, e.g., Azzouz, 2019: 108; Jenkins,

276 Conclusion

1997; 42; Viswanathan et al., 2021: 168). What scholars such as Masten have underlined, however, is the 'ordinariness' of resilience. Resilience, she argues, 'appears to be a common phenomenon that results in most cases from the operation of basic human adaptational systems' (Masten, 2001: 227). These systems, however, do not exist in isolation. This book has aimed to show that resilience, broadly, and the connectivity approach to resilience that it has developed and applied, more particularly, offer an important framework for thinking about how best to support both victims-/survivors of CRSV *and* the wider social ecologies with which their lives are interconnected.

Connectivity as a Novel Social-Ecological Approach

I began this book by describing my first meeting (during a previous research project in 2014–2015) with Džana, a Bosnian woman. It was partly because of the time that I spent with her and her family that I became interested in resilience – and curious as to why I had come across so little mention of it in my research on CRSV during the Bosnian war. My sense was that there were important stories of resilience – 'situated in everydayness' (Lenette et al., 2013: 639) – that had not been recognised or discussed as such. When I designed the study on which this book is based, purposely selecting three very different case studies to maximise comparative social-ecological analyses of resilience and to accentuate cultural and contextual factors, I wanted to capture and explore some of these stories. Chapters 5, 6 and 7 primarily presented the qualitative data from the study, namely 63 semi-structured interviews from BiH, Colombia and Uganda. As my analysis of the data progressed, I started to think about resilience itself as constituting a story, or rather a set of stories, about the relationships – and the stories of those relationships – between individuals and various parts of their social ecologies.

The research has examined this idea using the concept of connectivity. Reflecting the book's strong emphasis on the significance of social ecologies – and why they matter for how we think about resilience, CRSV and, ultimately, transitional justice – it has drawn directly on the field of ecology to think about connectivity. In so doing, it has developed (in Chapter 2) its own conceptual framework for studying and analysing resilience. This framework constitutes an original social-ecological approach to resilience in three main ways. First, it co-opts a set of concepts from ecology literature – structural and functional connectivity, fragmentation and dynamic connectivity – and adapts them for use in a social science context, thereby effecting a novel social-ecological fusion.

Second, it offers a holistic way of thinking about resilience that encompasses all of the following: (a) changes in the relationships that individuals have with their social ecologies (broken and ruptured connectivities [fragmentation]); (b) the multi-systemic resources that individuals can access within their social ecologies and how they actively utilise them (supportive and sustaining connectivities [structural and functional connectivity]); and (c) some of the ways that individuals forge new connectivities, including by giving back to their social ecologies (new connectivities [dynamic connectivity]). These storied connectivities also encapsulate important longitudinal dimensions of resilience, highlighting the fact that 'Resilient functioning is not immutable' (Cicchetti, 2013: 414).

Third, connectivities – and the stories of those connectivities – are deeply contextual. Some of the examples given of 'bad connectivities' (see, e.g., Chapter 6) illustrate this. The book's connectivity framework is therefore particularly suited for comparative cross-country research. Such research, in turn, is essential for further enriching some of the important work that has been done on cultural elements and expressions of resilience (see, e.g., Ryan, 2015; Ungar, 2010; Wexler, 2014).

Connectivity is significant, however, not only as a conceptual and analytical framework. It also has a practical relevance and application, linked to the idea of 'nudging'. Nudging is about subtly influencing the decisions and choices that people make (Thaler and Sunstein, 2008: x). Using the concept of nudging in a slightly different sense, I argue that the book's use of connectivity, as a way of framing the multiple relationships between individuals and their social ecologies, 'nudges' policymakers and scholars to think about the notion of a 'survivor-centred approach' to CRSV from a broader perspective.

The Wider Relevance of Connectivity for Conflict-Related Sexual Violence

In its Resolution 2467 – part of its Women, Peace and Security agenda – the UN Security Council (2019) recognised 'the need for a survivor-centered approach in preventing and responding to sexual violence in conflict and post-conflict situations'. The terminology of a survivor-centred approach is now widely used at the international policy level. What is lacking, however, is critical reflection on the concept – and its potential limitations. A notable exception in this regard is a report that resulted from the Wilton Park conference on CRSV in February 2019, organised in collaboration with the United Kingdom's FCO (which has since been renamed the Foreign, Commonwealth and Development Office). While endorsing a survivor-centred approach, the report also recognises that 'the current focus on an individual survivor's physical and psychosocial needs and access to justice for that individual risks overlooking the collective nature of harms experienced and the full range of victims of sexual violence' (FCO and Wilton Park, 2019: 2). It further emphasises that CRSV does not only affect direct victims-/survivors, but also 'families, communities and those who were forced to witness such crimes take place' (FCO and Wilton Park, 2019: 2). Beyond just the issue of harm, the larger point is that 'centring' potentially risks 'de-centring the "big picture"' (Cunningham and Williams, 1993: 429), in the sense of the social ecologies and structures that fundamentally shape, in multiple ways, the experiences, needs and priorities of individual victims-/survivors.

The limitations of 'centring' are not confined to CRSV. The 2030 UN Agenda for Sustainable Development, for example, states that 'On behalf of the peoples we serve, we have adopted a historic decision on a comprehensive, far-reaching and people-centred set of universal and transformative Goals and targets' (UN Department of Economic and Social Affairs, 2015: para. 2). An important question is whether and to what extent centring people is the optimal approach to achieving highly ambitious transformative goals relating to global issues, such as climate change. To be clear, this is not to say that 'centring' can never be transformative. As just one example of how it can be, Gobby et al.'s research discusses resistance efforts in Canada directed at extractive industries; and it emphasises 'the vast networks of frontline struggles joining forces, centring Indigenous struggles, and coalescing around transformative goals such as land restitution (#LandBack) and Indigenous self-determination' (Gobby et al., 2022).

As regards CRSV, the very concept of a 'survivor-centred approach' is itself transformative in the broader context of victims-/survivors' historical neglect and marginalisation (du Toit and le Roux, 2021: 117).[3] It is imperative, however, that the practical implementation of 'centring' victims-/survivors of CRSV does not push into the background wider social-ecological and contextual elements that are likely to be crucial to any fundamental transformation. An example of this, albeit not directly related, is Crooks et al.'s research on the impact of the COVID-19 pandemic on Black girls. Rather than centre the girls themselves, the authors explicitly adopted a social-ecological approach, explaining that this 'allows us to examine the intersection of systems and multilevel factors that lead to risk, produce inequities, and sustain inequalities, which are critical to addressing health disparities experienced within this population' (Crooks et al., 2022: 271).

Connectivity, as an intrinsically relational idea, 'nudges' towards a repositioning or relocation of survivor-centred approaches, both conceptually and operationally, within a wider social-ecological framework. Significant in this regard are the types of questions that we ask women and men who have experienced CRSV. The first edition of the International Protocol on the Documentation and Investigation of Sexual Violence in Conflict identifies three broad sets of questions, relating to 'the act', 'the context' and 'the perpetrator' respectively (FCO, 2014: 54–56). The suggested questions are aimed at gathering the legal evidence needed to prosecute CRSV in international law. More recently, the Murad Code (formally known as the Global Code of Conduct for Gathering and Using Information about Systematic and Conflict-Related Sexual Violence) underscores the need to ask open questions (Nadia's Initiative et al., 2022: Principle 10.6).[4] If, as Haraway (2018: 102) maintains, 'Storytelling is a thinking practice, not an embellishment to thinking', open questions allow this 'thinking practice' to unfold more freely.

Incorporating connectivity into some of the questions that we ask means giving victims-/survivors the space and opportunity to speak in more relational ways about their experiences, thus bringing into direct focus the social ecologies in which their individual lives are 'severally enmeshed' (Ingold, 2008: 1807). Such questions might include the following: *To what extent have your experiences had an impact on your relationships (e.g., with family, community) and, if so, how? How has war/armed conflict affected everyday life in your community? To what extent has war/armed conflict harmed the natural environment around you (animals, rivers, land, soil)? What resources/sources of support do you have in your life? If you think about your life and your relationships as forming a web, which threads of the web remain strong? Which threads have broken or become weak? What contact do you have with other victims-/survivors? What are the main resources available to people in your community?*

These are just a few suggestions, and they are not intended in any way to be prescriptive (or exhaustive). The bigger point is about how we stand with victims-/survivors of CRSV. The UN Secretary-General (2020: 3) has referred to 'contextualized solutions that build resilience', which he associates with a survivor-centred approach. Such solutions are not just about building resilience (and not everyone will necessarily regard this as a desirable goal). They are, however, the optimal way to support those who have suffered CRSV – or indeed any form of violence – which underscores the need for approaches that extend care and attention to individuals' social ecologies. This book has further argued that such approaches have a significant part to play within transitional justice.

New Directions for Transitional Justice

Teitel has identified and discussed three historical 'phases' of transitional justice. The first and 'postwar phase', characterised by a 'rush of internationalism', was followed by a second 'post-Cold War phase', which coincided with 'the post-1989 wave of democratization, modernization, and nation-building' (Teitel, 2005: 839). The third 'steady-state phase' began towards the end of the twentieth century, and Teitel (2005: 839) has associated it with 'contemporary conditions of persistent conflict which lay the basis for the generalization and normalization of a law of violence'.

Building on this transitional justice genealogy, Sharp (2013: 157) has pointed to a fourth phase – which he calls ' "fourth generation" transitional justice' – that is 'characterized in part by its increasing willingness to grapple with issues that continue to sit at the periphery of transitional justice concern'. These issues include economic justice and the relationship between the local and the international (Sharp, 2013: 157). In other words, this 'fourth phase' is fundamentally about pushing and expanding the boundaries of transitional justice. According to McAuliffe (2017: vii), moreover, 'A core element of this expansion has been to rewrite the dominant scripts evident in scholarship and practice'. These are scripts, he argues, that 'foreground familiar institutions (trials, truth commissions, reparations, lustration), familiar abuses (usually bodily integrity abuses) and familiar teleologies (liberal democracy, civil rights protection)' (McAuliffe, 2017: vii).

This book positions itself within this 'fourth phase' of transitional justice. Readers might nevertheless have expected it to give more attention to those dominant scripts that 'foreground familiar institutions', particularly in view of some of the important transitional justice developments that have taken place in BiH, Colombia and Uganda. Certainly, the research study on which this book is based could have been designed in a way that gave much more direct prominence to these institutions. For example, the focus could have been on investigating possible relationships between participation in (or, more broadly, individual experiences of) transitional justice processes – including through giving testimony in a criminal trial or helping to create a memorial – and resilience. This is a potential topic for future research and one that would represent a novel extension of existing work on transitional justice impact (see, e.g., Balcells et al., 2022; Dancy, 2010; Van der Merwe et al., 2009). Another angle might have been to examine how expressions of everyday resilience shape engagement with transitional justice processes and the possibilities that individuals have, through their social-ecological relationships, to 'actively claim and promote appropriate transitional justice mechanisms and ideas about justice' (Kastner, 2020: 382).

This research, however, has adopted a more conceptual approach, focused on exploring how the idea of social ecologies that is so fundamental to its analysis of resilience is also relevant to the field of transitional justice. It has linked the three elements of the book's connectivity framework – broken and ruptured connectivities, supportive and sustaining connectivities and new connectivities – to harm and relationality, adaptive capacity and mutuality; and it has reflected on how these concepts, in turn, potentially translate into new social-ecological ways of thinking about, and doing, transitional justice. Relatedly, it has incorporated ideas from resilience literature – including social-ecological systems (SES) and complex adaptive systems (CAS) – into its discussions about transitional justice, thereby forging new interdisciplinary syntheses.

Just as this research has drawn attention to some of the possible limitations of a 'survivor-centred approach' to CRSV, it has also raised questions about the notion of 'centring' in a transitional justice context (see, e.g., Nyseth Brehm and Golden, 2017; Robins, 2011). Balasco (2017: 4) maintains that 'survivor-centred justice need not be construed as just individual-centred'. She seeks to demonstrate this using her 'framework of reparative development', which makes clear that harms done to individuals also harm families and communities (Balasco, 2017: 2). This is itself a social-ecological argument, even if Balasco does not use this terminology. However, it captures only a small part of why social ecologies are important. Crucially, it is necessary to consider not only what a 'survivor-centred approach' to transitional justice might encompass, but also what it might neglect or leave out.

This book has placed a heavy accent on relationships and social-ecological connectivities – and the importance of bringing them more into the foreground of transitional justice processes. It has proposed conceptualising and thinking about societies that have experienced large-scale violence and rights abuses as SES. It has also accentuated the 'dynamism, feedbacks, and complex interactions' (Kittinger et al., 2012) that quintessentially define and shape these systems, thus further raising questions about 'centring' – and who/what should be centred. It has not specifically focused on relationships between human and more-than-human worlds, but it has underscored the largely unexplored significance of posthumanism for transitional justice theory and practice.

In this way, it ultimately points to a potential 'fifth phase' of transitional justice that would further extend the idea of developing the field in new social-ecological directions. This fifth phase would be a 'hybridised phase'. It would reject human exceptionalism and transcend human–nature binaries, and it would constitute a rupture with 'anthropocentric ideas about justice' (Celermajer et al., 2021: 121). It would be a more transformative justice, but not only in the sense that the term has been discussed within extant scholarship (see, e.g., Gready and Robins, 2014: 340). It would also be ontologically transformative, recognising relational subjects 'constituted in and by multiplicity' (Braidotti, 2013: 58).

Some Suggestions for Future Research

This book has primarily drawn on qualitative data, but the study on which it is based used mixed methods. The quantitative part of the research involved the design and use of a questionnaire, one of the aims of which was to 'measure' resilience. According to Prior and Hagmann (2014: 284), 'The discussion about whether to measure resilience is as old and as fraught as the concept's meaning'. They further underline that 'Even a basic exploration of what might constitute a measure (or index) of resilience . . . reveals the difficulty in establishing a measure that is both accurate and "fit for purpose"' (Prior and Hagmann, 2014: 284). One of the significant challenges is to capture the inherent fluidity of resilience, which makes prominent the value of longitudinal research. However, such research may not always be practical or feasible, and for this reason it is important to include longitudinal elements into measurement tools themselves.

As discussed in Chapter 3, this study used the Adult Resilience Measure (ARM; Resilience Research Centre, 2016), which measures a person's individual, relational and contextual resources. Future research on the ARM could usefully explore how to incorporate what this book has called storied connectivities into the scale. This would mean, for example, asking questions not only about current resources, but also about lost resources and, more broadly, changes in those resources. The statement 'My family have usually supported me through life', for instance, appears to assume that this support has been fairly constant and unchanging, which may not in fact be the case. Family can be an important broken and ruptured connectivity in a person's life, as Chapter 6 explored. In short, there is substantial scope for developing the ARM in ways that do more than give a snapshot of an individual's resources at a particular moment in time.

The framework that this book has developed tells a story about resilience through the dynamic connectivities between individuals and their social ecologies. Because these connectivities are conceptually broad, becoming fully 'storied' at an empirical level, the framework has a wide application and further research could adapt and utilise it in other contexts. As just one example, the current war in Ukraine will unquestionably generate a vast amount of academic research, including, potentially, research on Ukrainian refugees and resilience. Such research could incorporate the book's connectivity framework to explore, inter alia, how connectivities 'travel' – linking back to previously discussed associations within ecology scholarship between connectivity and movement. It could also examine how supportive and sustaining connectivities – and more generally what Reid (2009: 615) terms 'the multiplicity of routes of connectivity' – potentially change and evolve, in the sense of what they offer and how they are used, in situations of ongoing upheaval and displacement. Any such research, however, would also do well to make very clear that discussions about resilience in this context (and indeed in *any* context) should not be construed as 'de-vulnerabilizing' (Krause and Schmidt, 2020: 30) individuals or diminishing the horrors that they may have gone through. Krause and Schmidt (2020: 30) make the point that 'refugees can be vulnerable to assaults or marginalization, but they can also learn to cope with traumatic experiences . . . as well as establish economic collaborations [an example of new connectivities]'.

That resilience has received very little attention within scholarship on CRSV sowed the idea for this study. More research – and in particular comparative research – will be important for further exploring how individual victims-/survivors deal with their experiences, and how their relationships and interactions with their social ecologies shape this process – positively and/or negatively. Gilmore and Moffett (2021) have looked at some of the ways that victims and survivors of violence (but not specifically CRSV) engage in acts of 'self-repair', and in so doing they make a linkage between repair and resilience. 'At the heart of our article', they argue, 'is the aim of conveying the resilience and agency of victims and survivors to repair and cope with their harm in the absence of state action to provide assistance or reparations' (Gilmore and Moffett, 2021: 459). Their discussion of resilience is to be welcomed. It is, however, unfortunate that they frame resilience as a response to state failures, as this does nothing to challenge neoliberal critiques (which are not mentioned or acknowledged in the authors' research). It is essential that any future research on resilience and CRSV addresses such critiques – as this book has done – and does not inadvertently or indirectly feed into them.

This research has focused on interviews with direct victims-/survivors of CRSV. Future studies could also experiment with different methodologies that bring individuals' social ecologies more squarely to the forefront. In their research in north-eastern Nigeria, for example, Njoku and Dery (2021: 1792) conducted interviews with male victims-/survivors of CRSV, as well as with 'one community leader, ten NGO workers, and three security agents who knew or may have worked with male survivors'. Greater use of ethnographic methods that enable researchers – where it is feasible and safe to do so – to spend time with victims-/survivors in their 'own' environments, and thus to directly learn more about their social ecologies, will also be important. Although this research did not use such methods, the relationships that I personally developed with several of the interviewees gave me some very privileged and first-hand insights into their lives and family dynamics.

Finally, there is unquestionably a need for further research to be done on resilience and transitional justice. Two suggestions have already been made in the context of McAuliffe's (2017: vii) aforementioned reference to 'dominant scripts'. The book's proposed social-ecological framing of transitional justice also offers many potential avenues for new research. Certainly, it is hoped that others will build on and develop some of the arguments made, adding their own thoughts and reflections. There are also some larger issues relating to transitional justice that merit attention and exploration. It is sufficient to mention three of them.

First, this research has stressed that social ecologies matter for transitional justice, just as they matter for resilience and for CRSV. Highly pertinent in this regard, thus, is Held's (1995: 131) argument that 'care is the wider moral framework into which justice should be fitted', which raises the important question: how might transitional justice interventions and mechanisms practically extend care to individuals' social ecologies? Relatedly, and as part of a potential future 'fifth phase' of transitional justice, how can processes of dealing with the legacies of rights abuses and violence help to build 'networks of interspecies care' (Voinot-Baron, 2020)? Second, what is the relationship between resilience and transformative justice? In particular, how might attention to and efforts to foster resilience contribute to developing 'a transformative approach' to justice that 'works at multiple levels' (Wakefield and Zimmerman, 2020: 157)? Third, the book's discussion (particularly in Chapter 8) about story-telling, story-sharing and story-building invites the broader question: how can transitional justice processes create space for 'storyscapes', meaning 'the surrounding landscape of interconnected stories with which we inevitably interact' (Cense and Ganzevoort, 2019: 572)?

★★★

According to Haraway (2016: 35), 'It matters what stories tell stories'. As an expression of the concept of connectivity that is such a pivotal part of this book, participants in the reflections workshops that took place in 2021 were invited to write (or to verbally express, in cases of illiteracy) any messages of support that they would like to convey to other victims-/survivors of CRSV, in their own countries and/or in other parts of the world (including in BiH, Colombia and Uganda). These messages also tell stories, not least in the sense that some of them strongly reflect the influence and/or significance of the individuals' social ecologies.[5] Sharing these messages, which were also communicated to the study participants, feels like a fitting way to end this book.

Messages from BiH

'Our entire life is a fight for survival, both when we win and when we lose. When we experience someone humiliating and or devaluing us, we ourselves have to set goals that will lead us to success and a way out. And help in reaching those goals can only come from family, if we still have one. My guide to salvation is my son'.

'Have faith in yourself and good people. There are still some'.

'It's important to be continuously occupied with some work or activity and not to have too much time to think about what we survived. That was a long time ago'.

'We are weak without the [spider's] web. We need strong solid networks that do not break'.

'Greetings to all victims throughout the world. Let's unite. Together we are stronger'.

'The worst is over. With the help of good people, there has to be faith in a better future'.

'My message to anyone who has survived sexual violence and mistreatment is let's unite. Let's be strong'.

'This is my message to all survivors and victims. Spread love, care and solidarity to all victims, wherever they are'.

'To all women – regardless of their skin colour, name or surname – who have survived violence, let's all stand together. Let's go forward'.

'To all survivors, I want to say that you have support from women in Bosnia-Herzegovina to be strong and brave in the fight for your rights'.

Messages from Colombia

'A hug to all my sisters in pain and sadness due to this war that affects us all. But we are not going to allow ourselves to be defeated. Remember, united we will win. By persevering and resisting, and with loads of love, we will know how to get ahead, showing that we are capable of resisting since we are not afraid. Remember that we have sisters, friends, colleagues united in the same walk for our rights and together we will continue to move forward. Always together'.

'We the women of the world are strong and brave'.

'Hello. As a woman victim of violence, I want to give a few words of encouragement to those who have gone through the same thing as me, in any part of the world they are in, to keep going and not give in to anything or anyone. As women, we are worth a lot and we cannot fall with the obstacles that lie ahead of us in life. Encouragement to all warrior women. Greetings to all'.

'We have been violated and raped by different kinds of groups. As a result of those violations, we had sons and daughters. They have led us to resist, persist and never give up because when we can tell our stories, we are healing from within to move on and to be able to know ourselves, to recognise the pain of others'.

'This is for all women who have been victims of the armed conflict. Let's get together to ask the government for social justice because they finance the war, but women are the ones who pay the price'.

'I want to send this message to all women in the world and to boys, girls and adolescents. Let us denounce all these acts of violence. Let us not be silent. Let us share everything we learn in organisations. Our life is only ours. There is no justification for another human being to violate our body, our dignity. As a woman and as women, we are committed to preserving the memory of the women who have been disappeared, and together in chorus let us shout justice, justice, so that they do not violate us anymore. We are not a weapon of war'.

'Dear women from all over the world. I know that, like me, some of you have been victims of sexual violence, but united we are strong and courageous. Fighting, resistant women. Women who fight for their rights. We must be brave to fight for our *compañeras* [sisters]. United we are strong'.

'We are with you, we also go through the same. But God is with everyone, God bless you and us. Let's fight for our rights and achievements, for our mental health, and those around us will succeed'.

'When you feel lonely, I am here for you'.

'First of all, we thank the Women's Network for keeping an eye on every woman in this country, Colombia. For teaching us every day to defend our rights. All that we have learned in each of the meetings helps us a lot. And putting into practice all the teachings that they give us in *Ruta Pacifica de las Mujeres* does us a lot of good'.

'Hold onto what makes you happy'.

'Strength. God is with you at all times'.

'Life goes on and we have to fight for what we want and feel. Learn to value every situation no matter how difficult it may be. Things happen when they have to. Only God knows what the goal is'.

'Every obstacle in life is a learning experience. We are different because we are survivors'.

Messages from Uganda

'Dear friend, colleague, sister, mother, aunt, niece: I encourage you to be strong. Do not let anything tear you apart. Hold yourselves together with one another. Because together we are strong'.

'If you have any resource, make good use of it. See, I am using my garden to farm so I can meet my food needs. Do not get discouraged by any negative words being said. Bear a strong heart'.

'I wish to encourage people who might have gone through experiences like mine during armed conflict. These things have happened to many people in many parts of the world. You are not alone. Look at me: I came back from captivity already infected with HIV, but I am moving on with my life. My body looks healthy. So, in case you acquired a similar health problem like I did during war, do not allow it to take over your life'.

'My experiences are now things of the past. Let the past be the past. If things are not good, you should leave them to God. Do the same when things are bad. Leave them to God, even when the past has left scars that you see every day. True, one may never forget the scars, but try and move on with your life'.

'I want to encourage people who might have suffered similar fates as me. Press your heart [persevere] because you were not the only one. Countless people have suffered these things'.

'If the world has become unbearable, carry a strong heart. Press your heart. You see, if a person starts suffering at a tender age just like I did, that person can easily give up on life'.

'First, if you have experienced what I did, get someone to talk to you and counsel you properly. Second, put whatever skills you have acquired to good use. Do not sit on them. And, finally, know God. God's love and mercy is the best. Knowing God is one of the most important things that can help you'.

'I came back with my son from captivity and he is HIV positive. The stigma he suffers from the community is unbearable, but I have moved on with a positive attitude towards people. I decided to be free and live positively for my sake and my child's. So, be positive and live free. Once you do that, people will automatically start treating you better, and with time things will normalise'.

'The atrocities we suffered during war happened to other people elsewhere too. There is always the good and the bad. I have learned to let go of the bad. It is what the world should be doing'.

'Joining hands with others is important because it can be of help to you'.

Notes

1   In contrast, the first edition of the International Protocol on the Documentation and Investigation of Sexual Violence in Conflict does not mention resilience at all (FCO, 2014).

Conclusion 287

2 The aforementioned Special Representative of the Secretary-General on Sexual Violence in Conflict, for example, has stated:

> Consider the plight of a woman who has been raped, cast out of her home and community due to stigma, and forced to fend for herself and her dependent children in an environment of ongoing insecurity. This woman will confront greater threats and be forced to take greater risks because the basic needs of her family are not being met.
>
> (Patten, 2018)

3 It is important to stress, however, that the marginalisation of some victims-/survivors of CRSV, including men, largely persists (see, e.g., Grey and Shepherd, 2013: 116; Schulz, 2018: 587).

4 The Code points to 'the potential harmful impact of closed questions on the survivor and on the accuracy and detail of information collected that way' (Nadia's Initiative et al., 2022: Principle 10.6).

5 It is important to note that some of the Ugandan participants found it difficult to think of messages that they wanted to send to other victims-/survivors of CRSV, due to ongoing challenges and adversities in their lives. One of them, for example, noted that just a few days earlier, a cattle raid had taken place in her community, during which three women were gang raped. Hence, not every participant articulated a message.

References

Anderson B (2015) What kind of thing is resilience? *Politics* 35(1): 60–66.

Aroussi S (2018) Perceptions of justice and hierarchies of rape: Rethinking approaches to sexual violence in eastern Congo from the ground up. *International Journal of Transitional Justice* 12(2): 277–295.

Azzouz A (2019) A tale of a Syrian city at war: Destruction, resilience and memory in Homs. *City* 23(1): 107–122.

Balasco LM (2017) Reparative development: Re-conceptualising reparations in transitional justice processes. *Conflict, Security & Development* 17(1): 1–20.

Balcells L, Palanza V and Voytas E (2022) Do transitional justice museums persuade visitors? Evidence from a field experiment. *The Journal of Politics* 84(1): 496–510.

Braidotti R (2013) *The Posthuman.* Cambridge: Polity Press.

Brassett J, Croft S and Vaughan-Williams N (2013) Introduction: An agenda for resilience research in politics and international relations. *Politics* 33(4): 221–228.

Brown K (2014) Global environmental change I: A social turn for resilience? *Progress in Human Geography* 38(1): 107–117.

Celermajer D, Schlosberg D, Rickards L, Stewart-Harawira M, Thaler M, Tschakert P, Verlie B and Winter C (2021) Multispecies justice: Theories, challenges and a research agenda for environmental politics. *Environmental Politics* 30(1–2): 119–140.

Cense S and Ganzevoort RR (2019) The storyscapes of teenage pregnancy: On morality, embodiment and narrative agency. *Journal of Youth Studies* 22(4): 568–583.

Cicchetti D (2013) Annual research review: Resilient functioning in maltreated children – Past, present and future perspectives. *The Journal of Child Psychology and Psychiatry* 54(4): 402–422.

Crooks N, Sosina W, Debra A and Donenberg G (2022) The impact of COVID-19 among Black girls: A social-ecological perspective. *Journal of Pediatric Psychology* 47(3): 270–278.

Cunningham A and Williams P (1993) De-centring the 'big picture': *The Origins of Modern Science* and the modern origins of science. *The British Journal of the History of Science* 26(4): 407–432.

Dancy G (2010) Impact assessment, not evaluation: Defining a limited role for positivism in the study of transitional justice. *International Journal of Transitional Justice* 4(3): 355–376.

Dolan C (2016) Inclusive gender: Why tackling gender hierarchies cannot be at the expense of human rights and the humanitarian imperative. *International Review of the Red Cross* 98(902): 625–634.

du Toit L and le Roux E (2021) A feminist reflection on male victims of conflict-related sexual violence. *European Journal of Women's Studies* 28(2): 115–128.

EC (2022) Address by Mr Janusz Wojciechowski on the adoption of the European Commission communication 'Safeguarding food security and reinforcing the resilience of food systems'. Available at: https://ec.europa.eu/commission/presscorner/detail/en/SPEECH_22_1991 (accessed 31 March 2022).

FCO (2014) International Protocol on the Documentation and Investigation of Sexual Violence in Conflict: Basic Standards of Best Practice on the Documentation of Sexual Violence as a Crime under International Law. 1st ed. Available at: https://assets.publishing.service.gov.uk/government/uploads/system/uploads/attachment_data/file/319054/PSVI_protocol_web.pdf (accessed 2 October 2021).

FCO (2017) International Protocol on the Documentation and Investigation of Sexual Violence in Conflict: Best Practice on the Documentation of Sexual Violence as a Crime or Violation of International Law. 2nd ed. Available at: https://assets.publishing.service.gov.uk/government/uploads/system/uploads/attachment_data/file/598335/International_Protocol_2017_2nd_Edition.pdf (accessed 2 October 2021).

FCO and Wilton Park (2019) Sexual violence in conflict: Delivering justice for survivors and holding perpetrators to account. Available at: www.wiltonpark.org.uk/wp-content/uploads/WP1651-Report-1-1.pdf (accessed 23 October 2020).

Fernández-Prados JS, Lozano-Díaz A and Muyor-Rodríguez J (2021) Factors explaining social resilience against COVID-19: The case of Spain. *European Societies* 23(1): 111–121.

Gilmore S and Moffett L (2021) Finding a way to live with the past: 'Self-repair', 'informal repair' and reparations in transitional justice. *Journal of Law and Society* 48(3): 455–480.

Gobby J, Temper L, Burke M and von Ellenrieder N (2022) Resistance as governance: Transformative strategies forged on the frontlines of extractivism in Canada. *The Extractive Industries and Societies* 9: 100919.

Gready P and Robins S (2014) From transitional to transformative justice: A new agenda for practice. *International Journal of Transitional Justice* 8(3): 339–361.

Grey R and Shepherd LJ (2013) 'Stop rape now?': Masculinity, responsibility and conflict-related sexual violence. *Men and Masculinities* 16(1): 115–135.

Haraway DJ (2016) *Staying with the Trouble: Making Kin in the Chthulucene.* Durham, NC: Duke University Press.

Haraway DJ (2018) Staying with the trouble for multispecies environmental justice. *Dialogues in Human Geography* 8(1): 102–105.

Held V (1995) The meshing of care and justice. *Hypatia* 10(2): 128–132.

ICRC (2018) ICRC strategy on sexual violence 2018–2022. Available at: www.icrc.org/sites/default/files/topic/file_plus_list/icrc_strategy_on_sexual_violence_2018-2022_-_en.pdf (accessed 14 March 2022).

Ingold T (2008) Bindings against boundaries: Entanglements of life in an open world. *Environment and Planning A: Economy and Space* 40(8): 1796–1810.

Jenkins JH (1997) Not without a trace: Resilience and remembering among Bosnian refugees (Commentary on 'A family survives genocide'). *Psychiatry* 60(1): 40–43.

Joseph J (2013) Resilience as embedded neoliberalism: A governmentality approach. *Resilience* 1(1): 38–52.

Kastner P (2020) A resilience approach to transitional justice? *Journal of Intervention and Statebuilding* 14(3): 368–388.

Keyes CLM (2004) Risk and resilience in human development: An introduction. *Research in Human Development* 1(4): 223–227.

Kittinger JN, Finkbeiner EM, Glazier EW and Crowder LB (2012) Human dimensions of coral reef social-ecological systems. *Ecology and Society* 17(4): 17.

Krause U and Schmidt H (2020) Refugees as actors? Critical reflections on global refugee policies on self-reliance and resilience. *Journal of Refugee Studies* 33(1): 22–41.

Lenette C, Brough M and Cox L (2013) Everyday resilience: Narratives of single refugee women with children. *Qualitative Social Work* 12(5): 637–653.

Marchini S, Zaurino E, Bouziotis J, Brondino N, Delvenne V and Delhaye M (2021) Study of resilience and loneliness in youth (18–25 years old) during the COVID-19 pandemic lockdown measures. *Journal of Community Psychology* 49(2): 468–480.

Massad S, Stryker R, Mansour S and Khammash U (2018) Rethinking resilience for children and youth in conflict zones: The case of Palestine. *Research in Human Development* 15(3–4): 280–293.

Masten AS (2001) Ordinary magic: Resilience processes in development. *American Psychologist* 56(3): 227–238.

McAuliffe P (2017) *Transformative Transitional Justice and the Malleability of Post-Conflict States.* Cheltenham: Edward Elgar.

Nadia's Initiative, International Institute for Criminal Investigations and the Preventing Sexual Violence in Conflict Initiative (2022) Global code of conduct for gathering and using information about systematic and conflict-related sexual violence (Murad Code). Available at: www.muradcode.com/murad-code (accessed 24 April 2022).

NATO (2022) Statement by NATO heads of state and government. Available at: www.nato.int/cps/en/natohq/official_texts_193719.htm (accessed 1 April 2022).

Nitschke JP, Forbes PAG, Ali N, Cutler J, Apps MAJ, Lockwood PL and Lamm C (2021) Resilience during uncertainty? Greater social connectedness during COVID-19 lockdown is associated with reduced distress and fatigue. *British Journal of Health Psychology* 26(2): 553–569.

Njoku ET and Dery I (2021) Spiritual security: An explanatory framework for conflict-related sexual violence against men. *International Affairs* 97(6): 1785–1803.

Nyseth Brehm H and Golden S (2017) Centering survivors in local transitional justice. *Annual Review of Law and Social Science* 13: 101–121.

OSRSG-SVC (2021) SRSG Pramila Patten, video remarks international conference on 'the principle of credibility as a tool against impunity for sexual violence', 9–10 December 2021, Guatemala City. Available at: www.un.org/sexualviolenceinconflict/statement/srsg-pramila-patten-video-remarks-international-congress-on-the-principle-of-credibility-as-a-tool-against-impunity-for-sexual-violence-9–10-december-2021-guatemala-city/ (accessed 28 January 2022).

Patten P (2018) Ensuring that survivors of conflict-related sexual violence are not left behind in the sustainable development agenda. Available at: www.un.org/en/chronicle/article/ensuring-survivors-conflict-related-sexual-violence-are-not-left-behind-sustainable-development (accessed 16 September 2021).

Prior T and Hagmann J (2014) Measuring resilience: Methodological and political challenges of a trend security concept. *Journal of Risk Research* 17(3): 281–298.

Reid J (2009) Politicizing connectivity: Beyond the biopolitics of information technology in international relations. *Cambridge Review of International Affairs* 22(4): 607–623.

Resilience Research Centre (2016) The Resilience Research Centre Adult Resilience Measure (RRC-ARM): User's manual. Available at: https://cyrm.resilienceresearch.org/files/ArchivedMaterials.zip (accessed 9 October 2021).

Robins S (2011) Towards victim-centred transitional justice: Understanding the needs of families of the disappeared in postconflict Nepal. *International Journal of Transitional Justice* 5(1): 75–98.

Ryan C (2015) Everyday resilience as resistance: Palestinian women practising *sumud*. *International Political Sociology* 9(4): 299–315.

Schulz P (2018) The 'ethical loneliness' of male sexual violence survivors in northern Uganda: Gendered reflections on silencing. *International Feminist Journal of Politics* 20(4): 583–601.

Sharp DN (2013) Interrogating the peripheries: The preoccupations of fourth generation transitional justice. *Harvard Human Rights Journal* 26: 149–178.

Simić O (2018) *Silenced Victims of Wartime Rape*. Abingdon: Routledge.

Teitel R (2005) The law and politics of contemporary transitional justice. *Cornell International Law Journal* 38(3): 837–862.

Thaler RH and Sunstein CR (2008) *Nudge: Improving Decisions about Health, Wealth, and Happiness*. New Haven, CT: Yale University Press.

UN Department of Economic and Social Affairs (2015) Transforming our world: The 2030 agenda for sustainable development. Available at: https://sdgs.un.org/2030agenda (accessed 2 April 2022).

UN Secretary-General (2020) Conflict-related sexual violence: Report of the United Nations Secretary-General. Available at: www.un.org/sexualviolenceinconflict/wp-content/uploads/2020/07/report/conflict-related-sexual-violence-report-of-the-united-nations-secretary-general/2019-SG-Report.pdf (accessed 19 June 2021).

UN Secretary-General (2021) Conflict-related sexual violence: Report of the UN Secretary-General. Available at: www.un.org/sexualviolenceinconflict/wp-content/uploads/2021/04/report/conflict-related-sexual-violence-report-of-the-united-nations-secretary-general/SG-Report-2020editedsmall.pdf (accessed 8 September 2021).

UN Security Council (2019) Resolution 2467.

Ungar M (2010) Families as navigators and negotiators: Facilitating culturally and contextually specific expressions of resilience. *Family Process* 49(3): 421–435.

Ungar M (2013) Resilience, trauma, context and culture. *Trauma, Violence & Abuse* 14(3): 255–266.

Van der Merwe H, Baxter V and Chapman AR (eds.) (2009) *Assessing the Impact of Transitional Justice: Challenges for Empirical Research*. Washington, DC: United States Institute of Peace.

Viswanathan M, Aly HF, Duncan R and Mandhan M (2021) Unequal but essential: How subsistence consumer-entrepreneurs negotiate unprecedented shock with extraordinary resilience during COVID-19. *The Journal of Consumer Affairs* 55(1): 151–178.

Voinot-Baron W (2020) A bitter taste of fish: The temporality of salmon, settler colonialism and the work of well-being in a Yupiaq fishing village. *Ecology and Society* 25(2): 4.

Wakefield S and Zimmerman K (2020) Re-imagining resilience: Supporting feminist women to lead development with transformative practice. *Gender & Development* 28(1): 155–174.

Wexler L (2014) Looking across three generations of Alaska natives to explore how culture fosters Indigenous resilience. *Transcultural Psychiatry* 51(1): 73–92.

Zembylas M (2021) Against the psychologization of resilience: Towards an onto-political theorization of the concept and its implications for higher education. *Studies in Higher Education* 46(9): 1966–1977.

Appendix 1

The Interview Guide

A. Life Today

1 Can you start by telling me in a few sentences something about your life today?
2 If you were to tell the story of your life, what title would you give it?
3 What are the main difficulties that you currently experience in your everyday life?
4 Can you think about the last time that you experienced something very stressful that you feel comfortable sharing; how did you deal with that experience and who did you turn to?

B. War Experiences

5 Could you briefly tell me your story relating to the war/armed conflict?
6 Are there parts of your war story which are important to you and which you are never asked about? Can you tell me more?

C. Sexual Violence

7 How has your experience of sexual violence impacted on your life and your relations with others?
8 As someone who has suffered sexual violence, can you give me three words that you would use to describe yourself?
9 Can you tell me a little more about the three words that you have chosen to describe yourself?
10 Some people describe those who have suffered sexual violence as victims. How do you understand the term 'victim'?
11 Some people describe those who have suffered sexual violence as survivors. How do you understand the term 'survivor'?
12 Do you see yourself as a victim, as a survivor, as a victim and a survivor or as neither a victim nor a survivor?

D. Resources and Support

13 What resources do you have that help you to deal with challenges (e.g., your own inner resources, services within your community, government institutions)?
14 What do you do to get the resources you need?
15 Who or what are the sources of support in your life?

E. Resilience and Coping

16 After everything that you have gone through, what are the factors that have been most important in helping you to rebuild/start to rebuild your life?
17 What are the factors that have made it difficult for you to rebuild/start to rebuild your life?
18 Do you think that being a man/woman has influenced how you deal with challenges and adversity in your life? If yes, can you give me an example?
19 Do you think that being a X [reference to ethnicity] has influenced how you deal with challenges and adversity in your life? If yes, can you give me an example?
20 Has the place where you grew up, or the place where you currently live – if different – affected how you deal with challenges and adversity in your life? If yes, can you give me an example?
21 Given all that you have been through, how well do you think you are doing? Would you say that you are doing better than expected, as expected or worse than expected?
22 What words do you use to describe people who do better than expected after experiencing many challenges in life?

F. Justice

23 In societies that have experienced war, armed conflict and large-scale human rights abuses, people often talk about the need for 'justice'. Thinking about your own life, what does 'justice' mean to you?
24 Transitional justice refers to the process of dealing with past human rights abuses in a society. It can take many forms, including criminal prosecutions, truth commissions and reparations. Have you experienced any form of transitional justice?
25 If yes, did it change your life in any way and how?
26 What do you need from transitional justice (or still need) for it to make a meaningful difference to your life and why?
27 Reparations are an important part of transitional justice because they seek to repair some of the damage that has been done to victims of crimes and their communities. Reparations can be individual (e.g., the payment of

monetary compensation) and/or collective (e.g., the building of a school). What sort of reparations would mean the most to you and why?

G. Closing questions

28 Is there anything else that you would like to share with me today?

29 At the start of the interview, I asked you to tell me what title you would give your life story. You answered 'XXX'. If I ask you the same question again now, would you answer it differently? If yes, can you tell me why?

30 Finally, how was your experience of talking to me today and telling me your story?

Appendix 2

Rape Cases in Bosnia-Herzegovina

The commonly cited figure of 20,000–50,000 wartime rapes in Bosnia-Herzegovina (BiH) is usually attributed to one of two main sources. The first source is the United Nations (UN). Trial International (2020), for example, claims that 'According to the United Nations, between 20,000 and 50,000 women and men were raped or sexually assaulted during the 1992–1995 war in Bosnia and Herzegovina' (see also Husarić, 2021). It is the case that the UN Commission of Experts used the figure of 20,000. As background to this, between 29 June and 9 July 1993, the Commission sent an investigative team to Sarajevo to conduct a pilot study on the issue of rape. Its report notes that:

> In Sarajevo, the investigative team obtained all the relevant information from the database of the War Crimes Commission of Bosnia and Herzegovina. The database lists 126 victims, 113 incidents, 252 alleged perpetrators, 73 witnesses and 100 documents. Of these, there were 105 rape cases.
> (UN Commission of Experts, 1994: para. 239)

It goes on to underline that in the challenging circumstances in which the investigative team was working, 'it was not practicable to gather precise information leading to possible *prima facie* cases' (UN Commission of Experts, 1994: para. 240). Nevertheless, a footnote in the report – discussing the scale of victimisation (not only related to sexual violence) in the former Yugoslavia – states that 'the earlier projection of 20,000 rapes made by other sources' is 'not unreasonable considering the number of actual reported cases' (UN Commission of Experts, 1994: 84, n87). It is important, thus, to underline that the figure of 20,000 refers not just to BiH but to the whole of the former Yugoslavia, and that it originally came not from the UN Commission but from 'other sources', which the Commission's report does not name.

In 1996, a preliminary report of the Special Rapporteur, Linda Chavez, on the situation of systematic rape, sexual slavery and slavery-like practices during periods of armed conflict noted that:

> The Special Rapporteur of the Commission on Human Rights on the situation of human rights in the territory of the former Yugoslavia has

reported that between 1992 and 1994 in the former Yugoslavia, rape of women and girls occurred on a large scale, with possibly as many as 20,000 victims.

(UN, 1996: para. 9)

No reference for this statistic is provided, although there is a reference at the end of the paragraph to an earlier 1993 report by the Special Rapporteur of the Commission on Human Rights, Tadeusz Mazowiecki. That report states:

The Special Rapporteur feels that it is not possible at present to determine the number of victims of rape in this conflict [referring to the former Yugoslavia]. However, it is clear that there are large numbers involved and care for them must be the first priority.

(UN, 1993: para. 86)

The second main source frequently cited regarding the number of rapes in BiH is the Council of Europe. An Amnesty International (2017: 16) report, for example, acknowledges that the precise number of female victims of conflict-related sexual violence in BiH is 'widely disputed' and maintains that the figure of 20,000 given by the Council of Europe is the 'most reliable estimate'. The figure of 20,000 is not, however, an 'estimate' made by the Council of Europe. What the Parliamentary Assembly of the Council of Europe stated (referring to 'the Balkan wars') is that 'To this day, the exact figures are disputed' (Parliamentary Assembly, 2009: para. 6). It also noted: 'but it is estimated [it is not clear by whom] that upward of 20 000 Bosniac, Croat and Serb women were raped, often gang raped and sometimes sexually enslaved and forcibly impregnated in so-called "rape camps" by armies and paramilitary groups' (Parliamentary Assembly, 2009: para. 6).

The figure of 20,000 rapes has also been attributed to a European Community (EC) investigative mission – headed by the late Dame Anne Warburton, Britain's first female ambassador (to Denmark) – into the treatment of Muslim women in the former Yugoslavia. Noting that 2.6 million people had been displaced by November 1992, the investigative mission's report commented that accurate statistics on the crimes being committed were 'not available' (EC, 1993: para. 10). It further emphasised that 'the inherent difficulties in compiling statistics on rape and other sexual abuse have been hugely accentuated in the current chaotic conditions' (EC, 1993: para. 10). It concluded, thus, that it would 'probably never be possible to calculate precisely the number of victims involved', while also accepting – on the basis of its investigations[1] – that 'it is possible to speak in terms of many thousands. Estimates vary widely, ranging from 10,000 to as many as 60,000' (EC, 1993: para. 14). It further added that 'The most reasoned estimates suggested to the mission place the number of victims at around 20,000' (EC, 1993: para. 14). It is unclear, however, how it adjudged these estimates as being 'the most reasoned'.

Rape Cases in Bosnia-Herzegovina   297

In short, some of the claims relating to statistics – and in particular claims that 20,000 to 50,000 individuals were raped during the Bosnian war – have a thin evidentiary basis. This is not to say that they are wrong or inflated. The aforementioned UN Commission of Experts (1994: para. 234) itself commented that 'it is very difficult to make any general assessment of actual numbers of rape victims'. It is, though, important to note that the issue has become a broader 'numbers game', in which Bosnian politicians have themselves been deeply complicit. This, in turn, highlights the frequent instrumentalisation of wartime rape in BiH[2] and, by extension, the instrumentalisation of the women who 'helped to create a national image of the enemy as well as the image of the nation as victim' (Kašić, 2002: 198; see also Berry, 2018: 188).

Notes

1   The mission made only short visits to the former Yugoslavia – to Zagreb from 20 to 24 December 1992 and then again from 19 to 21 January 1993, and to BiH from 22 to 26 January 1993 (EC, 1993: para. 3).
2   On 24 August 1993, the Bosnian Ambassador to the UN, Muhamed Sacirbey, delivered a speech to the UN Security Council and declared that:

> Bosnia and Herzegovina is being gang raped . . . I do not lightly apply the analogy of a gang rape to the plight of the Republic of Bosnia and Herzegovina. As we know, systematic rape has been one of the weapons of this aggression against the Bosnian women in particular.
>
> (cited in Hansen, 2000: 62)

This is just one illustration of how 'Images of Bosnian [and specifically Bosniak] women as wartime rape victims have come to symbolize the victimization of Bosnia as a whole' (Björkdahl, 2012: 302; see also Helms, 2013: 25).

References

Amnesty International (2017) Bosnia and Herzegovina: 'We need support not pity': Last chance for justice for Bosnia's wartime rape survivors. Available at: www.amnesty.org/en/documents/eur63/6679/2017/en/ (accessed 8 May 2021).

Berry ME (2018) *Women, War and Power: From Violence to Mobilization in Rwanda and Bosnia-Herzegovina*. Cambridge: Cambridge University Press.

Björkdahl A (2012) A gender-just peace? Exploring the post-Dayton peace process in Bosnia. *Peace & Change* 37(2): 286–317.

EC (1993) European Community investigative commission into the treatment of Muslim women in the former Yugoslavia. Available at: https://digitallibrary.un.org/record/160501/files/S_25240-EN.pdf (accessed 6 June 2021).

Hansen L (2000) Gender, nation, rape: Bosnia and the construction of security. *International Feminist Journal of Politics* 3(1): 55–75.

Helms E (2013) *Innocence and Victimhood: Gender, Nation and Women's Activism in Postwar Bosnia-Herzegovina*. Madison, WI: University of Wisconsin Press.

Husarić A (2021) Bosnian war rape survivors 'still afraid to speak out'. Available at: https://balkaninsight.com/2021/03/03/bosnian-war-rape-survivors-still-afraid-to-speak-out/ (accessed 6 July 2021).

Kašić B (2002) The dynamics of identifications within nationalistic discourse: From archetypes to promising female roles. In: Iveković R and Mostov J (eds.), *From Gender to Nation*. Ravenna: Longo Editore, pp. 189–200.

Parliamentary Assembly (2009) Resolution 1670 (2009): Sexual violence against women in armed conflict. Available at: http://assembly.coe.int/nw/xml/XRef/Xref-XML2HTML-en.asp?fileid=17741&lang=en (accessed 3 June 2021).

Trial International (2020) Wartime sexual violence survivors: Bosnia and Herzegovina's forgotten ones. Available at: https://trialinternational.org/latest-post/25-years-after-the-war-rights-of-victims-of-sexual-violence-are-still-not-guaranteed-in-bosnia-and-herzegovina/ (accessed 2 June 2021).

UN (1993) Report on the situation of human rights in the territory of the former Yugoslavia, submitted by Tadeusz Mazowiecki, Special Rapporteur of the Commission on Human Rights, pursuant to Commission resolution 19992/S-1/1 of August 1992. Available at: https://digitallibrary.un.org/record/226088?ln=en (accessed 31 May 2021).

UN (1996) Preliminary report of the Special Rapporteur on the situation of systematic rape, sexual slavery and slavery-like practices during periods of armed conflict. Available at: https://digitallibrary.un.org/record/236621?ln=en (accessed 31 May 2021).

UN Commission of Experts (1994) Final report of the Commission of Experts established pursuant to Security Council Resolution 780 (1992), S/1994/674. Available at: www.icty.org/x/file/About/OTP/un_commission_of_experts_report1994_en.pdf (accessed 28 August 2021).

Index

Page numbers in *italics* indicate a figure; and n indicates a note on the corresponding page.

ABColombia 70, 110, 111
Abdi S 220
abduction 205–6
ABiH see Army of Bosnia-Herzegovina
    (ABiH)
Abonga F 220
Acholi *manyen* 119
Acholi people 114
Acosta M 111
adaptive capacity 253–5
adaptive cycle 26–7, 31, 52–3, 192
Adger WN 6, 25, 28, 36, 37
Adult Resilience Measure (ARM) 30,
    73–4, 78, 81–2, 84, 91n11, 138, 154,
    175, 281–2
Agarwal B 52
Akhavan P 115
Alaimo S 61n4
Allen B 102, 122n3
Allen CR 26
Allen T 115
Amnesty International 101, 113, 115, 118,
    134, 296
Anderson B 287
Andreas P 98
Antonovsky A 190
Apio EO 9, 231n8
Army of Bosnia-Herzegovina (ABiH) 101,
    138, 148
Army of *Repubika Srpska* (VRS) 101,
    122n2, 148
Aroussi S 275
AUC see United Self-Defence Forces of
    Colombia (AUC)
Auma A 114, 114–15
Australia 28

Autesserre S 60n2
Auto 092 (Colombian Constitutional
    Court) 90n1, 110

back loop 192
Baines E 2, 119, 228, 230, 232n13, 232n17
Balasco LM 280
Balint J 248
Barnes GD 51
Barnes-Lee AR 180
Barrios RE 31, 32
Bećirević E 105
Béné C 33
Benzies K 208
Berkes F 31
Berry ME 150, 159
BiH see Bosnia-Herzegovina (BiH)
Bimeny P 254
Binder CR 47
Blackie LER 190
Bodin Ö 47
Boesten J 47, 69, 80
Bonanno GA 2
Borbasi S 8
Bosnia-Herzegovina (BiH): Bosnian
    war 14, 70, 76, 98–101, 101–6,
    144, 149, 297; broken and ruptured
    connectivities 136–43; children and
    connectivity 145–7; civilian victim of
    war status 155; community relationships
    136–8; connectivity stories 134–60;
    contextualisation of violence 134–6;
    demographics 122n1; friction sources
    157–9; genocidal rape claims 102–3;
    health 140–3; health services and
    providers 149–51; interview ethics 87–8,

300 Index

89, 91n9; meaning making 152–3, 191; messages from 284; new connectivities 151–60; overview 98–106; political context 154–6; rape cases in 102–3, 295–7; selection for study 70; sexual violence 101–6; sexual violence by all sides 103–6; spouses/partners 144–5; supportive and sustaining connectivities 143–51, 187; transitional justice in 242, 243; unanswered questions 153–6; unemployment 161n8; women's and non-governmental organisations 184

bouncing back 24, 31, 73, 90n3

Bourbeau P 4, 35

Boutron C 197n15

Bradfield P 261n4

Bradley M 262n22

Braidotti R 262n19

Bralo case 103

Branch A 215

Brassett J 35

Braun V 84

Bringa T 136

Brockmeier J 188

broken and ruptured connectivities: in adaptive cycle 192; in Bosnia-Herzegovina 136–143; community relationships 136–8; in Colombia 173–180; discussion of 57–8; embodied ruptures 177–9; forced displacement 173–4; harm 247–52; health 140–3, 177–80, 212–15; linked to fragmentation 57–8; loss of loved ones/broken families 174–7; lost opportunities 207–10; relationality 247–52; repair of 216–17; social-ecological health 179–80; social interactions 138–40; stigma 210–12; support networks 59; in Uganda 207–15; uprooting 173–7

Bromage A 161n5, 161n11, 197n9, 197n20

Bronfenbrenner U 49

Brown C 220

Brown K 287

Brysiewicz P 59

Bunnell SL 89

Burton T 179

Buss DE 262n13

Cabrera L 110

Calhoun D 196n8

Calhoun LG 190

Calić MJ 99

Campbell CA 180

Campbell R 86

Canada 60, 61n5, 278

captivity 205–6

care/acts of care: definition of 228; holistic 185; importance of 228; as moral framework 283; as stewardship 174

Carlson K 123n17

case studies, selection of 8, 69–71

Cassidy L 51

Cecez-Kecmanovic D 49

Celermajer D 250

centring concepts 252, 277–8

Češić case 104

Céspedes-Báez LM 58

Četniks 122n4

Chambers-Ju C 197n21

Chandler D 32, 35

Chaskin RC 219

Chavez L 295

Child and Youth Resilience Measure (CYRM) 74, 82

children: in Bosnia-Herzegovina 146–7; in Colombia 179; refugees 254; research on 3, 13, 21, 145–6; resilience of 22–3, 29, 37; supportive and sustaining connectivities 145–7, 180; transitional justice and 254; in Uganda 116, 118, 208

Chinkin C 102–3

Clarke V 84

CNMH see National Centre for Historical Memory (CNMH)

Cole SM 56

collapse and release phase, of adaptive cycle 26, 53

Colombia: armed conflict 106–9; broken and ruptured connectivities 173–80; connectivity stories 169–97; contextualisation of violence 170–3; everyday violence 171–2; forced displacement 173–4; guerrillas 106–8; health services and providers 149; interview ethics 87, 88, 89; land 174, 195; La Violencia 106–8; loss of loved ones/broken families 174–7; meaning making 154, 188–95; messages from 284–5; National Liberation Army 107, 108; paramilitaries 108–9; peace agreement 14, 71, 106, 113; reparations 242; research priorities 76; Revolutionary Armed Forces of Colombia 106, 107, 108–9, 112,

123n10; selection for study 70–1; sexual violence 108, 109–13; social-ecological health 179–80; social-ecological thinking 240–1, 244; Special Jurisdiction for Peace 113, 241; transitional justice in 113, 241, 242, 243, 244; United Self-Defence Forces of Colombia 109; witnessing violence 170–1; women's and non-governmental organisations 184–7, 192, 193
Colombia Diversa 91n8, 187
colonialism 110, 248
community 136–8, 219–22
comparative case study approach 69–71
competence 22
complex adaptive system (CAS) 26, 31, 253
conflict-related sexual violence (CRSV): in Bosnia-Herzegovina 101–6; in Colombia 108, 109–13; connectivity and 47, 277–9; contextualisation 134–6, 170–3, 205–7; continuum of violence 47, 113, 135, 172; cultural factors 189; definition of 15n1; faith and spirituality 181–3; structural factors 189; and 'survivor-centred approach' 4, 252, 277–8, 280; in Uganda 118–22, 123n17; witnessing 170–1, 206–7; *see also* sexual and gender-based violence (SGBV)
connectivity: in Bosnia-Herzegovina 134–60; 'bad connectivities' 176, 177, 179, 277; broken and ruptured 57–8, 136–43, 173–80, 207–15, 247–52; in Colombia 169–97; as conceptual framework 5–7, 46–50, 55–60; conflict-related sexual violence and 277–9; definition of 47, 52; dynamic nature of 7, 58–60; ecology and 5–7, 13, 46, 48, 49, 50, 54, 55–60, 85, 136, 276; family-related 143–7; functional 6–7, 55–7; gender and 51–2; and fragmentation 7, 57, 136; hyperconnectivity 46–7; as multi-systemic concept 49; new 58–60, 151–60, 188–96, 223–34, 255–60; as novel social-ecological approach 276–7; reason to study 47–50; resilience and 50–55; supportive and sustaining 55–7, 143–51, 180–8, 215–23, 253–5; structural 7, 55–56; thematic analysis 84–5; transitional justice and 240; in Uganda 204–31

Conservation of Resources (COR) theory 142–3
conservation phase, of adaptive cycle 26, 53
COR see Conservation of Resources (COR) theory
Cote M 32
Coulter C 2, 188
COVID-19 81, 111, 180, 258, 273, 278
Crellin RJ 249
Creswell JW 71
Croatian Defence Council (HVO) 101, 138
Croatian Defence Forces (HOS) 141
Croatia (war in) 99
Crooks JA 46
Crooks N 278
Crosby A 250, 256, 262n14
CRSV see conflict-related sexual violence (CRSV)
Cruikshank J 249
cultural stereotypes 189
CYRM see Child and Youth Resilience Measure (CYRM)

Davidson DJ 37
Davoudi S 33
Dawney L 72
de Finney S 61n5
De Greiff P 11
Democratic Republic of Congo (DRC) 60n2, 85, 117, 250
Derickson KD 31
Dery I 283
Destrooper T 240
Deterding NM 82
Devas N 232n21
De Welde K 178
differential impact theory 180
differentially-impactful resilience enablers 180
Dolan C 117, 120, 121, 151, 224
domestic violence 111, 135, 180
Donnelly P 123n18
Doom R 114, 123n13
Dowds E 226
Draucker CB 89
DRC see Democratic Republic of Congo (DRC)
Duffield M 21, 34
Dunn KC 116
Dworkin G 262n17
dynamic connectivity 7, 13, 58–60, 276, 277

302 Index

Eaton K 197n21
Ebila F 227, 231n1
ecofeminism 61n4, 523
Ecological Thought, The (Morton) 54
Edkins JE 90n4
Edström J 2, 120
education 208–9, 255
Ekblad S 214
Elbers E 177
Ellis BH 220
ELN see National Liberation Army (ELN)
embodied resilience 177
embodied ruptures 177–9
engineering resilience 24
Ethical and Safety Recommendations
    for Researching, Documenting and
    Monitoring Sexual Violence in
    Emergencies 86–7, 89
ethics of research 85–90
euphemisms 227
Evrard E 251, 261n12
experiential solidarity 185–7, 192

Faguet JP 107
faith 140, 180–3, 225
false positive crimes 176, 197n11
family resilience 143–7, 215–18
FARC see Revolutionary Armed Forces of
    Colombia (FARC)
Feitosa C 52
femicide 111
feminist framework 47
Ferizović J 105
Fetters MD 73
Finland 49
Fiske L 263n29
Fletcher LE 251
Flisi I 111
Flomo VK 263n34
Folke C 26, 28, 37
forced displacement 173–4
Forero JE 176
Foster JE 86, 89
fragmentation 7, 57, 136
Fragmentos 259
friction sources 157–9
functional connectivity 6–7, 55–7
Funk J 150
future research suggestions 281–4

Gamble A 4
García-Godos J 109

Garmestani AS 28–9, 49
Garmezy N 22–3
gender: Colombia sub-committee
    197n15; connectivity and 51–2, 60;
    fish processing and 56, 60; hierarchy
    211, 275; inequalities 33, 172, 221;
    interviewee selection and 78; resilience
    and 33, 51; traditional roles and 112;
    transitional justice and 247–8, 262n15;
    Uganda Local Council system 232n21;
    Yugoslavia policy 161n3; *see also* sexual
    and gender-based violence (SGBV)
genocidal rape 102, 103, 105
genocide: Bosnia-Herzegovina (BiH)
    105, 148; Canada 61n5; *mens rea* 105;
    Rwanda 59, 262n13; Srebrenica
    101, 105
Gerber LR 49
Gillum TL 180
Gilmore S 282
Global Code of Conduct for Gathering
    and Using Information about Systematic
    and Conflict-Related Sexual Violence
    86, 262n26, 278
Global Network of Victims and Survivors
    to End Sexual Violence in Conflict
    (SEMA) 257
Global Survivors Fund 135, 246
Gobby J 278
God, importance of 224–5
Gordon E 197n11
Grant U 232n21
Gready S 245
Green J 82
growth and exploitation phase, of adaptive
    cycle 26
Guatemala 250, 251, 256, 261n12, 274
Gunderson LH 25
Gustavsson M 120
Guterres A 274

Hagmann J 281
Hansen L 102, 144
Haraway DJ 59, 250, 278, 283
harm: gender-based 247–8; posthumanism
    and 250; relationality and 249–52;
    social-ecological systems and 250–2;
    transitional justice critiques 247–9
Harris OJT 249
Hašečić B 159
Hastings A 54
Hawke S 253

Index   303

health: in Bosnia-Herzegovina 140–3; in Colombia 177–80; embodied ruptures 177–9; physical performativity 212–14; individual health legacies 212–14; mental health 150, 156; social-ecological 179–80, 214–15; in Uganda 212–15, 214–15
Heckman S 61n4
Held V 283
Helms E 9, 91n12, 102, 103, 159, 161n3, 161n6
Henriksen D 262n18
Henry M 80
Henry N 262n15
Herman A 37
Herremans B 240
Herrera N 112
Hertz T 5
Hess JJ 148
hierarchy of victims 26, 103, 275
Hinton AL 243, 251
Hoare MA 99
Hobfoll S 142, 143
Holling CS 6, 22, 24–5, 38n2
Holy Spirit Mobile Force (HSMF) 114–16
Hooke J 59
Hopwood J 222
Horstman HK 151
HOS see Croatian Defence Forces (HOS)
Hovil L 121
Howe K 121
Howell A 36
Hronešova J 161n10
HSMF see Holy Spirit Mobile Force (HSMF)
Huck A 53
Human Rights Watch (HRW) 180, 261n3
Huneeus A 250, 252
HVO see Croatian Defence Council (HVO)

ICC see International Criminal Court (ICC)
ICRC see International Committee of the Red Cross
ICTY see International Criminal Tribunal for the former Yugoslavia (ICTY)
India 52
Indigenous peoples: in Canada 61n5, 278; in Colombia 9, 76, 106, 110–11, 174, 241, 250; ecological thinking and 241; in Guatemala 274; identity and 197n18; relationality and 249; resilience and 32;

spirituality and 261n2; transitional justice and 248, 250
individual resilience 274–5
interdisciplinary approach 49–50
International Committee of the Red Cross (ICRC) 274
International Criminal Court (ICC) 226
International Criminal Tribunal for the former Yugoslavia (ICTY) 1, 98, 103–4, 105, 226, 242
International Protocol on the Documentation and Investigation of Sexual Violence in Conflict 274, 278
intersectionality 47
Irazábal C 174
Ivankova NV 72

Janssen MA 47, 60
Jayawickreme E 190
Jenkins K 51
JEP see Special Jurisdiction for Peace (JEP)
Johnson RB 71
'Jokers' 103–4
Jonsson M 109
Jordan JV 57, 255, 256
Joseph J 34, 275

Karadžić R 101, 105, 123n7
Karkkainen BC 27, 31
Kartalova-O'Doherty Y 156
Kastner P 11
Kaufmann M 46
Kent L 58
Khadiagala L 219
Kiconco A 210, 232n18
King ML Jr 257
Kolb DG 57
Kony J 9, 71, 115, 116, 119, 123n13, 211
Koos C 2
Kostovicova D 161n9
Kramer S 119
Krause U 282
Kreft AK 113, 184, 189
Krieger N 212
Kunarac et al. case 105, 226
Kurtović L 261n10
Kuru N 254
Kvočka et al. case 103

Lakwena A 114
Lawson ES 263n34
Lederach AJ 174

304 Index

Leech NL 72
Legerski JP 89
Leiby ML 8
Lemaitre J 174, 186
Leopold A 249
Levine SZ 191
Lewis 85
LGBT community 91n8, 112, 187, 211
liberalism 11, 248, 251
Lid KNO 109
Liebenberg L 3, 30, 74, 81
Lima JB 169
Lord's Resistance Army (LRA): abductions 118, 123n14, 205, 205–6, 207, 208, 209, 210, 216, 226, 231n9; Acholi *manyen* 119; emergence and evolution of 115–16; forced marriage 118–20; international context 116; objectives 115, 119; regional context 116; sexual violence 118–20, 209, 210, 216, 226; in Sudan 116, 119; violence and 115, 116, 117, 213, 224, 232n19
lost opportunities 207–10
LRA see Lord's Resistance Army (LRA)
Lundy P 58
Lunn J 181
Lykes MB 250, 256
Lyons K 250, 262n21

MacKinnon CA 102, 122n5
MacKinnon D 31
Majstorović D 153
male rape 59, 121, 206, 211
Manyena SB 22
marriage prospects 209–10
Martin LK 231n10
Massad S 275
Masten AS 27, 60, 276
Mazowiecki T 296
Mazurana D 123n17
Mbazumutima T 263n32
McAuliffe P 279, 283
McCauley DJ 59
McDowell S 32
McRae BH 6, 7
meaning making 151–3, 188–91, 223–34
Meger S 60n2
Mertens C 250, 252
Meyers JA 262n24
Miller SC 11
Minwalla S 86, 89
mixed methods approach 9, 71

Mkutu KA 233n26
Mladić R 100, 122n2, 123n7
Mlinarević G 105
Močnik N 76, 91n12
Moffett L 282
Moore JC 3, 74
Mootz JJ 123n15
Moreno Sandoval CD 10
motherhood 2, 146, 147, 228, 260
Mucić et al. case 104
Mukamana D 59
Mukwege D 134, 246, 257
Mukwege Foundation 257
Mumby PJ 54
Murad Code 86, 255, 262n26, 262n27, 278
Murad N 134, 246, 254–5
Museveni Y 114, 115, 117, 121, 206
Musinguzi LK 232n25
mutuality: interviewees and 12; through giving back and story-making 258–60; through solidarity and story-sharing 256–8
Mychasiuk R 208
Myrttinen H 135

Nadia's Initiative 254–5
National Centre for Historical Memory (CNMH) 110, 123n12
National Liberation Army (ELN) 107, 108
National Resistance Army (NRA) 114, 120–1
natural environment 148–9, 262n20
neoliberalism 4, 11, 34–5, 36, 275
new connectivities: in Bosnia-Herzegovina 151–60; in Colombia 188–96; cross-ethnic solidarities 155; economic collaborations 282; fighting for change 191–5; friction sources 157–9; linked to dynamic connectivity 58–60; meaning making 151–3, 188–91, 223–34; mutuality and 12, 255–60; reaching out 159–60; rebuilding 227–30; reconnection with life 156–7; renewal 229; resistance to 230; as re-storying 151; social ecologies and 277; socio-cultural importance of women 228–9; in Uganda 223–31; unanswered questions 153–6; wider context 194–5
NGOs see non-governmental organisations (NGOs)
Nieto Valdivieso YF 123n12
Nightingale AJ 32, 56

Njoku ET 283
non-governmental organisations (NGOs)
   184–7, 192
NRA see National Resistance Army
   (NRA)
Nthakomwa M 210, 232n18
nudging 277

O'Brien A 250
Observatory of Memory and Conflict
   (OMC) 123n12
Okello ES 214
Okello MC 121
Oliveira C 2, 228, 230
OMC see Observatory of Memory and
   Conflict (OMC)
Ong DM 252
Ongwen D 114, 118, 119–20
Onwuegbuzie AJ 72
Oosterom M 221
O'Reilly M 159
Orjuela C 255
O'Rourke C 207
Oslender U 174
'over-researched' 86

Palestine 35
panarchy 26, 27–8, 31
Pardy M 250, 252
Park CL 154
Pastor L 261n2
Patten P 274, 287n2
Patterson JM 175
Payne WJ 112
Pelkmans M 179
Perez C 33
Peruvian Truth and Reconciliation
   Commission 247–8
Perz SG 53
Pescosolido BA 231n10
Pham PN 116
Pinzón JC 106
Pipher M 151
Porch D 112
pornography 102–3, 122n5
Porter HE 119, 121, 225
posthumanism 12, 249, 250
post-traumatic growth (PTG) 190–1
Preiser R 253
Prior T 281
Prunier G 115
PTG see post-traumatic growth (PTG)

Quinlan AE 84

Randle JM 53
rape: in Bosnia-Herzegovina 9, 101–6,
   161n6, 295–7; in Colombia 169, 171,
   172, 175, 176, 177, 178, 179; 181, 182,
   198; definition of 226; euphemisms 227;
   as genocide 102, 103, 105; legal cases
   103–6, 226; LGBT community 211;
   male rape 59, 121, 206, 211; marital
   consequences 144; marriage prospects
   and 209–10; representations 102; in
   Rwanda 59; statistics 109–10, 172, 295–7;
   stigma 150, 210–12, 221, 231n10;
   strategic rape 50, 61n3; survival sex
   121; in Uganda 206, 209–10, 211, 216,
   226; as weapon of war 262n13; see also
   conflict-related sexual violence (CRSV);
   sexual and gender-based violence
   (SGBV)
RCT see Relational-Cultural Theory
   (RCT)
Refugee Law Project 120
Reid J 36, 282
Reilly RC 256
Relational-Cultural Theory (RCT) 48,
   50–1, 255, 256
relationality 249–52
religion 181, 224–5; see also faith;
   spirituality
religious coping 183
'remember' phase, of adaptive cycle 27
reorganisation and renewal phase, of
   adaptive cycle 26, 53
reparations: co-creation and 246; collective
   versus individual 245–6; in Colombia
   242; as enabling 13, 259; in Guatemala
   261n12
Republika Srpska (RS) 76, 100, 137
research methodology: challenges 75;
   coding 82–4; comparative case study
   approach 69–71; ethics issues 85–90;
   interviewees 78–9, 79; interview guide
   292–4; interviews 79–81, 85–6, 88;
   limitations 76; mixed methods approach
   71; participants 77–8, 77; priorities
   75–8; qualitative data 82–5; qualitative
   phase 78–81; quantitative data 81–2;
   quantitative phase 73–8; questionnaire
   73–5; reflections workshops 81; risks
   of retraumatisation 87–90; thematic
   analysis 84–5

resilience: assumptions of 31; controversies 3–4; critical views of 31–8; definitions of 4, 21, 22, 23, 24, 275; development of field 22–5; ecological strand 24–5; framing beyond individual-centred 274–6; gender and 33, 51; holistic view of 276–7; inequalities 33; motherhood and 2, 146, 147, 228; multi-systemic approaches 26, 37, 47, 49, 54; navigation and negotiation 29; neoliberalism and 3–4, 34–36, 50, 225, 274–5, 282; as policy 36; psychological strand 22–4; as social-ecological concept 21–38; through connectivity 46–60; transitional justice and 11, 12; of what? 32–4; for whom? 34–5

resilience scales 73–4
resource caravans 143
retraumatisation 87–90
'revolt' phase, of adaptive cycle 26–7
Revolutionary Armed Forces of Colombia (FARC) 71, 106, 107, 108–9, 112, 123n10, 173
Rew L 51
Robbins J 263n35
Rodriguez Castro L 194
Rodriguez SP 123n8
Roelvink G 240
Rondón G 51
Ross H 31
RS see *Republika Srpska* (RS)
Rueda Sáiz P 250, 252
Ruhl JB 37
Ruiz L 7
Ruta Pacífica de las Mujeres 81, 159, 187, 194
Rutter M 23
Rwanda 59, 147
Ryan C 35

Saab BY 108
Sachseder J 197n17
Sackellares SN 144
Salcedo D 259
Saldaña J 82
Salt D 73, 251
salutogenesis 190
Sanchez-Barrios LJ 197n12
Sandercock L 263n31
Sandvik KB 186
Santamaria A 261n2
Scarry E 178
Schacter DL 240

Scheffer M 54
Schmidt H 282
Schulz P 59, 75, 120, 121, 187
self-repair 282
SEMA see Global Network of Victims and Survivors to End Sexual Violence in Conflict (SEMA)
Sense of Coherence (SOC) 190
SES see social-ecological systems (SES)
sexual and gender-based violence (SGBV): by all sides 103–6, 111; in Bosnia-Herzegovina 101–6; causal complexity 103–6; in Colombia 109–13, 112–13, 171–2; connectivity and 47, 144; domestic violence 111; femicide 111; against men 111, 120, 211; rape representations 102; transitional justice and 247–8, 262n15; in Uganda 118–122; *see also* conflict-related sexual violence (CRSV); rape
SGBV see sexual and gender-based violence (SGBV)
Shackel R 263n29
Sharp DN 279
Simić O 76
Simpson A 6
Skjelsbaek I 91n9
Slovenia (war in) 99
Smyth I 33
Snaga Žene 2, 81, 91n8, 155
SOC see Sense of Coherence (SOC)
social-ecological framing of transitional justice 5, 10–13, 14, 231, 240, 246–260, 276–7
social-ecological health 179–80, 214–15
social-ecological systems (SES): adaptive capacity 26; as complex adaptive systems 253; definition of 5, 252; description of 25–6; feedbacks and 5, 25, 26, 30, 48, 251, 252, 253, 281; harm and 250–2; rupture in 192; transitional justice and 252
social ecologies: care and 228, 279, 283; definition of 4; future research on conflict-related sexual violence 283; reparations and 13, 245–6; resilience and 4–7, 8, 29, 30, 36, 46, 48, 49, 122, 169, 188, 196, 239, 276–277; spider's web and 10; supporting victims-/survivors of conflict-related sexual violence 50, 254, 276, 279; transitional justice and 11–12, 14, 36, 239–60, 280, 283

Index   307

social resilience 37
solidarity 185–7, 192, 256–8
Spannring R 253
Special Jurisdiction for Peace (JEP) 113, 241, 244, 261n9
spiders 10, 223, 224, 228
spider webs 10, 205, 207, 211, 223, 284
spirituality 180–3, 224–5
spouses/partners 144–5
Srebrenica 101, 105, 123, 148
Staub E 240
stigma 210–12, 221, 231n10
Stites E 121
story-building 259, 260
story-making 258–60
story-sharing 256–8, 263n32
story-telling 278
strategic rape 50, 61n3
structural connectivity 6, 55–7
structural violence 248
Suarez AV 46
Sudan 116
Sultana F 33
Summerfield D 160n1
supportive and sustaining connectivities: adaptive capacity 253–5; in Bosnia-Herzegovina 143–51; children 145–7; in Colombia 180–7; community 219–22; emotional support 217; faith and spirituality 180–3; family 143–7, 215–18; financial support 217–18; health services and providers 149–51; land 222–3; linked to structural and functional connectivity 55–7; men 186–7, 195; natural environment 148–9; spouses/partners 144–5; in Uganda 215–23; wider families 145–7; women's and non-governmental organisations 184–7, 192, 193
survivor-centred approach 4, 252, 277–8, 280–1
Sviland R 177
Swaine A 50, 61n3, 135
Sweetman C 33
Szoke-Burke S 245

Taylor AW 108
TEC see Traumatic Events Checklist (TEC)
Tedeschi RG 190
Teitel RG 248, 279
tek-gungu 120–1, 206, 211

Tengö M 47
Theidon K 188–9, 247
Theron L 29–30, 49, 180, 259
Thylin T 112
Touquet H 75
Tovar-Restrepo M 174
transformative justice 248, 281, 283
transitional justice: adaptive capacity and 253–5; in Bosnia-Herzegovina 242, 243; in Colombia 113, 241, 242, 243, 244; connectivity and 240; definition of 10; future research 283; harm-based critiques 247–9; interviewees' reflections on 241–7; legacy and 57–8; liberalism and 11, 248; mutuality and 255–60; nature and 262n20; new directions for 279–81; phases of 279–80, 281; posthumanism and 12, 250; relationality and 249–52; resilience and 11, 12, 239, 246; sexual and gender-based violence and 247–8; social-ecological systems and 252, 281; social-ecological framing of 5, 10–13, 14, 231, 240, 246–260, 276–7; structural violence and 248; in Uganda 117, 242–3; *see also* reparations
trauma 74, 89, 90n4, 142, 150, 160n1, 175, 240, 252, 263n29
Traumatic Events Checklist (TEC) 74, *74*, 175
Tremaria S 108
Tripp AM 231n1
Tronto JC 228
Tsing AL 157
Tynan L 249

Uganda: abduction and captivity 205–6; Acholi people 114; Agreement on Accountability and Reconciliation 11; Amnesty Act 123n16, 242; broken and ruptured connectivities 207–15; cattle rustlers 121, 206–7; community 219–22; connectivity stories 204–31; contextualisation of violence 205–7; education 208; forced marriage 118–20; God, importance of 224–5; health 212–15; health services and providers 149; interview ethics 88; Kony J 115, 116; land 222–3; Local Council system 221–2; Lord's Resistance Army 114–16, 118–20, 123n14; lost opportunities 207–10; mass displacement 117–18; meaning making 191, 223–34; messages from 285, 287n5; National Resistance Army 114, 120–1; new connectivities 227–30; Ongwen D 118, 119–20; payment of *luk* 211, 232n11; peace agreement 116; 'protected villages' 117–18; Refugee Law Project 120; religion 224–5, 232n23, 232n24; renewal 229; research priorities 76; roots of war 113–14; selection for study 71; sexual violence 118–22, 123n17; socio-cultural importance of women 228–9; stigma 210–12, 221; supportive and sustaining connectivities 187, 215–23; transitional justice 117, 242–3; Ugandan National Liberation Army 114; Uganda People's Defence Forces 115, 116, 121; Village Savings and Loan Associations 185, 229

Ugandan National Liberation Army (UNLA) 114

Uganda People's Defence Forces (UPDF) 115, 116, 121

Ukraine 273, 282

UN Agenda for Sustainable Development 278

unanswered questions 153–6

UN Commission of Experts 104, 122n6

Ungar M 4, 6, 8, 22, 29, 53, 73, 81, 161n7, 180, 232n22, 254

United Self-Defence Forces of Colombia (AUC) 108, 109, 112

UNLA see Ugandan National Liberation Army (UNLA)

UPDF see Uganda People's Defence Forces (UPDF)

Uprichard E 72

Uribe MV 171

Valdovinos MG 10

Valiñas M 261n9

Van Acker F 115

van Breda A 49

Van Rensburg AC 73, 91n11

Vaughan-Williams N 35

victim hierarchies 26, 103, 275

Vietnam 28

Vlassenroot K 114, 123n13

VRS see Army of *Repubika Srpska* (VRS)

Wade P 197n16

Wakefield S 192

Walker BH 24, 47, 73, 251, 262n24

Walker M 256

Walsh-Dilley M 27

Walsh F 147, 160

Waters MC 82

Weins, JA 55

Weinstein HM 251

Welker M 240

Weston C 82

WHO see World Health Organization (WHO)

Wiebelhaus-Brahm E 239

Wienand S 108

Williams LH 232n24

Wilton Park conference 277

Wine B 117

Wolford W 27

women's organisations 184–7, 192, 193

Wood EJ 172

World Health Organization (WHO) 86–7, 89

Xie C 59

Yamaoka M 52

Yoshida K 58

Yugoslavia 98–9; *see also* Bosnia-Herzegovina (BiH)

Zalesne D 110

Zambia 56

Zraly M 2, 146, 147

Zulver JM 171, 192